Ellesmere Island

Eureka

Thule Airbase

GREENLAND

Grise Fjord   Craig Harbour

Devon Island   Dundas Harbour

Baffin Bay

Godhavn

Lancaster Sound

Fort Ross

Arctic Bay   Pond Inlet

Clyde River

Davis Strait

Sondre
Stromfjord

Boothia ninsula

Spence Bay

Baffin Island

oa Haven

Padloping Island

Pangnirtung

Repulse Bay

Foxe Basin

Frobisher Bay

Cape Dorset

Southhampton Island

Lake Harbour

Atlantic Ocean

Baker Lake

Coral Harbour

Hudson Strait

sterfield Inlet

Wakeham Bay

Ungava Bay

Hebron

Point

Fort Chimo

Port Harrison

Indian House Lake

LABRADOR

Goose Bay

Hudson Bay

rchill

Mecatina

ort Nelson

QUEBEC

Mingan

ONTARIO

BA

Moosonee

NORTHERN CANADA

CIRCA 1930-1950

SOVEREIGNTY OR SECURITY? GOVERNMENT POLICY IN THE CANADIAN NORTH, 1936–1950

Sovereignty or Security? explores the numerous and diverse influences responsible for the dramatic change in the Canadian government's northern policies during the 1940s and their subsequent impact on the Yukon and the Northwest Territories. Apart from concern for the social, economic, and political development of the North, two major issues emerged which became central to policy initiatives during the war and postwar years—maintaining optimum sovereign control and providing adequate defence against possible enemy attack. As a result, Ottawa abandoned its former laissez-faire approach to northern affairs and adopted an active interventionist role, accompanied by unprecedented financial support.

Pressure for change in government attitude and policies came from the private sector, but recent archival research in Ottawa, London, and Washington has revealed that military considerations and foreign relations had a far greater impact on final decisions. In this context, Grant examines the process of policy-making, with particular emphasis on the roles played by key individuals and institutions: Hugh Keenleyside, Arnold Heeney, Lester Pearson, Major-General William Foster, High Commissioner Malcolm MacDonald, Brooke Claxton, Jack Hickerson, and Major-General Guy Henry, as well as the Permanent Joint Board on Defence, External Affairs, Mines and Resources, the Advisory Committee on Northern Development, the Canadian Institute of International Affairs, the Arctic Institute of North America, and the United States State Department, to name only a few.

The circumstances leading to various war and postwar agreements are also studied, particularly the Ogdensburg and Hyde Park agreements, the 1947 joint defence pact with its "civilian cover" addendum, and the Anglo-American negotiations on atomic research and allocation of Canadian uranium resources. These events and others had a direct bearing on Ottawa's increasing involvement and financial investment in the northern territories.

Relative to the current debate over Arctic sovereignty and northern defence, this book provides an important new insight into the strategies and commitments of the 1940s, which are crucial to understanding the basis of the dilemma facing Canadians today.

SHELAGH GRANT teaches history and Canadian studies at Trent University.

ERRATA

PHOTO CREDITS

National Archives of Canada: Plate 5, PA-45057 *should read* Plate 4; Plate 16, Paul Horsdal, PA-102187 *should read* Plate 18; R. M. Anderson Collection—Plate 4, R. M. Anderson, C-85994 *should read* Plate 5; Indian and Northern Affairs Collection—Plate 6, O. S. Finnie, PA-100458 *should read* Plate 14; Plate 14, D. L. McKeand, PA-102187 *should read* Plate 6; National Film Board Collection—Plate 18, C-85693 *should read* Plate 16

ILLUSTRATIONS

4 is 5; 5 is 4; 6 is 14; 14 is 6; 16 is 18; 18 is 16

Sovereignty or Security?

GOVERNMENT POLICY IN THE CANADIAN NORTH, 1936–1950

Shelagh D. Grant

University of British Columbia Press
Vancouver 1988

Canadian Cataloguing in Publication Data
Grant, Shelagh D. (Shelagh Dawn), 1938–
  Sovereignty or security?

Bibliography: p.
Includes index.
ISBN 0-7748-0306-1

  1. Canada, Northern – Politics and government.
2. Canada, Northern – History. I. Title.
FC3963.G72 1988   971.9′02   C88-091608-7
F1090.5.G72 1988

This book has been published with the help of a grant from
the Social Science Federation of Canada, using funds
provided by the Social Sciences and Humanities Research
Council of Canada.

International Standard Book Number 0-7748-0306-1
Printed in Canada

To John Wendell Holmes
1910–1988

Contents

Photo Credits

Arctic Institute of North America, Plate 42, *Arctic,* 20 (1966)
National Archives of Canada: Plate 5, PA-45057; Plate 7, PA-45061; Plate 16, Paul Horsdal, PA-102187; Plate 20, C-5229; Plate 25, Arthur Roy, C-5337; Plate 28, C-25752; Plate 29, R. Jacques, C-80775; Plate 40, C-29466; Plate 45, Acme Newspictures Inc. C-23285; Plate 46, *Paris Matin,* C-31312; Plate 47, C-24826
R. M. Anderson Collection: Plate 4, R. M. Anderson, C-85994
Duncan Cameron Collection: Plate 48, PA-121702; Plate 50, PA-121698
Department of National Defence Collection: Plate 52, PA-66445
A. D. P. Heeney Collection: Plate 19, C-44767
Indian and Northern Affairs Collection: Plate 1, PA-118126; Plate 2, R. Tash, PA-102315; Plate 3, M. Haycock, PA-102648; Plate 6, O.S. Finnie, PA-100458; Plate 8, M. Meikle, PA-101791; Plate 9, M. Meikle, PA-101617; Plate 10, PA-101811; Plate 11, M. Meikle, PA-101853; Plate 12, M. Meikle, PA-101908; Plate 13, M. Meikle, PA-101789; Plate 14, D. L. McKeand, PA-102187; Plate 15, M. Meikle, PA-135778; Plate 17, M. Meikle, PA-101975; Plate 24, M. Meikle, PA-101863; Plate 51, M. Meikle, PA-101883
W. L. M. King Collection: Plate 49, C-27905
National Film Board Collection: Plate 18, C-85693; Plate 21, Frank Tyrell, PA-130488; Plate 23, R. Jacques, PA-130474; Plate 26, Harry Rowed, PA-113193; Plate 27, Harry Rowed, PA-113194; Plate 30, Nicolas Morant, PA-121715; Plate 44, C. Lund, PA-129003; Plate 54, W. Doucette, PA-144766; Plate 55, W. Doucette, PA-111208
National Archives in Washington: Plate 22, photo collection, 80-G-225196; Plate 53, State Department records, RG 59, PJBD series, vol. 2, file "Fort Churchill"
Prince of Wales Heritage Centre, Yellowknife: R. Finnie Collection, Plates 34, 35, and 36
Private sources: H. L. Keenleyside, Plate 37; Trevor Lloyd, Plates 31, 32, 33, 38, and 43; Elizabeth Pound, Plate 41
Royal Commonwealth Society Library: Plate 39

Illustrations

Figures and Maps

Tables

Foreword

At the end of the 1980s, Canadian attention has been drawn to its Arctic frontier for many urgent reasons. Perhaps not since the 1940s, with which this book is concerned, have the dilemmas of policy been so baffling. The acute sensitivity of Canadians to sovereignty issues and American "challenges" was evident in the instance of the voyage of the *Polar Sea* in 1985. Similarly, renewed concern for defences against aircraft or missiles of advanced technology and the possible complications of the American Strategic Defence Initiative pose again the ambiguities of alliance obligations and the maintenance of sovereign authority. To complicate things further comes a new prospect of arms control agreements between the superpowers and an extraordinary shift in Soviet positions on the Arctic. Not only in his speech in Murmansk in September 1987, but also in his proposals for a conference of sub-Arctic countries and a bilateral treaty with Canada, Mikhail Gorbachev is floating ideas similar to those Canada proposed over forty years ago. The fact that these new developments are hopeful and encouraging does not make them any the less difficult, for we have to move on from the intellectual comforts of the status quo.

All this is happening at a time when, partly because of its own stances in the United Nations and the Commonwealth, Canada is obliged to direct much greater attention to the historic rights of the native peoples and is finding that the will is easier to achieve than the way. The internationalization of the Arctic community is being pioneered by the Inuit themselves. It is notable that, even in hot and cold wartime, as Shelagh Grant illustrates, there was in the bureaucracy and that small elite interested in the North, great concern for the health and welfare of the people who lived there and a continuing effort to reconcile this concern with strategic demands. There was little expectation then that the Arctic might be a source of rich energy supplies in a world badly in need of them. Although expectations that this northern Mediterranean Sea might become a Persian Gulf have diminished, they cannot be absent from our economic and strategic calculations.

It is a tangled web. The issues cannot be clarified without a grasp of history, in particular the history of the wartime and postwar periods when Canadians, and their allies as well, were trying to cope with the implications of the removal of an impenetrable glacial barrier on the northern frontier. Now that archival records are open, it is possible to reveal the considerations of a period in which future policies and perceptions were established. This illuminating account has been broadened by the author's search of records in Britain and the United States and by her diligent interrogation of many of those involved, including present inhabitants of the Arctic regions. At a time when such subjects were the concern of a few and the requirements of confidentiality pressing, personalities were important. They were a remarkably able lot, as the author vividly illustrates. The issues were and are complex, and Mrs. Grant has clarified without simplifying them. She has an obviously deep concern for the welfare of the region and its peoples, an awareness of the international pressures and obligations, and an understanding of the strange mythical element in Canadians' approach to what Franklyn Griffiths has called "the Arctic sublime."

John W. Holmes
January 1988

Preface

The decade of the 1940s was a landmark in the evolution of government policy in the Canadian north. Concentrated into a very short time were many momentous events and changing economic circumstances, as well as important technological advances and altered geopolitical factors, all of which directly affected the nature of government involvement in the Yukon and the Northwest Territories. A closer look at the issues, influences, and personalities involved in the years before, during, and after World War II, provides a new insight into the rationale motivating those policy decisions which inevitably determined Ottawa's hidden agenda in the future conduct of northern affairs.

The study of this particular place and time in Canadian history is more pertinent now than when my research began in 1979. At that time, interest in the north evolved around such questions as the environment, oil and gas development, native land claims, and proposed constitutional changes. More recently, the issues of Arctic sovereignty and northern defence have attracted increasing attention in the news media and academic journals, and in 1987 they formed the core debate in two important works: *Politics of the Northwest Passage,* edited by Franklyn Griffiths, and John Honderich's *Arctic Imperative: Is Canada Losing the North*[1] There is a touch of irony, however, in the fact that the same questions, objectives and dilemmas, involving the same nations, were the subject of major controversy some forty years earlier. To comprehend fully the complexity of the sovereignty or security debate and the compromise solutions, one must reconstruct the influences, circumstances, and commitments that ultimately created the quandary facing Canadians today.

From Confederation to the end of 1950, the shifts in perceptions and priorities that shaped northern policy were a result of the complex interrelationship of three major issues: sovereignty, stewardship, and national security. Sovereignty and security emerged as top priority considerations among senior statesmen in the 1940s, with the question of stewardship responsibilities arising out of increasing social consciousness and public pressure. Here, definitions of sovereignty and stewardship are taken in their broadest context. For the most part, threats to northern sovereignty were perceived in *de facto* terms of United States dominance or encroachment on Canada's military, economic, and political authority, although there were a few instances when Canadian territorial claims within the Arctic Archipelago appeared in jeopardy. The term "stewardship" is also employed in a general sense to cover the full range of federal responsibility in administering the domestic affairs of the northern territories for the welfare of all residents, indigenous and Euro-Canadian alike. Thus, stewardship or governance involves all aspects of the political, economic, and social concerns. On the other hand, the need to provide adequate military defence for reasons of "national security" is straightforward, arising originally out of the Japanese attack on Pearl Harbor and becoming a matter of increasing significance during the Cold War as a result of advanced aviation technology and the threat of nuclear war. By virtue of its uranium resources and strategic location, Canada's north was central to the foreign policy discussions involving continental and imperial defence schemes and the control of atomic energy. While the title, *Sovereignty or Security?* may seem to imply an "either—or" situation, in essence, it simply reflects the two sides of the debate involved in the search for a compromise that would provide maximum security with minimal loss of sovereignty.

As a result, federal policy in the north shifted dramatically in less than a decade, from the somewhat laissez-faire attitude of the 1930s to one of active intervention involving massive increases in expenditure and major reorganization. All this came about with the support of a southern electorate who were excited by the vision of a new northern frontier, yet who were also apprehensive of any major American military presence which might diminish Canada's sovereign rights or control. But by 1950, the fear of a nuclear war overrode all other concerns.

Where possible, events and influences are correlated chronologically with changes in attitude and policy. An overview of the period from Confederation to the Depression illustrates previous patterns of government response with reference to the relationship of Arctic sovereignty and the "myth of the north" in the psyche of Canadian identity. Administrative policies and private development in the two territories during the 1930s are equally critical in evaluating the changes which occurred in the next decade, as are the complexities of Anglo-Canadian-American relations and the unique character of Ottawa's wartime civil service. Following the Japanese bombing of Pearl Harbor, the prolific growth of "joint" defence projects throughout the Canadian north led to "the crisis of 1943" when Ottawa was alerted to a potential American threat to northern sovereignty. The study of subsequent reaction emphasizes the diverse influences directing government debate and decisions, with particular focus on the crucial move in November 1946 to peacetime collaboration with the United States in northern defence. For three short years, from 1947 to 1949 inclusive, when Hugh Keenleyside was deputy minister of the Department of Mines and Resources, social and economic reform appeared to have an unusually high priority in government policy. The failure to sustain this progressive centralized approach to territorial government is examined in terms of events, personalities, and shifting priorities. In conclusion, the patterns of decision-making from 1936 to 1950 are interpreted in relation to domestic and external influences, and their relevance to the overall evolution of northern policy. While concern for the future of the Canadian north may have been rooted in nationalist pride, government policy change was more often provoked by international circumstance and pressure.

The idea of "north" has many meanings and boundaries, but in terms of government policy, it should be defined in political terms—the land beyond 60° north latitude. In terms of military planning, however, northern Canada includes sections of British Columbia, Alberta, Saskatchewan, Manitoba, and Quebec. In the public perception, a more abstract interpretation encompasses the various images and myths of "north" inbred in the Canadian ethos. Recognition of these diverse meanings is important in understanding the conflicts and confusion in the minds of many policy-makers. Louis Edmond Hamelin has argued that "two extreme opinions emerge: an over-idealized vision and an excessive pessimistic view."[2] William Wonders emphasized the same contradictions when he wrote, "magnificent and miserable, exhilarating and depressing, beautiful and ugly—the north is all of these."[3] These contrasts were particularly evident in the 1940s, as is reflected in the enthusiastic optimism of the would-be architects of a "new north" and compared to the cool, pragmatic calculations of the military planners.

Researching such a broad topic provided an infinite challenge. There appeared no obvious place to start, and certainly there is no defined end. For domestic issues, the records of departments most active in northern affairs were correlated with manuscript sources of those individuals and institutions instrumental in promoting new policies. The rationale behind decisions of the northern administration was determined through careful examination of the minutes and reports of the Northwest Territories and Yukon Councils. To affirm and expand information derived from archival sources, additional data was obtained through personal discussions and correspondence with individuals actively involved in northern affairs during the crucial periods. As expected, published accounts and official speeches often betrayed some of the real concerns and objectives of politicians and public servants. Curiosity drew me to the scattered communities of the Yukon and the Mackenzie Val-

ley and eventually to the eastern Arctic, where interviews with longtime residents of diverse occupations and ethnicity were invaluable in verifying conditions as they existed against the statements in government reports. Local
records were equally revealing.

In evaluating the influence of international affairs, the documents of Canada's Department of External Affairs, the Privy Council Office, the Prime
Minister's Office, and various manuscript sources were compared with their
appropriate counterparts at the Public Records Office and Royal Commonwealth Society Library in London and the National Archives and Library of
Congress in Washington. Research also included extensive reading of articles and books written during the period as well as more recent accounts
and analytical assessments. Not surprisingly, the historiography of the Canadian north is quite fragmented, focusing primarily on economic, regional,
scientific, military, social, or political developments.

As happens in researching any topic which represents only a minor part of
a rather large controversial subject, I found it difficult to refrain from going
off on tangents which were fascinating in themselves but of little significance
in terms of northern policy. Similarly, the problems of government in attempting to co-ordinate domestic and external demands through numerous
departments and agencies often complicated my effort to record the sequence
and significance of shifting priorities into a cohesive account. These internal
conflicts and tensions were further confused by the competing objectives inherent in Anglo-Canadian, Anglo-American, and Canadian-American relations.

In some instances, the records in London and Washington confirmed what
was little more than speculation based on the records of External Affairs and
the Privy Council Office in Ottawa. Noticeable patterns of priorities and
responses began to take form, giving rise to the possibility of subconscious
motives attached to northern policy decisions. Further questions should be
raised, seriously considered, and earnestly debated. This volume is merely a
beginning—an examination of government and public reactions from 1936 to
1950 and their relationship to similar situations in the past. Direct comparison to the present is purposely avoided because of restricted access to
comparable government records.

Canada's north provides an infinite challenge for historians who attempt to
explain its mystique in terms of Canadian identity or government policies in
terms of public opinion and political pressures. In my own experience, historical research and associated travel stimulated an even deeper appreciation
and concern for what most Canadians describe as "our north." While the related myth continues to have a powerful influence on public perception, only
through broader knowledge and understanding of the past can we hope to im-

prove on the present, to accommodate the needs of all northerners with those of the nation, and at the same time fulfil the dreams of many Canadians by preserving much of the north as a place of true wilderness.

ACKNOWLEDGMENTS

For assistance in my research, I am indebted to a number of individuals who were more than generous in their support of my endeavours: in the National Archives of Canada there was James Kidd from the Manuscript Division; from Government Documents, Terry Cook, Tom Nesmith, Mark Hopkins, David Smith, and their assistants; in the Historical Division of External Affairs, Dacre Cole; in the northern territories, the staff of Prince of Wales Heritage Centre at Yellowknife, and Diana Johnston of the Yukon Archives; in Britain, Donald Simpson of the Royal Commonwealth Society Library and Margaret Gowing, official historian of the British Atomic Energy Authority; and in Washington, Sally Marks of the National Archives, responsible for the diplomatic records of the State Department. With respect to personal inquiries, special thanks are due to those who took the time to discuss or write of their knowledge and experience: René Fumoleau, Maxwell Dunbar, Escott Reid, Graham Rowley, Louise Parkin, and Sheila Lougheed, sister of the Rt. Hon. Malcolm MacDonald, British High Commissioner to Canada during the war years. Very sincere appreciation goes to Trevor Lloyd who spent long hours in discussion and correspondence, continually adding new insight into the accumulated research and allowing the use of his original maps; to J. Lewis Robinson for his interest and editorial suggestions in the early stages; and, in the final hour, to Hugh Keenleyside who so kindly helped locate photographs, then read the entire manuscript for accuracy of detail. Thanks also to Margaret Tully and Lilian Rankin for their typing and retyping of the numerous drafts, to Betsy Struthers and Nicola Jarvis Jennings for their assistance in proofreading, to Louis Taylor, Barbara Fox, and Barbara Pitt of Trent University's Graphics Department, to Doug James for his cartography, and to my editor, Jane Fredeman, who deserves a very special mention for her ongoing encouragement and guidance. A number of my colleagues in history and Canadian Studies, including the late Brian Heeney, also offered their help and advice. To Bruce Hodgins, particularly, I owe an especially warm debt of gratitude for the initial inspiration and direction and his confidence in my ability to undertake the task at hand.

Over the past several years John Holmes played the role of critic and mentor with great patience and equal enthusiasm. Indeed, if it were not for his persistent encouragement that the story be told, this book might never have been completed. His passing this summer was a particularly sad moment in the lives of so many. Most certainly he will go down in history as a "great Canadian," but for myself, I will never forget how genuinely and deeply he cared about people, things, and most of all, his country.

Lastly, but with heartfelt sincerity, I thank my family, and especially my husband, for their patience and understanding when my academic pursuits too often took priority over other matters.

S.D.G.
August 1988

Sovereignty or Security?

The eagle may soar;
beavers build dams.

JOSEPH S. NYE, JR.

1

A Historical Perspective, 1867–1930

Concern about the North in the past could be correlated closely
with the fear of losing it.

Trevor Lloyd, 1946

Over the years, Canada's "north" became an integral part of the national
identity—"the true north, strong and free"—implying a promise of freedom
and prosperity, a land of opportunity, and an open frontier. Some claimed
that the nation's northernness directly influenced its society and economy by
imparting a unique identity distinct from the rest of North America. Others
thought the country was still in adolescence and that the key to maturity lay
in the development of the northern hinterland. These intangible notions are
sometimes referred to collectively as the "myth of the north" that somehow
explains Canadian identity and so became a recurrent theme in nationalist
rhetoric. Common to most perceptions was the conviction that the sparsely
populated Arctic Archipelago and adjacent mainland were irrevocably a part
of the Canadian entity and therefore that any threat, or even perceived threat,
to sovereignty was a serious matter demanding government action. It was a
land of potential resources to be exploited by southerners, but prior to World
War II there seemed little chance that the frozen wastelands would have any
immediate agricultural, political, or strategic value. As a consequence, government policy appeared inconsistent: at times somewhat laissez-faire, but
quite reactive when faced with a possible challenge to sovereign authority.

I

The symbiotic relationship between national identity and northern sovereignty had its origins in the pre-Confederation era. By the late 1850s, reports

of a potential fertile belt in the lands held under charter by the Hudson's Bay Company caused earlier reservations and pessimism to give way to unconcealed optimism among the entrepreneurially minded in Canada West. By 1857, the acquisition of the northwest was a key issue in the Reform Party's platform, and the aim quickly gained popularity across partisan lines. Countless speeches, newspaper articles, and pamphlets promised growth and prosperity rivalling that of the United States. As expected, the idea of a "Nova Britannia," "a Great Britannic Empire of the North," predicated on the northwesterly movement of Christian civilization, inspired patriotic fervour among English-speaking colonists.[1] It was an imperial vision, a Canadian version of the British Empire, with confident expectations that Canada would eventually be an equal partner in an imperial federation. It was also an effective counter-argument to America's "manifest destiny" and the pro-annexationists.[2] At about the same time, a similar image of their provincial "north" as a land of opportunity and future settlement was promoted by certain members of the Catholic clergy in Canada East, who claimed "notre Ouest, c'est le Nord" in hopes of reinforcing French-Canadian nationalism and stemming the migration to New England.[3] Thus, even prior to the birth of the new dominion, English- and French-speaking colonists had integrated a northern ethos into their nationalist rhetoric.

During the Confederation debates, both George Brown and John A. Macdonald argued that acquisition of the "old Northwest" was crucial to prevent American territorial expansion and exploitation of potential resources rightfully belonging to the proposed dominion. It was a theme which encouraged unity among the divisive political factions and regional interests, inspiring visions of a great new nation and appealing to Loyalist sympathies throughout British North America. Attention initially focused on sparsely populated British Columbia, where American miners had already settled in alarming numbers, on the Red River district eyed by United States commercial and railway interests, and on the prairie lands that offered such great agricultural potential. Ironically, Canada's imperial vision faced its first challenge on the 1st of July 1867, when the United States purchased Alaska from the Russians and it appeared that America's dream of "manifest destiny" would directly conflict with Canada's hopes for a nation stretching "from sea to sea." In a countermove, Rupert's Land and the remainder of the North-Western Territory were officially transferred to Canada in 1870, and in the same year, the province of Manitoba was created to encompass the settlements in the Red River district. British Columbia entered Confederation the following year.

Meanwhile, the concept that Canada's northern character affirmed its uniqueness in North America continued to fire patriotism and national unity. In 1869, Robert G. Haliburton claimed that "the peculiar characteristic of the new Dominion must ever be that it is a Northern Country," and he predicted a special destiny for the nation because of its location, rigorous climate, and heritage of northern races.[4] This theme was promoted vigorously in the early 1870s by members of the Canada First Movement, who continued to emphasize the vision of a great "British" empire of the north, thus raising the ire and distrust of French Canadians. Naturally, the Canada Firsters found fertile ground in the rapidly expanding community of Winnipeg, and soon the social Darwinian concept was incorporated into the rhetoric and boosterism of the western expansionists.

Up to that point, the British-held Arctic islands seemed to offer little in the way of short-term economic benefits or opportunities, that is, until 1874, when American interests requested mineral rights on Baffin Island. Negotiations began immediately for the transfer of the Arctic Archipelago to Canada. As one member of the British Colonial Office remarked, the main object in turning over the islands was "to prevent the United States from claiming them, not from the likelihood of their being any value to Canada."[5] To clarify the boundaries of Canadian authority, an imperial order-in-council of 31 July 1880 transferred to Canada "all British Territories and Possessions in North America, not already included in the Dominion of Canada, and all islands adjacent to any such territories or possessions" (noting the exception of Newfoundland and its dependencies), stating also that they be "subject to the laws for the time being in force in the said dominion."[6]

Although territorial expansion was a priority concern during the early years of Confederation, there was no thought of developing or settling the Arctic or sub-Arctic regions. Government attention was centred on the arable prairie lands, which were governed by the lieutenant-governor of Manitoba until the Northwest Territories Act of 1875 provided a resident lieutenant-governor and a five-member appointed council. Only the newly formed District of Keewatin, stretching from the Manitoba border to the Arctic coast, remained under the province's jurisdiction. Then in 1882, the southern regions of settlement were set up as the provisional districts of Athabaska, Saskatchewan, Alberta, and Assiniboia. By the same dominion order-in-council, policy regarding administration of the remaining lands to the north was explicit: "that no steps be taken with the view of legislating for the good government of the country until some influx of the population or other circumstance shall occur to make such provision more imperative than it would at present seem to be."[7] Perhaps it was merely a coincidence, but concurrent discussions in Berlin related to the status of African states were leading toward "effective possession" as the criteria for full sovereign control.[8]

It was more than a decade before "circumstances" were sufficient to require any government action in the far north. In the opinion of political economist Kenneth Rea, the unsettled hinterlands "were in practice virtually ungoverned frontier areas possessing neither population nor economic significance until the late 1890s in the case of the Yukon, and until the early 1920s in the case of the Northwest Territories."[9] At those times, increased population and economic potential were indeed key considerations in instituting changes in northern government, but in both cases a perceived American threat to Canadian sovereignty was the major catalyst prompting Ottawa to take decisive action.

By the mid-1880s, the western expansionist movement had aroused enough interest in the economic potential of a railway link from Winnipeg to a northern trade route through Hudson Bay, prompting several official scientific expeditions to investigate the resource potential and feasibility of navigation in the region. The jingoism in the propaganda supporting the proposed Hudson's Bay Railway surpassed even that of the Confederation era, as illustrated in Charles Tuttle's gilt-edged, leather-bound, *Our Northland*, which described in much exaggerated terms the unlimited potential of marine and land-based resources with continual reference to "Anglo-Saxon supremacy" and the northwesterly direction of "the general course of human progress." Apart from providing access to the unexploited wealth of the north, Tuttle maintained that the rail line to Churchill would ensure Canada's rise as a powerful and prosperous nation, with Manitoba at the centre.[10] In 1888, Senator John C. Schultz, a former Manitoba MP and a staunch backer of the Hudson's Bay Railway, headed a special Senate inquiry into the resource potential of the Great Mackenzie Basin. No doubt influenced by him, the committee reported that the region probably possessed "the most extensive petroleum field in America, if not the world," with the added recommendation that government authority be extended "to safeguard the national interest."[11] Ottawa's response was to continue the endless task of mapping and scientific exploration under the direction of the Geological Survey, but there was no support for a railway that would encourage commercial and industrial development of Manitoba at the expense of Ontario and Quebec.

As the nineteenth century drew to a close, Ottawa's attention was gradually drawn to the Pacific Northwest and, to a lesser degree, to the eastern Arctic. The first indication of a potential problem arose in 1893 from a report submitted by a government land surveyor, William Ogilvie. Based on first-hand observations during fieldwork, Ogilvie recommended that immediate steps be taken to establish authority over the unsettled regions north of British Columbia owing to the increasing numbers of American prospectors in the area. The next year, a police inspector and a staff sergeant were sent to investigate, and in 1895 a detachment of twenty North West Mounted Police was sent to establish a more permanent police post, and the Yukon was declared a provisional "District" along with Franklin, Mackenzie, and Ungava. The latter move was apparently designed to create an illusion of active government jurisdiction, for there were no associated administrative changes, and the handful of police were left with the entire responsibility of enforcing Canadian law and order. Ogilvie returned to the Klondike area in 1896 to continue his survey work in the event of any future disputes, although no one seemed concerned that the boundary location in the access area of the Alaska Panhandle was still unresolved.[12]

Meanwhile, missionary reports had reached Ottawa that American whaling activities in the western Arctic were depleting the supply and having a detrimental effect on the Inuit; there were warnings of similar conditions in the eastern Arctic. In both regions, it was now common practice for the whalers to winter over, causing concern that their presence might be construed as effective occupation according to international law. By 1896, for example, it was estimated that twelve hundred American whalers had remained on Herschel Island in the Beaufort Sea.[13] In 1897, the new Laurier government sent Captain William Wakeham on a reconnaissance expedition to Hudson Bay and Baffin Island. At a remote whaler's base at Kekerton Harbour, he made a formal declaration of Canadian sovereignty over Baffin Island and all adjacent territory, the first official proclamation after the transfer of the Arctic islands to Canadian jurisdiction seventeen years earlier.[14] This action drew little attention, for there were far more exciting, yet disturbing, events occurring elsewhere.

In the summer of 1896, a major gold discovery was reported along Bonanza Creek, a tributary of the Klondike and Yukon Rivers. In anticipation of a stampede similar to the California gold rush of 1849, Clifford Sifton, minister of the interior, appointed a retired police officer, J. M. Walsh, as commissioner of the Yukon. Accompanied by former boundary commissioner W. F. King and William Ogilvie, Sifton set out the next spring with Walsh's party of officials and police to assess the situation first-hand. Immediately, he ordered police posts armed with maxim machine guns to be set up in the two major passes, a precautionary measure prompted by reports that four companies of United States Infantry were on their way to the ports of Skagway and Dyea. Arriving several months later, the American commanding officer initially challenged Canada's right "to exercise civil and military authority over American Territory, or on Territory at least in question," but he was later overruled by a superior who accepted the validity of the Canadian claim.[15]

Hoping to create an all-Canadian route to the gold fields and thus avoid the American ports in the Panhandle, Sifton at once began negotiations to build a narrow-gauge railway connecting a point on the Stikine River in northern British Columbia to Teslin Lake in the Yukon. Although the bill passed in Parliament, it was delayed for six months in the Conservative-dominated Senate, by which time construction had already begun on an American-financed rail line following the shorter White Pass route through the Alaskan

Panhandle. In anticipation of difficulties in maintaining civil order, Sifton again expanded the law enforcement agencies. Thus, before the main rush occurred in the summer of 1898, the police force had been increased to 239 and soon received the additional support of 200 militia men, including Royal Canadian Dragoons and Artillery. In explaining his actions to Parliament, Sifton claimed that the precautions were necessary, a "case of possession being ten points in the law, and we intend to hold possession." He also believed that if American troops had got as far as Bennett Lake, "it would have taken twenty years of negotiating to get them out, in fact I doubt if we would ever have got them out."[16]

Persistent pressure from the miners and the new residents of Dawson City forced further changes in government institutions. In 1898, an "Act to Provide for the Government of the Yukon Territory" was passed that allowed for a commissioner, a six-man appointed council, and judicial offices. This act was amended over the next ten years to provide two elected council members in 1900, a seat in Parliament in 1902, and a fully elected council by 1908. Significantly, only British or Canadian subjects received the federal franchise, a prudent measure since in 1901 over 32 per cent of the estimated twenty-seven thousand newcomers still remaining were foreigners.[17] In hindsight, this event did not constitute a serious sovereignty crisis, but in 1896 there was just reason for concern. The crucial question facing the Laurier government was whether its authority would be accepted by the large number of Americans whose very nationality originated from the perceived right to revolt against British colonial rule. Sifton's sensitivity to any possible challenge to Canadian authority was roused again in 1901 with rumours of a miners' uprising. In response, more Mounted Police were sent to the territory, which in turn provoked an equally determined President Theodore Roosevelt to move more American troops into the Panhandle.[18] Fortunately, Sifton's strategy proved adequate and Canadian authority was accepted, although at times reluctantly. Then, as the gold supply was depleted and the Americans withdrew, the structure of government was adjusted to suit the dwindling population and economy. The council was reduced to three elected members in 1919, and the duties of commissioner and administrator were assigned to the gold commissioner. By 1932 the responsibilities of all three offices were delegated to the controller.[19]

Of additional concern was the question of the boundary location in the Alaska Panhandle. The Anglo-Russian Treaty of 1825 had defined an approximate border which was recognized by Canada at the time of American purchase, but there had been no official survey to verify its location. Thus, when gold was first discovered in the Cassiar Mountains of northern British Columbia, both Canada and the United States interpreted the original boundary definition in the Panhandle to their own advantage. The Klondike discovery created further dissension over the ports at the head of the Lynn Canal which gave access to the mountain passes leading into the Yukon interior. In 1899 a Joint High Commission attempted to resolve the dispute by declaring Pyramid Harbour a Canadian-controlled port and creating a corridor into British Columbia. Though the two governments were unable to reach an accord, a provisional boundary was eventually agreed upon until the issue could be officially settled. Canadian claims were based on rather tenuous grounds, but with nationalist sentiment on the rise, Sifton was not prepared to compromise.

In 1903, the two countries agreed to place their cases before a tribunal composed of three American, one British, and two Canadian jurists. En route to the hearings in London, W. F. King, the chief astronomer and former member of the 1893–1895 Alaska Boundary Commission, warned Sifton that Canada's sovereign claims were equally weak elsewhere in the north, with specific reference to the American whaling activities on Herschel Island. Alarmed, Sifton asked King to prepare a detailed document outlining the situation for future government consideration. Roosevelt's pressure tactics at the proceedings in London only served to increase concern, particularly his threat to back the American claims with military force and rumours of his attempt to purchase Greenland from Denmark.[20]

As expected, Canadian politicians and journalists reacted with anger and indignation when Lord Alverstone, the British jurist, supported a last-minute compromise solution, reportedly in the interest of preserving friendly Anglo-American relations. The decision not only fired strong anti-American sentiments, but it also raised the question of Britain's loyalties and caused Sifton to conclude that "the British connection must become much more informal, a thing of self-interest and sentiment, in no way binding or constricting Canadian growth." Regretting the "cold-blooded and somewhat supercilious conduct of our English friends," he was even more fearful of American motives. In a letter to friend and editor of the *Winnipeg Free Press*, John Dafoe, he argued that "the Yankees have simply got a lust for power territory & expenditure, & they are going to be the biggest bully the world has ever seen."[21] Sifton was not alone in his fears; many others in Ottawa believed that firm defensive action would be required simply to maintain the status quo.

Though Sifton's role as protector of northern sovereignty has generally been overshadowed by emphasis on his immigration policies, his biographer, D. J. Hall, gives full coverage to this aspect of his career, claiming that "Sifton can be credited nevertheless with making some of the earliest attempts to establish a credible, continuous Canadian presence in the far north." Hall also contends that the minister of the interior took a much stronger anti-American stand than the prime minister, that while "Laurier appeared cowed by American bluster and threats, Sifton stood firm in assert-

ing Canadian rights." In later years as chairman of the Conservation Commission, Sifton also stood firm against free trade, believing that its purpose
was to give the United States access to Canadian forests and that it would
lead to eventual annexation.[22]

II

Meanwhile, the situation in the eastern Arctic appeared to be worsening.
In addition to the American whaling activities, there were increasing reports
of foreign explorers cruising the waters of the Archipelago, the most serious
being the attempts of Peary and Cook to reach the North Pole and Otto Sverdrup's discovery of three large, uncharted islands to the west of Ellesmere.
At Sifton's urging and with the reluctant support of Prime Minister Laurier,
an official reconnaissance expedition set out in 1903 under the command of
A. P. Low of the Geological Survey, and accompanied by six Mounted Police; its purpose was merely to patrol the waters of Hudson Bay in hopes of effecting "quasi-occupation" by showing a presence of authority. With the
Alaska Boundary Tribunal not yet underway, Laurier was concerned that the
American whalers might take offence at paying customs duties. At the same
time, he was reluctant to make a formal declaration of sovereignty lest they
had already established permanent posts unknown to Ottawa.[23] Once the
boundary dispute was settled, a police post was set up at Fullerton Harbour
on Hudson Bay, and the next spring Low, aboard the *Neptune*, proceeded
northward through Baffin Bay until he reached Cape Herschel on Ellesmere
Island where a flag was raised and a document declaring Canadian possession of the island deposited in a cairn. A similar ceremony was conducted on
Somerset Island. After compiling a number of scientific reports and surveys,
the ship returned to Hudson Bay before heading south to Halifax.[24]

Also in 1903, Royal North West Mounted Police posts were established at
Fort McPherson and Herschel Island in the western Arctic. According to anthropologist Diamond Jenness: "By establishing these three police posts,
Canada for the first time openly served notice on the world that she was accepting the responsibilities of sovereignty over the arctic mainland and the islands beyond it, was integrating that region with the rest of the country, and
would enforce there her laws. But what plans she entertained, if any, for the
welfare of its Eskimos she wrapped in silence."[25] In light of the concern expressed for enforcing Canadian authority, it was perhaps no coincidence that
Superintendent Charles Constantine, the man responsible for maintaining
law and order at the height of the Yukon gold rush, was despatched to oversee the establishment of the two new posts. Yet in contrast to the Klondike
experience, assertion of authority in the western Arctic was more symbolic

than real. Little revenue was collected from licences or customs duties, and other than forbidding the sale of liquor, there was certainly no attempt to isolate the Inuit from the "detrimental" influence of the whalers. Moreover, having lost a good portion of their supplies en route, the two men assigned to Herschel were almost completely dependent on the American whalers for survival over the first winter. Luckily, the industry was already in decline, and the debauchery reported by the missionaries appeared of far lesser importance than the epidemics which had wiped out entire Inuit communities in the Mackenzie Delta.[26]

In the eastern Arctic, American whalers were now resorting to casual trading with the Inuit to bolster the flagging industry. As a consequence, the police report of the 1903 expedition recommended further patrols and the establishment of eight new posts.[27] The next year another expedition was commissioned, this time under the command of Captain J. E. Bernier. In contrast to previous ventures, which had included a fair measure of scientific research, the purpose in 1904 was clearly political. As described by the official historian attached to the patrol: "This time the purpose of the expedition would be, at last, to take official possession, in the name of Canada, of that great heritage so graciously given to us by England more than twenty years ago, a territory which today is very much prized by foreign nations. Let us remember the boundaries of Maine, the West and of Alaska."[28] On this occasion, the ship carried an officer and ten Mounted Police, whose duties included collecting customs duties, issuing whaling licences, and compiling reports on all foreign activities. Much to Bernier's disappointment, he was ordered to confine his activities to Hudson Bay where whalers had established their winter stations. Alas, these efforts were considered still inadequate according to Chief Astronomer King. In his 1905 published report on the legitimacy of Canadian claims in the Arctic, he recommended that even greater effort must be exerted to establish authority in the far north. Thus Bernier again set out in 1906, this time with orders to formally annex all new lands "by leaving proclamations in cairns at all points." He was also assigned other duties, including that of fisheries officer, justice of the peace, and protector of wildlife,[29] and although it was not in his official instructions, he also took the precaution of removing records left by previous foreign explorers lest they be used to dispute Canadian claims.[30]

In 1907, Senator Pascal Poirier proposed that the "sector theory" be officially declared as the basis for Canadian claims in the Archipelago. Laurier rejected the idea, claiming that sovereignty could only be maintained by officially exerting authority to create a semblance of quasi-occupation; that is, providing no foreigners permanently settled on the islands.[31] Declaration of discovery was still considered a crucial first step, however, so Bernier once again headed out, this time to place cairns and flags on the western islands of the Archipelago. In a formal ceremony at Winter Harbour on Melville Island, he unveiled a tablet on 1 July 1909 that officially laid claim in the name of the Dominion of Canada to "the whole 'Arctic Archipelago' lying to the north of America" from longitude 60° west to 141° west and on up to latitude 90° north. He made one further voyage in 1910–11, but failed in his objective of traversing the Northwest Passage.[32] Despite his passion for Arctic exploration, he resigned that fall after crew members accused him of using government supplies to trade for furs with the Inuit. Perhaps more importantly, his departure followed closely the defeat of the Laurier government, which had supported his expeditions over the past seven years.[33]

Despite its initial reservations, the new Conservative government under Robert Borden proved equally sensitive to the Arctic sovereignty issue. Concerned that uncharted lands might be discovered by an American-sponsored expedition, a special cabinet committee recommended that Vilhjalmur Stefansson's proposed Arctic expedition be fully financed if he would agree to discharge existing contracts with the American Museum of Natural History and the National Geographic Society.[34] Stefansson, Canadian-born but a resident of the United States for nearly his entire life, had no strong political loyalties. He readily accepted Canada's firm financial offer and proceeded to plan and execute one of the most ambitious explorations of its kind: the Canadian Arctic Expedition of 1913–1918. Despite the scandal and controversy surrounding the wreck of the *Karluk* and the loss of sixteen lives, its contribution in terms of scientific knowledge and mapping of uncharted shores was incalculable. Moreover, the discovery of four major islands— Brock, Borden, Meighen, and Lougheed—only confirmed the fear that there might be other islands lying to the north, undiscovered and unclaimed.

If Stefansson had been content to follow the traditional role of the explorer, the Canadian government would have been well rewarded for their investment. As it happened, Stefansson was also an ambitious visionary who had already discovered the usefulness of the press in gaining popular support for his ideas. Moreover, he was adept at lobbying influential individuals to force government action. In some instances, the results were positive. While he was still in the Arctic, his many letters to patrons on the potential of the region's unique wildlife resources resulted in an amendment to the Northwest Game Act in 1917, requiring all non-natives to be licensed for hunting and trapping.[35]

On his return, the charismatic Stefansson embarked on yet another campaign, this time to promote planned development of the Arctic beginning with a reindeer herding project and musk-ox farming. An even more ambitious scheme involved laying claim to and colonizing Wrangel Island, which he believed would make an ideal refueling base for future transcontinental flights over the North Pole. His pre-emptive move to settle Wrangel first and then force Ottawa to claim jurisdiction ended just short of an international fiasco, with the United States, Russia, Great Britain, and Canada all being reluctant competitors for the small, isolated island which lay well within the Russian sector of the Arctic waters. By 1924, Stefansson's penchant for dramatic publicity and his relentless lobbying had thoroughly alienated him from his former supporters in the prime minister's office, the Geological Survey, and External Affairs. In his detailed study of the Canadian Arctic Expedition, Richard Diubaldo sums up Ottawa's disaffection quite simply: "Stefansson had overstepped himself in his postwar years in Ottawa as government advisor and northern propagandist. He had underestimated the political realities within the Canadian bureaucracy and had assumed he could get his own way in the formulation of government policies."[36]

Bitter and resentful over the seeming indifference and disrespect, the tenacious explorer returned to the United States, where he took up permanent residence in New York City and continued his lecture tours and prolific writing on the "friendly Arctic." His predictions about the future potential of the Arctic seemed endless: discoveries of vast mineral and oil resources; visions of the Arctic Ocean becoming the Mediterranean of the future; commercial air routes crisscrossing over the polar ice cap; and thriving settlements, industries, and even agricultural development. Dubbed by journalists the "Prophet of the North," Stefansson continued to promote plans for the Arctic that demanded an entrepreneurial spirit and willingness to make major investments without guarantee of foreseeable return, characteristics quite alien to conservative Canadians. Nor was development of the Arctic very high on Ottawa's agenda in the inter-war years. But Stefansson did appeal to the American imagination, as evidenced by the popularity of his books and public appearances.[37] In Canada, as well, his ideas provoked curiosity and discussion, especially among the intellectual elite.

For the most part, the Geological Survey and the North West Mounted Police shared the responsibility and costs of Arctic expeditions prior to 1920. As a result, the administrative role of the Northwest Territories was considered of relatively minor importance. When the provinces of Alberta and Saskatchewan were created in 1905, the Northwest Territories Act was amended to provide for a commissioner and appointed council responsible to the Department of the Interior to govern the remaining lands. Yet the council was not set up for another fifteen years; instead, all legislative and administrative power rested with the commissioner, Lt. Col. Fred White, a former comptroller of the Mounted Police. This arrangement meant that the responsibility for the initiation, interpretation, and enforcement of territorial ordinances remained entirely in police hands; unrelated problems were referred to the appropriate federal agencies. But the task of administering the Northwest Territories did not appear particularly onerous: the commissioner's staff consisted of three clerks; his yearly budget never exceeded $10,000; and his major concern appeared to be the issuance of liquor permits and rotation of staff at the police outposts.[38]

Amid the publicity surrounding the Stefansson explorations, a seemingly minor incident arose over the use of Ellesmere Island by Inuit from Greenland. Ottawa informed the Danish government of regulations restricting hunting and trapping to only Canadian native residents and requested that the practice be curtailed. Quite unexpectedly, the noted ethnologist, Knud Rasmussen, who had lived with the Thule Inuit for several years, defended their right to hunt on Ellesmere, claiming that it was a "no man's land." The issue was settled amicably on a diplomatic level, but Ottawa was now convinced that a more visible Canadian presence along the eastern shores of Baffin Bay and the Lincoln Sea was required to deter further challenges. To do so, plans were set in motion to institute the Eastern Arctic Patrol on a yearly basis and to establish more police posts in the vicinity.[39]

III

The discovery of oil at Norman Wells in 1920 was the catalyst that brought about immediate and dramatic changes in the northern administration. Fearing an oil boom similar to the Klondike gold rush, Ottawa established a separate Northwest Territories and Yukon Branch within the Department of the Interior under the direction of O. S. Finnie, former gold commissioner of the Yukon. His first mandate was to establish offices in the Mackenzie District and posts in the Arctic islands, "where there was grave danger of our sovereign rights being questioned by foreign powers." To this end, Finnie immediately recruited a staff of administrators, mining engineers, scientists, and medical officers; then at Fort Smith, he began construction on the first permanent government buildings in the Northwest Territories. Within two years, the northern administration grew to include a staff of over sixty, with fewer than half located in Ottawa; the rest were stationed in Dawson, Fort Smith, and throughout the Northwest Territories.[40]

The first of the annual patrols in the eastern Arctic set out in 1922 under the command of the veteran Captain Bernier whose orders were to establish two new police posts at Craig Harbour and Pond Inlet on the east coasts of Ellesmere and Baffin Island respectively. Perhaps unrelated, it is still curious that Bernier's return to government service closely followed the Liberals' return to power in Ottawa. To give concrete evidence of "occupation" as well as the presence of authority, several Inuit families were moved to these previously uninhabited locations, and a press release was issued to explain the purpose of these measures. In the case of the *Ottawa Journal*, 17 October 1922, the news item appeared under the caption, "Canada's Northern Empire within 850 Miles of North Pole, Making Our Sovereignty Certain."[41] It was also recognized that exertion of authority depended on the co-operation of both native northerners and vested interests. As acknowledged by Superintendent D. L. McKeand, "the most important factor in maintaining British Sovereignty in the Eastern Arctic is the understanding and friendly relationship which exists between the administration and the fur traders, missionaries and eskimos."[42] It is not surprising, then, that the Hudson's Bay Company gained a singularly powerful influence over the conduct of northern affairs. Commonly referred to as "Here Before Christ" because its trading posts had preceded the missions, the "Company" was often perceived by the Inuit to be synonymous with the government of Canada.[43] Thus, as the Hudson's Bay Company expanded its trade throughout the Arctic and sub-Arctic, the "appearance" of Canadian jurisdiction and control increased with little effort or expenditure on the part of the federal government.

The decade of the 1920s marked the arrival of bush planes in the north, allowing prospectors ready access to formerly remote areas; it also saw the beginning of Canadian military involvement in the northern territories. In an attempt to gain adequate funding for the fledgling Royal Canadian Air Force, General A. G. L. McNaughton actively promoted northern training programmes which allowed numerous projects to be integrated with the requirements of civil agencies on a shared cost basis. With the Vickers Vedette designed specifically for northern flying, the air force initiated a programme of aerial photography in co-operation with the Topographical Service and the Geological Survey. Similarly, much-needed radio stations were established in the north to provide practical training for the Royal Canadian Corps of Signals, with costs shared by the Department of the Interior. Although initially few in numbers, these stations provided a communications system and basic meteorological reports for the growing commercial aviation industry. In addition, several small air bases were built in the Arctic.[44] While he admits that advances in aviation technology were a major factor in opening the north, McNaughton's biographer claims the general "speeded up the process."[45] It also established a precedent of combining civilian and military services in the north.

As director of the Northwest Territories and Yukon Branch, O. S. Finnie oversaw a number of notable achievements, including the establishment of new game regulations and preserves, the first official census and registration of births and deaths, the first hospital grants and recruitment of government medical officers, navigational aids along the Mackenzie River system, and increased scientific research.[46] As David Judd points out:

Once established, the Branch produced its own momentum and its own programme. The senior officers tried, with some success, to introduce new dimensions into northern administration. Much of the time was spent on clerical routine, but they were able to correct maps, to explore mineral resources, and to examine northern ecology. These expeditions were not simply the impulse of a few curious-minded civil servants; they were a conscious attempt to begin an inventory of resources and to gather information on which to base a new economic policy.[47]

However, the anticipated oil boom, the raison d'être for the new branch, never materialized. In addition to the disappointing results of preliminary tests, the introduction of new regulations intended to protect Canadian interests from speculators discouraged prospectors who discovered that three-quarters of any leasehold must be returned to the Crown in the event of discovery.[48] Furthermore, owing to the exorbitant cost involved in transporting the oil south and the lack of a sizable local market, the wells and small refinery were soon shut down. The Northwest Territories and Yukon Branch remained intact, but there was no increase in staff or responsibilities after 1928.

When it created the new administrative agency, Ottawa also expanded the legislative body by invoking the provisions of the 1905 Amendment to the Northwest Territories Act and appointing a six-member council made up of representatives from the Department of the Interior and the Royal Canadian Mounted Police. The deputy minister of the interior, W. W. Cory, was named commissioner, and Roy A. Gibson, assistant commissioner, was designated as "a full time administrative agent operating under the Commissioner and available to handle and plan day to day operations in the Northwest Territories."[49] At first the council was not a powerful body. According to historian Morris Zaslow, it was no more than "an inter-departmental advisory committee, co-ordinating the activities of several federal departments within the Territories; and its decisions, whether administrative or legislative, relied for implementation upon the funds and personnel of those departments."[50] Given the limited funds, most policy decisions were governed by cost factors and the interests of the fur trade. In the latter case, care was taken to avoid any changes which would alter the traditional life patterns of the natives or interfere with the supply of fur-bearing animals. Therefore, when Treaty Eleven was negotiated with Indians of the Mackenzie District in 1921, widespread hunting rights were granted, with the allocation of specific reserves deferred until deemed necessary. The purpose of the treaty was simply to extinguish aboriginal claims to the land, thus clearing the way for future sale to developers. In the meantime, new wildlife conservation measures were introduced to protect the availability of game for native hunters and fur-bearing animals for the traders.

Despite the reported success of the Eastern Arctic Patrol, there were still a number of uncertainties related to the sovereignty issue, the ongoing explorations of the veteran American explorer Donald B. MacMillan being only one. Rumours of his proposed flight over the North Pole with United States Navy Commander R. E. Byrd prompted an amendment to the Northwest Territories Act in 1925 that required all scientists and explorers to obtain a permit before entering the Canadian Arctic.[51] In the same year, a Northern Advisory Board, consisting almost entirely of deputy ministers having concerns in the north, was set up to study and report on all matters related to Arctic sovereignty. As a first priority, the board was asked to investigate Norway's claims resulting from the earlier Sverdrup discoveries. The subsequent report expressed grave doubts about the legality of the alleged British title, owing to the fact that there had been no formal declaration or exercise of jurisdiction. The special subcommittee which had met to consider possible courses of action unanimously agreed that O. D. Skelton of External Affairs should be given a free hand to settle the matter, a move that effectively placed the responsibility for northern sovereignty into the hands of the diplomats. When Norway officially dropped its claims after Ottawa paid $67,000 directly to Otto Sverdrup, the board believed that Canadian title to the entire Archipelago was finally secure.[52]

Meanwhile, as director of the Northwest Territories and Yukon Branch, O. S. Finnie was unsuccessful in his attempts to institute several new social programmes. In fact, his argument that territorial rights carried obligations and that the government should not relegate the responsibility for Inuit education and welfare to the fur traders and missionaries[53] appeared to have a negative effect, for in 1924, the minister of the interior pushed a bill through Parliament that transferred responsibility for the Inuit to the Department of Indian Affairs and outside of Finnie's jurisdiction. Six years later, "Eskimo affairs" were again reassigned, this time to the Northwest Territories Council. No one, it appeared, wished to assume the financial burden. A further dispute over the cost of native welfare in northern Quebec culminated in a Supreme Court case to clarify the status of the Inuit and designate responsibility. A decision handed down in 1939 ruled that Inuit were considered the same as Indians and thus wards of the federal government.[54]

Government policy in the 1920s was influenced more by economic considerations than social concern. As Finnie himself recognized, "the Canadian government subsidizes the Territories, not altogether in a spirit of philanthropy, but as an investment from which it will draw ample dividends."[55] Hence, since it was in the interests of the fur trade that the Inuit and Indians remain healthy, Finnie was able to convince the Northwest Territories Council to appoint several medical officers and to provide modest grants to the mission hospitals in an effort to control the increasing number of epidemics. Native education, however, was not considered essential to the fur trade, and so his plan to institute a programme of vocational training gained no support.[56]

Despite Finnie's more progressive attitude towards social responsibility and stewardship, the Northwest Territories and Yukon Branch did not have the power to influence northern policy. Using the phrase "a shackled administration," Diamond Jenness, then chief anthropologist of the National Museum, described the branch's role as

> merely an investigating and clerical agency that could study conditions there, register mining claims, licence trading posts, recommend such regulations as, in its judgement, would advance the interests of the territory, and act in general as a public front for the real rulers, the Northwest Territories Council and its on-the-spot administrators, the Royal Canadian Mounted Police. The latter's patrols in the Arctic were not responsible to the Council, but reported to and dependent for promotion on, their Assistant Commissioner who was only one of the Council's six members. . . . Thus the Arctic remained exactly as it had been since Low sailed north on the *Neptune* in 1903, under the control of the police.[57]

This was a harsh assessment, yet it concurs with W. R. Morrison's more recent interpretation that the federal government used the Mounted Police as "its main instrument" to spread it policies and authority throughout the north.[58] While Morrison describes government policy as one of "benign (or indifferent) neglect," both he and Jenness stress the delegation of power and authority to the police. Similarly, one could argue that the missionaries and fur traders were simply instruments for the implementation of social policy; considering the government's apparent deference to the needs of the Hudson's Bay Company, it was the laissez-faire approach to northern development that ultimately influenced the nature of health, education, and welfare services. For example, the new game regulations and the creation of large preserves for the use of natives and métis may have been recommended by the Wildlife Advisory Board and the Royal Commission on Reindeer and Musk-Ox Industries as conservation measures, but they also protected existing fur-trade interests against indiscriminate trapping by non-natives.[59] In most cases, an active government intervention involving new administrative infrastructures occurred only when there were perceived threats to sovereign rights, as in the instances involving American whalers, miners, explorers, and land speculators.

By 1930, the Depression overshadowed most other concerns, including interest in the far north. Since there was no immediate prospect of oil development and no impending challenge to sovereign jurisdiction, the extensive staff accumulated by Finnie was a convenient target for the new Conservative government's attrition policy and its drastic cutbacks in the civil service. As a result, the Northwest Territories and Yukon Branch was abolished, its director superannuated, and his key staff decimated. The consequences were later described by Finnie's son, Richard:

> Out with him in 1931 went all the key members of his staff, everyone of whom had spent the best years of his life in northern study and travel. They were administrators, surveyors, explorers, naturalists, geologists, each a specialist in his field, yet all having intimate and broad knowledge of the Northwest Territories. . . . Hardly a man was left who had ever lived in the North, or who had any first-hand understanding of conditions there. The men who were retained were minor clerks and executives.[60]

Finnie was distraught over the turn of events. According to Diamond Jenness, "he had honestly worked for the north country he loved, but he left the public service with a sense of frustration that darkened his last years and shortened his life."[61] Bennett's policy also had a direct impact on the Territories, where even the meagre health services were cut back in order to save a few thousand dollars.[62] For the same reasons, the government vessel used for the Eastern Arctic Patrol was retired, and space was leased on the Hudson's Bay Company's *Nascopie*. In the process, according to Jenness, the patrol lost its "semi-scientific" character and became "more a supply and relief operation."[63]

IV

Over the course of the first sixty-odd years since Confederation, knowledge of the Arctic and sub-Arctic regions had grown considerably, but perception of its immediate value changed only slightly. The myth of the north still provided Canadians with a unique national identity and a promise of future prosperity, but it was now enhanced by the ideology of the "wilderness appreciation" movement in the United States. By the mid-1800s, American philosophers such as Henry David Thoreau and Ralph Waldo Emerson began to write about the value of wilderness in terms of spirituality and transcendentalism. Others wrote of its influence in combatting the evils of urban industrialization, feeling that a wilderness experience developed strength and moral character in young men and women. Most believed that the presence of wilderness created a distinct American identity that differentiated the nation from the older, more settled European countries. Therefore, long before the excitement of gold discoveries, thousands of Americans had travelled by steamship to Alaska in search of a "wilderness experience,"[64] in spite of the fact that other pockets of wilderness could be found throughout their land, in New England, California, Minnesota, New Mexico, the Everglades, as well as Alaska.

In Canada, with the exception of the Maritimes, wilderness was north of everywhere, and interpretation of its meaning was increasingly related to personal experience. For the educated, the prolific literature on the Klondike gold rush added mystery and adventure to the Yukon in much the same way as the British Admiralty chronicles had romanticized the Arctic. By the early 1900s, Canadian authors began to adopt a more general northward focus, as in the case of the wilderness adventures by P. G. Downes and Arthur Heming or the unique wild animal stories of Ernest Thompson Seton, C. G. D. Roberts, and Grey Owl. Popular magazines, as well, reflected an increasing interest in wilderness experiences. Summer vacations were spent in the near north, in the Laurentians, Temagami, the Kawarthas, the Georgian Bay islands, Muskoka, and the Lake of the Woods region or, further west, in the Rocky Mountains. Youth camps for both the wealthy and the less privileged sprang up, as did adult hunting and fishing camps. Recreational canoeing became a popular pastime, particularly among the intellectual elite; national and provincial parks were created; and politicians began to talk more earnestly of the need for the conservation of wildlife. Gradually the north shed its fearful image for a more romantic vision, and the message was carried throughout Canada by the Boy Scouts and the YMCA, in textbooks and novels, in sermons, hymns, and theatre. It provided the inspiration for the Group of Seven, Tom Thomson, Emily Carr, and other landscape artists who celebrated the images of rocks, trees, and water as symbols of Canadian nationalism. Moreover, the wilderness ethic contained inherent moral and spiritual dimensions which encouraged adoption by most religious institutions.[65] Ultimately, in Canada, true wilderness became equated with the far north, especially in the imagination.

As long as Canada's "northernness" was a *prima causa* of national pride, the issue of sovereignty would have a strong influence on policy decisions. Until recently, historians have tended to minimize this aspect, perhaps because of the abstract qualities of the myth. Especially for the more empirically minded, it would be difficult to accept that a perceived challenge to northern sovereignty was virtually an attack on the heart and soul of Canadian nationality. But if the myth was an abstraction, the physical source of its inspiration was tangible.

By 1930, Ottawa believed the sovereignty issue was resolved, at least temporarily. All Arctic islands had been claimed as Canadian, either by right of discovery or by compensation to foreign explorers, and there was now a semblance of quasi-occupation and a presence of authority. The form of governance followed the British tradition of conservative paternalism, designed more for southern expectations than for the needs of northerners. There were no long-range plans or strategy laid down, but the pattern was set.

2

The Depression Years, 1930–1939

> The present tendency of the administration is to consider the Arctic as rather an embarrassing section of the country, the development of which, and of its inhabitants should be avoided as long as public opinion will permit.
>
> Tom Manning RCN, 1941

With few exceptions, conditions in the Canadian north changed little in the depression years. For those who defined progress in terms of government involvement, progress halted or, in some instances, was reversed. For the few who sought social reform, there was no improvement. Growth did occur in civil aviation and mining, but Ottawa's interest in the Yukon and Northwest Territories diminished significantly after 1930, and there were no incidents affecting sovereignty rights to arouse concern. The whaling industry was finished; the oil boom in the Mackenzie Valley had not materialized; American explorers had concurred with demands to seek official permission to enter the Canadian Arctic; and Norway's claims to the Sverdrup Islands were settled. The economy was the first priority, and it was politically expedient to cut back federal expenditure in the north.

I

Lack of government interest in northern Canada did not mean there was a completely static situation in Ottawa. Concern for the economy and the attendant social disorientation of the Depression drew an increasing number of academically oriented liberal reformers into the civil service.[1] Although most remained on the periphery of the Ottawa scene until war broke out, a few attempted to reform the system of government from within. These included O. D. Skelton heading up External Affairs, Clifford Clark in charge of the Department of Finance, Graham Towers as governor of the Bank of Canada, and Arnold Heeney in dual roles as clerk of the Privy Council and secretary to the Cabinet.

In the inter-war years, External Affairs was a small department, which slowly grew in power and prestige under Skelton's leadership. After introducing civil service exams to put an end to patronage appointments, the former professor of political science and economics at Queen's University successfully attracted a number of younger academics to the civil service. The result was the emergence of a "meritocratic elite," and in External Affairs they included Hume Wrong, Lester Pearson, Hugh Keenleyside, and Norman Robertson. According to J. L. Granatstein in *The Ottawa Men*, "ability was the key; capability a necessity. Influential friends could be important but by no means essential."[2] Described by John Holmes as a "new generation of Canadian nationalists," they sought autonomy to do things, not to keep out of things.[3] This more positive approach to government would have a direct bearing on the nature of policy changes and the rapidity with which they were implemented, a fact readily evident in the postwar conduct of northern affairs.

With few exceptions, these men were relatively young, highly educated, Anglo-Saxon, and Protestant. A large number had studied at Oxford; others had attended graduate schools in the United States. They were bright, aggressive, enlightened, and, above all, fiercely patriotic. Their shared belief in Canadian nationalism and the goal of world peace was a unifying bond, which resulted in their mutual participation in such organizations as the Canadian Club, the Canadian League, the Canadian Institute of International Affairs, and the League of Nations Society. In Granatstein's opinion, "the web of interconnections was intense, embracing family, class associations and work." Moreover, they truly believed that "public service was a civic virtue."[4] For the most part, these young men were social, economic, and political idealists, but they also had an eye to effective and responsible management of the government system. They were interventionists, centralists, proud nationalists, and at the same time committed to the concept of internationalism which emerged in the immediate postwar period. While their interests had little to do with northern Canada during the 1930s, their presence and influence created a propitious body for those hoping to initiate new ideas and policies at the federal level.

Prior to World War II, any criticism of government policy came from those with first-hand experience: scientists in particular, but also missionaries, medical officers, and occasionally the Mounted Police.[5] For British scientific explorers, the Arctic still held a magical allure in the tradition of the great Admiralty explorations of the mid-nineteenth century. Many eventually took up permanent residence in Canada and became active lobbyists for more government involvement in northern affairs.[6] Their educational background placed them in the same peer group as the Canadian-born intellectual elite in government, but they had little influence in Ottawa until the geopolitics of World War II brought the north into the centre of many military, political, and economic issues.

By the mid-thirties, the growing threat of a European war was a further distraction from any creative northward vision. Even though invasion of Canada seemed highly improbable, the Arctic was still considered to be a natural defence barrier. As one observer noted, northern policy in the 1930s appeared limited to "asserting authority; catching malefactors; trapping foxes; and saving souls." With pointed cynicism, he went on to explain that "the first two have been regarded as sufficient functions of Government, and the latter two have been handed over to private enterprise."[7] Although somewhat exaggerated, the remark reflects the frustration felt by a few individuals with respect to Ottawa's lack of interest in northern affairs. The experience of one British scientist in the Arctic prompted the complaint that "the Canadian government in the thirties maintained a low profile in the north, so low as to be practically indistinguishable."[8]

Changes in economic development and settlement patterns were a product of cyclic growth in the mining industry rather than government initiative in regulation or planning. Improvements in transportation and communications, in particular, were directly attributed to private enterprise or military training programmes. There was a decided ebb in public interest as well. Even the discovery of gold on the shores of Great Slave Lake failed to elicit more than a lukewarm response. And though it was unnoticed for the most part, the attrition and restructuring of the northern administration had a significant impact on Ottawa's ability to keep abreast of activities and issues directly affecting the two territories.

II

The implications of Prime Minister Bennett's cutbacks were not immediately discernible, since all previous responsibilities were redelegated rather than discharged. Reorganization aimed to achieve efficiency and consolidation, with multiple titles and tasks assigned to one or two officials. The result was a concentration of power in the hands of a few men, whose heavy workload meant that only urgent issues received attention. With diverse concerns spread across a vast area, there was bound to be an adverse effect on the process of decision-making. Inevitably, northern policies began to reflect the personalities, perceptions, and priorities of those holding the greatest power.

In 1931, responsibility for administration of the Yukon and Northwest Territories was assigned to a Dominion Lands Board under the Department of the Interior. Without altering the function, the title of the board was soon changed to the Lands, Northwest Territories and Yukon Branch.[9] When the Liberals returned to power in 1935, they disbanded the Department of the Interior, and while the northern administration suffered no further staff reductions, it was reduced in status to a mere bureau in the Lands, Parks and Forests Branch. This branch along with four others comprised the newly formed Department of Mines and Resources (see figure 1). Veteran politician T. A. Crerar was appointed minister, but he showed little interest or enthusiasm for northern affairs. Any initiative in planning or policy change was left to the discretion of the deputy minister, Charles Camsell, who was also commissioner of the Northwest Territories Council. This dual assignment made him responsible for both the administrative and legislative functions of northern government.

ORGANIZATION CHART: DEPARTMENT OF MINES AND RESOURCES, 1941

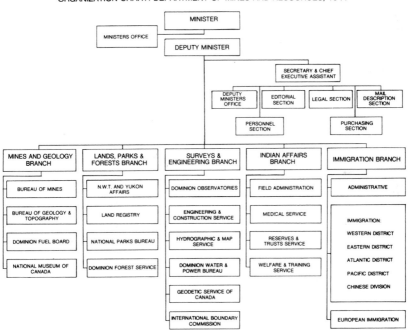

Figure 1 Organization Chart: Department of Mines and Resources, 1941 (from Department of Mines and Resources, *Annual Report, 1941*)

Camsell was born at Fort Liard in the Northwest Territories, the son of a Hudson's Bay Company Factor and Métis mother.[10] He received his basic education at St. John's School in Winnipeg and later at the University of Manitoba. As a member of the Geological Survey, he participated in several ex-

ORGANIZATION CHART, LANDS, PARKS AND FORESTS BRANCH, 1941-42.

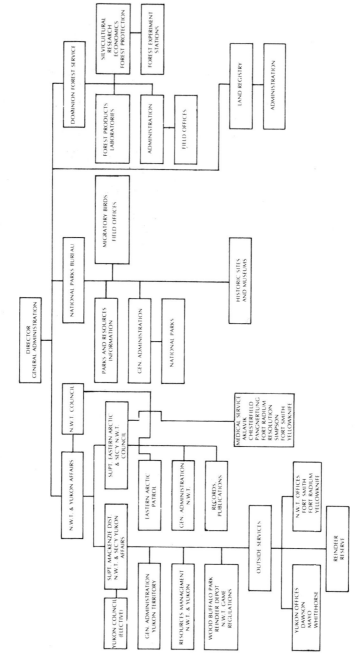

Figure 2 Organization Chart: Lands, Parks and Forests Branch 1941 (from Department of Mines and Resources, *Annual Report, 1941*)

ploratory expeditions before he was appointed deputy minister of the Department of Mines in 1920. Although highly regarded by his peers, he was considered by some critics to have little concern for the social needs of the native population.[11] This may appear surprising given his ancestry, but he never publicly acknowledged his Métis heritage, perhaps in a conscious attempt to be totally assimilated. Camsell's views were traditional and conservative, often at odds with the new generation of civil servants. His primary interest was geology, and when he was burdened with the heavy workload, he delegated most of the responsibility for northern administration to Roy A. Gibson, the director of the Lands, Parks and Forests Branch (see figure 2).

Gibson was born and raised in Brandon, Manitoba, and joined the federal civil service in 1908 at the age of twenty-three. He spent almost thirty years with the Department of the Interior, rising through the ranks from grain inspector to assistant deputy minister.[12] He was a hardworking, dedicated bureaucrat, but one who resented any interference or criticism from outsiders. Gibson distrusted those who might "upset his procedures and power," and on one occasion he was overheard remarking, "we don't want any goddamn scientists in our Arctic."[13] His fear of adverse comments concerning the administration led to an unofficial censorship policy, whereby all writers were required to submit their work to the Northwest Territories Council for approval prior to publication. In one instance, Gibson apparently tried to hire an outsider to prevent him from sending unfavourable reports to another department.[14] Professor J. Lewis Robinson, a former employee of the bureau recalled that "Gibson was a difficult man to assess. He was a dictator and an autocrat, the North was his kingdom and he ruled it. Virtually everything went across his desk for perusal and signature. He was hardworking, worked long hours and took great quantities of paper home every night."[15] Robinson did not doubt Gibson's sincerity, but he suspected that he "was manipulated (without so realizing it) by senior officials of the Hudson's Bay Company and perhaps the churches." Another observer described him as "quite useless in any creative sense."[16] Curiously, there is no record of the assistant deputy minister ever visiting the territory in the prewar period, a fact which was often noted by his critics.

Unfortunately, the two superintendents who reported to Gibson provided little leadership. According to Robinson, the head of the eastern Arctic was perceived as "a talkative bully who was not very bright." Moreover, "everyone in the Eastern Arctic laughed about him and derided him behind his back. The superintendent of the western Arctic was described as an "older man . . . who didn't seem to know what was going on."[17] The lack of capable lieutenants to provide Gibson with sound advice and direction was a major weakness in the organization, second only to the concentration of power.

Camsell's dual roles as deputy minister and commissioner were duplicated at the next level down by Gibson, who, as the director in charge of northern administration, also held the office of deputy commissioner of the Northwest Territories Council. Because of Camsell's tendency to delegate the major share of responsibility, Gibson became the most powerful man in northern affairs. In 1943, Trevor Lloyd, a geographer temporarily assigned to the bureau, described the administrative set-up as "extraordinarily complex because several men hold many quite independent jobs. In effect the whole show is a personal rule by Gibson with a group of selected men holding up to five separate offices."[18] Gibson's power of control also extended over the Yukon, where the decline of economic and political activity had resulted in the assignment of federal administrative responsibility to the Northwest Territories and Yukon Branch of 1921 and its successors.

Just as important as the reorganization of the administrative branch of northern government were the changes occurring in the roles of the two territorial councils. When the Yukon Act was amended in 1918, reducing the elected council to three members, it still retained its power to pass local ordinances as long as they did not involve borrowing or expenditure of funds. Such legislation could only be initiated by the commissioner or, after 1932, by the controller, who was appointed by and responsible to the ministry of Mines and Resources. The controller was not a member of the council, but he could refuse assent to any ordinance passed at its annual session. In this respect, the real power resided in his office, a position held by George Jeckell from 1932 to 1947. Officially he reported to Charles Camsell, but in practice he referred to Roy Gibson. According to a document prepared by the Department of Mines and Resources, this office was "responsible for business arising from the general administration of the Territory under the Yukon Act and Ordinances passed by the Territorial Council; for the disposal of lands under the Dominion Lands Act; for the administration of the Yukon Placer and Quartz Mining Acts; and for the collection of revenue."[19] There was one major exception to this rather all-encompassing jurisdiction; law enforcement remained the sole responsibility of the RCMP.

The same document stated clearly that the controller administered the Yukon Territory "under the instructions of the Minister of Mines and Resources." In addition, Jeckell was also the federal agent for public works, income tax inspector, chief registrar of land titles, and ex-officio mayor of Dawson. Moreover, he represented the interests of other federal departments and was directly responsible for allocation of government subsidies which supplemented the liquor revenues used to support local services.[20] One Ottawa observer declared that the Yukon government during this period was little more than a "benign dictatorship."[21] Similarly, one could argue that the "dictator" was little more than a puppet with strings attached to the director of the Lands, Parks and Forests Branch. While the Yukon had some aspects of representative government by virtue of its elected council and member of Parliament, it certainly did not have responsible government. Yet in contrast to the Northwest Territories, the controller and all council members were permanent residents of the Yukon.

The Northwest Territories Act, as amended in 1921, provided for an appointed commissioner assisted by a six-man council, one of whom could be designated as deputy commissioner. At that time, W. W. Cory, deputy minister of the interior, had been appointed commissioner and his assistant deputy, Roy Gibson, became deputy commissioner, an office he held until his retirement in 1950. Until 1947, the council consisted solely of federal officials who resided and met in Ottawa. The legislative powers granted to the commissioner-in-council were similar to those of a provincial assembly with the significant exception of borrowing privileges and jurisdiction over land and resources. Any ordinance could be repealed by the governor-in-council or, in effect, by the minister of mines and resources, up to two years after its approval by council. Under Section 2 of the Northwest Territories Act, the responsibility of administration was assigned to the commissioner, who was not bound by law to use the council as an executive body.[22] In practice, however, the major administrative responsibilities were delegated to Gibson, whose duties also included initiating council legislation.[23] This situation seriously complicated any attempt to bring about constitutional or administrative reform. Without representation in Parliament or elected members in council, the Northwest Territories could be accurately described as governed by a colonial administration.

The reorganization of the 1930s had a direct effect on the activities and functions of the Northwest Territories Council. The number of sessions dramatically increased compared to the previous decade, when meetings were held less than once a year, and minor decisions formerly handled in Finnie's office were now channelled through the council. The introduction of new ordinances and revisions of old ones gave the impression of renewed vigour on the part of the northern administration.[24] Appearances, however, can be misleading. While the council agenda included such items as executive orders, new legislation, area administration, education, health services, and game regulations, a great deal of discussion centred on trivial matters. At one session, there was a lengthy debate as to whether the tastier Alberta beer should be purchased instead of the cheaper Saskatchewan ale, followed by a heated discussion over the assignment of financial responsibility for the burial of two Alberta indigents who had died at Fort Smith.[25] Reports on native health and welfare might be tabled at the request of churches or medical officers, but items related to the fur trade or new mineral developments were the subject of more serious discussion.

Council meetings during the 1930s tended to be perfunctory. The majority of proposals placed on the agenda received approval; those provoking any debate or disagreement were usually deferred. Rarely did the Northwest Territories Council go on record as having opposed Gibson's views. Furthermore, many meetings identified in the minutes as "Special Sessions" were simply phone calls by Gibson, or occasionally Camsell, to a quorum of members, advising them of a problem and gaining approval for necessary action.[26] This method of avoiding open debate was very efficient, but it gave the false impression of council activity. The autocracy of the system was reinforced by distance, since the only means by which local residents could express their problems was to petition the council in Ottawa.

III

Settlement patterns in the two territories remained relatively unchanged during the 1930s with the exception of the new mining towns in the vicinity of Great Bear and Great Slave Lakes. Although expansion of civil aviation had encouraged exploration activities, actual development was confined to these two isolated areas. This form of "pocket" development differed greatly from traditional frontier settlement. Not only were fewer people involved and the company towns scattered, but costly transportation and poor communications reinforced localism and particularism, as evidenced by the lack of any co-ordinated effort between the residents of Fort Smith and Yellowknife when the two communities were petitioning for political reforms. In effect, there was no unified voice representing the Northwest Territories. Localism was also prevalent in the Yukon, where the elected council was frequently split owing to the traditional rivalry between the Dawson and Whitehorse districts. Legislative powers remained static during the inter-war years, coinciding with a period of no growth in the population or economy.

According to the 1941 census, the total Yukon population was 4,914 of whom 1,550 were classed as Indians.[27] Dawson City, the largest community with barely 1,000 residents, was a service and administration centre, as well as an entrepôt for the mining district. Whitehorse, with approximately 750 residents, was a transportation centre where the White Pass and Yukon Railway connected with the river system of the interior. Mayo Landing to the north was little more than a mining camp. The drastic decline in gold production was compensated for, to a degree, by discoveries of silver in the vicinity of the Stewart River. As a result, the society and economy of the Yukon were still based on resource extraction but with no perceptible internal growth.[28] Only a few local roads existed, and the movement of freight and people depended entirely on water and air transport.

The fur trade was still active in the Yukon, but it was not a major factor in the economy. There were no game preserves as established in the Northwest Territories, and although regulations on trapping seasons and game limits had been issued from time to time, it was not until 1933 that any serious consideration was given to limiting non-native hunting and trapping. The subsequent debate ended in an impasse. The recognition that native hunting and fishing should be protected from white encroachment to encourage retention of traditional lifestyles was countered by the argument that restrictions placed on land might prevent future mineral exploitation. A game ordinance was finally passed in 1938 which licensed trappers, but no land was set aside for limited use.[29] Although some Yukon Indians were still dependent on the fur trade, many were employed in wage labour: on riverboats, at wood camps, and as guides in the tradition of their forefathers during the gold rush era. The small native settlements attached to the trading posts and the missions were semi-permanent and located either across the river or at some distance from the predominately white mining towns. Only a few Inuit lived in the Yukon, and by virtue of their nomadic lifestyle, they were considered part of the Northwest Territories population. With the Indians in a decided minority, the Yukon was governed in the interest of the "white northerner," and the communities which had survived the gold rush became the mainstay of the Yukon society.

Most settlements in the Northwest Territories had originated as trading posts in the nineteenth century. Catholic and Anglican missionaries soon followed, and they were joined later by the Mounted Police. The growth rate of the communities varied according to their proximity to convenient transportation. Fort Smith became a government and transportation centre because of its location at the beginning of the Mackenzie River system; Aklavik and Port Brabant (later renamed Tuktoyaktuk) were direct links to shipping in the western Arctic. Unprofitable trading posts were abandoned, while new company towns such as Norman Wells and Port Radium grew out of the wilderness, providing relatively modern facilities for their transient Euro-Canadian workers. Yellowknife rapidly expanded into a large mining community, recording a population of more than a thousand by 1940. In sharp contrast, the trading post villages experienced little change, most having from ten to thirty permanent residents and a seasonal Indian population.[30]

Although the mining boom drastically altered the character of the region's economy, the impact on earlier settlements was isolated and minimal compared to the Yukon experience. According to the 1931 and 1941 census, the non-native and Métis population in the Northwest Territories had increased by only 1,277, with Indians and Inuit still comprising well over 80 per cent of the total. Most natives of the Mackenzie Valley were unaffected by the mining boom and depended entirely on hunting and trapping for their subsistence. The Métis, on the other hand, found work as pilots on the riverboats or as employees of the Hudson's Bay Company and the churches. The more educated were hired as interpreters or special constables for the RCMP.[31]

As the whaling industry declined, the Inuit became willing participants in the Arctic fur trade, which grew with the increasing demand for white fox. By 1941, the Inuit population was estimated at 7,700, scattered throughout the Arctic, Northern Quebec, and Labrador. Most were nomadic, but they tended to limit their migrations to regions adjacent to trading posts (see figure 3). The Inuit communities were much smaller than the Indian settlements to the south, and they had fewer permanent dwellings. In the western Arctic, the original Inuit population had largely succumbed to disease and were replaced by Alaska Inuit who migrated eastward to the vacant hunting grounds. Because of closer contact with the whalers and traders, most had adopted western traditions of food and clothing, and they tended to be more prosperous than their eastern counterparts.[32]

ARCTIC MISSIONS, RCMP AND TRADING POSTS

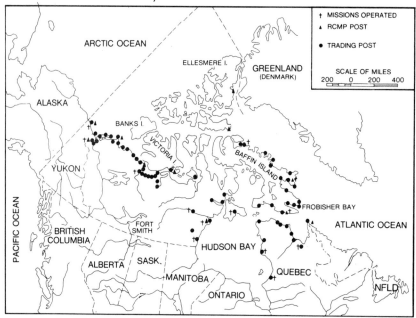

Figure 3 Arctic Missions, RCMP and Trading Posts (adapted from Diamond Jenness, *Eskimo Administration II*, 37)

Out of the total Inuit population, however, 80 per cent lived in the central and eastern Arctic, where they suffered acutely from food shortages and epidemics during the depression years. In an attempt to find a solution to their plight, Ottawa relaxed restrictions covering the Arctic Islands Game Preserve to allow for a Hudson's Bay Company experiment in which destitute Inuit were moved to a more northerly uninhabited region where there was thought to be ample fur and game. The plan was also justified as a means of reinforcing sovereignty through the creation of permanent settlements in the remote northern islands. In 1934, fifty-two Inuit were transported from Cape Dorset to Dundas Harbour on Devon Island, then moved to a series of locations in search of an area capable of supporting them. After thirteen years, they returned to the mainland; the experiment had failed. In retrospect, the project appeared to be designed less as a solution to Inuit destitution, than as a way for the Hudson's Bay Company to get around the restriction of new trading posts in the game preserve with the assertion of sovereignty as justification.[33]

In concert with the aims of traders and missionaries, government policies continued to encourage the Inuit to retain their traditional lifestyles. Although there was a popular consensus that both Indian and Inuit would eventually be absorbed into white civilization through intermarriage,[34] regulations actually promoted segregation and countered any hope of assimilation. Moreover, dependency on the fur trade and lack of educational opportunities gave the Inuit little means to adapt to or play a significant role in the white man's world. Lacking adequate medical services to combat the increasing number of epidemics, annihilation loomed as an even greater threat in the 1930s. Only visiting explorers, missionaries, traders, police, and medical officers seemed concerned, but their proposed solutions were often at variance.

In both the Yukon and Northwest Territories, responsibility for native health and education was left in the hands of the Catholic and Anglican missions, supported by small federal grants. Despite their honourable intentions, the churches came under severe criticism during the inter-war years. While admitting that the missions provided some elementary education and medical services to the natives, Richard Finnie believed that their primary goal was to gain converts and resulted in "enmity and competition between the two denominations: a savage game in which the natives are bewildered pawns. Catholics or Anglicans have sometimes been refused admission to institutions of the opposite faith, and money is wasted in the maintenance of double sets of schools or hospitals."[35]

Diamond Jenness also blamed Ottawa, stating that "government subsidies for schools and hospitals intensified the unconcealed rivalry between the two church organizations." Furthermore, the practice of removing young children to residential schools destroyed any cohesion that still remained in the

social structure of their lives.[36] In a recent interview, a Loucheux Indian recalled memories of his school years at the Anglican mission in Aklavik during the early 1940s: strict teachers who forced everyone to dress alike, having to wash floors and work in the garden, learning to mend socks over a
light bulb, and being forced to take a daily dose of cod liver oil. When asked
what he had "learned," he replied, "mostly about God and being good."[37] In
most Catholic schools, the nuns and Oblates taught in French, a language
which was of little value to the natives in later dealings with Hudson's Bay
Company or government officials.[38] Tom Manning, a British scientist who
spent a number of years in the Arctic, reported that while "some very good
work could be done by an enlightened missionary. . . the amount of harm
that is done by the average missionary of either denomination among the Eskimo far outweighs the good."[39] The only unqualified praise for the missions
appeared to come from the churches themselves, the southern congregations
who supported them, and government officials who saw economic benefit in
their operation of schools and hospitals.

Government grants to the mission schools came from two sources within
the Department of Mines and Resources: Indian Affairs, which was responsible officially only for those Indians covered by the Indian Act; and the
Northwest Territories administration, whose responsibility included the Inuit, Métis, and Euro-Canadian residents. In the Yukon, the schooling of non-
natives came under the jurisdiction of the territorial government. The public
schools, five in total, were quite advanced compared to the mission schools
which accommodated about one-fifth of the native children. Although most
Indians in the Yukon were not "treated," the Indian Affairs Branch did sub-
sidize two residential and four day schools operated by the missions. Prior to
1940 in the Northwest Territories, there were no "public schools," and non-
native children were expected to go "outside" for any formal education. Between them, the Catholic and Anglican missions operated nine day schools
and four boarding schools. These were all located in the Mackenzie District,
however, and provided education for just over 10 per cent of the native children. Responsibility for programmes, standards, and choice of location was
left entirely to the missionaries.[40] Apart from the subsidies provided by Indian
Affairs, government financial support was "negligible." The goal of the
churches was to teach Christianity, not to educate by southern standards, an
objective which suited the aims of both Ottawa and the fur traders in their
goal to keep "the natives, native."[41]

As in the case of education, financial responsibility for Indian and Inuit
health care was also divided. In the Northwest Territories, Indian Affairs
provided for the "Treaty Indians," whereas the territorial council was ac-
countable for the needs of the remaining population, including the Inuit.
With the exception of a few treated Indians in the southeast, the Yukon

council was officially responsible for supplying medical services to all its residents. In practice, Indian Affairs provided limited support to the missions.[42] Partly resulting from confusion over the status of the Inuit in northern Quebec prior to the Supreme Court decision of 1939 that "Eskimos were Indians," there was only the very minimum of health services available to natives of the eastern region: three mission hospitals opened in the 1920s under the Finnie administration and a medical doctor assigned to the Eastern Arctic Patrol. Despite glowing annual reports of its achievements, most observers believed the patrol could not begin to provide the health services required. Diamond Jenness argued that in the 1930s, it was little more than a supply mission.[43] A Catholic missionary stationed in Wakeham Bay was even more critical. In his opinion, the patrol visit was just a "show of face."

> It is true that the Chief of the Eastern Arctic Patrol makes a picnic of his inspection. He is installed on a trading ship, and when he arrives at different posts he sees everything shipshape. The traders must give a good impression to the visitors. Everything is in order; painted, polished, and the Eskimos dressed in the cleanest they can find. . . . That is why things are not as they should be; one must save "face"—appearances are good although conditions remain the same, and indeed sometimes grow worse.[44]

Even the "chief" of the patrol, D. J. McKeand, reported to Deputy Commissioner Gibson that the government medical services were totally unsatisfactory.[45] As a result of the unofficial censorship of reports written by visitors on the patrol, however, most Canadians were totally unaware of the poor health and poverty among the natives in the eastern Arctic. Conditions were only slightly better in the west.

The increase of government medical officers assigned to the Northwest Territories in the late 1920s had been hailed as a sign of great progress. In practice, however, these doctors were charged with various other administrative duties and could not begin to cover the health needs of the Indian and Inuit communities.[46] Furthermore, the cutbacks of the Depression had not only reduced their number, but had also decreased the administration staff in Ottawa. Funding which had been severely cut by the Northwest Territories Council was partially reinstated in 1934 at the urging of the various departments concerned with health, but this measure still proved inadequate to deal with the situation.[47]

According to a study by Richard Diubaldo, health care in the eastern Arctic was "in shambles," a consequence of poor organization to deal with an immense problem and the government's unwillingness to spend money. Yet, year after year, the *Annual Reports* of the Department of Mines and Resources reported that native health was "generally good" or "satisfactory," despite insider reports of starvation and destitution.[48] In 1939 the total cost of hospital services for the Inuit, Métis, and "indigent whites" amounted to only $28,700 in the whole of the Northwest Territories. Care of the Indians was subsidized by Indian Affairs under a separate budget. Self-supporting non-natives paid for their own health care.[49] Two "industrial homes" for the aged and infirm, attached to missions at Pangnirtung and Chesterfield, also received subsidies. These had been built under the Finnie administration, but plans for further facilities of this type were scrapped owing to the high costs.[50]

Dr. J. A. Livingstone, a medical officer with extensive experience in the eastern Arctic, had warned his superiors in 1929 that rigid measures must be taken to avoid degeneration of the Inuit. In a thirty-four-page report eight years later, he made special reference to the deterioration in health that had already taken place. Privately, he had also complained that his work was greatly hampered by the direction of Ottawa administrators who were advised by medical experts unfamiliar with "the special problems of the Arctic."[51] Other medical officers were equally concerned about conditions and the inadequate measures provided by the government, yet each year the advice was ignored and the medical reports shelved.[52] By sharp contrast, the health services provided by the companies at Norman Wells, Yellowknife, and Port Radium were found to be exemplary.[53]

In one instance, the Hudson's Bay Company took its own initiative to improve the health of the Inuit. At the company's request, a team of consultants from the Toronto Hospital for Sick Children was sent to the central Arctic in 1939. The findings of the study resulted in changes in the company's food stock to improve nutritional value and the introduction of a special Vitamin B enriched flour to offset vitamin deficiencies.[54] The Toronto hospital also sponsored a dental survey in the eastern Arctic. Unfortunately, after only a year it was cancelled by the Northwest Territories Council because of complaints about the lack of time during patrol stops to conduct satisfactory examinations.[55] Apart from limited funds, the administration's sensitivity to public criticism was a major factor in its reluctance to co-operate with the private sector to improve conditions in the Arctic.

The Hudson's Bay Company management may have been concerned about the welfare of the Inuit, but practices by some traders indicated the degree to which self-interest governed attempts to improve conditions. Where there were neither medical officers nor police, the responsibility for distribution of relief fell to the fur traders, and a number reportedly held back government rations in the belief that the natives would then work harder on their traplines in order to survive. Although these practices might have aroused concern among those suspicious of the Hudson's Bay Company monopoly a decade earlier, in the 1930s the territorial council looked on relief as a danger which might encourage laziness and dependence. The policy approved by the

Northwest Territories Council in 1933 stated explicitly that "wherever possible, relief is issued in the form of ammunition so that natives will be encouraged to get out and shift for themselves." But the council was also concerned that "competition in charity" be avoided; thus, while it was willing to provide relief in areas having more than one trading post, it was also asserted that "the larger trading companies undertake that where they enjoy a monopoly of trade there will be no need of the Government advancing relief to the natives."[56] In fact, government welfare payments to the Inuit were negligible. The total cost for relief in the King William Island area from 1933 to 1936, for example, amounted to only $477.33 spread among a hundred families.[57] Nevertheless, there was still concern that the system was abused. One missionary reported that some traders received credit for "poor relief" that was never passed on to the natives,[58] and on one occasion a government medical officer pleaded with his superiors that "unless rigid measures are taken for the control of relief, the Eskimo people are bound to degenerate."[59] Despite warnings, Inuit welfare remained a low priority in Ottawa. In the Mackenzie District, welfare relief for the Indians was handled by Indian Affairs, usually through an appointed agent who was either a government official or a member of the Mounted Police. In the Yukon, where industry was made up of small companies and free traders, the responsibility for Indian welfare relief was generally left to the missions.[60]

Although mining was the mainstay of the Yukon economy and of increasing importance in the Mackenzie District during the 1930s, the fur trade was the only real industry left in the Arctic after whaling all but disappeared. The effect on the Inuit was insidious. Not only had the fur trade changed their traditional nomadic hunting habits, but also their ability to trade was limited owing to the fact that white fox was the only fur of significant commercial value in the Arctic. Pursuit of this elusive animal left little time to hunt for seals and caribou if a hunter was to earn enough credit for rifles, ammunition, gasoline, and boats. Relying more and more on food supplies obtained at the post, the Inuit became increasingly dependent on the trader for survival.[61] The introduction of the debt system virtually cemented the relationship. Paternalism in excess was poignantly illustrated in the wording of the *Eskimo Book of Knowledge* published by the Hudson's Bay Company in 1931 and distributed to the Inuit, presumably among those who had been taught by the missions to read.

The Book of Knowledge is a token of friendship provided for you . . . and for your family by the Governor of the Company. He is a man of great understanding and wisdom who decides the difficult problems of the Company and directs the traders in their duties. . . . Take heed to what is written here, all you men and women of the North. Your people have not

derived good from the use which you have made of the White Men's
things. The things which have been brought to you are good things in
themselves, but you have misused some of these things, so that today you
are a feebler people than in the old days when your fathers did not know
the White Men. Your sons are less hardy, your wives bring forth fewer
children. There is sickness among some of you. Here you shall learn how
you have brought this weakness about.[62]

Although the book was designed to encourage more healthful living practices
and, indirectly, to increase fur production, it also illustrated the paternalistic
attitude of the trader. Although never expressed quite so arrogantly, the
views of many southern bureaucrats were identical. Any problems were
caused by the Inuit's inability to adapt, not the influence of the "white
man." Retention of traditional lifestyles meant more furs for the Hudson's
Bay Company, less responsibility for the government.

    During the height of the conservation movement in the 1920s, the govern-

GAME PRESERVES IN THE TERRITORIES CIRCA 1945

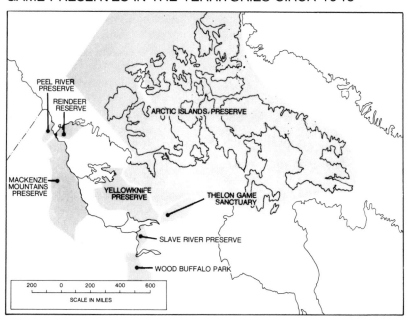

Figure 4 Territorial Game Preserves, 1945 (adapted from Trevor Lloyd, *The Geography and Admin-*
istration of Northern Canada, chapter 8)

ment had created large hunting preserves in the Northwest Territories to protect northern wildlife from exploitation by white hunters. Existing trading posts were allowed to continue, but new establishments were banned (see figure 4). Similarly, a number of game regulations were introduced to conserve the fur supply. Although these initially met with resistance from trading companies, actual enforcement would have been difficult without their support. Otherwise, responsibility fell on the Royal Canadian Mounted Police, who were faced with an impossible task given the few men and the size of the territory. During the early 1920s, those involved in the Arctic fur trade had enjoyed exceptional prosperity. Thus, the long-term objectives of the conservation measures were accepted, albeit at times reluctantly.[63]

Prosperity in the fur trade was shared by the native peoples as well. Many Inuit in the western Arctic were well clothed and fed; some owned motor boats; a few became independent traders. Companies competing with the Hudson's Bay Company also flourished, especially large operations such as the Canalaska Trading Company in the west and Revillon Frères in the east.[64] But there were problems on the horizon. The caribou herds, which were the traditional source of sustenance for the mainland Inuit, were rapidly declining in numbers. In addition, the trappers' increasingly poor health had a direct effect on fur production. Concern for the dwindling food supply led to renewed interest in the possibility of reindeer farms, an idea first advocated by Vilhjalmur Stefansson in 1919. A large herd was purchased in 1929 from Alaska, but it did not arrive in the Mackenzie Delta until 1935 and then it only provided food and clothing for those residing in the western Arctic. Government officials publicly claimed that there was a problem finding labour for the project, since few Inuit were attracted to this form of range farming. Some reports suggested that the Inuit might quickly deplete the herd and then expect more to arrive. As a consequence, the herd was managed under the close supervision of a government official, but even then, the project could not begin to supply the quantity of food required.[65]

The high price of white fox in the mid 1920s encouraged overtrapping and a sizable influx of Alaska Inuit and non-natives. This problem was intensified by the traders themselves, who advanced credit up to as much as $5,000 to entice more trappers to their posts. In 1926, however, the total catch was less than the previous year and divided among many more hunters. Overproduction lowered the price, which plummeted further during the Depression. By 1931, the price of white fox had fallen from a high of $40 to a mere $12 a skin. The traders began to decrease, or in some cases even refuse, credit when the natives were unable to repay their debt of the previous year. Already in serious debt, many Inuit were asked to pay cash for ammunition and supplies.[66]

During such periods of poor game supply and low fur prices, the Inuit were particularly vulnerable. When prices of white fox fell even further to reach a low of $8 in 1934, Inuit trappers in the eastern Arctic found themselves in dire straits and without caribou as an alternative food supply. Those in the Mackenzie Delta were relatively less affected because of their access to the reindeer herd and a more bountiful supply of fish and small animals.[67] Once independent, the Inuit now relied almost totally on the traders, missions, and to some extent the government for survival. Their living standards compared poorly with those of the natives of Alaska, Siberia, and Greenland. In 1939, the Russian Eskimos were piloting planes; the Alaskans operated businesses; and the Greenlanders were electing their own councils.[68] In Canada, the northern Indians and Inuit had no say in the economy, religious practices, education, law, or politics.

Whatever reasons contributed to the more successful adaptation of Inuit residing in other countries, the Canadian government showed little interest in studies or programmes to improve the welfare or status of their own northern natives. Outsiders with experience in the Arctic regions were extremely critical of government policy, especially the British scientists. Tom Manning, a biologist, argued that despite resource potential, "It is my contention that along with the development of mining, or preferably ahead of it, there should be a development of other resources and particularly of the native population." Manning also charged that "the present tendency of the administration is to consider the Arctic as rather an embarrassing section of the country, the development of which, and of its inhabitants should be avoided as long as public opinion will permit."[69] Richard Finnie, author and lecturer, was equally condemnatory when he wrote that, "today's Administration, clinging to its policy of laissez-faire, has abandoned the natives to moral and physical disintegration." He went on to criticize both the system and the men in charge.

> Some of the officials are fully aware of the short-comings of the system and privately acknowledge them. . . . Yet the men in charge are content to muddle along with the status quo from day to day, side-stepping responsibility, fearing criticism, and fervently hoping that they will not be saddled with embarrassing scandals. . . . Particularly evident in government circles is a dearth of vision and constructive imagination, and the Northwest Territories administration is no exception.[70]

By 1940, there was increasing evidence of government apathy in a number of areas other than the fur economy.

IV

The mining boom of the 1930s attracted little outside attention. When Gilbert Labine found pitchblende and silver on the shores of Great Bear Lake in 1929, there was only moderate reaction, even among prospectors. Despite a growing market for the radium found in pitchblende, this precious mineral lacked the magical appeal of gold. Moreover, times had changed since the Klondike days. Prospectors arrived with ease aboard ski and float planes; reporters suffered no time lag in getting news outside; and the Mounted Police and Geological Survey were soon on the scene in respectable numbers. Yet the noticeable absence of excitement and romance did not slow growth in the private sector. Eldorado Mines started operation in 1933 at Port Radium, and it was followed shortly by two others. The refinery and oil wells were reopened at Norman Wells, and commercial boat traffic increased along the Mackenzie. The production and transportation costs proved excessive, however, and by 1939, only the Eldorado mine remained in production.[71] At that time, there was no reason to suspect that the uranium content in the pitchblende ore would be of any commercial value.

One discovery led to another as mineral explorations expanded quickly with the aid of bush planes. The gold strike near Great Slave Lake in the midthirties brought another wave of prospectors and speculators north, but even the prospect of gold failed to excite the general public as it had in earlier years. In contrast to the placer gold of the Yukon, the mineral here was deeply imbedded in granite and not readily accessible to the amateur goldseeker. The setting was equally unattractive, with the bare rocky hills and stunted spruce providing little inspiration for writers and photographers. In the words of author Ray Price, "Yellowknife was dull. . . . The Dawson rush was like the careening gallop of a wild unbroken stallion, and the Yellowknife rush like the plodding of a horse cart."[72] Nonetheless, the first gold brick was poured in 1938, and Yellowknife soon became the largest community in the Northwest Territories.

In contrast to the preceding decade, the Yukon mining industry did better than average in the critical depression years. Although the early 1920s had been relatively prosperous for the Mayo silver mines, the next five years saw a general retrenchment as mergers and acquisitions created fewer, but larger, amalgamated companies to provide financing for new technologies. Still, the industry was in trouble. Government regulations were changed to provide some assistance, but only minimal financial support was offered. Then, as elsewhere in Canada, the Depression brought relative prosperity for the industry with the rise of gold prices. Production doubled in the decade, for the most part concentrated among the larger companies. Yet, it was hardly a boom period, and the high cost of new techniques provided little inducement for prospectors or developers.[73]

Considering Ottawa's previous response to mineral or oil discoveries in the far north, one might have expected growth of government infrastructures to support the developments occurring in the 1930s. But aside from provid-

ing law enforcement, geological studies, and a few minor officials, Ottawa
was reluctant to expand financial and human resources to assist the new communities, despite the fact that the value of mineral production in the Northwest Territories surpassed that of the fur trade by 1939. Some funds were allocated to improve local mining roads in the Yukon as well as new docks and
navigational aids on the Mackenzie River, but these expenditures were part
of a "make work" scheme to relieve unemployment and did not indicate a
specific initiative in northern development.[74]

In the Northwest Territories, this attitude did not adversely affect the private sector, which seemed capable of generating its own growth. The opening of mines at Great Bear Lake and Yellowknife prompted the expansion of
facilities at Norman Wells to fuel the growing river traffic. New transportation companies were formed, owned and operated by the mining concerns,
and for the first time in many years, the Hudson's Bay Company monopoly
on the Mackenzie was seriously threatened. River freight increased from
5,000 tons in 1929, to 21,000 tons in 1938.[75] In the Yukon, where transportation and service facilities were already established from earlier boom periods, there was little secondary economic growth.

Of greater significance was the role played by aviation. Scheduled air service began along the Mackenzie Valley in 1929, providing year-round acces-
sibility. Regular air service came later in the Yukon, although the mining
settlements were well serviced by charter flights. By the mid-1930s, freight
had become the mainstay of the small private airlines servicing the Canadian
north. Competing companies in the Northwest Territories were gradually absorbed by Canadian Airways, which merged with Grant McConachie's Yukon Southern to form Canadian Pacific Airlines in 1938.[76] Although civil
aviation stimulated private development, it had a mixed effect on government involvement. Morris Zaslow has argued that the increase in northern
aviation allowed activities of private prospectors to outdistance those of the
Geological Survey, a factor which ultimately contributed to the diminishing
importance of that agency.[77] On the other hand, civil aviation did benefit from
the various RCAF training programmes which continued on into the 1930s.
Apart from the extensive aerial photography and radio communications net-
works, the Air Force trained countless fliers who would become the bush
pilots of the north.[78]

Ottawa's reluctance to invest any significant sum in the territories also obstructed prewar attempts to build a highway from northern British Columbia
to Alaska. As early as 1929, the governments of British Columbia and the
Yukon had requested financial support from Ottawa for construction of a
road to link Canada's most westerly province with America's northernmost
territory. The idea was initiated by a group in Fairbanks, Alaska, and at the
outset of the Depression the project was strongly supported by British

Columbia's Premier S. F. Tolmie as a means to promote economic development and provide work for the unemployed. Although public interest was high, Ottawa had no interest in burdening itself with such a major expense. Northern development was particularly costly because of the need to adapt to climatic conditions, distance from market, inaccessibility, and scarcity of labour. Traditionally, the Canadian government was reluctant to give financial support to any enterprise which might have an element of risk.

By far the most dominant feature of northern policy in the 1930s was the government's preoccupation with restricting federal expenditures. Diamond Jenness described the effects of budget restraints:

> The times, in its [the council's] judgment, called for a rigid hold-the-line policy devoid of any new experiments or adventures that might involve government in extra expenditures. The police could continue as before to uphold Canada's sovereignty in the Arctic and maintain peace, enforce game regulations, collect the taxes on exported furs, distribute relief, and act in general as the Council's field administrations; the missions, supported by small subsidies could provide all hospitalization and rudimentary education that the Eskimos required; while the traders, gently regulated, could take care of their economic welfare.[79]

In this instance, "gentle regulation" meant that all applicants seeking to establish new trading posts "must assume full responsibility for the welfare of the natives" who traded with them and that any destitute natives must be maintained without expense to the department.[80]

"Without expense to the department" became a by-word in council discussions. On the one hand, nutritional studies funded by the Hudson's Bay Company received approval, but, on the other, Inuit were prohibited from travelling to Edmonton by air because of potential cost to the government. Gibson argued that although they might be able to afford a plane ticket at present, "subsequently they might apply for relief because of poor trapping seasons or low fur prices."[81] Even the white population had to bear the consequences of restricted expenditures. As one example, the application for a public school at Fort Smith was rejected on the grounds that it "would establish a precedent, and requests for schools at other points in the Mackenzie District would likely follow." As an alternative, Gibson suggested that parents should make their own arrangements for teachers.[82] The emphasis on financial restraint was also demonstrated in the council debate over the Supreme Court decision that "Eskimos were Indians" and thus a responsibility of the federal government. The administration's greatest fear was that it would be required to reimburse Quebec for previous welfare payments to the Inuit. According to the deputy commissioner, "a substantial amount

[$54,674.16] is involved. This factor should be considered when deciding whether an appeal should be made."[83]

The priorities inherent in government policy are clearly evident in a comparison of Canadian expenditures in the north with those of Alaska and Greenland.

TABLE I: Comparative government expenditures on the Inuit (per capita), 1939[84]

	Canada ($)	Greenland ($)	Alaska ($)
Police	17.00	0	.41
Education, health and welfare	12.00*	44.00	13.00

* Out of the $12, approximately $5 was paid indirectly by the Inuit through taxes on the furs sold.

Certainly, "showing a presence of authority" was unquestionably Ottawa's chief priority, but there were also disproportionate allocations of funds elsewhere. For example, in the 1939–40 fiscal year, the total budget of the Department of Mines and Resources amounted to over $23 million, of which less than $4 million was allotted to the Lands, Parks and Forests Branch. Of this latter amount, only 10 per cent was set aside for the Northwest Territories and Yukon administration combined, and of the $114,603.92 apportioned for medical services, schools, and welfare payments in the Northwest Territories, $25,000 went to the Hudson's Bay Company for use of the *Nascopie*.[85] Despite the popular argument that "financial stringency" was "the principal reason for the delays in instituting more progressive and far-reaching administrative programmes in the northland,"[86] one must conclude that by 1940 the "north" was a very low priority relative to other areas of government. Only in terms of the sovereignty issue did it take on any importance.

Financial reasons were also the basis for both rejection and approval of more representative and responsible government. In 1931, a petition was sent to Ottawa requesting a more democratic system with the seat of government and regional administration located in Fort Smith. The proposal was rejected by the Northwest Territories Council on the grounds that it was uneconomical.[87] In contrast, when the Yellowknife community demanded more local self-government in 1939 to counter what they perceived as Ottawa's "sluggish inactivity or evasion," they were granted the right to set up a Local Administrative Unit.[88] The new trustee board, which consisted of three appointed members plus the chairman and two elected representatives, was responsible for poor relief, health, education, fire regulations, sanitation, and public works. It was hoped that revenue from business licences and property and poll taxes would pay for the required services and alleviate demands on the northern administration.[89] By placing the financial responsibility on the shoulders of the local residents, the Northwest Territories Council hoped to divest themselves of the costs involved in providing social services for the rapidly expanding community. In this instance, a degree of local representative government was granted primarily because of monetary considerations rather than to institute a more democratic system.

Funds appeared to be equally restricted for assistance to private industry. It was not until 1941, and after concerted pressure from the company, that the Northwest Territories Council agreed to pay half the cost of the Consolidated Mining and Smelting Company's road construction in Yellowknife.[90] This decision, however, was more the exception than the rule. In most cases, grants for northern projects were more readily available from other branches of government. Between 1935 and 1936, over $2 million was allocated to the Geological Survey for field work in the far north, but again this was part of a make-work project.[91] By itself, economic development was not of sufficient priority to justify government expenditure.

V

During the early depression years, Ottawa's financial worries overshadowed the possible threat inherent in political events abroad. But with the failure of the League of Nations to implement a successful programme of economic sanctions against Italy and Japan, the prospect of further hostilities loomed on the horizon. Although most North Americans had hoped that an isolationist policy would prevent them from being drawn into another major conflict, politicians and military chiefs began to take stock of their home defence capabilities. Thus in 1936 the United States government again brought forward the question of an Alaskan highway. This time Canada's military advisers warned that if it were built with American money and war should subsequently break out between the United States and Japan, the highway would only serve as a justification for the United States to ignore Canadian neutrality. On the other hand, one report warned that if Canada proved incapable of defending the west coast, the American people were unlikely to tolerate neutrality on Canada's part. Instead, it was believed they would demand "what would amount to the military occupation of British Columbia by the U.S. forces."[92] Based on this premise, plans were devised to expand and modernize the Esquimalt naval base, but the highway proposal was put on hold. In 1937, there were further informal discussions between senior military representatives of the two countries, but there was no agreement on formal defence co-operation.

After a visit to Vancouver and Victoria in 1937, President F. D. Roosevelt personally brought up the question of a connecting highway to Alaska with British Columbia Premier T. D. Pattullo, who was in total agreement and wished to begin serious negotiations. When the idea was again dismissed by Mackenzie King, ostensibly because of cost, Pattullo headed to Washington where he personally lobbied the president and senior officials for a $15 million loan or grant. The prime minister reprimanded the overzealous premier, and with the full support of the federal cabinet, he firmly rejected any consideration of allowing American money to build a highway on Canadian soil. King warned of "financial penetration" and appeared unmoved by the argument that war with Japan was inevitable. Historian Robin Fisher argues that the military question was of lesser concern to the prime minister than the financial burden that would be assumed by the federal government. There were other concerns, such as the consequences of closer ties between British Columbia and the American west coast, not to mention the political ramifications if Central Canada perceived that Ottawa was spending an inordinate amount on British Columbia roads.[93]

Meanwhile, the issue of who was responsible for whose defence was still a sensitive issue for the prime minister. In August 1938, President Roosevelt made the famous speech at Kingston, Ontario, in which he asserted that the United States would "not stand idly by if domination of Canadian soil is threatened by any other empire." Although the press treated the statement as a friendly gesture of reassurance, two days later Mackenzie King replied, with dignity, that Canada would provide adequate defence to ensure there would be no threat. Writing in his diary, the prime minister appeared satisfied: "Good neighbour on one side; partners within the Empire on the other. Obligations to both in return for their assistance. Readiness to meet all emergencies."[94] Little did he realize what future "obligations" might entail.

Some weeks later, King did agree to set up a commission, comparable to the Alaska International Highway Commission appointed by Roosevelt, to study and advise on the proposal, but it was several months before he appointed its members. Reflecting the prime minister's lack of enthusiasm for the project, the commission's mandate was limited, covering the feasibility and approximate costs, but not the question of financing.[95] The political or military rationale and the matter of shared costs remained the sole preserve of the Prime Minister's Office and Cabinet.

American pressure for the highway did not come from the War Department, which had serious doubts about its military value,[96] but from two major lobby groups representing business and commercial interests: a group that later adopted the formal title of "The Alaska Northwest Defense Committee" supported a coastal route and represented Alaskan and Washington

State concerns; and a similar organization promoting an east-west interior route, calling themselves the "Wahpeton–Portal Highway Association," based in North Dakota, but supported by similar interests in Minneapolis, Indianapolis, Cincinnati, and Charleston, South Carolina.[97] Although the two groups were vying for the economic benefits to be gained from direct road access to Alaska, they both promoted the military value to encourage serious consideration and quick approval.

These discussions of the military advantages marked the first instance of national security being seriously considered in relation to Canada's northern regions, although fear of American domination or encroachment on sovereign rights still loomed as a far greater threat in the eyes of the King government. In all matters, the prime minister was keenly aware of the sensitivities of the Canadian electorate; thus he consciously avoided endorsement of any proposals which might be perceived as diminishing sovereign rights. In 1940, military historian C. P. Stacey wrote that to build "the road with American money would, it has been argued, tie Canada to Washington's apron strings in a manner she had never been tied, in modern times, to London's." As an afterthought, Stacey also cautioned that if a highway became essential to American security, Canada might be forced to reconsider the proposal.[98]

Prior to 1941, Ottawa seemed unconcerned or perhaps unaware of the potentially strategic importance of the far north. Stefansson, who had been commissioned by the U.S. Army Air Force to advise on conditions in the Arctic, attempted to explain the reasons for the apathy:

> Canada is less interested in her Arctic domain than most people suppose. The Dominion has only some 11,000,000 with which to people a territory the size of the United States, and most of these live in the country's southern fringe separated from the Arctic by a broad intermediate belt that has not been colonized. Canada has no immediate need for her Arctic region, and has thus far shown little interest in settling even this intermediate belt.[99]

The American military, on the other hand, viewed Alaska's vulnerability with increasing alarm. This isolated territory was considered "the Achilles heel of American defense," and so the entire north, including Canada, became an integral part of United States plans for continental defence. Thus, in 1940, when President Roosevelt finally introduced a bill in Congress authorizing construction of a highway to Alaska, it was stated that the route would be selected "as will best serve the needs of defense."[100] As a result, in consequence of Ottawa's refusal to give financial support to the project to advance economic development of the northwest in the 1930s, the proposed highway would be destined to follow a route most compatible with the needs of the United States Armed Forces.

There is no question that government interest in the north was relatively minor during the 1930s. True, the issue of national security surfaced in the Alaska highway debate, but even then it was superseded by concern over possible American economic domination or consequences of complicity in their defence activities in the North Pacific. Overall, the decade of the thirties denoted a period of relative apathy and financial restraint which laid the foundation for criticism of northern policy as being one of benign neglect.

3

The Ottawa Scene, 1939–1941

> The period in which we are living is... revolutionary; the outside
> world is beating upon Canada with unprecedented force; violent
> change is going on all around us; about the only prophecy we can
> safely make is that drastic changes are going to take place within
> Canada and in Canada's relations to the world outside her borders.
>
> Escott Reid, 1938

Since the frozen wastelands of the Arctic were still considered a natural barrier against a potential enemy invasion, concern for the security of northern
Canada was negligible at the beginning of World War II. Yet circumstances
and events during the war years would have a direct bearing on the changes
about to occur in northern policies. The continental defence and economic
agreements, in particular, eventually turned the focus of government attention northward as senior politicians and members of External Affairs began
to recognize some of the longer term implications. The international scene
was in a turmoil in 1940; in many instances, the strategies directing British
and American war policies were influenced as much by postwar objectives as
they were by the actions of the enemy. For this reason, the motivations behind the external pressures exerted by Washington and London are as critical
to understanding the rationale of policy decisions which ultimately affected
the future development of northern Canada as are the perceptions and priorities of the key actors in Ottawa. By 1940, the stage was set with the actors in
place, although neither they nor the audience had any foreknowledge of the
drama about to unfold.

I

During the period of Liberal hegemony from 1935 to 1957, the Ottawa
"mandarins" had an enormous influence on government policy, the peak of
their influence occurring in the forties. The formidable team of O. D.

Skelton, Clifford Clark, and Graham Towers, with their sub-lieutenants who had joined before the war, was strengthened immeasurably when the civil service opened its doors to fill the needs of a badly strained bureaucracy. During the war, the civil service exams were temporarily abandoned in External Affairs to allow for provisional appointments. As described by one member, "some twenty older men were brought in from the universities, from the professions and from business, and were given wartime assignments as Special Assistants."[1] Similar expansion occurred in other departments. Some were appointed to full-time positions; others were assigned to committees, boards, or specific tasks. The increase in the civil service was dramatic, rising from 46,000 in 1939 to 115,000 in 1945. Even the military were reported to have added members of the intellectual elite to their ranks, but owing to their lack of participation in domestic affairs, they were less involved or concerned with social issues. Moreover, the hierarchical nature of the system did not allow them to reach the upper echelons responsible for high policy decisions.[2] Of particular significance was the fact that many of the new civil servants were recruited from the membership of the Canadian Institute of International Affairs, thus increasing the importance of that organization as a liaison between government and men of influence in the private sector.[3]

The intellectual leaders of the wartime bureaucracy gave new direction to foreign and domestic policies, which in turn changed both the character of government and the part Canada would play in world affairs. Although most were nationalists rather than continentalists, ironically many were participants on the various joint Canadian-American committees which required closer co-operation between the two governments than ever before. The majority were also influenced by the emergence of a new social conscience, which would eventually lead to the beginnings of a welfare state. All believed in a strong centralized, interventionist government as the only efficient means to effect reform.[4] And, as Granatstein claims, "In the process they also created a central government structure and system in which great power and influence flowed to them as well."[5] During the war, the close co-operation between the more intellectually oriented within the civil service became "institutionalized," creating an informal, internalized "brains trust." Mackenzie King, at times sceptical of their idealism, referred to them simply as "the intelligentsia."[6] Their concerns, however, went far beyond domestic interests to embrace a new internationalism based on world peace, order, co-operation, and goodwill.

A number of these senior civil servants were actively involved in the debate over the future of northern Canada, but the two most influential in shaping the direction of government policy were Arnold Heeney and Hugh Keenleyside. They had different objectives and perspectives on the north, but they shared a common belief that close co-ordination of government agencies was essential for efficient and effective administration of the territories.

Arnold Danford Heeney, son of an Anglican clergyman, was born in Montreal in 1902 and raised in Winnipeg. In his view, it was the strong western influence of his undergraduate years that fostered his deep Canadian nationalism which was reinforced at Oxford.[7] Upon returning to Canada, Heeney entered McGill University to study law; then he set up practice in Montreal, where he took an active part in the Canadian League, the Canadian Institute of International Affairs, and in the informal discussions of the "Montreal Group" comprised mainly of Oxford and McGill graduates such as Eugene Forsey, F. R. Scott, Brooke Claxton, and Raleigh Parkin. In 1938 he joined the civil service as the prime minister's principal secretary, and within two years he was appointed clerk of the Privy Council and secretary to the Cabinet. In this dual capacity, Heeney brought organization and efficiency to these institutions, and at the same time he became one of King's closest and most trusted advisers.[8]

Hugh Keenleyside later described his former colleague as "coming as close as any man could, to being the ideal public official. He was intelligent without being arrogant, cool in judgment without being indifferent, kind without being maudlin."[9] Of additional importance was the fact that Heeney held an unprecedented degree of power, since all matters of prime ministerial and cabinet consideration was channelled through his office. By virtue of his dual role, he later became increasingly knowledgeable and concerned about problems occurring in northern Canada and strongly supportive of solutions advocated by those more directly involved.

Hugh Llewellyn Keenleyside figured even more prominently as an instigator of change in northern government. Born in Toronto and raised in Vancouver, he spent his graduate years studying history at Clark University, a Massachusetts college well known for its liberal orientation in the 1920s. Like many of his Ottawa colleagues, he spent several years in the academic profession before entering the Department of External Affairs in 1928. Following a six-year assignment with the Canadian Legation in Japan, he returned to Ottawa where he was attached to the Prime Minister's Office for a few months before his appointment as assistant under-secretary for external affairs in 1941. During the early war years, Keenleyside was a frequent emissary to Washington to prepare the way for high level discussions on naval defence and economic co-operation; he became permanently involved as a member of several committees, including the Permanent Joint Board on Defence and the Joint Economic Committees. His appointment as the representative for External Affairs on the Northwest Territories Council was Keenleyside's first introduction to some of the dilemmas facing the north. From this experience, he became increasingly involved, first as a private citizen and then as deputy minister of mines and resources from 1947 to 1950.

Influenced in part by a strong Methodist upbringing, Keenleyside was a man firmly committed to high ideals and principles. His penchant for intellectual analysis and at times rhetorical phrases gave rise to criticism that he was impractical and "up in the clouds." Similarly, his refusal to bend on issues related to social justice, individual freedom, and equality of opportunity occasionally earned him the reputation of being stubborn and rigid; his disdain for lesser values and compromise was sometimes translated as arrogance. Years later, Keenleyside admitted to a tendency to "overreact" and to "more radical views" in politics and economics, while professing to be conservative in matters of personal and social behaviour.[10]

Whereas Keenleyside was an idealist and an enthusiastic reformer, Heeney was perhaps more pragmatic and cautious; both sought change through reorganization and efficiency. In combination, the two would attempt to bring about progressive and effective administration of northern government. Members of External Affairs lent their full support, many of them motivated by concern for northern sovereignty. All were professed Canadian nationalists; yet because they also promoted a new internationalism which they believed would ensure the nation's autonomy, their plans for "a new north" became part of a much broader and more ambitious scheme of national and international postwar reconstruction. According to former colleague John Holmes, "new perspectives unleashed an unprecedented burst of zeal and invention in Ottawa, an enthusiastic participation in the raising of new structures, the adaptation of old ones, and then, soon after, their remodelling."[11] This attitude was also prevalent in other departments, particularly those involved with the introduction of social welfare programmes. Understandably, opposition to these innovations came from the traditionally conservative sectors of government, such as the Department of Mines and Resources and certain factions of the military, who saw the increasingly centralist thrust as a direct threat to their former preserves of authority. To overcome resistance to change, the liberal reformers often resorted to the use of the media and private associations to gain popular support for new ideas and thus facilitate acceptance by their political masters.

One of the country's most influential organizations during the war years was the Canadian Institute of International Affairs (CIIA). Founded in 1928 as a non-partisan, independent organization, the primary purpose of the institute was to provide a source of informed opinion for community leaders in hopes of encouraging the development of a responsible Canadian foreign policy. In contrast to the strategy of the British parent organization, which strictly preserved its impartiality and independence from possible government influence, the Canadian organization had "the closest direct relations with government of any of the old Commonwealth Institutes."[12] With branches from coast to coast, this organization attracted interested business leaders, academics, many senior politicians, party leaders, government officials, and virtually every member of External Affairs residing in Ottawa. The membership also provided a ready source of qualified candidates to fill the ranks of the expanding wartime bureaucracy; External Affairs, in particular, hired in succession the institute's first three national secretaries: Escott Reid, John Baldwin, and John Holmes. This active participation in the civil service, whether full-time or on temporary assignment, served to cement the close relationship between the institute and government.

Admittedly, the institute was elitist, but based on his experience as its executive director and later as a member of External Affairs, John Holmes justifies its role as a public forum for foreign policy debate. Noting that "the conduct of diplomacy and the discussion of international affairs always have been a preoccupation of an elite," he argues that "the responsibility of the intellectual elite is twofold. They stand to some extent between the government and the general public. On the one hand they have to assist the government in finding the answers and to criticize it responsibly... on the other hand they have to create a climate of public opinion which sustains wise policy with approval, and when required, sacrifice."[13] Particularly in the 1940s, the CIIA was a means by which the intellectual elite within and outside government could exchange views, share knowledge, and exert influence. According to Lester Pearson, the Department of External Affairs found the "well-thumbed volumes" of the institute's research studies of particular value. "We often learn from the experts what our policy has been, as well as what it should be."[14] Of additional significance was the fact that several members had serious concerns about the future of Canada's north and effectively used the organization as a vehicle to inform the public and at the same time lobby the government.

During the 1940s, the institute tried conscientiously to expand its public education programme. To this end, it sponsored several important high level conferences; conducted nationwide radio broadcasts; issued regular press releases, and published numerous pamphlets, books, and a quarterly academic journal. Its members had the added benefit of lectures, workshops, and regional seminars. The impact of such an organization on public opinion is impossible to measure, but its influence on politicians and senior government officials was undeniable during the war and postwar period. And although international relations still dominated discussion, the strategic location of the Arctic later emerged as an added consideration in determining the future role Canada might play in world affairs.

II

The neutrality debate of the prewar years reflected the traditional "schizophrenic pull between the imperialists and the continentalists,"[15] but the tension became more diffused and multidimensional during the war. Canadian

nationalism and traditional loyalties faded into the background when hopes
for immediate victory were replaced by the grim possibility of a British
defeat. Whereas the United States policy of neutrality had initially inspired
an all-out effort to encourage cordial Anglo-American relations, within a
year Canada urgently sought even closer ties with her southern neighbour as
insurance against enemy invasion of home territory.

From the beginning, Mackenzie King had hoped Canada would play the
role as a "linch-pin" in promoting more active American support for the
British war effort. Instead, Canadian efforts often had the reverse effect by
strengthening the neutralist cause among the American people. As stated by
one inside observer, "Canada was less a linch-pin than a nuisance in Anglo-
American relations," and in terms of the triangle concept, "not the intercessor, but the junior of two junior partners."[16] With the United States adher-
ing to terms of the Neutrality Act as revised in November 1939, relations between the two countries might be described as tenuous but not unfriendly.
Equipment and supplies were available to the Allied cause, but on a "cash
and carry" basis only. Washington had halted all discussion of co-operation
in North American defence; even the independent commissions set up to investigate routes for the Alaska Highway deferred submitting reports which
had been completed prior to Britain's declaration of war.[17] The United States
was determined to remain neutral, and Canada was obliged to respect its
rights.

Mackenzie King's attempt to play the role of intercessor was fraught with
problems from the beginning as a result of traditional trade rivalries between
the United States and Britain. Inherent in all negotiations prior to America's
entry into the war were the efforts by both parties to press for postwar benefits or at least for assurances that the other side would not gain an advantage.
Thus, while London believed that the Americans were intent on disbanding
the British Empire, Washington was pushing for future free trade provisions
and guarantees that Britain would abandon her colonial policy.[18] Caught in
between, Canada was aware that any appearance of Commonwealth
solidarity would be considered a direct threat to friendly Canadian-American
relations. As the British high commissioner to Canada reported to the Dominions Office, Canada's position would become impossible if rivalry existed between Britain and America because the latter was "so much more
powerful than herself"; thus, it was inevitable that "Canadians cannot afford
to alienate the sympathy of the United States."[19] There is no question that
prior to the bombing of Pearl Harbor, Washington held the trump card in negotiations for "neutral" support, and the hidden agenda underlying some of
the demands was not always palatable. But in 1940, Canada was unaware
that Washington needed certain natural resources and air bases located in the
northern territories in order to plan the defence of North America.

The motives driving the statesmen of all three countries caught in the diplomatic triangle were often in conflict, at times giving rise to "behind the scenes" suspicion and unease. The rifts within the State Department and Churchill's coalition Cabinet only compounded the confusion. Described by Dean Acheson as "a department without direction," State was split by personality and ideological clashes reflected in the feud between Secretary Cordell Hull and his "free traders" and Under-Secretary Sumner Welles.[20] As a consequence, Roosevelt virtually ignored the department when confronted with serious issues, relying on special advisers such as Harry Hopkins.[21] Winston Churchill was also known to have little respect for the Foreign Office, and his Cabinet was equally fractious according to one member, who claimed "we are all fighting each other instead of the enemy and with such zeal."[22]

The internal tensions only served to intensify the suspicions and distrust between the two large powers. Lord Halifax, British ambassador to the United States, described the Americans as "crude and uneducated"[23] and his dealings with the State Department as "a disorderly day's rabbit shooting."[24] The American diplomats, on the other hand, saw their British counterparts as "traditional tory aristocrats and imperialists," giving rise to Roosevelt's comment that "they are always foxey and you have to be the same with them."[25] Canadians were also the target of criticism by both the British and Americans. An intelligence report for the State Department described Canada's foreign policy as "a highly selfish one, bent on taking the best from all possible worlds and the responsibility for none."[26] At the same time, the British high commissioner refers to King's "sensitiveness" and his attitude of "timidity and reticence amounting to dumbness." And although he admits the Canadian prime minister is a "skillful, patriotic politician," he quite accurately describes him as "not endowed with the qualities of a war leader: there is in him no great dynamic energy, no genius for military affairs or statecraft of the highest order, nor gift of stirring oratory. He is somewhat pedestrian."[27] On the other hand, the under-secretary of the Foreign Office, Lord Cadogan, dismissed all Commonwealth high commissioners as "undependable busybodies" with "really not enough to do."[28] Meanwhile, King suffered the ignominy of American highhandedness on one side and British paternalism on the other. He also lost one of his most valued advisers with the sudden death of O. D. Skelton in January 1941. Norman Robertson took over the position of under-secretary while External Affairs underwent a reshuffling which brought many of the younger generation into key positions (see figure 5).

Despite tensions behind the scenes, Churchill, Roosevelt, and King managed to portray an illusion of friendly solidarity. In fact, their ability to ride above the dissension in high-level negotiations was probably the key to their success. Churchill, at least, displayed some sensitivity to the importance and perhaps impossibility of Canada's position when he appointed one of his cab-

Department of External Affairs   Ottawa - 1941

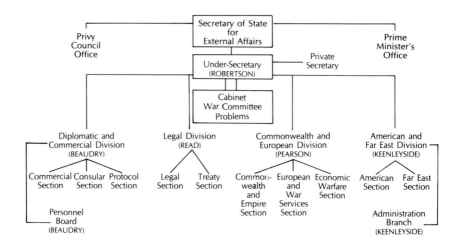

Figure 5 Department of External Affairs, 1941 (adapted from Hugh Keenleyside, *Memoirs*, Vol. 2, 118)

inet ministers, the Rt. Hon. Malcolm MacDonald, as high commissioner to Canada in February 1941. The son of Britain's first Labour prime minister, MacDonald had an unusually close relationship with Mackenzie King, beginning in 1924, when he was invited to stay at Kingsmere following a tour of Canada with the Oxford debating team.[29] He was first elected to the British Parliament at the age of twenty-eight, and as a member of the National Labour Party he held a variety of offices in the coalition government, including secretary of state for Dominion Affairs and minister of Health.

When MacDonald returned to Canada, he was warmly welcomed into government social circles by his former Oxford classmates, Arnold Heeney and Norman Robertson.[30] His role was not only of critical importance as a mediator, facilitator, and investigator for Britain, but also as an unofficial guardian of Canadian interests in matters related to uranium production, Arctic airfields, and American military activities in the northwest. His attachment to Canada was evident when he refused Churchill's request to return to a major post early in 1945 and was later confirmed when he took up residence in Ottawa upon his retirement in 1969.[31] In many respects, it was MacDonald rather than King who would succeed in playing a peculiar, but effective, role as a "linch-pin," warning his superiors of their oversights and paternalism, while alerting the Canadian government to potential American abuse of authority, especially in the north.

By the spring of 1940, it was increasingly evident that hopes for an early Allied victory were unrealistic, and serious thought was directed toward the possible consequences of a German triumph. Despite direct representations by Prime Minister King and members of External Affairs, President Roosevelt rejected pleas for assistance which might contravene the terms of neutrality. At the same time, however, Washington made it quite clear that the United States would not only take full responsibility for the protection of Greenland from enemy invasion, but also had the exclusive right to do so under a 1920 agreement with Denmark.[32] With Italy's declaration of war in June, the prospects were grim. The Allies were now desperate for aircraft and supplies. Churchill pleaded directly for the "loan" of forty or fifty destroyers in May, but not until 15 August was there an offer and then only on specific terms. Britain was to provide leases for American military bases in Newfoundland, Bermuda, and British possessions in the Caribbean, in addition to assuring that the British fleet would not be surrendered to the Germans in event of defeat.[33]

The request for military bases came as little surprise to Mackenzie King. At Ottawa's urging, meetings had been held between senior staff of the Canadian and American military in July, and it was readily apparent that the United States was more interested in the possibilities of establishing bases in Labrador, Newfoundland, and the Maritimes than in serious discussion of co-ordinated defence of North America.[34] At the same meetings, the American assistant chief of staff for the War Plans Division asked for and received the agreement that, if attacked, Canada would allow the United States to take command over operations in certain defined regions within the Dominion.[35] In essence, the Canadian military had agreed to what amounted to U.S. military occupation in the event of invasion prior to any formal defence agreement. Washington was demanding concessions with far-reaching implications. But in the summer of 1940, there appeared to be few alternatives.

In Canada, meanwhile, public opinion was mounting for some form of security arrangement with the United States in the event of Britain's surrender. The national secretary of the Canadian Institute of International Affairs wrote to its president, E. J. Tarr, on 4 July 1940, describing the mood of the country. "I think that opinion is swinging steadily towards the North American outlook for Canada and while there would be a natural reaction of an emotional type once the battle of Britain begins, I feel it will not interfere with the general trend. You yourself would be amazed at some of the statements that have been made to me in the last few weeks by persons whom I have classed hitherto as staunch imperialists."[36]

That summer a group of concerned individuals, some from the academic community and the civil service but mostly CIIA members, met at the Chateau Laurier on 17 and 18 July to consider future strategy should Britain fall. Edgar Tarr, George Ferguson, Bruce Hutchison, Norman Lambert, A. R. M. Lower, R. A. MacKay, and O. D. Skelton's son Alex were among the organizers. The product of these private meetings was a policy paper titled "Program of Immediate Canadian Action," which outlined the need for a continental scheme of economic and military integration. The proposal demanded prompt action on the premise that, if Canada did not seek joint co-operation, the United States might demand it, and as a consequence the Dominion could lose its "independent identity." Among the twenty signatures were such familiar names as R. B. Bryce, Brooke Claxton, James Coyne, Davidson Dunton, Paul Martin, Raleigh Parkin, F. R. Scott, and Jack Pickersgill. The paper was circulated to the prime minister, to the under-secretary of state for external affairs, and others involved in major policy decisions. According to Hugh Keenleyside, who was present at the meeting, the paper "undoubtedly assisted in the clarification of thinking and contributed to the rapid development of government policy toward the United States."[37]

Washington was also aware of the changing mood among Canadians. In a letter to the American secretary of state, the United States minister to Canada reported a growing public demand for "some form of joint defence understanding with the United States," even among those who "have been least well disposed towards us such as the Toronto public and the English-speaking sections of Montreal."[38] In fact, influential leaders in both countries believed that close co-operation in continental defence was inevitable. The only apparent uncertainty remaining was over who would take the initiative and who would be in a position to dictate the terms.

Adolf Berle, assistant to the secretary of state and one of Roosevelt's economic advisers, was reported to have a rather ambitious plan in mind as the situation unfolded. In a memo to the prime minister on 12 June 1940, Canadian reporter Bruce Hutchison wrote of an interview in which Berle had related his vision of a "new American Empire." Hutchison went on to report that Berle claimed to be working "on the reorganization of the economy of all North and South to make it independent of the world."[39] This was an implied economic union predicated on British defeat. Hugh Keenleyside also reported to External Affairs that it was "no longer any secret that the government of the United States has been giving detailed and serious consideration to the possibility of re-organizing the whole economic life of the Western Hemisphere." On the other hand, Keenleyside believed it unlikely that Washington would continue to offer indirect assistance and security guarantees to Canada without some formal agreement and urged that Ottawa seriously consider negotiating a "specific offensive-defensive alliance."[40]

Viewing the prospects from a different angle, a report by the Bank of Canada predicted that a British defeat would have disastrous effects on the country's economy and inevitably result in need for direct American financial assistance.[41] While fear drove Canadians to consider closer ties with the United States, many believed that autonomy could be preserved if agreements were negotiated prior to a state of emergency.

What worried Canadians did not know was that Roosevelt and King had already discussed the defence of North America in the President's swimming pool at Warm Springs, Georgia, in April of that year. As King reported to Malcolm MacDonald in a private dinner conversation, the two heads of state had laid out the basis for a joint United States-Canadian agreement while basking in the warm waters, "stark naked except for little belly bands."[42] In this instance, it would appear that both King and Roosevelt had waited for public opinion to support them in a policy decision agreed upon months before. On 17 August 1940 the two leaders met at Ogdensburg, New York, ostensibly to discuss the co-ordination of defence planning and the establishment of an advisory board. The initiative had been Roosevelt's and without apparent pressure from his military advisers, who at that point were more concerned with Central America. It was not considered a formal alliance, but simply a statement of principle supporting mutual co-operation in the defence of North America. The creation of the Permanent Joint Board of Defence, however, gave official substance to the intent of the "informal" accord.

There was no time lost once the agreement was signed. The membership of the joint board was announced five days later; the first meeting was held on the 26 August 1940. The structure, similar to the International Joint Commission set up in 1909, was a prototype for future joint committees, with separate sections for each country. The Canadian section was chaired by Colonel O. M. Biggar and included Brigadier Kenneth Stewart, deputy chief of general staff; Captain L. W. Murray, deputy chief of naval staff: Air Commodore A. A. L. Cuffe; and Hugh Keenleyside, the Canadian secretary and representative of External Affairs. Colonel G. P. Vanier, who would later become governor general, was added two months later. Mayor Fiorello La Guardia of New York city headed the American section, which also included Lieutenant General S. D. Embrick; Lieutenant Colonel J. T. McNarney; Captain H. W. Hill and Commander Forrest P. Sherman, both of the Navy; and J. D. Hickerson, the American secretary and assistant chief of the European division of the State Department. The original chairmen and secretaries remained in their positions until the summer of 1945, with frequent changes in the military representatives. Meetings alternated between Montreal and New York, their frequency dictated by the urgency of the agenda. Decisions were based on a majority vote, but often as a result of lengthy discussions leading to an acceptable consensus. According to Keenleyside, disagreements tended to occur between services, rather than countries, with the good humour of the American chairman largely responsible for defusing serious rifts. Recommendations were forwarded to the Cabinet War Committee in Canada and directly to the President of the United States.[43] The Ogdensburg Agreement was the first step in the evolution of formal wartime co-operation; the Hyde Park Declaration the following April was merely an economic corollary to the military pact.

III

Following the recommendations of the Permanent Joint Board on Defence, the Canadian government authorized the building of a series of airfields to connect Edmonton, Alberta, to Fairbanks, Alaska, along a route used by Grant McConachie and his Yukon Southern Air in the 1930s. Construction began early in 1941 with Canadian labour, under Canadian direction, and with Canadian financing. According to American sources, the purpose of these air bases was to "permit aircraft to be deployed rapidly to northwestern Canada and Alaska in time of emergency, and allow men and supplies to be moved to the region by air." In addition to fields at Grande Prairie, Fort St. John, Fort Nelson, Watson Lake, and Whitehorse, two additional fields were constructed at Prince George and Smithers in British Columbia to connect Edmonton to Prince Rupert on the coast. Access for workmen and equipment proved extremely difficult either by water in the Yukon or over winter haul roads in British Columbia. Yet despite the problems, these bases were completed for daylight use by the end of 1941. Prior to the Soviet-American Lend-Lease agreement in the summer of 1942, the route was used entirely to transport United States troops and supplies to Alaska.[44]

Before the creation of the Permanent Joint Board on Defence, Canadian defence strategists did not appear concerned about the possibility of an enemy air or sea invasion from the north.[45] Quite understandably, all efforts to defend home territory centred on the maritimes or southern British Columbia. American military planners were much less complacent, especially after reports of increased Japanese and Russian activity in the North Pacific. In December 1938 a United States Navy report declared that military bases in Alaska "would be essential in time of war" and recommended construction of both submarine and naval air facilities. The signing of the Russo-German non-aggression pact in August 1939 heightened these fears, and construction of Alaskan bases began, first at Kodiak Island and Sitka, then at Anchorage and Fairbanks.[46] The first troops of the new Alaska Defence Force arrived at Anchorage on 27 June 1940, and within a year the numbers grew from approximately eight hundred to eight thousand. Meanwhile, $48 million was appropriated for the Civil Aeronautics Board, a research station was established at Ladd Field near Fairbanks, and plans for larger military bases began to take shape.[47]

The proposed Alaska Highway, however, appeared to be temporarily stalemated. In June 1940, when the delegate for Alaska submitted a bill to Congress authorizing its construction, the legislation was rejected on the advice of the secretary of war, who believed the highway to have little value as a defence measure. In April 1941, the United States secretary of state made a personal plea to Mackenzie King, who still refused to consider the matter, this time regarding the highway as unnecessary because of the airfields.[48] The proposal was again put before Congress in February 1941 and was referred to the Army's War Plans Division, which initially advised against it.[49] The Federal Works Agency also advised deferral since "plans looking to a working arrangement with the necessary authorities in the Dominion of Canada... have not yet matured sufficiently." Meanwhile, reports from both the Canadian and American commissions were tabled offering two alternative routes. Vilhjalmur Stefansson, who had been appointed to the United States War Department as a special adviser on the Arctic, provided yet another.[50] Ottawa was now accused of stalling, but Canadian officials insisted that the road was not immediately critical to defence. Then, in August 1941, President Roosevelt himself requested that a survey of the road begin at once, a proposal which was once again refused consideration by External Affairs unless the American military declared it necessary for reasons of national security.[51]

Overall, plans for defence in the North Pacific progressed at a steady but conservative pace. Prior to December 1941, American military strategists were hesitant to approve projects without extensive study and discussion, particularly in the far north, where extravagant expenditures would be of questionable benefit in peacetime. This reticence did not go unnoticed by Stefansson, who warned that "only the Soviets are utilizing the resources of the Arctic and sub-Arctic on a large scale" and predicted that "presumably the other circumpolar countries will undertake extensive projects within their Arctic territories only if they became convinced that military necessities demanded it."[52] When the United States government did proceed cautiously, their activities came under severe criticism by the Japanese. In 1941, the newspaper *Hochi* reported distress over American plans to build a military highway to Alaska with accompanying air bases and warned that "American measures in this direction will be regarded as a continuation of the horseshoe-shaped encirclement of Japan by the Washington Government."[53] Yet in spite of appearances, the United States had more immediate plans of higher priority.

Throughout 1941, the United States gradually exercised its declared right to direct and control continental defence. Beginning in April, a formal agree-

ment was signed with the Danish minister in Washington that resulted in the
establishment of American air bases in Greenland. Then, in July, Roosevelt
announced that American forces would replace the British garrisons in Iceland. The United States Army also requested permission to survey landing
fields at Frobisher Bay, Fort Chimo, and Padloping Island to expand the
northeastern staging route.[54] In August, however, the set plans for North
American defence were temporarily thwarted by Ottawa's prior negotiation
for leasing rights to a site on the Northwest River in Labrador. Against the
expressed wishes of the United States Army Air Force, who believed divided
responsibility was unworkable, the Canadians insisted on building the Goose
Bay airfield. Since it proved too small to accommodate the traffic, the
USAAF established its own base at the same site.[55] The Goose Bay air base
was not only critical for defence purposes, but was also the key link in the
northeast staging route which provided refuelling bases for American-built
planes en route to Scotland (see figure 6). A number of weather stations with
"observation and radio facilities" were also built and operated by the United
States Army Air Force to support the ferry route. The original northeast airway was modest in contrast to the two alternate routes which included air
bases at Fort Chimo, Frobisher Bay, and Coral Harbour on Southampton Island, later constructed at an estimated cost of $40 million. Originally, Chimo
and Frobisher, Crystal I and Crystal II respectively, were planned as simple

AIR FERRY ROUTES TO BRITAIN, 1941-45

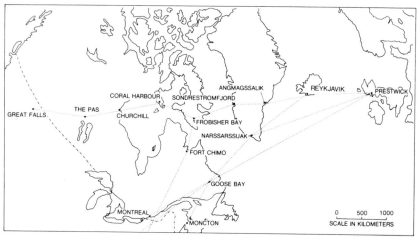

Figure 6 Air Ferry Routes to Britain, 1944 (courtesy Trevor Lloyd)

radio and weather stations, but they were expanded substantially after the United States entered the war. Slightly smaller in size than the west coast Greenland base at Sondre Stromfjord (Bluie West), they were never used extensively for ferrying planes. Their purpose was primarily to provide defence, and if necessary to receive wounded evacuees from Europe.[56]

The joint military operations in 1941 were carried out in the name of "wartime emergency," but if Adolf Berle was to be taken seriously, there may have been underlying motives. In reference to the importance of the air bases in Greenland being under American rather than Canadian control, Berle's diary entry of 13 February 1941 read as follows: "I am glad there is not very much territory in the Arctic, and so few people there that it does not complicate the course of world affairs as it does in West Europe. But it is, I think, a distinct new step in the American position. For the first time, the Monroe Doctrine has been implemented militarily on a frontier."[57] Berle's interpretation of the Monroe Doctrine implied blatant imperialist designs aimed for the moment at the Arctic regions of North America. But to the world at large, the United States was providing much needed support to the Allies, within the accepted limits of neutrality. Moreover, the plan of joint defence of Canada and the United States, commonly referred to as ABC 22, was approved by the British-American Joint Chiefs of Staff Committee and eventually by the United Kingdom War Cabinet.[58] The first indication that there may have been a misunderstanding in the intent of the defence agreement occurred in the fall of 1941, when the United States War Department rejected Ottawa's request to set up a Canadian military mission in Washington to facilitate participation in policy discussions.[59] It was soon apparent that the term "joint" had its limitations and did not include a permanent Canadian presence on American soil. This incident was only a forewarning of future trends in Canadian-American "friendly relations."

IV

Within months of the signing of the Ogdensburg Agreement, it became apparent that other infrastructures were necessary to integrate the defence requirements of the two countries. Significantly, it was Hugh Keenleyside who requested study into "the coordination and rational integration of the war industries of Canada and the United States" following discussions at the first meetings of the Permanent Joint Board on Defence.[60] On 18 March 1941, he met with Adolf Berle to discuss the War Cabinet's recommendation that studies be initiated into the possibility of continental economic integration. Berle's reaction was ecstatic, as his diary entry reveals:

They have proposed a study of economic pooling between the United States and Canada. . . . But the rest of it goes much farther. Keenleyside realizes that this is now one continent and one economy; that we shall have to be integrated as to finance, trade routes and pretty much everything else; and in this I so thoroughly agree with him that it is refreshing. We talked long and happily about it—though much lies in the realm of dreams. This at least is a new order, which can exist without hatred and can be created without bloodshed, and ought to lead to production without slavery.[61]

Again Berle was thinking in terms of a North American empire. Little did he realize that while Canadians might be willing to accept plans for economic integration as a wartime necessity, national pride would precipitate actions to reverse the trend once the crisis had passed. Nor did Mackenzie King see wartime economic integration as either permanent or strictly continental, but as a step towards future worldwide co-operation, understanding, and mutual aid. In later years, Keenleyside also denied he ever entertained thought of long-term continental integration. "For war purposes we were prepared to go as far as would be beneficial for our joint effort to defeat the worst threat ever faced by Western civilization."[62] In more pragmatic terms, the key motivation behind Ottawa's initiative was a balance of payments deficit that could be alleviated by the United States purchase of Canadian raw resources and excess war production, especially since the lend-lease agreement passed by the Congress a week earlier offered no relief to Canada's shortage of American dollars and meant probable liquidation of capital invested in the United States.[63]

The Hyde Park Declaration, signed by King and Roosevelt on 20 April 1941, was an agreement in principle "that in mobilizing resources of this continent each country should provide the other with defence articles which it is best able to produce. . . and that production programs should be coordinated to this end."[64] The British high commissioner passed on his own observations to London, claiming that while the agreement was "natural and inevitable" under the circumstances, it was now doubly important for London to make an all out effort to "keep alive British ideas and culture" in Canada. His lengthy report at times verged on sarcasm, however, as he described the incident as a "love affair," with the prime minister behaving like "any infatuated swain." On a more thoughtful note, he suggested that the agreement was "just one important part of that process which Mr. Churchill described as the affairs of Britain and the United States getting somewhat mixed up together" and concluded that "what the distant future may bring is still inscrutable."[65]

As a result of the Hyde Park Declaration, several co-ordinating agencies were set up including the Joint Economic Committees which were initially charged with studying the efficient use of combined resources during the war and postwar period.[66] Within months, the Joint War Production Committee was set up as a separate body, thus changing the mandate of the Joint Economic Committee to encompass only postwar planning. In some quarters, there was obvious confusion as to the exact role these committees were expected to play. A year and a half after they had received their new mandate, Mackenzie King still referred to the old terms of reference which focused on wartime co-operation and study of "the possibility of reducing the probable post-war dislocation,"[67] whereas Carl Goldenberg of the Treasury Department explicitly informed the Canadian chairman on 21 June 1941 that the "function of the Joint Economic Committees, as now amended, is to explore the possibility of a greater degree of economic cooperation between Canada and the United States."[68] The summer of 1941 was also the height of American pressure to have postwar reciprocity included in the lend-lease agreement with Great Britain. In time it would become clearer that the American long-term vision of ending the British preferential tariff and bringing about continental economic integration was not what Mackenzie King had in mind when he signed the Hyde Park Declaration.

Following the sudden death of R. A. C. Henry within months of his appointment, the Canadian section of the Joint Economic Committees was headed by W. A. Mackintosh, on temporary leave from Queen's University and assigned as a special assistant to the Department of Finance. The others included D. A. Skelton, chief of the research department of the Bank of Canada, and J. G. Bouchard, assistant deputy minister of agriculture. When it was considered appropriate, Hugh Keenleyside and Adolf Berle were nominated to attend meetings as a representatives of External Affairs and the State Department respectively. Alvin Hansen, professor of political economy at Harvard, chaired the American section, which included representatives from the Tariff Commission, the Federal Reserve Board, and the War Production Board. For the most part, the committees met only rarely as a joint body.[69] Several sub-committees were set up to study specific proposals, such as the Sub-Committee on Bilateralism, with Tariff Commissioner E. Dana Durand in charge.[70] The fact that the American committee was made up of a goodly number of avid "free traders," such as Berle, H. D. White, and Will Clayton, and was assigned to the Treasury Department, which was dominated by Morganthau and his "empire builders," fully explains the Americans' preoccupation with long-range economic integration.[71] Although Keenleyside claims the Canadian section became little more than a clearing house and did not seriously study the possibilities of postwar co-operation,[72] the records of the American Committee and sub-committees indicate quite the contrary, at least in terms of their own activities.

The American section wasted no time in submitting studies and reports to the Canadians for discussion. On 2 September 1941, Charles Kindleberger of the Federal Reserve Board submitted a lengthy draft report on "Long-Run Economic Collaboration between Canada and the United States" to Alex Skelton for his comments and contribution. The report recommended as minimum objectives: Canada's continued reliance on resource export and increased import trade with the United States; a move towards reducing tariff barriers; new regulations to restrict Canadian monopolies; a joint immigration policy; a move toward equalization of the two countries' social programmes for the poor, aged and unemployed; a similar move toward equalization of taxes; and freer passage across the border. The "maximum objectives" amounted to commercial and socioeconomic union.[73] This committee was not considered important to Canadians, but for the Americans it provided a means to explore the extent to which Ottawa might agree to continental economic integration and, of particular interest here, the possibility of sharing northern resources. As in the case of the Permanent Joint Board on Defence, the role of the Canadian committee was essentially to approve, alter, or reject American proposals. Only a few recommendations reached the Cabinet War Committee, but one of these would prove very significant in terms of the future of Canada's north. In this respect, the Hyde Park Declaration, like the Ogdensburg Agreement, resulted in convenient infrastructures which ensured that Canada would have the opportunity to learn what the Americans were planning, just as the Americans were able to "test the waters."

V

Ottawa's apparent enthusiasm for the joint economic and defence agreements was shared by the majority of Canadians. Only occasionally was there concern expressed for possible adverse effects, such as an article which appeared in *The Canadian Forum* that suggested the United States was looking upon wartime co-operation measures as long-term arrangements. "They are hinting more and more openly that Canadian-American plans, military and economic, are not merely for the duration of the war."[74] Others were more cautious, with public opinion generally appearing to favour the agreements.

Of greater concern to Canadians was the issue of national security, particularly in relation to the Pacific and Atlantic seaboards. Although not considered of great importance, the possibility of an Axis air attack from bases established in the Arctic was the subject of a number of articles appearing in the *Vancouver Province*. Most accounts rejected the idea as either impossible or unrealistic, but there were some interesting observations. One article reported that "the Royal Canadian Mounted Police had taken precautions to prevent any attempted enemy airplane flights over the north by destroying commercial gasoline caches." As an example, it was stated that "hundreds of gallons of aviation gasoline" had been dumped into the waters of Repulse Bay on the western shore of Hudson Bay. A less reassuring article appeared some months later, noting that "along the east coast of Hudson Bay from Cape Smith on the extreme northern tip, to Cochrane . . . the sole government law enforcing agency consists of one member of the Royal Canadian Mounted Police." A report by the "Bishop of the Arctic" seemed even more disconcerting when he advised that "a single Eskimo would travel for days to tell the authorities of any mysterious vessels, planes, or persons he might happen to see." As a result, argued the Reverend Mr. Fleming, "Ottawa would know in no time at all, if anything was going on."[75] These reports may seem humorous today, but they point out the reality of the situation in 1941. Without the aid of the American military, Canada would have had to rely on a few Mounted Police, an occasional fur trader or missionary, and a number of quick-footed Inuit, to "stand on guard" in the Arctic.

As the months wore on, there appeared to be some awareness about the new significance of the polar regions. On 15 November 1941, the *Montreal Gazette* carried a lengthy story describing the Arctic in terms of the new air routes and the presence of unexploited mineral wealth. A map explained the new strategic significance and included a Stefansson-style prophecy (see figure 7). "As the war and its involutions spread out over the globe, the mysterious, white-shrouded Arctic's strategic importance is becoming more and more evident. This map is drawn in the projection which serves best to give a true conception of the struggle's relationship to the Far North. Study it carefully, You'll hear more of the Arctic later on."[76] Of special significance was the lack of "ownership" assigned to the Arctic and the omission of any Canadian involvement. On the map there appear to be only two countries concerned with the defence of the Arctic: the United States and the Soviet Union. The prediction in the caption may have seemed a remote possibility to some, inevitable to others.

Perhaps understandably, the issues of American dominance and Arctic sovereignty were of low priority when a foreign aggressor was directly threatening national security. With all efforts aimed at encouraging optimum United States participation in the Allied cause, the initial influx of American forces into the Canadian north was of little consequence compared to their contribution in preventing a German victory. Many years later, Escott Reid recalled the nature of Canadian-American relations prior to the United States official entry into the war. "Looking back at it, we had a very close relationship with the Americans during the period of American neutrality." He went on to explain that "we were grateful to the Americans for leaning over back-

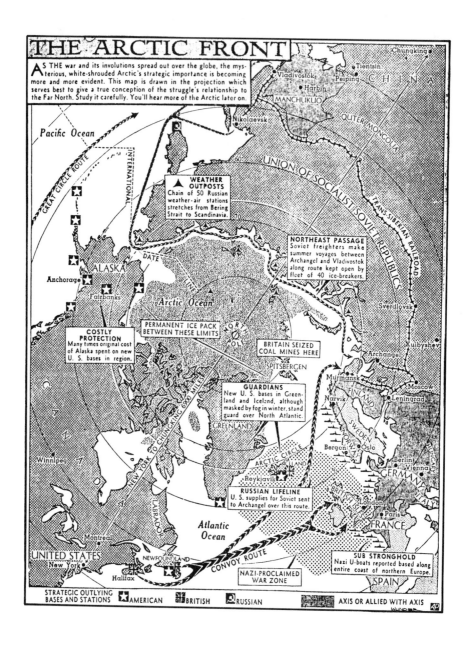

Figure 7 Media View of the Polar Regions (*Montreal Gazette*, 15 November 1941)

wards in interpreting or misinterpreting the neutrality legislation to make things easy for us and they did. Then when they entered the war the situation changed."[77]

Prior to December 1941, Washington appeared content to confine American defence strategies in the Canadian north to the development of the air routes and the erection of weather stations. The stage was set, however, for the visionaries of a "new American empire" to use the pretext of continental defence to forward their ambitions. Ottawa was not totally unaware of these pretensions, but the view from Laurier House revealed greater perils on the horizon.

4

The Northward Winds of War, 1941–1942

> They [the Americans] have apparently walked in and taken posses-
> sion in many cases as if Canada were unclaimed territory inhabited
> by a docile race of aborigines.
>
> Vincent Massey, 1943

The bombing of Pearl Harbor on 7 December 1941 created ripple effects throughout the entire world by expanding the participants and parameters of World War II. The impact on the State Department was immediate; its former hemispheric outlook shifted to a global vision, accompanied by a change in attitude that raised serious concern among members of External Affairs. At the same time, Canadian perception of the war also took on a new dimension with the realization that North America was no longer protected by the neutralist policies of the United States. In the minds of senior politicians and military officials of both countries, time was of the essence. For the sake of efficiency, discussions were kept brief; plans were approved and implemented with minimum delay; cost considerations were of lesser importance. All available manpower, supplies, and technology were directed towards a single goal: victory. Quite apart from formal agreements, the people of Canada and the United States were philosophically united in a common cause, and their resources were mobilized to mutual advantage. The United States at once assumed the responsibility for planning the defence of North America, and military projects proliferated to protect the land, sea, and airspace of the continent. As a result, External Affairs found that its time and efforts were increasingly centred on preserving national sovereignty.

While the impact of the war on Canada was minimal compared to that felt by European countries, the lasting effect of American military activities in the north was greater than any previous event in the region's history. With a few exceptions, the "joint" defence projects were designed, financed, and built under American leadership, employing American military and civilians, with American technology and equipment, and located in sparsely inhabited areas remote from government and population centres. All activities were sanctioned under the terms of the Ogdensburg Agreement. However, in the opinion of one former member of External Affairs, the agreement in its practical application "involved the United States in the defence of Canada, but it did not involve Canada in the whole of United States strategy."[1]

Although there was no official American military occupation of northern Canada, there was certainly an illusion of occupation by virtue of their dominant presence and their assumption of command. Specific plans were recommended by the Permanent Joint Board on Defence, then approved by the Cabinet War Committee, whose full agenda left little time for study or discussion of issues. As a consequence, it was over a year before Ottawa fully comprehended the enormity of some projects in terms of cost, manpower, and the area affected. Local problems arising out of the northern military activities were primarily the responsibility of the territorial councils, who dealt with specific issues on an ad hoc basis and with little consideration for the overall impact. External Affairs and the War Committee attended to national and international questions. Meanwhile, serious concerns for some of the long-term implications were raised by private individuals and by British officials, who were increasingly apprehensive about the ever-tightening economic and military ties. Never before had Ottawa been asked to make so many northern policy decisions, all based on a southern perspective. The sixteen-month period following the American entrance into the war was one of rapidly changing circumstances and priorities which directly and indirectly affected the future of northern Canada.

I

After 7 December 1941, there was an immediate change in attitude among members of the State Department. Within weeks, Norman Robertson warned the prime minister of a growing tendency on the part of the United States "to regard Canada as an internal domestic relationship rather than an international one." Moreover, the Americans' renewed sense of "manifest destiny" was being translated into a more aggressive assertion of their influence in world affairs.[2] By mid-January, Escott Reid wrote of "the tendency on the part of the government of the United States to order Canada around" and called for a change of position on Ottawa's part. "We are being treated as children because we have refused to behave as adults."[3] From Washington, Hume Wrong wrote that there had been a serious loss of Canadian influence.[4]

The situation worsened. On 7 April 1942, Wrong warned of growing American support for the neo-isolationist argument which advocated hemispheric imperialism to divide the world in half, "with the United States dominating the two Americas and isolated from the other great land masses."

> For protection, according to this concept, the United States must control the approaches to her territory. For them the position of Canada is altered from a good neighbour with a lauded undefended frontier to a menace to American security whose territory must be protected by the United States in her own interest. Some of the former isolationists now seem to look on Canada almost as an undeclared colony of the United States. The logic of this imperialism is that, if Canada will not freely let her destinies be controlled from Washington, she must be made to do so; failure to meet any demands from the United States becomes a sort of rebellion. These views are now held only by a small minority, but should the war not end in complete victory, they might well become the opinions of a majority.[5]

In 1942, there was not the remotest chance that Canada could provide adequate defence of the far north, and the future prospects appeared equally grim in terms of available manpower and financial limitations. Almost overnight, the once neutral "good neighbour" became a superpower at war, and as such it began to redefine the relationship of those dependent on her military and economic support. To Washington, "mutual co-operation" did not mean equal partnership, as shown by the assumption that all Canadian west coast army and naval units would be more effectively utilized if placed under United States command.[6] Although the idea was rejected out of hand, the incident served as a warning that Canada's autonomy had acquired a new vulnerability from the economic and military agreements.

Most members of External Affairs were acutely aware of the problem, and many offered short term solutions. Looking further to the future, Escott Reid suggested that the only answer was to work out a new scheme of Canadian-American co-operation, "if possible within the framework of a collective system," in which "a small state like Canada would have an opportunity to exert a reasonable amount of influence in international politics."[7] In the early months of 1942, these and other ideas began to take form and eventually gave birth to the functional approach advocated by the postwar internationalists, when Canada once again attempted to gain more independence, this time from the nation which had provided an effective counterbalance to British paternalism in the inter-war years.

The whole question of North American defence also took on a new perspective. In John Holmes' view, the war in the Pacific "led Canadians to a new look at their own geography and their own vulnerability. It not only made them more aware of the Pacific as a frontier; it also led them to look upon the North with new eyes. . . . Maps with polar projections began to replace the traditional perspectives of Mercator. Collective security took on a new meaning if Canada itself was open to direct attack."[8] Recognition of the north's new strategic significance coincided with a number of equally disturbing circumstances which temporarily thwarted any constructive plan to deal with the consequences. Resistance to conscription and increasing financial limitations meant that few troops or funds could be spared for northern defence at a time when the weak Allied position on all fronts provided little hope for an early conclusion to the hostilities. Amidst a seemingly endless array of crises in Europe, North Africa, and the South Pacific, the United States War Department submitted numerous requests for approval to build substantial defence facilities throughout the Canadian north, but concentrated in the northwest. Caught between two conflicting objectives, the Cabinet War Committee attempted to balance the priorities of military necessity and sovereign control. The lack of Canadian participation in the "joint" projects was only of concern in the more populated areas such as Edmonton. The lessons learned from the Alaska boundary dispute regarding the importance of effecting "a presence of authority" and "quasi-occupation" were long forgotten.

II

During the early 1940s, Vilhjalmur Stefansson was reported to have had a major influence on the direction of North American defence policy. Purely by coincidence, an article describing his role as Arctic adviser to the United States Army and Navy was published the very day the Japanese attacked Pearl Harbor. Referring to the veteran explorer as "the Prophet of the North," the author claimed that the American military now relied on his knowledge and experience in planning for Arctic defence.[9] Considering his futuristic visions of Arctic development, it was natural that Stefansson's recommendations would attempt to fulfil wartime needs and at the same time provide ample opportunity for future growth and settlement. Nor was it surprising that he hired "as his Canadian representative and editorial assistant" the son of the former director of the Northwest Territories and Yukon Branch, Richard Finnie, who, like Stefansson, was a severe critic of former government neglect.[10]

In Stefansson's opinion, the construction of a land bridge from the United States to Alaska was crucial to the defence of the territory, and in November 1940, he toured the area to study all possible routes.[11] His first choice was a route from the end of rail north of Edmonton, following the Mackenzie River system, past Norman Wells, then across to Fairbanks, Alaska. Although of no value to British Columbia or the American west coast, the route would

STEFANSSON'S PROPOSED ROUTES TO ALASKA

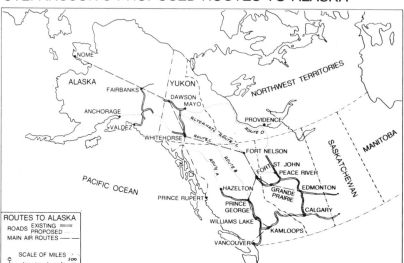

Figure 8 Proposed Routes to Alaska, 1940 (adapted from V. Stefansson, "Routes to Alaska," *Foreign Affairs* [July 1941]: 864)

have given the Alaskan military bases direct access to Canadian oil and at the same time provided a direct link between the Northwest Territories, the Yukon, and Alaska. In effect, this route would have encouraged closer integration towards development of a more autonomous region[12] (see figure 8).

On 11 January 1942, the proposal of combining a highway to Alaska with oil production was brought to public attention in an article written by Richard Finnie, "Sub-Arctic Canada's Oil Field May Supply Alaskan War Bases," which appeared in the New York *Herald Tribune*. According to Finnie, the inland route to Alaska would allow for the exploitation of two oil fields, Norman Wells and the Athabaska tar sands, and at the same time improve access to the gold and silver resources at Dawson and Mayo respectively. Although not stated, the proposed road would also have provided land access to a United States Navy petroleum reserve which covered a thirty-five-thousand-square-mile area on the north Alaskan coast near Point Barrow,[13] a factor which may have contributed to the plan's rejection. The highway and pipeline were projects designed for the benefit of the United States Army Air Force, not the Navy. There were other objections to the ambitious proposal, notably by Standard Oil of California, which was in direct competition with Standard Oil of New Jersey. The former supplied American naval operations in the Pacific; the latter owned the oil fields in the Mackenzie Valley.[14] In spite of his reported "power of influence," Stefansson's recommendations would be compromised. Agreeing with the Arctic adviser's rationale but not his route, the American military elected to embark on two separate projects—a highway and a pipeline—neither of which followed his route. Recognizing the priorities of both governments and the lack of concern for the region itself, Stefansson later wrote that "we shall come to know the Arctic because the highways take us through it to where we want to go."[15]

Top priority was given to the Alaska Highway after study by a special cabinet committee set up by Roosevelt. At the outset, the War Department realized the highway could not be completed in time to allay the immediate crisis and instead justified their recommendation for government approval on political grounds rather than military need. Aware that Canada would reject the proposal unless it was considered vital to security, the War Plans Division recommended that highway construction be presented "in the interests of national defense" and thus "take advantage of the present war to secure the necessary agreements from Canada to start work now and finish perhaps many years to come." Unless viewed in terms of commercial aviation, this strategy at first appears illogical, since the routes of economic benefit to Alaska, British Columbia, and the west coast states were rejected in favour of a road connecting the airfields of the Northwest Staging Route. In a matter of only two days, the assistant chief of army engineers drew up a survey and construction plan which followed the existing military airfields and bypassed Dawson, the capital of the Yukon. Roosevelt granted immediate approval.[16]

On 12 February 1942, the Cabinet War Committee agreed to what they were informed was simply a "request to survey," not the actual construction of the highway. The formal written request presented to the under-secretary of External Affairs the next day, however, included reference to "a pioneer road" which the United States minister to Canada defined as "a rough working road . . . considered part of the survey." This subterfuge succeeded, and the army engineers were ordered to proceed as planned.[17] Having previously met to discuss strategy and terms,[18] the Canadian members reluctantly agreed to recommend approval for actual construction at the 25–26 February meeting of the Permanent Joint Board on Defence, but only on the proviso that the Americans would undertake the full responsibility for the cost, construction, and maintenance for the duration of the war and that the Canadian portion of the highway would be turned over to Canada at its end. According to the secretary of the Canadian section, Hugh Keenleyside, the recommendation was based purely "on political, not strategic grounds"; in his opinion, the defence argument was "a most dubious egg"; and the highway would become little more than "a white elephant." Robertson was equally sceptical of the need, but he agreed "that on political grounds we cannot be put in the position of blocking its construction."[19] And so it happened that the Army of Engineers arrived in Dawson Creek and began work two days before the Cabinet War Committee approved the project and two weeks before the details of the agreement were confirmed by an "exchange of notes" on 17–18 March 1942. It was a significant, and indeed a rather ominous, beginning of what would become a proliferation of "joint" defence projects in the Canadian north.

Mackenzie King was equally suspicious of the circumstances surrounding the highway's approval. In later discussion with Malcolm MacDonald, he claimed that the highway "was less intended for protection against the Japanese than as one of the fingers of the hand which American is placing more or less over the whole of the Western Hemisphere."[20] Considering the method employed to gain approval, his concerns were well founded. The events of the next two years would only confirm them. Years later, Escott Reid recalled how the Americans employed "various devices" to bring pressure on Ottawa for approval of northern defence projects. "One device was to say that we're terribly sorry but we don't see any possibility of the press not learning of this difference of opinion. Then if we didn't do what they wanted, they would leak the story to the press."[21]

The tactics employed in the case of the Alaska Highway were certainly not "above board," but the terms of the agreement were probably the best possible under the circumstances: the pioneer highway was to be built by American troops, with the cost of construction and maintenance borne by the United States government; Canada would provide right of ways, waive import duties and taxes, and allow use of timber and gravel along the route; and the Yukon, Alberta, and British Columbia portions of the road would revert to Canadian control six months after the war, at which time the road would "become in all respects an integral part of the Canadian highway system" with no discriminatory regulations for American civilian traffic.[22] Significantly, this was a departure from earlier policy to pay for all fixed defence facilities on Canadian soil, and it created a precedent for future agreements as American requests proliferated at an astounding rate over the next year.

The pioneer road covering 1,420 miles was completed by the United States Army Engineers in October 1942. The whole project had been carried out in relative secrecy as far as the south was concerned. For all intents and purposes, the region was treated as a United States military zone, and only scant details reached the media before November 1942, at which time the press were invited to official opening ceremonies. The small Canadian delegation was headed by the Hon. Ian Mackenzie, minister of pensions and health, with General George R. Pearkes representing the Canadian armed forces and accompanied by a contingent of Royal Canadian Mounted Police. In addition to the many soldiers on location, the American representation included the governor of Alaska, area army commanders, and the district engineer of the

Captain Joseph Elzéar Bernier, aged 71, on board the CGS *Arctic*, 1923. Bernier made numerous expeditions in the Archipelago between 1906 and 1911 to claim the Arctic islands for Canada and between 1922 and 1925 on the Eastern Arctic Patrol.

The *Arctic* at anchor near Godhavn, Greenland, ca. 1924. Originally built for a German Antarctic expedition, the ship was purchased by the Canadian government in 1904.

The patrol ship SS *Beothic,* chartered from a Newfoundland sealing company for the Eastern Patrol from 1926 to 1931, is pictured here anchored off Pond Inlet.

RCMP barracks at Fort Smith, NWT, 1927.

"Main Street" of Pond Inlet on Baffin Island, July 1928. Inuit houses and tents are shown in the foreground with the Hudson's Bay Company post and RCMP detachment in the distance.

RMS *Nascopie* anchored off Pond Inlet in 1936. From 1933 until this HBC supply ship sank off Cape Dorset in the summer of 1947, the Eastern Arctic Patrol rented space aboard.

The first government buildings in the Northwest Territories were constructed at Fort Smith in 1922. This picture, with the tennis courts in the foreground, was taken in 1927.

Hudson's Bay Company buildings at Fort Smith, ca. 1941.

Typical log buildings of the Athapaskan Indians, Fort Good Hope, NWT, in the early 1940s.

Catholic mission hospital at Fort Smith, ca. 1942.

Catholic mission buildings at Fort Resolution, NWT, showing (*left* to *right*) the church, residence, school, and hospital, July 1941.

The isolated Indian village of Rae is situated on a small inland lake northwest of Yellowknife.

The first public school in the NWT, photographed here with its first class, was built in 1940.

O.S. Finnie was director of the Northwest Territories and Yukon Branch of the Department of the Interior from 1921 to 1931. Here he examines the contents of a gold pan near the mouth of Bear Creek in the Yukon.

Reindeer herds in corrals on Richards Island in the Mackenzie Delta, July 1937. As part of the Canadian Reindeer Project, a herd was purchased in 1929 from the Lomen brothers in Alaska.

Hugh L. Keenleyside, assistant undersecretary of state for external affairs, 1941–44; Canadian ambassador to Mexico, 1944–47; commissioner of the NWT and deputy minister of mines and resources, 1947–49; and deputy minister of resources and development until October 1950.

The gold mining community of Yellowknife, 1940.

Charles Camsell, deputy minister of mines and resources and commissioner of the Northwest Territories from 1936 until his retirement in December 1946.

Mackenzie King and A.D.P. Heeney, 1941. Heeney, clerk of the Privy Council Office and secretary to the Cabinet from 1940 to 1949, became a trusted adviser to the prime minister.

Public Roads Administration. The ceremony was formal, but small in scale to adapt to the wilderness location on a mountain pass above Lake Kluane in the Yukon; the atmosphere was definitely collegial and intensely patriotic. For the Americans, this was their highway even if it passed through Canada, an understandable perception considering the lack of Canadian participation (see Appendix C).

Travel was restricted to military and construction personnel with special permits required for local civilian travel. The rough, single-track road had been pushed through rock, muskeg, and permafrost at phenomenal speed by seven regiments of General Service and Combat Engineers—three regiments having black troops and white officers—and assisted by several civilian crews provided by the Public Roads Administration. By the next spring, stretches of the highway were impassable owing to melted permafrost, with one section near Beaver Creek having virtually disappeared. The Public Roads Administration immediately began building a permanent structure using both Canadian and American contractors. Construction also commenced on the Haines Cutoff to provide a more direct access to the Pacific. The final cost of the road was over $135 million, and the Haines Cutoff another $13 million, a far cry from Roosevelt's estimated $25 million in 1940 and almost double the $80 million price-tag of 1942.[23] Alaska's Governor Ernest Gruening believed the army had made a "colossal blunder" in selection of the route, and he proposed that Washington should arrange a deal with Canada to trade the Skagway access for sixteen thousand square miles of land surrounding the Haines Cutoff and west to the Alaska border, thus providing an all-American route from Haines to Fairbanks. The request was politely ignored by Washington, who apparently considered it more important to deny the Yukon a direct link to the Pacific.[24]

Within weeks of granting approval for the pioneer road, Ottawa received a number of requests for expansion of existing airfields and construction of new bases, first in connection with the northwestern ferry route and then followed a few weeks later with extensive expansion plans in the northeast. The cost estimates were large, ranging from several million to approximately $200 million. Initially, members of External Affairs questioned the size and permanence of the projects which, in Hugh Keenleyside's view, were intended for postwar commercial use rather than being a wartime necessity. For this reason, he strongly recommended that Canada should continue the policy employed in the original building of the Northwest Staging Route and pay for all construction of airfields to prevent the Americans assuming "proprietary and perpetual interests." On two occasions, Colonel O. M. Biggar, Canadian chairman of the Permanent Joint Board on Defence, referred the question to the Cabinet War Committee for direction before discussion at the full meeting of the board. In both instances, it was argued that despite the political implications, the costs were now far beyond Canada's means. Understandably, the strongest arguments against Canada's assumption of full financial responsibility came from J. L. Ilsley, minister of finance; C. D. Howe, minister of munitions and supply; J. L. Ralston, minister of national defence; C. G. Power, minister of national defence for air; and C. P. Edwards, deputy minister of transport. The compromise agreed upon was specifically designed to show evidence of "joint participation in the south" rather than "a presence of authority in the north," despite the reservations expressed by Colonel Biggar, Keenleyside, and the Royal Canadian Air Force. Canadian labour and contractors were to be employed at Edmonton, Alberta, The Pas in Manitoba, and Mingan, Quebec, whereas the Americans were responsible for construction, operation, and defence of the airfields in the remote northern regions.[25]

Warning that the written assurances might not be adequate to prevent American claims to postwar rights came on 13 January 1943, when the American chairman of the Permanent Joint Board on Defence, Mayor La Guardia, declared that "of course American planes would be able after the war to use the bases in Canada which are being built by American money." This resulted in attempts by Ottawa to renegotiate the terms of operational control and postwar disposition of the air bases. By agreement, Canadians would assume control of bases jointly used by the two countries, but Americans would exercise authority over the airfields used only by the United States Army Air Force.[26] No sooner had this problem been partially solved than the United States War Department requested further expansion of facilities in the northwest, with accusations that delays by Canadian contractors were hindering American efforts to supply its Alaskan bases and ferry planes to Russia.[27] This latest submission was directly in response to Norman Robertson's insistence that control over construction must remain in Canadian hands, a policy which was thwarting the United States War Department's attempts to take over contracts which had been let out to Canadian contractors by the Department of Transport.[28] A definite pattern seemed to be developing. Should Canada stall on requests from the War Department, new demands involving sizable expenditures and use of manpower were submitted, forcing Ottawa to agree to a compromise involving minimal cost to Canada. The "eagle" was indeed soaring, and because of wartime rationing, the "beavers" were now relying on paper rather than material of more substance to build their dams.

III

During this period, the efforts of External Affairs and the Cabinet War Committee were directed toward preserving sovereign authority, at least in principle, but with little concern for the direct effect the military activities might have on the residents of the northern territories. The problems were particularly acute in the Yukon, where there was no direct line of communication between the appointed liaison officer and those approving the various projects as was the case of the Northwest Territories where a member of External Affairs sat on the territorial council. Local problems in the Yukon were the responsibility of Controller G. A. Jeckell, who resided in Dawson, and Liaison Officer C. K. LeCapelain, posted at Whitehorse. Both would refer specific items of business to the appropriate agents of federal departments, in addition to keeping Director Roy Gibson of the Lands, Parks and Forests Branch informed of the ongoing situation. Although relatively minor compared to those baffling the diplomats, the many issues were all related to the pressures of the American projects on transportation and communications services, on the limited food supply and small arms ammunition rations, on water supply and sewage facilities at Whitehorse, on the health of the Indian communities along the highway, on fire protection, and many other aspects of Yukon society and economy. The mining industry, in particular, was not only competing for transportation and equipment allocations but also suffering from labour shortages owing to the more lucrative employment offered in the rapidly expanding service sector.[29]

Beleaguered by the responsibility and frustration of dealing with complaints from both local residents and the military, LeCapelain sent a plea to Gibson in March 1943, suggesting that the controller "should pay more frequent visits to Whitehorse to find out for himself and at firsthand the real situation." Aware that Canada's sovereign rights must be upheld, LeCapelain warned against the Americans being allowed to take over fire protection and the cleaning up of garbage "without properly constituted Canadian authority." Admitting the benefits of the military's willing assistance, he was nevertheless concerned for "their apparent assertiveness and of pushing Canadian authorities aside."[30] It is doubtful that LeCapelain's complaints went further than Gibson's office; if they did, they found little sympathy in the federal government. When Deputy Minister Charles Camsell went on an inspection tour that summer with the British high commissioner, they touched down in Whitehorse for lunch with Controller Jeckell, LeCapelain, and George Black, the Yukon member of Parliament. Camsell reported receiving considerable information on the highway project, whereas MacDonald observed that Jeckell "rules the country with the help of a small local advisory council under general direction of the authorities in Ottawa" and appeared to be resolving the problems related to the presence of the United States Army "in a spirit of friendly co-operation." A brief lunch was followed immediately by a flight to Dawson City, well away from the major centre of highway construction.[31]

The sewage, water, and sanitation problems encountered at Whitehorse appeared to be the major source of the army's complaints, giving rise to such comments as Whitehorse being "one vast cess pool" and Dawson Creek as "just above a primitive level." Undaunted, the American medical officers set about to look after their own and Yukoners as well. In addition to aiding Canadian authorities in attempts to clean up sanitary conditions, the 58th Medical Battalion shared their temporary aid stations, dispensaries, and permanent hospital facilities with local residents in need.[32] Yet, despite the army's attempt to execute an exemplary programme of preventative medicine, even to the point of separating "residents from construction forces to prevent the exchange and spread of disease," the native communities along the highway suffered greatly from a variety of infectious diseases.[33]

In early March 1943, Jeckell reported that dangerous sanitation problems at Whitehorse required immediate attention to prevent an epidemic. As a result, a study was carried out by the Department of Pensions and National Health.[34] A year later, frustrated by lack of assistance from the Yukon Council, local residents petitioned the prime minister directly. Gibson's demand for a full and frank account from Jeckell resulted in a tirade of disclaimers and accusations, included the rejoinder that it was "unseemly and unnecessary that I have to use part of my valuable time to contradict statements made by Mr. LeCapelain." Jeckell denied knowledge of the federal agency's report and stated that paving the streets and a new water and sewer system were "beyond the present resources of the Territorial Government." Moreover, he claimed that Whitehorse should be incorporated as a town and made responsible for its own improvements. The "ruler" of the country seemed to have suffered a decided lack of "friendly co-operation," as knowledge of the political rift between Dawson and Whitehorse residents spread to the outside world.[35] Eventually the United States Army would allow the town to link up to its modern sanitation system, but of more serious significance were the reports that in many instances the medical facilities they shared with Yukon residents were of better quality "than had previously existed in local communities."[36]

Meanwhile, members of the Cabinet and External Affairs kept a close watch over "more serious matters" such as the proposed official name change from the original "Alcan" to the more commonly used "Alaska Highway." Although there was no quarrel with the name itself, the prime minister was particularly concerned that the change was not attended by "too much fuss" nor given the honour of being passed as a congressional bill.[37] Other business continued throughout 1942 and into the next year, with the Cabinet War Committee granting approval only if agreements included specific guarantees against any attempt to claim postwar rights.[38] The first indication that Washington might wish to alter the terms arose in March 1943, when the United States Army requested revision of the original agreement to "cover the post-war use of the connecting roads and of the Highway itself, by the United States military." On the advice of the chiefs of staff, the Cabinet War Committee concluded that "no commitment should be made regarding post-war military use of the highway and connecting roads."[39] Also of direct concern to the Yukon was Washington's "anxious" request to come to an agreement on a thirty-eight-year-old controversy related to the Alaska boundary settlement of 1903, reportedly for the purpose of preparing naval charts. At issue were the boundary line extensions from Dixon Entrance of the Portland Channel and on the northern coast into the Beaufort Sea. In light of strong objections by the attorney general of British Columbia and puzzled by the sudden urgency, Ottawa suggested the issue be deferred until after the war. The request was initially refused, but after months of fruitless negotiations the matter was dropped.[40] Forty years later, the location of the boundary extensions had still not been resolved.[41]

Within months of the commencement of highway construction, it was readily apparent that the "pioneer road" and expanded ferry routes were only a beginning. Ancillary projects proliferated at an unbelievable rate. There were telephone and telegraph lines, emergency airfields, radio stations, and new wharf facilities at Skagway and Prince Rupert, as well as railway spurs at the latter port. In connection with the Northeast and Northwest Staging Routes, existing structures were expanded to accommodate the increased traffic, and numerous weather stations were built and manned primarily by United States military personnel. Both governments had also agreed to undertake a location survey for a military railway to connect Prince George to Fairbanks. Construction, which was to begin in May 1943 at an estimated cost of $230 million, was cancelled when the crisis eased on the Pacific Front, although events occurring at the same time may suggest other reasons for the cancellation. By far the most ambitious undertaking was the construction of an oil pipeline from Norman Wells to Whitehorse. "Canol," a shortened version of "Canadian Oil," was estimated to have cost over $134 million.[42]

Prior to the war, the first and only oil pipeline built in the far north was a relatively short, eight-and-a-half-mile-long, two-inch diameter line to skirt the rapids of the Great Bear River. Constructed in 1933, the line was used in conjunction with sternwheelers and barges to deliver oil from Norman Wells to the mines on Great Bear Lake. In comparison, the laying of four-inch pipe from Norman Wells to Whitehorse proved to be a formidable task. On the advice of Colonel James Graham, dean of engineering at the University of Kentucky, the project was approved by the United States Army on 9 April 1942, after one day of discussion. Approval was justified on the grounds that the pipeline would guarantee a continuous supply of fuel to the Alaska Highway and adjacent airfields should the Japanese effectively halt all tanker traffic in the Pacific. The original plans included over 550 miles of line and road, the drilling of new oil wells within a fifty-mile radius of Norman Wells, and construction of a new refinery at Whitehorse. Despite reservations, first by Charles Camsell, who claimed that at least thirty more wells would be needed to produce the target production of three thousand barrels a day, and then by Imperial Oil representatives who advised that the necessary equipment would not be available to accommodate freight demands, the project went ahead as scheduled at an estimated cost to the American government of $30 million, an estimate which would prove to be over $100 million short.[43]

When it was finally operational in the spring of 1944, the Canol Project had expanded to include a series of airfields along the Mackenzie Valley, importation of additional river transport, numerous construction camps and pumping stations, expanded facilities at Norman Wells, winter roads, telephone lines, and supplementary pipelines from Skagway to Whitehorse and along the length of the Alaska Highway (see figure 9). The problems of labour, transportation, and construction seemed insurmountable, but the American Army and the civilian contractors were determined to see it through. One observer wrote that despite the mountain barriers, "the engineers who are tackling the job of fetching oil from Norman to Alaska exclaimed 'to Hell with the Mackenzie Mountains.'"[44] Little thought had been given to geography or climate. Quite apart from the intense cold of winter and the hordes of insects arriving with the heat of summer, the contractors were totally unprepared and inexperienced in dealing with muskeg and permafrost.

Yet haste was essential, and like the Alaska Highway, the project was underway in advance of the exchange of notes. The American War Department granted approval on 4 April; the Cabinet War Committee agreed in principle on 16 May; the first American troops reached the end of rail at Waterways on 4 June; and the formal notes of agreement after details had been negotiated were exchanged on 27 and 29 June 1942. The terms of postwar disposition were only slightly different from those agreed to on the Alaska Highway project. Warned by the deputy minister of mines and resources that the pipeline would not be financially feasible in peacetime, the Cabinet War Committee granted approval with certain limitations. Although the United States assumed responsibility for construction and costs of the pipeline, ownership of the line and refinery would remain in American hands only until the end of the war. At that time Canada could claim prior right of purchase before the matter of disposition was referred to the Permanent Joint Board on Defence. Canada agreed to waive royalties on all oil produced during wartime in addition to providing sites and right of ways. On the other hand, the United States government could not purchase land or leases, a provision

JOINT MILITARY PROJECTS

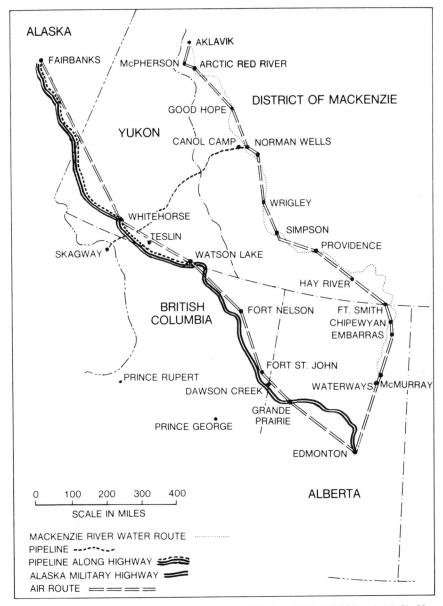

Figure 9 Military Projects in the Canadian Northwest, 1943 (from NAC, RG 36/7, vol. 14, file 22-3, "Defence Projects in Canada")

which was occasionally ignored.[45] In the final analysis, the pipeline would cease to be the property of the United States government at the conclusion of the war, but Canada would not be required to purchase or maintain it if it proved to be another "white elephant" as was already suspected.

Initially, Ottawa showed only moderate interest in the pipeline project. Reports submitted to the Northwest Territories Council in June, August, and December 1942 contained general information concerning the purpose, plans, and terms of the agreement, with emphasis on the fact that the construction would be carried out by the United States Army Engineer Corps with the assistance of American contractors, Bechtel-Price-Callahan and an imported labour crew. Significantly, there was no mention of a completion date. The oil-drilling programme was contracted out to the Northwest Company, a subsidiary of the Imperial Oil Company, which in turn was owned by Standard Oil of New Jersey. The message was clear: this was an American project which would not drain Canadian manpower or financial resources needed for the overseas war effort. The August report made mention of three thousand American troops in the area, and the December update noted a major delay owing to problems in transporting the equipment from the end of rail at Waterways. What they did not report was that the tugs imported from Missouri had been unequal to the task of towing the heavily laden barges over the hazardous waters of Great Slave Lake.[46] The official tour by Camsell and MacDonald in the summer of 1942 was dutifully reported at the council meeting in late August with no concern expressed for the extent of the American activities or the presence of new airfields along the river system. At that time, the only reported problem was the bootlegging by locals who purchased liquor with their permits, then resold it to the U.S. Army Engineers.[47] More serious difficulties were arising elsewhere.

Despite their efforts to protect sovereign jurisdiction, External Affairs were continually plagued with irregularities in procedure. By October 1942, it was apparent that a number of works had been initiated ahead of, or without, approval: the airfields along the Mackenzie, the pipeline from Watson Lake to Whitehorse, and various ancillary roads.[48] The informal documents passing between officials of the two countries reflected Ottawa's increasing embarrassment at being notified of plans after the Americans had taken unilateral action.[49] Behind the scenes, anger and frustration were slowly building up. Years later, Escott Reid explained the problem:

> One thing we didn't know about the Northwest was the amount of discretion that was left to the American General in the field . . . and the degree of independence of the Defence Department from the State Department. We would work out an agreement with the State Department on American activities in the North and then discover months later that the Americans

were not acting in accordance with the agreement we'd reached in Washington, but were extending their jurisdiction well beyond what they had agreed to.[50]

Richard Finnie, who was hired as a consultant and liaison officer by the civilian contractor working on the pipeline, later verified that some activities might have commenced without formal authorization, as in the case of the Mackenzie Valley airfields. He also admitted that the officer in charge, Colonel Theodore Wyman, Jr., was "not noted for his tact or diplomacy," but he argued that "if the U.S. War Department neglected to obtain specific authorization from Ottawa, it may have been with the assumption that it already had blanket authorization from Ottawa to resort to any reasonable means of completing the Canol Project in the cause of joint U.S.–Canadian defence."[51] Hugh Keenleyside, as a member of the Permanent Joint Board on Defence, was not as charitable, claiming that American officials tended "to act first and seek approval after—if at all."[52] Regardless of their reasons, in 1942 many Americans in the field assumed they had the same powers as a military occupation.[53]

Informed of the grievances, Washington agreed to follow proper authorization procedures. Further requests continued, including a proposed extension of oil drilling rights to encompass an area bounded by the Arctic, the 60th parallel, the 112th meridian, and the continental divide. Pierrepont Moffat, the American minister in Canada, urged immediate consideration of the wildcat programme as a precaution in the event that the supply of oil at Norman Wells proved inadequate to meet the needs of the United States military.[54] Canadian Oil Controller G. R. Cottrelle was sceptical, but he reluctantly agreed since Ottawa's hands were so inextricably tied by the Hyde Park agreement that Canadian oil was "considered on a parity with that of the United States." He cautioned, however, that there was a growing interest in Washington for wider development of Canadian resources by Americans.[55]

Censorship was exceptionally rigid at this time, and apparently a number of senior Washington authorities complained that they were equally uninformed about the details of the project. Vilhjalmur Stefansson reported in March 1943 that one of the "highest officials" had stated "that the suppression of the Mackenzie appeared to be the deepest military secret in Washington, for he had been able to penetrate every other secret the existence of which he suspected."[56] The American military had good reason to remain silent. Costs had escalated beyond their wildest expectations. By December 1942 there were more than fifteen thousand American military and civilians stationed in the Canadian northwest. Six months later, the over thirty-three thousand Americans would far exceed the local Canadian population. Some estimates placed the figure at forty-three thousand.[57] Even though the threat of a Japanese invasion had abated, the construction crews continued the slow process of building a pipeline and road over the Mackenzie Mountains. The original purpose of defence appeared to have been replaced by concern to save face.

IV

The reaction of the Northwest Territories Council was at first ambivalent. When informed of the United States plans to expand radio and meteorological facilities in the Arctic, Deputy Commissioner Gibson argued that Canadians, not Americans, should build and man the proposed weather stations. Keenleyside, as the council member representing External Affairs, agreed to consult the Permanent Joint Board on Defence on the matter, knowing full well that there were no Canadians with the necessary skills available.[58] By the end of 1942, the Mackenzie District experienced similar problems. Yellowknife, in particular, reported that labour shortages had resulted in the closing of mines and many local enterprises. According to one report, "the U.S. Army projects at Fort Smith and down river have drained this area of practically all casual labour and the rumoured attractive wages have induced a number of tractor and truck operators to leave this area."[59] And there were other effects, such as the drastic reduction in freight and passenger space on the Eastern Arctic Patrol and the necessity of acquiring a special permit for civilian air travel throughout the north.[60]

A most revealing report of American activities came from the Superintendent of the Eastern Arctic Patrol in the summer of 1942. Major D. L. McKeand had arrived at Churchill to find it a hive of activity. To his complete surprise, he found that the ship customarily used for the patrol, the *Nascopie*, had been requisitioned by the United States armed forces to carry building material, supplies, equipment, and personnel for the new weather stations at Fort Ross and Arctic Bay. In a confidential letter of explanation for the delay incurred, McKeand expressed serious concern for the lack of communication and government representation in the area.

> With Radio Operators, R.C.M.Police, etc., building materials and food supplies arriving at Churchill almost every day and without any advice, we have cooperated with each other to make the best arrangement possible. You may not be aware of it but the United States Army is in supreme command here and is acting on instructions from Washington. . . . I have had some field experience in wartime to appreciate the difficulties that arise at headquarters without much notice. But unless we in

the field are kept reasonably informed of what to expect there is [*sic*] bound to be misunderstandings.

To emphasize the strain put on existing facilities, McKeand claimed "everything that can be made to float is being shoved into the water."[61] According to the confidential report submitted on his return, the American military seemed to be everywhere, busily occupied with the construction of new facilities or expansion of existing ones. In a carefully edited report for press purposes, the military activities were mentioned very briefly and then only in reference to the building of a new weather station and the "two experts from Washington" who were assisting in the installation of equipment and its operation. Otherwise, there was no indication that a single American soldier was present in the Arctic that summer.[62] Some of the best kept secrets of the war lay hidden in the land of snow and ice, out of public view.

The police and government officials were expected to co-operate with the Americans as part of the "war effort," with the result that most changes to territorial regulations were related to adjusting the activities of the existing residents to those of the invited guests. Generally, policy decisions of the northern administration were still based on cost and fur-trade considerations, but at times even traditional concerns took a back seat, as in the case of hunting and fishing permits for those employed at the Arctic weather stations. Despite warnings that hunting and casual trading would "seriously affect game resources in some areas and upset trading in others," the Northwest Territories Council agreed to allow American personnel to hunt and fish in the Arctic Islands Preserve, lest denial of such privileges might "endanger the policy of granting government employees complimentary 'limited' hunting and trapping licenses." The fact that the requests were submitted by the United States minister to Canada by way of the Department of External Affairs may also have been a factor.[63]

McKeand's report also revealed the priorities and perspectives attached to the welfare of the Inuit. He noted with satisfaction that the Inuit migration "to more favourable locations" had been successful, since those who had moved from Frobisher to River Clyde reported an "all time record high fur catch." Moreover, he proudly reported "encouraging signs of thrift" among the more "intelligent," who had followed advice of the traders and were now "proud owners" of motor boats and sewing machines. Many had cleared their debt and were now placing prepaid orders for goods such as new rifles, woollen underwear, flour, tea, and so forth. Ironically, there was one side effect of the successful fur catch that had not been anticipated; the women and children had been so busy dressing the furs that they were unable to fill the Hudson's Bay request for three thousand sealskin boots for export trade. McKeand also reported that "the policy of relieving the hunters of the responsibility for their aged, crippled, and hospital cases, has contributed to the successful hunt of the past year,"[64] a statement which partly explains the generous funding of the two industrial homes when funds were denied for welfare elsewhere.

McKeand claimed that the presence of the armed forces camps were a direct threat to the fur trade, but he reported that he had encouraged American officers and contractors to keep the Inuit away from army settlements so that they would continue to hunt and trap. Noting that a few natives had been temporarily employed by the Americans at Southampton Island, Fort Chimo, Frobisher, and Exeter,* he reassured the council that the "novelty of fixed hours, high wages and weekly payments was gradually wearing off." Whether in the interests of the fur trade or military secrecy, it was reported that "surplus native population from government radio stations" had been transported "to locations where children have better opportunities to follow their mode of life."[65] As a further guarantee that any temporarily employed Inuit would return to their traditional lifestyle, the northern administration and the Department of Transport jointly sponsored a motion to limit the length of native wage employment in the eastern Arctic to a period of not more than two or three years. Council granted unanimous approval.[66]

A number of health problems were brought to the council's attention in 1942, eliciting rather inconsistent responses. Cutbacks on hospital grants prompted the advisement that "Indians who can be cared for by relatives at home should not be admitted." Yet two months later, Deputy Commissioner Gibson reported deep concern for the poor health among the Inuit of the eastern Arctic. His underlying motives were rather suspect, however, for he went on to complain that "this condition reflected adversely on the Administration and urged the appointment of resident medical officers to study the situation and to make recommendations as to what should be done to improve conditions."[67] "Government studies" appeared to be the standard procedure in dealing with suggestions or problems reported by external sources. For example, when Keenleyside inquired about the possibility of council taking over all educational and health services in the Northwest Territories, the deputy commissioner supplied a detailed report recommending that medical care was best left to the missions. Not only was it less costly, but "hospitalization was synonymous with the advancement of civilization and Christianity."[68]

---

*Exeter no longer appears on the map, but it was the location of a small Inuit settlement near the weather station being built on Padloping Island in the vicinity of Exeter Bay and Exeter Strait.

Newcomers to the Arctic with a sense of social responsibility would have disagreed with Gibson's assessment. The severity of Inuit health problems requiring attention were beyond the capacity of the missions. From 1941 to 1943, more epidemics were reported among the natives involving influenza, tuberculosis, and spinal meningitis.[69] There was also a cruel irony in McKeand's own statement that medical services were inadequate and federal grants insufficient to meet the "unavoidable epidemics" which followed the annual visit of the patrol ship.[70] In this respect, the arrival of the United States Army was a blessing. As had occurred in the Yukon, American medical officers stationed in the Northwest Territories volunteered their services to both native and white inhabitants, but much to the consternation of the northern administration, they frequently notified Canadian authorities of the highly unsatisfactory conditions.[71] Yet despite awareness of inadequate health services, there was little attempt to remedy the situation. The proposed reconstruction budget set down in the spring of 1943 still allotted only minimal funds for health and education, even though there were large increases for the construction of administration buildings, improvements to mining roads and airports, studies on potential development of natural resources, dock facilities and navigational aids, as well as grants for geological surveys, topographical mapping, geodetic studies, and aerial photography.[72]

There were other reported incidents which reflected the priorities of the Northwest Territories Council. To meet the needs of the American soldiers and construction workers, a new liquor depot was opened at Fort Smith in the spring of 1942, resulting in enthusiastic reports of increased revenue at the August council meeting. The "influx of strangers" was also given as the reason for passing "An Ordinance Respecting the Prevention of Venereal Disease." Expenditure without promise of revenue was another matter, and it was not until January 1943 that the Department of Mines and Resources appointed a qualified geologist, Dr. J. S. Stewart, as a liaison officer to report on American drilling operations at Norman Wells. If the need was considered critical, savings could be found elsewhere; in this case the department decided not to send geological crews to the Mackenzie District that summer, since Imperial Oil planned to have ten parties working in the area. For the most part, however, it was business as usual. Regardless of the fact that there was a war going on, the council still found time to debate whether the weekly Saturday night dance at the Yellowknife recreation hall should close its doors at midnight.[73] Meanwhile, revenues were extracted where possible; ordinances were passed to prevent problems which had already occurred; and expenditures were kept to a minimum. Inherent in all policy decisions was the aim to keep up the public appearance that all was well and everything under control in Canada's north, an objective shared by the members of External Affairs and the Cabinet War Committee.

While the United States Army of Engineers were busily fulfilling the intent of the Ogdensburg agreement, the economic experts were equally engrossed in integrating the production and resources of the two countries. Of particular relevance to the Canadian northwest, in light of the oil at Norman Wells and the uranium at Port Radium, was a proposal put forward to the Joint Economic Committees by the U.S. National Resources Planning Board in September 1942. The North Pacific Planning Project was officially reported as a study into "the extension of wartime collaboration to the peacetime development of the vast region of northern British Columbia, Yukon Territory and Alaska." The committees agreed to sponsor the study with the understanding that the planning board, which was established in 1938 by President Roosevelt and reported to the board of governors of the Federal Reserve System, would pay the costs and provide the "full time assistance of its Alaskan regional office staff" with James E. Rettie as director.[74] The Canadian chairman of the committees, W. A. Mackintosh, believed the study fell within the terms of reference and did not seek the approval of the Canadian government.[75]

After receiving approval, Rettie wasted little time in submitting his first full-length report on 8 October. It recommended the construction of a "Trans-Canada-Alaska Railroad," initially for military purposes, but also to stimulate postwar mineral production, settlement, and tourism. He then proceeded to Ottawa on 12 October, where he discussed the project with senior representatives of various agencies and departments, such as the Geological Survey, Transport, Civil Aviation, Immigration, and Mines and Resources. When he visited the United States Legation, Moffat warned him that Canada would be apprehensive of providing the manpower required for railway construction and suggested the use of United States Army Engineer troops if Canada could be induced "to see the whole problem from the standpoint of national wartime interests." Moffat also noted that while Canada had "cooperated wholeheartedly in the war effort," there had been "some irritation" which created "a delicate situation" because of "pressure tactics" by United States airlines attempting to gain permission to operate across Canada to Alaska, a problem which had been "temporarily shelved by militarization of the airlines." Rettie's visit with Mackintosh was less encouraging as far as any expectation of immediate action. Believing the study should be centred on possibilities of resource development, the Canadian chairman argued that ad hoc committees should be set up to "check views and help revise tentative reports" on coastal shipping, air transport, land and agriculture, mineral and industrial development, and trade.[76] Unknown to Mackintosh, Rettie had a much more comprehensive study in mind and was not prepared to wait for sub-committee input and consensus.

On 6 December 1942, the *Sunday Oregonian* gave full front page coverage to the proposed development of "CANASKA—A Wide and Wealthy Northern Empire," which was "receiving intensive study by the authority of both governments" through sponsorship of the Joint Economic Committees (see figure 10). A large full-coloured map carefully located the resources of the area, including the radium, oil, and gold fields of the Mackenzie Valley, and the article emphasized the exploitation of a wide variety of resources: fishing, lumber, precious minerals, coal, iron, oil, and finally the mountains and lakes for tourism. Rettie, described as a graduate of Yale and the London School of Economics, was quoted as saying "that if the northern empire is not developed, then we shall not deserve to hold it." Referred to as "an eloquent demonstration of international cooperation," the purpose of the project was stated as "an urgent need for backing up the military defense with a strong transportation system and a better balanced civilian economy." The similarity of the ambitious scheme to earlier Stefansson visions was no coincidence; the article devoted four paragraphs to his ideas and comments, including his call "for the use of this empire as an artery to the orient, carrying a stream of supplies to the heart of Siberia and China."[77]

Not content with local coverage, Rettie arranged for the regional chairman of the National Resources Planning Board to present the full study plan to the Eighth Study Conference of the Institute of Pacific Relations, hosted by the Canadian Institute of International Affairs and held mid-December at Mont Tremblant, Quebec. Provided with detailed maps and a complete outline by the project's director, Benjamin Kizer gave a paper entitled "The North Pacific International Planning Project" to a round-table session attended by a number of important figures including D. A. Skelton, Hugh Keenleyside, M. J. Coldwell, and F. H. Soward.[78] Added to the original scope of the study were "adjacent areas," which, according to the map, included the whole of the Mackenzie Valley as well as Great Slave Lake, Great Bear Lake, and the Coppermine region. As one might expect, all proposed railways, air routes, and highways led to Washington and Oregon states.[79] The paper prepared for distribution described in explicit detail a proposal of Canadian-American cooperation in settlement, transportation, development of resources, and defence of the northwest. The primary motive, as stated, was to provide military security in North America as a key factor "in the postwar system of world security." Economic integration of the region was the second objective, followed by "a better balanced continental economy," and "an economic opportunity for some of the displaced peoples of the world who are adaptable to this region." Implementation of the plan, it was suggested, would be carried out by a "Canadian-United States Development Authority."[80]

Five days after the conference, on 17 December, and with a press release enclosed, Mackintosh wrote to Arnold Heeney to describe the project ap-

Figure 10 Front Page of *The Sunday Oregonian*, 6 December 1942

proved by the joint committees and to suggest that "the Prime Minister, and if he thinks best the War Committee, should learn of the study directly rather than in the press."[81] Perhaps owing to his secret knowledge of the significance of Canada's uranium or aware that British preferential trade and colonial policies had come under severe attack by the Americans at the Mont Tremblant Conference, King reacted with exceptional cynicism and distrust. When he recorded the incident in his diary, he related how he had firmly resisted the proposed study because of his suspicions about the "ultimate design of the Americans" and wrote that he viewed the project as part of a plan "by the Americans to control developments in the country after the war and bring Canada out of the orbit of the British Commonwealth of Nations into their own orbit." Almost as an afterthought, he concluded that he wanted "to see Canada continue to develop as a nation to be, in time, as our country certainly will, the greatest of nations of the British Commonwealth.[82]

The issue was debated at the next two Cabinet War Committee meetings, with King arguing that "to safeguard Canadian interests" at least the project "should be on a basis of equal participation."[83] Rettie was notified of the complication and rather graciously agreed to have Charles Camsell made co-director.[84] The War Committee subsequently approved the plan, and on 25 January 1943, the North Pacific Planning Project was officially announced to the Canadian and American public.[85]

The press release referred to "the first international planning project of such magnitude in history," but the emphasis was on "study" rather than "planning," and "joint participation" as opposed to "co-operation." There was no direct reference to military strategy or economic integration. The preliminary draft submitted to the Joint Economic Committees, however, included evaluation of the economic potential of all natural resources, study of "measures conducive to freer trade"; "integration of water routes, railroads, highways and airways"; potential for internal migration and immigration to the northwest; and a specific section to study "practical solutions" to the development and conservation of petroleum resources.[86]

Of particular relevance was the reason advanced for expanding the regional development studies of Alaska into a joint Canadian-American project. According to a "confidential" progress report, the chairman of the National Resources Planning Board along with regional officers and "with the approval of the State Department and the War Department" had toured the Canadian Northwest in June 1942. As a result of this trip, it became apparent to members of the planning board that the wartime projects had "a significance that reaches far beyond immediate war interests."[87] Not mentioned was the fact that the Canadian resources of key importance to the Americans in the summer of 1942 were oil and uranium.

The British Columbia press initially greeted the project with enthusiasm, with the *Vancouver Daily Province* on 25 January 1943 claiming a "new economic empire for B.C." in the proposed development scheme which could prove to be "an economic empire twice as large as Norway, Sweden and Finland combined." The editorial the next day, while still extremely positive, noted with some resignation that the war had "brought about a tremendous tangling of Canadian and American interest in the country north of 54:40 and it will probably be much easier to continue the co-operation after the war than to attempt an unscrambling of interests." The *Edmonton Journal* reflected more moderate reaction, claiming interest in the part Alberta might play in "joint economic undertakings" but firmly rejecting the idea of any "joint political administration" as suggested in an Ottawa despatch.[88] The *New York Times* considered the proposed co-operation as an inevitable extension of wartime collaboration and noted that unofficial informed sources claimed that the development of the area's "immense" resources would best be undertaken through joint administration. The other issue of importance was the wartime air routes, which were also described as better handled by "joint authority." The editorial comment the next day again stressed the importance of Fairbanks as a future "world junction point" in commercial aviation and applauded the breaking down of boundary barriers. While admitting that "boundary lines will continue to exist" and that they are "convenient and have sentimental values," the editor suggested that the economic advantages might be so advantageous that "political boundary lines may simply become less important."[89] The *Financial Post* some months later reported that some members of British Columbia's coalition government were expressing resentment of being bypassed in "negotiations between Ottawa and Washington" but that the reduction of U.S. tariffs and equalization of exchange rates would be of great advantage in promoting the province's manufacturing sector.[90] The editor of the *Vancouver Sun*, re-examining the project after a look at a preliminary report, noted that the dramatic wartime growth of the west coast manufacturing industries posed a problem during the reconstruction phase of peacetime and that suggestions of utilizing the natural resources of the Northwest, including the hydro-electric potential of the Columbia River, to produce a strong manufacturing export industry were as relevant to British Columbia as to the northwestern states. More important than developing international markets, the article cautioned, the entire future of a manufacturing sector in British Columbia depended solely on the reduction of American tariffs.[91]

After his presentation at Mont Tremblant, Kizer was approached by the American Council of the Institute of Pacific Relations with an offer to publish his paper in book form. The chairmen of the two economic committees gave their consent, Mackintosh insisting that Charles Camsell's name should appear as a co-director and the "planning" aspect be downplayed.[92] Thus, in

April of the same year, *The U.S.–Canadian Northwest* appeared in print, outlining plans of "collaboration" in postwar development, with special attention to the role of air transport, which the author claimed should be studied "carefully" in preparation for diplomatic negotiations. Discussion of oil resources included the suggestion that *only* if the Norman Wells fields proved to be too small to supply American needs should further exploration proceed in Alaska. And while plans of "military collaboration" were stated as being beyond the scope of the project, it was noted that with "the growing effectiveness of air power, the mutual interdependence of Canada and the United States with respect to security in the North Pacific is obvious." Recommendations included an extension of the Alaska Highway to connect directly with the coastal highway systems, the establishment of strong land-sea-air military bases, the export of British Columbia's iron ore to support an American west coast steel industry, freer trade between the two countries, and a railway line from Fairbanks to Prince George which would connect to lines in the south. More disconcerting to some Canadians was the map showing proposed transportation routes connecting the uranium, oil, and gold fields of northwestern Canada to American west coast cities.[93]

One important objective of the project was to investigate means of increasing settlement in the American northwest through postwar immigration. The implications of limited population in northern Canada already greatly concerned some Americans. According to Isaiah Bowman, the political geographer, president of Johns Hopkins University, and wartime adviser to Franklin Roosevelt, Canada's "almost empty northland" was potentially a "dangerous military vacuum... should Russian expansion ever become a menace to the Western Hemisphere." Bowman went on to argue that "it is of great moment that Northern Canada be fully developed as fast as possible so that population increases and there is more general distribution of settlement."[94] The words had a strange echo of those uttered a half century earlier when Canadians used the identical rationale for rapid settlement of the prairies to forestall the threat of American expansion.

Showing apparent enthusiasm for the project, Hugh Keenleyside, under the alias of John Hughes, wrote an introduction for Kizer's book and for a similar article appearing in the *Far Eastern*, 8 February 1943. While emphasizing the scientific aspects of the study, he praised the fact that "political boundaries were forgotten except insofar as it was necessary to obtain the cooperation of the respective political authorities." He stated that it was a great achievement to have set aside nationalism for the advancement of the "good life" for the common man.[95] In later years, Keenleyside replied to the subsequent criticism that he had been in favour of continental integration leading to a customs union by saying that "this was not then, never has been, and is not now my position." He went on to clarify his stand. "It is still my view that mutually advantageous co-operative arrangements between Canadian and American industries could be designed. But they would have to contain strong guarantees that Canada would enjoy a reasonable proportion of the continental market in the commodities involved. The simple abolition of tariffs in a customs union, on the contrary, could in many instances bring disaster to the Canadian economy."[96] Like many intellectuals during the early war years, Keenleyside had an inherent distrust of nationalism, which in turn gave the impression that he favoured continentalism. Equally suspicious of American imperialism in the postwar period, most would seek internationalism as the more acceptable alternative.

Keenleyside's support for the North Pacific Planning Project coincided with other attempts on his part to devise a plan of development for northern Canada. On 3 March 1943, he wrote to Dana Wilgress at the Canadian embassy in Moscow to request any pertinent information on Russian settlement in their polar regions.[97] At the same time, he hired a professional geographer to undertake a study of comparative development in Arctic regions with particular emphasis on the Soviet experience. Trevor Lloyd, an English-born Canadian currently teaching geography at Dartmouth College, was officially assigned to the Wartime Information Board, but unofficially his mandate was to provide Keenleyside with background information towards a long-range development strategy for Canada's north.[98] Although his actions were prompted by American interest, this instance marked the first initiative on the part of a senior civil servant to consider planned development of the Canadian north seriously.

V

At a time when most considered problems in northern Canada of minor importance compared to depression and war, there were a few private citizens who shared a broad interest in its potential. From different walks of life, they had a common concern for Ottawa's apparent unwillingness to effect responsible administrative practices and development strategies. Many had firsthand experience in the Arctic or sub-Arctic regions through scientific exploration or military experience. A few developed interest purely from an intellectual perspective; some were motivated by social conscience; others were involved through government; and many feared the potential threat of American imperialism.

A central figure among the promoters of a "new north" was George Raleigh Parkin, son of the renowned educator and staunch imperialist, Sir George Robert Parkin. A graduate of McGill and Oxford, Raleigh Parkin was employed as a senior executive of the Sun Life Assurance Company located in Montreal. In the image of his father, he was a devout Canadian nationalist, yet at the same time an active participant in both the Canadian Institute of International Affairs and the Institute of Current World Affairs (ICWA). His interest in northern affairs grew out of social and intellectual concerns; he had never once visited the Yukon or Northwest Territories. Professor Maxwell J. Dunbar, who knew Parkin during the 1940s, attempted to explain his motives and methods:

> Raleigh Parkin's interests were both broad and deep; what interested him he explored deeply. He was extremely articulate and a marvelous conversationalist. . . . it was his awareness of history and environment (time and space) in the general sense, no doubt that brought his attention to the North. A region hitherto thought of as remote, hostile, almost legendary, was fast becoming close, relevant, and in urgent need of scientific attention. . . . The thing about Raleigh and others of his leadership qualities was that they decided to do something *outside Government circles*. This was important.[99]

Parkin was not politically ambitious. He did not enjoy being in the limelight, but he thrived on taking ideas and putting them to practical purpose. He was an initiator who preferred to remain behind the scenes.[100] His success was partly related to his influential ties in government, business, and academic circles which opened up direct channels of communication.

Parkin's interest in the north first arose through his association with the Institute of Current World Affairs, commonly referred to as the Crane Foundation. This organization was established for the purpose of collecting and distributing information on international affairs. Towards this goal, young men were sent to various countries to gain further education and knowledge that might promote a better understanding of foreign relations.[101] In 1936 Parkin was intrigued by an idea put forward by the foundation's director, W. S. Rogers, that an extensive study of the underdeveloped regions in northern Canada would provide insight into some of the complex problems of more advanced societies. Parkin's thoughts went beyond this concept. He was convinced that a man trained as an "Arctic generalist" could later assume a responsible position in the Canadian government "to give effective expression of his ideas and experience" in northern affairs.[102] In an attempt to gain support for a proposed "Institute for North Atlantic Studies," Parkin invited senior academics and Ottawa officials to attend dinner meetings in the spring of 1940 and again in April 1941. Despite impressive guest lists, his proposals received little encouragement. In recalling the apathetic response some years later, he claimed it was "the typical [Canadian] reaction to any problems which do not literally stare us in the face."[103] That same month, Parkin also met with the deputy commissioner of the Northwest Territories to explore the possibility of government co-operation for detailed study of the Arctic. At the time, Parkin referred to the potential candidate as "having a breadth of view and a delicate sense of proportion" and mentioned that the name of Trevor Lloyd of Winnipeg had been submitted to the institute. The report of the meeting was duly noted at the next council meeting, but it elicited no comments and was simply tabled.[104]

Although initially discouraged by the lack of interest, Parkin persisted in his efforts to find a suitable candidate to study the problems of northern Canada. His search brought him in contact with a number of Arctic specialists: Diamond Jenness, Trevor Lloyd, Tom Manning, Erling Porsild, and Maxwell Dunbar, all of whom freely commented on their experience and concerns. In turn, Parkin furnished the Arctic scientists with letters of introduction to those with influence in Ottawa.[105] Of particular significance was the favourable impression and subsequent friendship that developed from an interview in November 1942 with Trevor Lloyd. Lloyd related to Parkin his experiences on the Mackenzie the previous summer when he had observed the military activities involving the Canol Project. In notes taken after the meeting, Parkin expressed deep concern over the extent of the project and the apparent lack of Canadian involvement.[106] Subsequently, Parkin contacted Malcolm MacDonald and that, in turn, led to several briefing sessions between Lloyd and the British high commissioner's assistant secretary, Ian M. R. Maclennan. Lloyd also discussed the situation with Hugh Keenleyside.[107] Parkin, meanwhile, brought the matter to the attention of other influential contacts in Ottawa: Arnold Heeney and Brooke Claxton; Robert Beattie, the director of research for the Bank of Canada; and Group Captain William Hanna of the Royal Canadian Air Force. He also communicated his concerns to Joseph Willets of the Rockefeller Foundation and W. S. Rogers of the Institute of Current World Affairs.[108]

Over the succeeding months, Parkin became increasingly uneasy over the steady American encroachment on matters he believed should be left to Canadians. In reply to a letter from Benjamin Kizer concerning the North Pacific Planning Project, Parkin reminded him that there was "room for independent work and study by both Americans and Canadians," that "some sectors will be primarily Canada's responsibility," and that "there are quite a number of Canadians with wide experience and knowledge of Arctic matters." He also insisted that such a study required a more "academic or intellectual" approach to assist in shaping "immediate social, economic and political policies."[109] The following day, 18 March 1943, Raleigh Parkin took more positive action.

As a member of the Research Committee, Parkin proposed that the Canadian Institute of International Affairs sponsor Trevor Lloyd in an extensive study of problems related to northern Canada. He noted that the research could take as long as seven years to complete and that it would cover political, economic, social, transportation, and resource related issues.[110] The proposed "Arctic Study" as it was commonly called, received formal approval in June 1943, with the Rockefeller Foundation providing 50 per cent of the funding. The Research Committee of the CIIA justified their support, of what might be considered a domestic concern, in terms of the north's new strategic significance and its possible effect on future Canadian external relations.[111] Lloyd was more explicit in defining his objectives. In his opinion, the main purpose was "to inform Canadians about conditions in the northern part of the Dominion so that they will support plans for its proper development."[112] Regardless of their diverse motives, Parkin and Lloyd effectively utilized the institute as a vehicle to promote public and government support for changes in northern policy.

VI

While Canadian diplomats worried about changing attitudes in the State Department and American free traders were planning economic integration of the Pacific Northwest, the war continued on far-flung fronts. One scene of battle which received little attention in the Canadian newspapers was located in the Aleutian Islands, the chain of volcanic remnants belonging to Alaska and stretching over a thousand miles into the Bering Sea. As a diversionary tactic in June 1942, the Japanese bombed the army and naval bases at Dutch Harbor, some 850 miles southwest of Anchorage, and took possession of two of the more distant islands, Attu and Kiska. In response, the Americans built bases on Adack and Amchitka. A naval battle off the Russian Komandorskis Islands just east of the Aleutians in March 1943 marked the last important skirmish in the area, and the two occupied islands were recaptured that spring and summer. Reclaiming Attu cost the Americans 560 lives, the Japanese over 2,300. The assault on Kiska, in which the Canadian Air Force participated under American command, was an anticlimax. Completely undetected, the Japanese had effected a total evacuation a week prior to the Allied landing.[113]

Although no major battles were fought, the minor clashes gave just cause for concern over the security of Alaska. As a consequence, numerous military bases were hastily erected on both the mainland and islands (see figure 11), and an Alaska territorial guard was formed, nicknamed the "Tundra Army" and comprised of twenty thousand Inuit, Indians, and Aleutians. In comparison, Canadian participation in defence of the North Pacific was described as primarily limited to "a rear-areas security force," providing

Figure 11 Military Bases in Alaska and the Yukon, 1943 (map by D. James)

mainly reconnaissance and backup squadrons in the event of attack. Now
referred to as "the forgotten war," the fight for control of the Aleutians may
have been of relatively minor importance, but to the residents of Alaska it
was real, and it was memorable. Aircraft carriers brought fighters and, in
their wake, bombers and paratroopers. The once remote and inaccessible islands were now direct links in the wartime network of communications and
transportation.[114]

By the spring of 1943, high-level officials in London, Washington, and
Ottawa began to consider the long-term uses of the air bases. There was a
general consensus that these air routes would eventually become commercial
ones providing either benefits or disadvantages depending upon the perspective of the country involved and a number of questions surfaced in relation to
future control and regulation. Of critical concern was the uncertainty surrounding Washington's expectations regarding the American-built military
fields around the world.

In January 1943, Vincent Massey, the Canadian high commissioner to the
United Kingdom, received some rather disconcerting news. With obvious

distress, he wrote in his diary of conversations with a senior official of the Hudson's Bay Company concerning the problems at the American air bases in northern Canada.

They have apparently walked in and taken possession in many cases as if Canada were unclaimed territory inhabited by a docile race of aborigines. Our Government people have obviously been slack in allowing American exploitation to get out of control. Large numbers of men have been discovered well established in certain parts of the North without Ottawa knowing anything about the matter at all or any permission asked or given. It is true the work is all in aid of the war effort but it does not follow from that Canadian sovereign rights should not be jealously safeguarded. This is particularly necessary in view of the fact that the Americans quite clearly have in mind the use of air routes for commercial purposes after the war.[115]

Although the criticism was harsh, the concern was valid. Those most responsible for acceding to American pressure for increased facilities in the Arctic had no conceptual understanding of the situation. No senior member of External Affairs, let alone the prime minister, Ilsley, Howe, or Ralston had ever visited any part of the northern military operations. What they could not see did not concern them as long as sovereignty was guaranteed on paper.[116] The intensity of Massey's concern, however, was likely related to his having a very persuasive brother-in-law, Raleigh Parkin.

The fear of American postwar intentions in the matter of civil aviation was not without some foundation. Adolf Berle outlined Washington's strategy, as he perceived it, in a letter to his secretary of state on 9 September 1942, claiming that "aviation will have a greater influence on American foreign interests and American foreign policy than any other non-political consideration." For reasons of defence and commerce, Berle argued that air power would become as important as sea power had been in the past, and he recommended close study of "territorial relationships, certain international objectives and diplomatic strategy. . . . We cannot remain unconcerned as to location of airports, present and post-war control of these, and arrangements by which they are controlled and maintained."[117] If the United States had designs on air bases throughout the world for their postwar use, there was no reason to believe the Canadian ones would be exceptions. On the other hand, it would have been a gross diplomatic error to question the intentions of one's strongest ally on the basis of mere speculation.

Canada's north seemed far removed from the battlefronts, although nationalist sentiment was beginning to stir again in the face of growing American aggressiveness and paternalism. One of the special assistants in External Affairs observed that "our Canadian nationalists are now looking southward with all the terror they previously reserved for their eastward glances." His own sympathies were quite clear when he charged that Ottawa was "letting the Americans get away with things that would have broken the Commonwealth in little pieces if London tried them."[118] Other diplomats in External Affairs were viewing their loss of prestige in Canadian-American relations with similar apprehension. Lester B. Pearson wrote from Washington of the American tendency to consider Canada either as "one of themselves" in direct negotiations or as a colony of the United Kingdom in matters of representation on combined boards. As a consequence, he warned that "we are going to have a difficult time in the months ahead in maintaining our own position and standing on our own feet." He also admonished Canadian negotiators for sounding firm then giving way under the slightest show of American pressure, but he warned against forcing issues of little importance because of the United States' new power and influence. "It will be therefore necessary," he wrote, "to have an unanswerable case, or one in which some really vital Canadian interest is at stake, if we are to 'go to the mat' with Washington."[119] What Ottawa lacked was a focal point upon which to protest the rights of an independent nation. Not until the spring of 1943 would Malcolm MacDonald provide Canada with a worthy cause.

5

The Army of Occupation, 1943–1944

> Everywhere these Americans are talking eagerly about the development of the North-West and their words are being translated into deeds. The American Army calls itself "the Army of Occupation."
>
> Malcolm MacDonald, 1943

By the spring of 1943, Canadian diplomats and politicians were increasingly uneasy about the attitude of the State Department and the proliferation of requests to expand the northern defence facilities, but they appeared quite unaware of the magnitude of the projects, the breadth of penetration, and the dominant presence of the United States Army Air Force throughout the northern territories. The few individuals who did have first-hand knowledge only saw a small part of the whole, and in most cases, they had little influence on Ottawa policy decisions. Although as minister and deputy minister of mines and resources they had toured the northwest the previous summer, neither Thomas Crerar nor Charles Camsell possessed the sensitivity, foresight, or initiative displayed by Clifford Sifton and William Ogilvie fewer than fifty years earlier. Sifton's claim that "occupation [was] ten points of the law" was either ignored or perhaps simply forgotten. In Ottawa, sovereignty was viewed in the abstract sense of rights, control, and jurisdiction, unrelated to actual place. As long as the Canadian government held paper guarantees of authority and the majority of American troops remained hidden from public view, there seemed to be little reason for concern. Only one man had the combination of wit, motive, and power to change the course of events. Ironically, he was not a Canadian, but the United Kingdom's high commissioner to Canada.

By February 1943, Anglo-American relations were rapidly deteriorating, partly as a result of the United States Army's refusal to share scientific knowledge or to release uranium supplies to the British atomic research programme. The secrecy involved required initiative and ingenuity to avert an impending crisis. In hopes of exerting indirect pressure on Washington and at the same time to gain sympathy and support in Ottawa, the resourceful high commissioner embarked on an "impertinent, if not to say unconstitutional"[1] plan of action which led to his submission of an extremely critical report to both the Cabinet War Committee and the Dominions Office. The controversial "memorandum" set into motion a chain of events which led to closer co-operation between the British and the Americans and somewhat more estranged relations between Canada and the United States.

I

From the outset of the European war, events were taking place in Britain and the United States that would ultimately have a profound influence on the future of Canada in the scheme of world affairs and indirectly bring a new significance to its northernmost regions. From their beginnings in 1939, scientists in England and the United States appeared to be progressing slowly in their work on nuclear fission, but a report released in the summer of 1941 showed the British team to be well ahead of the Americans. Although willing to share information, London's subsequent refusal to participate in a joint pilot project located in North America caused the Americans to proceed ahead at a feverish pace. Within a year, they had managed to outdistance the British team, and this time Washington refused to consider belated overtures of participatory co-operation at a time when there was growing fear for the safety of the research facilities in England.[2]

Excitement over the progress of nuclear studies was tempered by the immediate problem of gaining control over sources of uranium production. Canada's mine at Port Radium on Great Bear Lake in the Northwest Territories was the only major source in allied possession; the one other field of any account was located in the Belgian Congo (now Zaire) and under threat of enemy invasion. In the early summer of 1942, it was agreed that the British high commissioner should be brought into the picture to act as a high-level liaison in Canada. His first mandate was to secure government control of Canada's uranium production. Thus, on 15 June, Malcolm MacDonald, along with the British scientific liaison officer in Ottawa and the deputy director of the atomic research project, met with Mackenzie King to explain the vital role of uranium in the study of potential war and postwar applications of nuclear fission and to explore possible means for government control of its production and sale. Agreeing wholeheartedly with the importance of the "Tubes Alloy" project, as it was called, and the necessity for utmost secrecy, King suggested that discussion of the matter be limited to the minister of munitions and supply, C. D. Howe, and Dean C. J. Mackenzie, the president of the National Research Council. MacDonald also put forward the idea of transferring the British research facilities to Canada and received tentative approval.[3]

Considering the confidential nature of the issue, Howe was reluctant to employ wartime expropriation powers to acquire control of uranium production, but he advised that the Canadian government would have no problem purchasing a majority holding in the company. King agreed "so long as the Americans were advised in advance of the intention."[4] The deputy director of the British project continued on to Washington, where he received "strong personal approval of the Anglo-Canadian action" from the director of the American research, Dr. Vannevar Bush.[5] Behind the scenes, however, the American Army immediately contracted for 350 tons of uranium oxide from the Eldorado company, enough to cover at least a year's production.[6] In mid-July, after confirming plans to move the British team to the "Montreal Lab" and placing an order for twenty tons of uranium oxide, MacDonald was informed of the American purchase. Further negotiations that autumn resulted in an agreement that Britain would receive five tons of the order right away and that the remainder would be delivered to the Montreal Lab by the end of December. For the time being, the potential conflict appeared resolved. Howe and MacDonald were responsible for the broad policy decisions of their respective governments; Mackenzie had authority over the research team working within the structure of the National Research Council.[7]

Rivalry between Great Britain and the United States for Canadian resources in the Mackenzie Valley dated back to 1921 when Winston Churchill, then First Lord of the Admiralty, had advised that any oil pipeline from Norman Wells should remain in Canadian territory rather than pass through the Alaska Panhandle to the Pacific. During World War II, however, British interests were not consulted or represented in the negotiations which had integrated the resources and production needs of Canada and the United States. By designating Canada as the sixth district of the United States Petroleum Resources for War Program, Washington made it abundantly clear that it considered Canadian oil a continental, if not domestic, resource.[8] By 1942, however, the Mackenzie Valley offered a second valuable resource: uranium. The old radium mine, which had been closed in the summer of 1940 with adequate stockpiles to furnish its southern refinery for at least three years, was opened again in the summer of 1942. That August, Camsell reported that it was "working to capacity and producing about 100 tons of ore a day."[9]

Shortly after learning details of the American contract for the Canadian uranium, MacDonald left for a tour of the northwest which included a visit to the "radium" mine on Great Bear Lake and several sites of American military projects. Although it is not fully documented, the tour appears to have been initiated by MacDonald, with Clement Attlee as secretary of state for dominion affairs having granted him authority "to have a look at military and other developments."[10] En route to Edmonton, he stopped over at Winnipeg as the guest of Lieutenant-Governor R. F. McWilliams, where he dined with Edgar Tarr, former national president of the Canadian Institute of International Affairs, and other members such as John W. Dafoe, James Coyne, Phil Chester, and George Ferguson. With reference to there being "no livelier or more stimulating, original and creative intellectual group in Canada," MacDonald made special note in his personal diary of their open "criticism of government," which he termed "free men's inalienable right."[11] Although he was on loan from the British Parliament as part of the war effort, there is no question that the high commissioner had become an integral member of Doug Owram's "government generation of intellectual elites." In Mackenzie King's opinion, "there was no one individual who, by temperament, background, outlook and conviction, has been a more staunch friend of Canada."[12]

Accompanied by Charles Camsell, Thomas Crerar, and his secretary, Ian Maclennan, MacDonald left for Edmonton on 7 August 1942 for a circle tour of the Yukon and Mackenzie District. Travelling in an amphibian plane, they stopped at Grande Prairie, Fort St. John, Watson Lake; lunched briefly at Whitehorse; then flew on to Dawson City, Old Crow, Aklavik, Norman Wells, Port Radium, Yellowknife, and Fort Smith.[13] The experience was stimulating, but for MacDonald, with his eye on political implications, it proved equally disconcerting. From his diary notes he prepared a lengthy report for the Dominions Office, which was later presented and tabled at a British War Cabinet meeting in October 1942. The aim of the trip was stated clearly in the official report as having a dual purpose: "The first was to inspect the progress of the Alaska Highway and other works.... Our second purpose was to have a look at the conditions and prospects of fur-trading, mining and other activities there." For those aware of the importance of the uranium mine at Port Radium, the last sentence had a more subtle meaning.

MacDonald's analysis of the situation was recounted with the candid humour and keen perception that marked his style. Reporting on the progress of the Alaska Highway and Canol pipeline, he noted that they were "being unnecessarily extravagant and making some mistakes," yet he was nonetheless admiring of their "imagination, boldness and mechanical resource." In reference to the oil production at Norman Wells, he discreetly questioned the need for an expanded drilling programme since he had information that enough had already been discovered to meet the original requirements. The pipeline project itself had been delayed owing to serious forest fires, inadequate transportation facilities, and severe difficulties encountered in crossing Great Slave Lake where "six precious bull-dozers and some other vehicles are already nestling in the mud at the bottom." As a result, completion date for the pipeline was now set for the fall of 1943.

MacDonald's most serious concern, however, was related to the airfields of the staging routes, which he begged "the Air Ministry to keep a close eye on." Noting that the agreements stated that they were to revert to "the unqualified ownership of the Dominion" at the end of the war, he was dubious that the guarantees were adequate.

> I confess that I do not trust all the responsible authorities amongst our American allies, and I saw enough in the north-west to give me an unpleasant feeling that they will seek to use their power after the war to gain control of these vital air-routes. Mr. Crerar and I have communicated our opinions on this to members of the Canadian Government. It is primarily for them to defend British interest in Canada, but I trust that in Britain we shall be alert to stimulate and support them in any efforts that may be needed. [14]

The use of the particular phrase "to stimulate" in the last sentence suggests that MacDonald, like Roosevelt, was not prepared "to stand idly by" if Canadian interests were threatened by a "foreign power."

MacDonald reported a few minor difficulties, including the extravagant wages paid to American workers, that were double those paid to Canadians, and the fact that "some of the Americans throw their weight about in an unfortunate manner." As an aside, he also commented on "the customary troubles connected with wine and women." He had great difficulty restraining his sense of humour, even to the War Cabinet, when he described the insect problem as a consequence of "Nature sending her air-squadrons to attempt to defeat the violation of her virgin wilderness." Remarking on their "devilish size," he claimed that one was reported to have landed on a runway and "filled up with eighty-seven gallons of petrol before the airman realized it was a mosquito."

Almost as an afterthought, on the very last page he made a statement accentuated by its very simplicity: "At Great Bear Lake we saw the radium miners hard at work." Its significance was understood by only a very few, including Sir John Anderson, Lord President of the Council, who held the ultimate responsibility for Britain's atomic research. [15] In his personal diary, MacDonald described in detail the bustling activity of the mine, noting that approximately a thousand tons of ore were required to produce one gram of radium. Below in large block letters was the single word "URANIUM" with an annotation on the importance of this mining as "a piece of war work." [16]

In the United States, responsibility for atomic research was under the authority of the national Defense Research Committee, which was chaired by

James B. Conant and which reported to the Office of Scientific Research and development directed by Dr. Vannevar Bush.[17] By the fall of 1942, the overall responsibility had been assigned to the Military Policy Committee, which meant that the atomic research programme was now controlled by the United States Army, under the direction of Major General L. R. Groves of the Engineers Corps. Driven by the commitment to maintain optimum secrecy, Groves instituted a policy of internal compartmentalization which discouraged even the various American teams from sharing information with each other. When the nuclear pile at Stagg Field near Chicago went "critical" in December, the army adopted additional measures to protect their short-term military and longer-term economic advantage.

The first sign of problems occurred in the late fall when the American Army began to pressure Howe for use of the fifteen tons of uranium reserved for the British.[18] Then in a concise, definitive statement, Washington laid down the ground rules whereby the Canadians and British were urged to contribute as much information as possible, but the arrangement was not to be reciprocal. The rationale was simply that co-operation towards the war effort was urgent, but because of the lag in British research, sharing of American information or resources would only be of postwar benefit.[19] Long forgotten was the fact that the current success of the United States team was partially a result of earlier knowledge shared by the British scientists.

The director of the "Tubes Alloy" project, W. A. Akers, kept Mac-Donald "fully posted" about the frustrations encountered in his attempt to improve relations. Of critical concern was the U.S. Army's refusal to release the promised allotment of uranium, which was urgently needed to begin work at the Montreal Lab. When the situation worsened, MacDonald offered to cable Sir John Anderson for assistance.[20] This in turn brought Churchill into the picture, who then discussed the problem with Harry Hopkins, Roosevelt's personal aide, and received assurances that the matter would be resolved. General Groves, meanwhile, had convinced Roosevelt that the Anglo-Canadian research would be of no value to the war effort.[21] When there was still no indication of a change in American attitude according to information received from MacDonald and Anderson, Churchill sent an urgent telegram on 27 February, protesting the president's apparent decision to support the policy of top secrecy. A request for more information was provided in a detailed document, yet there was still no hint of any forthcoming change in attitude.[22] Concerned about a number of contentious issues, Churchill sent Anthony Eden, secretary of the Foreign Office, to Washington on 12 March for discussions on a "variety of topics," which included postwar planning.[23]

The fall and winter of 1942–1943 also marked a period of increasing rivalry between Britain and the United States over potential postwar economic advantages. At the Mont Tremblant conference in December 1942, the American attitude was extremely hostile to British colonial policy, prompting one observer to remark that it was "Britain against the field."[24] The growing competition in atomic research only served to intensify the tension until, according to the official historian of the United Kingdom Atomic Energy Authority, Anglo-American relations had reached a state of crisis by the spring of 1943.[25] The deteriorating situation was also the topic of discussion between MacDonald and a variety of people, such as Wendell Wilkie and Brooke Claxton,[26] and the subject of yet another lengthy report to the Dominions Office.

In a "Memorandum" on "the post-war position of Great Britain and the British Commonwealth... with particular reference to the position of Canada," MacDonald defended the Dominion's increasing dependence on the United States as inevitable and placed the onus on Britain to encourage traditional loyalties by showing more consideration, respect, and recognition. Stressing the importance of co-operation, he claimed that despite suggestions to the contrary, Canada could and should act as an effective "interpreter." In this regard, he made special reference to the great influence of "a group of high officials who are still comparatively young—mostly in their early or middle forties." It was time, warned MacDonald, for Britain to carefully review the need for improved "co-operation and consultation" and "maximum cohesion." It was the responsibility of Britain, not Canada. The implications of the Hyde Park Declaration now posed a serious problem to British statesmen, who, according to MacDonald, were increasingly aware that Britain's postwar position as a world power would depend, not only on the strength and unity of the Commonwealth, but also on the ability of Great Britain to remain its central member.[27]

The problem of access to Canada's uranium production was particularly frustrating, since the strict secrecy attached to the nuclear research projects made direct confrontation impossible. In 1942, aside from the scientists and project directors, there appeared to be only four men in Ottawa who were aware of the ultimate purpose of the Tubes Alloy and American Manhattan Projects: Mackenzie King, C. D. Howe, C. J. Mackenzie, and Malcolm MacDonald.[28] Howe and Mackenzie were unwilling to take any action which might adversely affect future Canadian-American relations.[29] King remained true to character and was silent. MacDonald, although still recovering from minor surgery, planned to do some investigating of his own before taking action.[30]

II

MacDonald's second trip to the Canadian northwest was neither official nor leisurely. Nor was it quite as impulsive as it later appeared. On 26 February, he outlined his purpose to Lord Halifax, the British ambassador to Washington: "Immense developments in the way of road-making and the construction of air routes by the Americans are taking place there, and I want to try to find out exactly what they are. I have a feeling that this may be more important than anything else that is happening in Canada at the present time."[31] The day after Anthony Eden's arrival in Washington, MacDonald wrote the foreign secretary to arrange for his attendance at a Canadian Cabinet War Committee meeting on his way back to London.[32] The next step in his plan required careful timing, initiative, and complete disregard for diplomatic discretion.

With his plans now set, MacDonald left Ottawa on, or about, 20 March accompanied only by his newly appointed secretary, Mr. Cyril Costley-White, and headed for Edmonton and points north (see figure 12). Stopping only for sleep, refuelling, and inclement weather, the two men headed straight for Port Radium, arriving on 23 March. Here MacDonald noted that work was "proceeding as rapidly as ever" but that women and children had now joined the miners to give an air of permanence to community life.[33] After a day trip to Coppermine, where they discovered only a small isolated Inuit community, the two returned to Norman Wells where they parted company. Costley-

NORTHERN TOURS BY THE RT. HON. MALCOLM MACDONALD

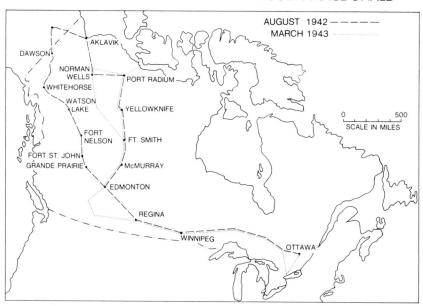

Figure 12 Northern Tours by the Rt. Hon. Malcolm MacDonald (drawn from M. MacDonald, *Down North,* frontispiece)

White headed north for Aklavik "to look at developments in that region" while MacDonald flew south "in order to get back to Ottawa in time."[34]

Arriving in Ottawa on the evening of 27 March, the high commissioner went directly from the airport to see the prime minister at Laurier House. An account of the impromptu meeting was entered in King's diary: "A long talk with Malcolm MacDonald who had just returned from Edmonton. Says Americans sending 46,000 workers to construct another highway along Mackenzie river. I said to him that we were going to have a hard time after the war to prevent the U.S. attempting control of some Canadian situations. He said already they speak jokingly of the men as an Army of Occupation."[35] The prime minister's fears of American intentions echoed those expressed by Clifford Sifton during the Yukon gold rush. Yet, whereas Sifton's concerns were expressed as justification for his measures to prevent American encroachment on Canadian jurisdiction, King's apprehension arose from the consequences of his government's failure to take adequate steps to avoid the problem.

Without mentioning that he had already discussed the matter with the prime minister, MacDonald met with Norman Robertson and several others to relay his concern for "the completeness of American penetration" and to recommend "local assertion of Canadian interests in the area.[36] Then, as so carefully planned weeks earlier, MacDonald and Eden attended a regular meeting of the Cabinet War Committee on 30 March 1943. Norman Robertson, Hume Wrong, and Lester Pearson of External Affairs were also asked to sit in.

At the request of the prime minister, MacDonald presented a most undiplomatic report on the impact of the U.S. military activities in the northwest. Stating that American "undertakings were being planned and carried out with a view to the post-war situation," he claimed that the few Canadians in the area "were quite unable to keep control or even keep in touch with day to day developments."[37] Then, in response to King's suggestion, MacDonald wrote a detailed account of his observations, ostensibly for two audiences: the Cabinet War Committee and the Dominions Office in London.[38] A copy of the lengthy memorandum, dated 6 April 1943, was sent to Clement Attlee, with a letter explaining his actions. "I fear that it may be impertinent, not to say unconstitutional, for a High Commissioner to send such a 'Note' to the Canadian Government," wrote MacDonald, "but the situation in the North-West is so disturbing that I felt something had to be done." He also noted that he had "probably understated, rather than overstated the case."[39] Once Ottawa and London were notified, MacDonald attempted to achieve his third objective. On the same day he forwarded his written report, he also contacted C. D. Howe to request immediate delivery of the promised uranium oxide.[40]

The "Note" was indeed controversial and profoundly anti-American.

Under-Secretary Norman Robertson immediately advised the prime minister that the extra copies should be withheld from circulation to prevent the United States government from learning that the British high commissioner had taken the initiative in such a matter.[41] The military projects were described as "colossal," their significance as "far reaching," and the motives of American interests as suspect. MacDonald warned that the lack of Canadian presence could have serious consequences.

> Everywhere you travel north of Edmonton there are large numbers of American military officers troops, and airmen and civilian workmen, and representatives of American business and finance. Everywhere these Americans are talking eagerly about the development of the North-West, and their words are being translated into deeds. The American Army calls itself "the Army of Occupation.". . . The inhabitants of those regions are beginning to say that it seems that the Americans are more awake to the importance of the Canadian North-West than are the Canadian authorities. This state of affairs tends to play into the hands of those Western Canadians who are inclined to assert that the West receives little sympathy and help from Eastern Canada, that its destiny lies in incorporation with the United States of America.[42]

The domestic political implications touched on a particularly sensitive issue. Just prior to MacDonald's report, the Wartime Information Board had distributed the results of a December survey which showed that an average of 31 per cent of all Canadians favoured the postwar union of their country with the United States. Furthermore, the poll indicated that the idea of union was most popular among prairie residents.[43]

Other observations were equally disturbing. While in theory the joint projects implied equal partnership, MacDonald argued that "in practice American authorities had gained increasing control" and had proceeded to build roads and airfields without Canadian participation and at times without authority. He reported that American officers had stated frankly that the works were designed "to be of particular value for commercial aviation and transport after the war, and for waging war against the Russians in the next world crisis." Furthermore, in addition to extensive aerial photography by the air force, American oil interests were closely watching the drilling programme and "will seek to gain control there." And in Edmonton, where there were thirteen thousand American military and civilian employees, Canada's liaison office consisted of one man, who was a consulting mining engineer and secretary of the Alberta Chamber of Mines. MacDonald then listed a number of recommendations including a concerted effort to increase visible evidence of Canadian participation and the appointment of a special commissioner reporting directly to the government. He also suggested that two or three men be sent north to verify his report.

The document was not presented to the Cabinet War Committee, but it was forwarded to Hugh Keenleyside and Arnold Heeney for comment. Keenleyside's intitial response was somewhat defensive. He claimed that while concern was quite justified, the situation was not as deplorable as MacDonald had implied.[44] In accordance with the high commissioner's suggestion, two internal reports were submitted to the War Committee. John Baldwin of External Affairs concurred that there were serious problems:

> The United States has undertaken the economic development of one of Canada's largest and strategically most important areas, without any measure of Canadian participation or control of development. U.S. interests are gaining a permanent foothold in Canada in the development of certain resources. In addition, the U.S. government is establishing its influence in an area of great strategic importance to it in the event of any future conflict with an Asiatic power.[45]

Robert Beattie, director of northern research for the Bank of Canada, also sent a lengthy memorandum to Keenleyside with his assessment of the economic implications after a short trip along the Alaska Highway. Although he noted the dominant American presence, Beattie expressed greater concern over the huge financial investment by the United States, which he claimed was "equivalent to perhaps a quarter of the whole of Canada's wartime capital expansion." Referring to reports that between fifty and seventy-five thousand Americans were expected in the area that summer and that the projects "might run well over $500 million," he contrasted these figures to Canadian participation. The resident population, he claimed, was probably about ten thousand, and the Canadian government's total expenditure around $5 million a year. The long-term view looked even more disconcerting. Beattie reported that Department of Transport officials "were alarmed at the known ambitions and aggressiveness of the American private airlines operating in the north under the Army's wing" and feared "that the Americans will never, in fact, relinquish their present control of air transport in the area." While agreeing that liaison and control were important, Beattie also suggested that serious investigation be made into a long-term plan of northern development. Otherwise, he argued, Canada "will never again regain effective control of that region, nor will she deserve to."[46]

In a note to Norman Robertson, Keenleyside admitted that Beattie's report was "a very sound appraisal," but he expressed cynicism about his "faith in the efficacy of governmental planning as a solution to Northwestern problems." Referring to his experience on the Northwest Territories Council, he pointed to the problem of "limited budgets" and of previous failure to convince the commissioner to prepare a plan which could be "sold to the government." He claimed that while he agreed that "planning should be undertaken on a larger scale and with greater urgency than has so far been the case... no amount of blue printing is going to make the Northwest anything but a 'frontier' for a long time to come." Yet in spite of his scepticism, Keenleyside did add in closing that the memo "should be a real help in bringing the problem more effectively before the responsible people here."[47]

Heeney agreed with the seriousness of the situation and suggested that a commissioner be immediately appointed with a "dual function" of representing the government and making recommendations for solutions to the problem. Although the order-in-council might define the new position in general terms, "as a measure of Canadian cooperation with the United States," the cabinet secretary argued that the commissioner should be directed by "confidential instructions... to review the whole situation from the point of Canadian war and post-war interest and submit recommendations to the War Committee without delay." In the meantime, the Cabinet War Committee would be presented with a "factual statement of the American projects" prepared by the Department of Mines and Resources.[48] Thus, on 16 April 1943, the committee unanimously approved in principle "the appointment of a commissioner, responsible directly to the War Committee," not merely as a government representative, but with authority to make recommendations in accordance with specific instructions.[49] With the exception of physically increasing Canadian participation, MacDonald's recommendations would be adopted with the support of External Affairs. The extra copies he had supplied were not distributed to the Cabinet War Committee, however, which may explain why MacDonald's direct approach to C. D. Howe on the subject of uranium did not achieve the expected results.

MacDonald's report provided the "unanswerable case" of vital national interest that only weeks earlier Lester Pearson had stated was necessary "to go 'to the mat' with Washington." Now that Canada had been alerted to the Americans' postwar intentions, the scoreboard stood at a tie, with both Britain and the United States hoping to gain economic benefit. The playing field was the north, and it was now up to Canada to keep the game under control by enforcing home rules.

The first concrete action came almost immediately. At the next meeting of the War Committee, the suggestion was put forward that Canada should reimburse the United States for the costs of all airfield construction to avoid any question of postwar benefits for American commercial airlines.[50] For the same reasons, the committee did not grant Washington's request to extend the Mackenzie air route to the Beaufort Sea as an alternative to the Northwest

Staging Route. Avoiding outright rejection, the issue was repeatedly deferred that spring until the U.S. Northwest Service Command finally withdrew its plan.[51] In addition, the United States Army had requested "as a matter of great urgency" that engineer troops be allowed to take over all construction on the Northwest Staging Route which involved improvement of existing facilities and the building of emergency airfields. Again, approval was deferred pending investigation of economic implications and the guarantee of Canadian control. To complicate the issue, the Yukon mining industries complained of a Canadian labour shortage because of higher wages paid by American contractors. The terms of the agreement negotiated in June for the upgrading and new construction on the airfields provided a partial remedy. All sites in Alberta would be selected by Canadian authorities, and construction would be carried out by Canadian contractors and workers. Conversely, only American army and civilian labour would be employed in northern British Columbia and the Yukon.[52] This move followed a now familiar pattern of presenting an image of "joint participation" in more populated areas, similar to the prime minister's agreement to Canadian participation in the Aleutian campaign in "token proportions" as a means of showing visible "partnership in defence of the Northwest" and countering the impression of American dominance.[53] A firmer attitude began to emerge when Ottawa refused the State Department's request for approval of postwar military use of the Alaska Highway and redefinition of authority over the airfields.[54] Similarly, requests which previously had been quickly approved on the recommendation of the Permanent Joint Board on Defence were now being questioned and deferred for further study.

Meanwhile, the matter of British access to Great Bear Lake uranium remained unresolved. Despite the Canadian government's acquisition of controlling shares in the Eldorado Mining and Refining Company, its president announced in May that the entire production in the foreseeable future had been promised to the United States Army. When the news was cabled to Winston Churchill, already in Washington for high-level talks, he was said to have remarked that C. D. Howe had "sold the British Empire down the river," a statement which threatened to cause a rift in Anglo-Canadian relations when it was related to the minister of munitions and supply.[55] Lord Cherwell, Churchill's personal adviser, brought up the matter with Mackenzie King, who replied rather importantly that MacDonald had already apprised him of the situation.[56] Churchill then discussed the problem directly with Roosevelt at the Washington talks, or Trident Conference as it was called. Although Dr. Bush continued to argue that Britain only wanted to exploit nuclear energy for postwar benefit, Roosevelt finally gave verbal assent to full co-operation.[57].

A period of tension followed, with Canada frequently irritated by the tact-

less and high-handed attitude of the British. MacDonald was particularly
concerned over what he believed was a "bottled up" resentment over numerous incidents involving lack of consultation.[58] The dissension was finally
eased when an agreement to collaborate on atomic energy research was
signed by Roosevelt and Churchill at the Quebec Conference in August
1943. Canada did not take part in these negotiations, but Mackenzie King
was informed of the draft agreement before final signatures were affixed, and
he agreed to have C. D. Howe sit on the proposed six-member Combined
Policy Committee. Howe's appointment was clearly a functional one, related
to the key part of the committee's mandate: "to allocate materials, apparatus
and plant, in limited supply, in accordance with the requirements of the programme agreed by the Committee."[59] Although the effectiveness of the committee, and Howe's contribution in particular, is a matter of dispute, Canada's presence on it nevertheless established a precedent for future representation on the United Nations Atomic Energy Commission. Meanwhile,
the Canadian government took effective control over distribution of all
radioactive substances. All shares in the company were finally expropriated
in January 1944, and Eldorado Mining became a crown corporation. In June,
a Combined Development Trust with six appointed members was created to
acquire control of world uranium and thorium supplies. When Belgium was
liberated that fall, the Congo mine was reopened, thus bringing an end to
Canada's monopoly on uranium production.[60]

III

In the spring of 1943, other matters relating to the Canadian north required
immediate attention. Now that the extent and potential liabilities of the
American defence projects were revealed, close monitoring of the situation
was crucial. The Department of External Affairs and, ultimately, the Cabinet
War Committee were responsible for finding solutions, but it was important
that their judgment be based on first-hand factual information, from Canadian, not American, sources. For this reason, the role of the observer was as
critical as that of the decision-makers. On 5 May 1943, the prime minister
announced the appointment of Brigadier-General W. W. Foster, who was
soon promoted to Major-General, as "the special commissioner for defence
projects in northwest Canada." The task at hand would prove as unwieldy as
the title of office.

Historians in the past have tended to describe Foster's position as one of
liaison or "watch-dog,"[61] yet examination of government records indicate a
much broader and more influential role. Confidential instructions were forwarded in a personal letter from Mackenzie King that outlined "the consider-

ations the government had in mind in appointing a Special Commissioner, and the specific duties which they desire you to perform," which included submission of special reports evaluating the situation and making recommendations. Moreover, Foster was given the authority to "take such further action as may be appropriate under the terms of the Order in Council and the foregoing instructions."[62] Of particular significance was the fact that the special commissioner reported directly to the Cabinet War Committee through its secretary, Arnold Heeney, who was a most enthusiastic supporter of his efforts and proposals. This reporting structure also allowed for expedient and influential channels of communication to External Affairs.

Heeney's interest in northern affairs was primarily motivated by his aim to improve government administration for the purpose of building a strong independent nation.[63] This latter emphasis was reflected in his letter to Foster regarding "questions of staff and of the administrative machinery of government required for the overall development of that area. . . . This is one of the most delicate and yet important problems involved, and I hope as your work proceeds, you may be able to make valuable suggestions to the government in this connection."[64] Whereas Heeney sought to reorganize the northern administration, others had different priorities. From External Affairs, John Baldwin forwarded the suggestion of general research related to postwar economic and defence matters and a specific study into "how far the costs of northern development can be justified by the gain of National Sovereignty and self-respect, attendant upon a policy of vigorous exploration of this part of the continent."[65] In addition, the special commissioner was not only to act as liaison between all agencies and departments involved in northern affairs, but also as co-ordinator of federal and provincial relations.[66]

Meanwhile, the War Committee was kept informed on all aspects of the defence projects, including their social, economic, and political impact, by way of detailed monthly reports, which on occasion were over sixty pages in length. In turn, Heeney forwarded copies to ministers of the relevant departments: External Affairs, Defence, Finance, Munitions and Supply, Mines and Resources, Transport, and Labour. The formal reports were supplemented by frequent correspondence between Foster and Heeney, both official and personal. The voluminous files of incoming and outgoing mail reflected the formidable chore of liaison work.[67]

A major portion of the commissioner's official duties was related to ensuring that all American activities received proper authorization and abided by Canadian regulations. The American legation was informed that all proposals submitted to the Canadian government must be referred to the special commissioner "at an early date," so that he would have the opportunity to present his views to the War Committee.[68] Coincident with Foster's appointment, new procedures were set down for authorization of military projects that ap-

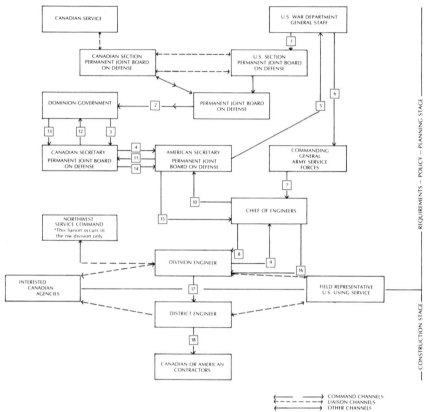

Figure 13 Military Authorization Procedures, 1943 (from NAC, Special Commissioner's Records, RG 36/7, vol. 14, file 28-6)

peared to be designed to discourage, rather than facilitate, any further planning. From the initial submission of a proposal by the United States War Department to the commencement of construction, there were no fewer than eighteen stages of planning and policy approval (see figure 13). At the same time, the United States legation was informed that all new projects and major modifications must be approved by External Affairs, the State Department, and the Permanent Joint Board on Defence. Minor alterations were to go directly to Foster.[69] Other time-consuming duties of the commissioner's office involved censorship of all press releases and the issuance of travel permits.

The most important responsibility assigned to the special commissioner was the mandate to suggest appropriate policy and action to protect Canadian sovereignty and at the same time ensure optimum progress in the development of the northwest. In his first report to the War Committee, Foster submitted twelve formal recommendations on issues ranging from takeover

plans for the Alaska Highway to the protection of oil interests in the Mackenzie Valley, future civil aviation policy, and environmental measures.[70] These
and other early recommendations offered an unofficial military perspective
over and above that provided by the Permanent Joint Board on Defence.
Later proposals focused on the needs of new communities and the administrative changes required to adapt to the increased population. In this regard,
the special commissioner was fulfilling a role that would normally have been
the responsibility of the Department of Mines and Resources. A measure-
ment of Foster's achievements is found in a prepared analysis of cabinet
response to his forty-one recommendations submitted over a period of eighteen months. Almost half the proposals were approved, others were referred
to departments, a few were deferred, and only one was rejected outright.[71]
The fact that a number were never implemented after they were deferred reflected the resistance by various government bodies to any externally suggested changes within their jurisdiction.

Foster's office was also responsible for the protection of the physical environment, an assignment which fell under the broad category of "all matters
related to the defence projects." In his second report, the special commissioner recommended that regulations be drawn up requiring United States
contractors and army engineers to restore sites to their original condition. He
was particularly troubled by "American carelessness" in fire prevention as
reported by regional liaison officers and the Mounted Police. One observer
commented that "it seems to be the opinion of the troops to let the country
burn, it's no good anyway."[72] At Foster's urging, new regulations were introduced and a fire protection service was created in the Yukon in 1943. A similar agency was established two years later in the Northwest Territories.[73]

In many respects, Foster became the unofficial guardian of the northwest
between 1943 and 1945. Described by Heeney as "a man who knew and
loved the Canadian North,"[74] he was a veteran of two world wars, had twice
been awarded the D.S.O., was a keen outdoorsman, and had participated in
several geographical explorations in Alaska and the Yukon. During the inter-
war years, he had been a construction engineer and at one time was deputy
minister of public works for British Columbia. His qualifications were exceptional, but in terms of practical politics, his appointment may have been
related to the fact that he was a close friend of Keenleyside's father.[75] Although Foster shared their ideals and objectives, the disparity in age, his military connection, and the location of his headquarters in Edmonton effectively discouraged any close association with the concerned individuals in
Ottawa who hoped to provoke the government into adopting new approaches
to northern policy.

Foster's private image of the north contrasted sharply with his official recommendations, which encouraged northern development, a duality that he

expressed in a speech to the Ottawa Branch of the Canadian Club in January 1945. Claiming that because of the northern defence projects, Canada was "assured of the development of its existing unique political and geographical position," he concluded his remarks by quoting lines from Robert Service's "The Land of Beyond," which he perceived as having "a far wider application today than when they were written."

> Thank God there is always a land of beyond,
> For those who are true to the trail,
> A vision to seek, a beckoning peak,
> A freedom that never will fail.[76]

Major-General Foster viewed the north from two perspectives: a place of wilderness and a land of future settlement. Such conflicting images were common among those directly concerned with northern affairs, and they often resulted in confusion in the direction of new policies.

IV

After MacDonald's stern warning, Ottawa's immediate priority was to find a method of countering the American impact. One of the first steps in the strategy proposed by Keenleyside was to promote the potential of northern development in the hope that public support for the advantages to be gained from the military activities would defuse criticism of excessive American involvement.[77] Although details of the northern defence projects were still classified, several articles appeared in newspapers in early April 1943 with the obvious aim of encouraging public interest in the far north. Most appeared within weeks of MacDonald's verbal report to the War Committee.

Under the headline "War Unlocks Our Last Frontier: Canada's Northern Opportunity," the *Financial Post* predicted the migration of thousands of young men to the new industrial north which would grow out of the wartime transportation advances. The report was profoundly optimistic and contained a number of erroneous impressions. The accompanying map showed a network of highways, one from Fort Nelson to Norman which was in reality no more than a temporary winter road, and another along the Canol pipeline route which was still under construction (see figure 14). In the same issue, an article by Lieutenant Colonel George Drew described Canada as the logical centre of Commonwealth aviation activity. Drew claimed that "the air could become to Canada what the sea has been to Britain."[78] A short article appearing in the *Montreal Gazette* only two weeks after MacDonald's report announced that Charles Camsell was departing for the west to make arrangements with the British Columbia and Alberta governments for "assembling and studying data for use in planning the future orderly development of territory adjacent to the Canadian section of the Alaska Highway." With only a passing reference to the American section of the North Pacific Planning Project as "directing similar work in connection with United States territories along the highway route," the Department of Mines and Resources declared that "it is immediately essential" that plans for development of this region "be considered by proper governmental authorities."[79] In contrast to the press release concerning the North Pacific Planning Project issued only months earlier, the emphasis was now on Canadian development rather than continental integration of economic resources and transportation systems.

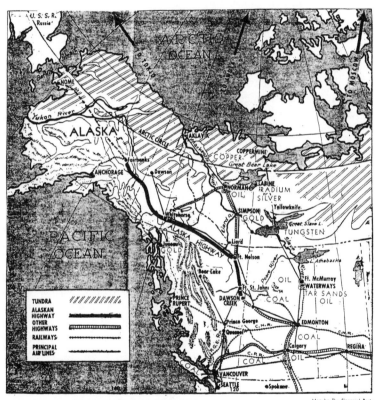

Highways, Airways, Railways and Waterways Await the Settler

War Unlocks Our Last Frontier-- Canada's Northern Opportunity

Figure 14 Optimism in the Press (*Financial Post*, 3 April 1943)

Not all newspapers were so co-operative, as is indicated by the 30 April 1943 issue of the *Vancouver Sun*, which reported a quite different picture under the headline "Baghdad on the Saskatchewan."

> The Americans have landed, are landing and will continue to land in Edmonton in numbers which are a military secret and a source of civilian astonishment. Perhaps Edmontonians will retain their individuality but there are doubts. In some quarters its [*sic*] wryly said that the Americans captured Edmonton without firing a shot. They say that seaports no longer make cities but airports do. A city within a city is practically completed now by U.S. War Department engineers. Urgency is the motto of the American movement and money is no object.

In response, Keenleyside recommended that the Wartime Information Board institute an aggressive publicity drive to draw attention to the terms of the joint agreements which protected Canadian interests in the postwar period, with special focus on those activities in which Canada had fully participated.[80] The board responded immediately with the suggestion that aside from the usual press releases, arrangements be made with the National Film Board for still photographs and movies of Canadians at work on the joint defence projects.[81] The initial promotion was successful. The Wartime Information Board opinion survey published in late June reported that the issues of postwar aviation and northern development had been given considerable coverage in the press and that there now appeared to be less sympathy for union with the United States.[82]

It was during this same period that Keenleyside temporarily assigned Trevor Lloyd to the Wartime Information Board for the purpose of conducting a study of "various phases of northern development" with particular emphasis on the Russian experience.[83] Although this assignment seemed quite unrelated to the jurisdiction of the public relations board, which was established in September 1942 "with the object of ensuring an informed and intelligent understanding of the purposes and progress of the Canadian war effort,"[84] Keenleyside believed that attachment to this agency would enable Lloyd to conduct investigations without hindrance from the priorities and biases of other departments.[85]

In the course of investigations, it soon became apparent that the Americans were far advanced in their study of the Canadian Arctic. In a memo to John Grierson, director of the Wartime Information Board, Lloyd warned that the American Army "was deeply entrenched in the north" and that "they have first class research facilities and an Arctic information centre. We have nothing." To remedy the situation, he suggested the creation of an "Information Centre on Northern Canada" as a means of co-ordinating the research of the numerous agencies involved, "to see that information available is distributed where it will be most effective, and to keep in close touch with activities of other nations in similar areas."[86] Lloyd also suggested that the proposed centre could "undertake research either when an apparent need exists or at the special request of a government department."[87]

The proposal was discussed at length, and it was supported by a number of officials in the Privy Council Office, the National Research Council, the Navy and the Air Force, with most agreeing that Canada had fallen far behind the United States in research. Brooke Claxton, then parliamentary secretary assigned to the prime minister, reminded Heeney that he had suggested the establishment of a northern research centre as far back as 1938. "We have neglected it shamefully. Unless we use our opportunities now, the Americans who already have some people better informed than we have, will edge us out."[88] The idea received general approval, but a major controversy arose concerning the appropriate jurisdiction for the proposed agency. The issue was deferred to the Department of Mines and Resources for further study, and there, as one cynical observer predicted, the idea became "absolutely stillborn" when it was passed on to director R. A. Gibson.[89]

During his two-month assignment with the Wartime Information Board, Lloyd received numerous reports of public reaction to the military activities in the northwest. One such item was particularly alarming:

> The Americans in Edmonton are openly describing themselves as an "Army of Occupation"—indeed that is the way the telephone switchboard is answered. . . . They have built a hospital for themselves, taken over acres of land, and generally absorbed the whole community. Not only in Edmonton, but the whole of the West is feeling this problem, and is really concerned about it, and is inclined to take the attitude that the government is closing its eyes to these dangers in order to achieve what is accepted as essential, namely cooperation of the U.S. in building the Highway.[90]

Such comments not only confirmed MacDonald's observations, but served to reinforce the argument for more drastic measures than simply the appointment of a special commissioner.

By the summer of 1943, a number of rather optimistic articles began to appear in newspapers from coast to coast. An item in the *Edmonton Bulletin* claimed that the opening of the northwest was "just as important to this age as the opening of the prairie farmlands to the people forty years ago. . . . An Empire is being born."[91] An article written by an Alberta correspondent for *The Times* of London described the Alaska Highway as a "new Northwest Passage," comparable in effect to the transcontinental railways of an earlier

era.[92] A number of articles appeared in *Maclean's* Dominion Day edition that
stressed the new strategic significance of the north and the potential importance of postwar civil aviation. Trevor Lloyd's "Canada: Mainstreet of the
Air" ended on a rather sombre note, warning against extensive American involvement in northern Canada, which "was in effect sublet for the duration
[of the war] with a saving clause in the lease which stipulated that the
premises be vacated with all movable property six months after the end of the
war." Despite this fact, Lloyd argued that a grave situation existed and that
Ottawa would have to assume greater responsibility in the area.[93] Again, the
timing of this renewed media interest in the north was not accidental; it was
orchestrated through press releases and contacts.

MacDonald may have been indiscreet in his report to the War Committee,
but he was less so in his full-length book, *Down North*, published in 1943.
Still, the inferences were clear. Describing his visit to Norman Wells, he
noted that "modern industry is despoiling aged Nature there and the methods
employed are not leisurely." He also referred to Alaska as "Uncle Sam's
great estate" and to the work of the bulldozer as "an outrageous piece of interference with Nature."[94] His analysis of the overall situation was serious
and perceptive: "Delicate and difficult problems exist in the north which will
require wise statesmanship for their happy solution—such matters as the care
of the health, education and well-being of the Indian and Eskimo peoples, the
definition of proper status and functions of the religious missions, the prudent planning of the coming economic development and the friendly adjustment of Canadian and United States interests."[95] The book made it obvious
that there was very little "British" to be found there, but it was apparent that
the trip had inspired an unusual fascination and empathy for the north. Similar enthusiasm for the indigenous peoples and their land appeared in articles
MacDonald wrote for newspapers in his home riding of Ross and Cromarty
in northern Scotland.[96]

During this same period, government officials expressed serious concern
about items appearing in American newspapers. In June 1943, an Associated
Press release directly countered Ottawa's plans to focus on Canadian participation in the joint military activities by stating that "the Canadian Northwest
was a wilderness a year ago. Now a military area, it is under the control of
the United States Army and will remain a restricted area until the war is
over." External Affairs considered this a breach of the censorship agreement
and demanded tighter regulations requiring the authorities of both countries
to approve any visit or publication of any article related to the northern
defence projects.[97] Unfortunately, regulations do little to change popular
opinion, and distorted views continued to appear in the American newspapers. This was apparent when a public opinion survey in July 1943 indicated that 72 per cent of United States citizens did not know whether or not

Canadians paid taxes directly to England, a misconception which was considered responsible for such comments as "Britain should hand over Canada in payment of war debts."[98] Publicity was not enough.

Keenleyside continued his efforts to arouse government interest in northern research. At the June meeting of the Northwest Territories Council, he proposed "a programme of study and planning" to devise a strategy "for the long-term development of our northern areas."[99] Unknown to Trevor Lloyd, he also suggested that both Lloyd and Tom Manning be hired for the project. A confidential inquiry revealed that Dartmouth was unwilling to release Lloyd from his teaching duties,[100] and the geographer returned to the American university at the end of June where he continued to work on the "Arctic Study" for the Canadian Institute of International Affairs. Tom Manning also refused full employment with the northern administration, but he agreed to be seconded from the Navy for a summer assignment.[101] On Lloyd's recommendation, however, the Bureau of the Northwest Territories and Yukon Affairs hired a young geographer, J. Lewis Robinson, to carry out further studies.

Over the next five years, Robinson wrote many articles on the north for the *Canadian Geographical Journal*. Based on a combination of field work and information gathered from internal reports, the accounts focused on the history, geography, settlement, and resource potential of the various regions. Occasionally, he referred to the adverse climatic conditions which restricted settlement and to the lack of government funds and personnel to provide adequate services. Of greater significance was the fact that his articles educated the public to the reality, rather than the romance, of the north.

In the summer of 1943, however, the visible American dominance could not be solved by media propaganda or diplomatic guarantees. By June, official figures estimated that well over thirty thousand United States Army troops and personnel were employed on the northern defence projects. With American civilians added to the number, the total was thought to be closer to forty-three thousand.[102] Following a visit to the northwest by members of the Permanent Joint Board on Defence, Keenleyside reported to the prime minister on the great "disparity between the contribution of Canada and that of the United States." After viewing the Alaska Highway first-hand, he was far more pessimistic about its postwar potential, claiming that the permanent road was only half completed and could never be used extensively by tourists. He warned that inaccurate publicity would raise false expectations among Canadians. "Its only justification is the military necessity which prompted its construction."[103] This news put the situation in a new light, and the diplomats began to explore various means to protect Canadian jurisdiction in the longer term, including possible compensation for the construction costs of the American-built facilities.[104]

Meanwhile, journalists and editors were cautioned against encouraging unrealistic expectations. In an effort to correct misconceptions, a lengthy editorial in *Maclean's* emphasized the military purpose of the highway and cautioned readers against optimism as to its potential in opening the north. Referring to the "rosy dreams of many people," the editor argued that great expense and considerable time was necessary before it would benefit civilian or tourist travel. "And whether or not the results would justify the expenditures is a matter in which there is room for considerable difference of opinion."[105]

V

The need for more serious study of suitable development for the northern frontier appeared only partially resolved with the preliminary investigations and inquiries carried out that summer on behalf of the North Pacific Planning Project. Although R. K. Odell of the Department of Mines and Resources was delegated the responsibility of collecting the Canadian data, the preliminary report issued in May 1943 showed that most of the work was being carried out by the Americans. The Canadian contribution appeared minimal despite Camsell's hopes that the studies would provide a major breakthrough in long-range planning.[106] Moreover, Yukon officials viewed the project with a fair degree of suspicion. Controller Jeckell, in particular, argued that, regardless of the wartime boom, mining would continue to be the only industry of any account. For this reason, he declared that Ottawa's objectives need only centre on new roads and cheaper transportation.[107]

Concern for the northern economy was a topic of more serious discussion among members of the Department of External Affairs. In July 1943, Norman Robertson proposed the idea of a chartered company as the best means to stimulate rapid development of the north. Escott Reid, one of the more creative members of the department, expanded on the idea. He suggested that a "Company of the North" be governed by a board of directors composed of parliamentarians and representatives of relevant departments, but without direct ties to the ministry of Mines and Resources "in view of the weakness of this department." Apart from aiding development, Reid believed that a public corporation responsible for "the opening up of a new frontier in the Canadian North" would inspire support as a "national objective."[108]

This proposal was resurrected in February 1944 following the expropriation of Eldorado Mines. Understandably, there was no reference to Canada's newest crown corporation, but discussion did focus on future government involvement in both the oil and airline industries in the Mackenzie Valley.

Reid stated that the primary objective would be "the optimum development of the North in the interests of the people of Canada." He went on to argue that in addition to benefits for local residents, there was the "purely economic interest of maximizing the national income by the widest possible exploitation of the resources of the area." But of greater importance were the issues of sovereignty and national unity, which were essentially the basis of Reid's rationale for suggesting unprecedented government encroachment on free enterprise in the north.

> Politically it is desirable that Canadian activity in the Far North be such as to discourage other nations from attempting to dispute Canada's claim to sovereignty over all the land between the mainland of Canada and the North Pole. There is also the possible national interest to be served by making the development of the North an inspiring and somewhat romantic national objective for the people of Canada.[109]

Plans for the "Company of the North" were not implemented, but the objectives are of significant interest in themselves. The emphasis on the exploitation of the hinterland for the economic advantage of the south appeared to have changed little from the reasons for western expansion expressed by George Brown and John A. Macdonald in the Confederation debates, with one major difference. In the 1940s fear of American domination and eventual absorption had replaced the nineteenth-century threat of outright annexation.

Suspicions about American postwar intentions were drawn to Heeney's attention in a confidential memo from Foster. Referring to a visit by United States senators to the northwest in the summer of 1943, he reported that the Americans appeared to discount boundary lines in their discussion of potential oil and mineral resources in the Mackenzie District.[110] Heeney decided to see for himself and set out in September on an inspection tour accompanied by the commissioner and Group Captain William Hanna of National Defence Headquarters. In eight days they visited twelve communities: McMurray-Waterways, Fort Smith, Fort Simpson, Norman Wells, Camp Canol, Whitehorse, Watson Lake, Fort Nelson, Fort St. John, Dawson Creek, Grande Prairie, and Edmonton, the headquarters of the Northwest Service Command. Upon his return, Heeney reported to the Cabinet War Committee that American troops indeed dominated the Canadian northwest. He suggested that the erection of official Canadian signs and the flying of the red ensign might help to counter the predominance of the "Stars and Stripes," but apart from recommending the establishment of a branch office for Foster at Norman Wells and the stationing of more Canadian troops throughout the area, he was unable to offer any further ideas which might alter the visual effect of "American occupation."[111]

Foster and Heeney were confronted with additional irritants which had occurred in their absence. On 26 September, an article appeared in the Canadian press purportedly written by an Ottawa reporter and entitled "The 49th
State—Edmonton." Foster described the offending news item in a letter to
Heeney: "Amongst other extravagant statements is the one that the Mayor
turned over to the U.S. the keys to the city and that Americans have new telephone, sewer, gas services and other privileges denied to Canadians; the article ending with alleged quotation "This is the 49th State. God Bless America."[112] As public opinion mounted against the American presence in the
northwest, Ottawa was having its own problems with United States officials.
After a visit to the northern airfields, Senators Owen Brewster and Richard
Russell were reported to have urged Washington to take immediate action to
obtain an agreement with Canada for postwar use of the American-built facilities for commercial aviation.[113] Then in September, Ray Atherton, the newly
appointed American ambassador to Canada, made a speech to the Ottawa
Branch of the Canadian Club in which he not only extolled the benefits of
continentalism, but also went on to assert that "the best thing for the United
States and Alaska is also the best thing for Canada."[114] The gauntlet had been
dropped; it was now Ottawa's turn to respond.

6

Pressures for Change, 1943–1945

> The whole future of the North is increasingly coming under con-
> sideration both inside and outside Canada and there has been a
> good deal of evidence for some time that certain organizations and
> individuals in Canada have become very reluctant to see any
> detached study of the problems that are occurring.
> Raleigh Parkin, 1944

After negotiating the gradual withdrawal of the Americans from the northwest, the Department of External Affairs appeared to have resolved the perceived sovereignty crisis of 1943. But other issues emerged during postwar
planning discussions, resulting in demands for major policy changes on the
domestic side of northern affairs. Much of the pressure came from the private
sector. As Trevor Lloyd recalled, "new ideas about the Northern Administration came from the outside and had to be fed into the power system by any
route available. This also had to be backed up by drum-beating on the outside."[1] Sympathetic support came from those departments most directly involved in the sovereignty debate, with the Bureau of the Northwest Territories and Yukon Affairs remaining stubbornly opposed to any departure from
the status quo. As discussions continued, it became increasingly apparent
that either a crisis or stronger leadership in Ottawa would be required to bring
about any dramatic change in domestic policy. From December 1943 until
the conclusion of World War II, there was neither. Within government, the
primary focus of northern interest still centred on international issues.

I

Ironically, the event which effectively halted further expansion of American military involvement in Canada originated in Washington, not Ottawa.
In September 1943, a special committee of the United States Senate chaired
by Harry S. Truman was set up to investigate the escalating costs of the Na-

tional Defense Program. One of the primary targets was the Canol Project, which had incurred extravagant expenses owing to multiple delays and cost overruns. The whole operation appeared fraught with poor planning, undue haste, and inordinate waste. In Ottawa as well, its basic objectives came under suspicion when it was discovered that the newly erected refinery had a capacity much larger than the pipeline could possibly supply, even including the oil shipped in via Skagway.[2] Before the senate committee's recommendations were announced, it was apparent from reports leaked to the press that the United States government would try to renegotiate the wartime agreements in order to obtain an adequate return on American investments. Alerted in advance, Canadian officials had their policy and strategy well planned before the State Department called a high-level meeting on 2 December 1943.[3]

There was no attempt to hide the purpose of the discussions; the request was clear and simple: the United States government wanted a share in the postwar commercial development of the Norman Wells oil field, justified as compensation for its sizable wartime expenditure. Although Norman Robertson headed the Canadian delegation, it was Hugh Keenleyside who advanced the strongest arguments against the American proposal. Citing his experience as the Canadian secretary of the Permanent Joint Board on Defence, he declared that the Canol project was approved solely as a defence measure and that it "should not be considered as a commercial investment." Speaking for the Canadians present, who included Heeney, Foster, and Hanna among others, he concluded that they would likely advise their government against any modifications in the agreements.[4] In a move to further discourage American expectations of peacetime advantages, the Cabinet War Committee the next day approved the recommendation to reimburse the United States for costs incurred in the construction of the Mackenzie Valley airfields.[5]

In support of the argument that Canada must stand firm, Keenleyside prepared a confidential report on 11 December 1943, titled "Evidence Relating to United States Efforts to Obtain Post-War Advantages from Wartime Expenditures in Canada." Stating that the "legislators and people of the United States have begun to think in terms of postwar advantage," he went on to report that "the interpretation or misinterpretation of the principles underlying Lease-Lend, have led to a popular feeling in the United States that the Administration will be failing in its duty if it does not now provide for the acquisition of post-war profit from the wartime expenditure in foreign countries." After reiterating a number of examples of American expectations of gaining postwar benefits, Keenleyside emphatically recommended that Ottawa must do "everything possible to reduce the number and the relevant importance of defence facilities in Canada for which the United States taxpayer has to foot the bill."[6] The process of identifying and verifying the problem would prove to be far simpler than finding a viable solution.

The official report of the Truman Commission published in January 1944 strongly recommended that "every effort should be made to obtain at once a revision of those contracts which will provide proper postwar rights and safeguard the interests of the United States."[7] Although the initial decision to build the pipeline had originated with the United States Army, now public pressure demanded that the State Department rectify the error. Negotiations continued on the disposition of Canol and other wartime facilities, with the prime minister and key members of External Affairs remaining firm in their resolve to remove the American presence from the Canadian north.

After discussing the Canol issue at the War Committee meeting on 14 February 1944, Mackenzie King wrote in his diary that he "held strongly with one or two others to the view that we ought to get the Americans out of further developments there, and keep complete control in our own hands." He also recognized potential dangers. "Canada holding a position geographically advantageous in air routes as well as resources, there will be a demand on this country to make very great concessions to other nations." Echoing the sentiment expressed less than a year earlier by Lester Pearson, King concluded that "with the United States so powerful and her investments becoming greater in Canada we will have great difficulty to hold our own against pressure from the United States."[8] The next few months proved to be a crucial phase in negotiations related to postwar disposition of the defence facilities and the control of international civil aviation. A new aggressiveness and attitude of superiority in Washington met with equally strong resistance and resentment by Ottawa. As King was reported to have exclaimed: "Canadians were looked upon by Americans as a lot of Eskimos."[9] Numerous challenges loomed on the horizon, and there were no guarantees that Ottawa could succeed in untying the bonds of Hyde Park and Ogdensburg.

Before oil ever reached the Whitehorse refinery from Norman Wells, Mackenzie King informed the United States ambassador that his government desired the American Army's total withdrawal from the Canol Project at the end of the war. He did agree, however, that there might possibly be provision for a strategic reserve to satisfy the needs of continental defence.[10] In his diary, King explained his reasons for allowing private enterprise, rather than government, to control the pipeline and Norman Wells oil production:

Broadly the decision was to recognize the need for pursuing development of oil in that region, first because of the need of oil for defence purposes, and for the opening-up of new resources which might be all important in that region. Equally the necessity of going ahead because we had become dependent on the United States for oil from California to meet our needs, and that supply is becoming limited and Americans are urging that unless

we develop our fields, we may be cut off from theirs. . . . I felt clear in my
own mind it was necessary to have private enterprise make a beginning.[11]

Thus, it became Liberal party policy to encourage oil exploitation by private
enterprise under "obligations. . . to see that development was made in a way
that would give Canada benefits," a policy which remained intact until the
energy crises during the 1970s demanded a re-evaluation of the situation. After months of negotiation, agreement on the disposition of Canol was finally
concluded with an "Exchange of Notes" on 7 June 1944. The terms included
the early withdrawal by the United States government, Canada's first right of
refusal in the event of sale, and the creation of a strategic reserve for the purpose of North American defence.[112]

Within weeks, negotiations were also concluded for Canada's reimbursement for American costs incurred in permanent construction elsewhere.
These agreements excluded the Alaska Highway and Canol, but covered
items such as the airfields, weather stations, port facilities, and telephone-
telegraph lines. A supplementary agreement in 1946 added the weather stations along the Alaska Highway and a few miscellaneous items. In total, the
United States had been involved in the construction of twenty-eight airfields
and fifty-six weather stations. The cost to Canada, including the assumption
of $29,599,963 of debt for work done on the behalf of the United States,
amounted to over $123.5 million. There was an estimated additional Amer-
ican expense of $60 million not included in the reimbursements.[13]

While most government efforts were directed towards the steady withdrawal of American investment and military personnel, the position on the
Alaska Highway differed slightly. When Washington proposed in September
1944 that Canada take over its final construction and maintenance, the offer
was rejected. The original agreement had stipulated that the United States
would complete the road to approved standards, and Ottawa argued that extensive rebuilding was still required to fulfil the terms of that agreement.[14]
Eventually the Canadian portion of the highway would be turned over, less
than a year after the war had ended. Because of its poor condition, however,
it remained a military road maintained by the Canadian Army. To have
opened it to tourist traffic would have proven embarrassing in light of the
overly enthusiastic promotion during the summer of 1943.[15]

As part of the "Canadianization" strategy, plans were also underway to
have the Department of Transport and the RCAF take over control of all
weather stations and airfields. Ottawa soon discovered, however, that it was
difficult, if not impossible, to find adequately trained staff to fulfil the obligations. Most returning soldiers had little desire to spend a year, or even
months, at remote Arctic posts with the same predominantly male compan-

ionship they had left behind in Europe. The Canol Project was more easily resolved. The pipeline from Norman Wells to Whitehorse was finally closed down in the spring of 1945 after a short, lacklustre performance complicated by breakdowns, leaks, and spring floods. Described as "a monumental junkyard to military stupidity" by one cynic, the assets of the pipeline were then sold piecemeal for a fraction of their $134 million cost.[16] The disposal of American-built defence facilities was a tangible problem; other, more insidious threats of American encroachment posed a greater dilemma.

II

One serious complication in the process of eliminating possible American postwar advantages was Washington's refusal to accept Canadian claims to title over all the islands in the Arctic Archipelago. Nor was discussion of the issue confined to diplomatic circles. An article entitled "Ownership of Land in Arctic Sought" appeared in the *Journal of Commerce* on 9 March 1944. The dateline was Washington.

The State Department and the Canadian Government are seeking to determine the ownership of lands in the Arctic regions, north of Canada, it was learned today.

Interest in the area has been stirred by the need for clarification of postwar controls over air routes which will extten [sic] over the top of the world.

According to airline methods of mapping the world, it is claimed that the shortest air routes from New York to Asia or to the East Indies, India and even Moscow lie directly over Arctic territories claimed by Canada.

The claim is based on the "sector principle" which many countries, including the United States, do not recognize as valid. This principle implies a declaration of ownership of lands without exploring or policing them. The United States has never claimed territory north of Alaska. But it does not recognize other claims to the area.

The State Department has scrutinized the possibilities of the need for postwar air bases, meteorological stations, repair depots, and freight in these areas and finds that unless sovereignty be established, it will be impossible for United States airlines to develop these short routes to other parts of the world.

Apart from future military considerations, the United States is believed not to be interested [sic] in ownership of any land in the area, believing that the cost of maintaining control would be excessive. But if any other country exercises such control, difficulties may develop, it is said, so that American airlines could not operate in competition with those of other countries.

To most Canadian nationalists, this position represented outright American imperialism and potentially a direct threat to Canada's sovereignty claims. For this reason, control of all northern defence installations and direct representation in the civil aviation negotiations were now considered crucial. While there was as yet no official challenge, the threat remained, dormant but alive, until the issue again surfaced after the war had ended.

Before the development of intercontinental aircraft, all northern nations believed that postwar commercial routes would be established over the polar regions, requiring elaborate bases, weather stations, and navigational aids. Rumours about the ambitions of large American commercial aviation interests ran rampant; many believed that private United States interests would demand the right to use the wartime airfields "in perpetuity." After extensive study, Mackenzie King announced in Parliament on 2 April 1944 that to preserve the nation's autonomy Canada would seek international collaboration as a means to regulate commercial air transport.[17] The basis of this policy was in line with more general discussions about how Canada might overcome the threat of American domination through active participation in all forms of international organizations.[18]

The future regulation of commercial aviation was a minor concern compared to the fear that the Americans might demand the right "to construct a Maginot line of air defences in the Canadian North," thus preventing any attempt to remain neutral if the United States became involved in a war. Control of the airways by an international authority was therefore an important first step to gain "greater freedom of action" and offset American dominance. In particular, there was great fear that in any bilateral negotiation the United States might exert pressure to build northern airfields for commercial international flights, then demand rights for military use because of their financial contribution.[19] Unfortunately, Canadian hopes for a fully international regulatory body were incompatible with Britain's plans for special intra-Commonwealth agreements. As in the case of the uranium crisis of 1943, northern Canada was once again the object of rival claims by Britain and the United States. For this reason, it was crucial that Canada have direct representation at the international aviation negotiations, and not simply be regarded as a member of the British Commonwealth. Britain, on the other hand, was pressuring for a unified Commonwealth consensus as bargaining power against the aggressive American negotiators.

Meanwhile, Washington had begun its own secret investigations into the possibility of a continental air policy involving a bilateral agreement with

Canada. Unknown to Ottawa, back in February 1943 the United States Civil Aeronautics Board had been requested by the American section of the Joint Economic Committees to prepare a report on "United States–Canadian Airway Cooperation." The report submitted in June of that year was almost three hundred pages in length and fully documented with maps and inventories of all Canadian airfields and weather stations. The author made specific note of the fact that Ottawa's greatest asset in negotiations would be the right to freedom of transit but warned that there was little benefit for Canada in the proposed plan. He also noted that he was prohibited from discussing the subject with Canadian officials.[20]

Discussion and study continued in Washington until Roosevelt finally succumbed to demands by the senators who had toured the American air bases in connection with the Truman Commission. In October 1943 he announced his government's policy for postwar commercial aviation which included four main points: the United States government would retain full control of all internal aviation; commercial and passenger routes would be left to private enterprise; the government would consider subsidies for American airlines competing with low-cost foreign service on international flights; and foreign planes crossing United States territory would be granted privileges for refuelling and flyover only.[21] Three divergent views began to take shape: the United States agreeing to very minimal international authority, Britain desiring to protect the right to special Commonwealth agreements, and Canada advocating complete internationalization.

British concern about the future status of Canada's northern airfields prompted a third trip north by the British high commissioner in the summer of 1944, this time to the eastern Arctic. Malcolm MacDonald was accompanied by his secretary, a commanding officer of the USAAF, members of the RCAF, and several unnamed civilian experts. The specific purpose was to examine the American-built airfields of the northeast staging route: The Pas, Churchill, Coral Harbour, Frobisher Bay, Chimo in Ungava, Goose Bay in Labrador, as well as Mingen and Seven Islands (Sept Isles) in Quebec. In an official report to the Dominions Office, MacDonald described the airfields as "striking examples of the American nation's magnificent impertinence, imaginativeness, energy, mechanical skill and extravagance." He made special reference to "the small town" of Frobisher, built to accommodate eight hundred people with such luxuries as hot and cold showers, a library, and a circular, well-stocked bar.

> Besides the runways, an operations building, a hangar, a workshop and the other appurtenances of a modern aerodrome, there are various establishments in the station. These include barracks, mess-rooms and kitchens; a twenty-five bed hospital with a completely up-to-date operating

room, X-ray department and dentist's quarters; a shop and coffee-house; a theatre furnished for film shows, the legitimate drama and concerts; a laundry, a barber's shop and Turkish bath-house.

Describing the Arctic airfields as a "colossal piece of over-insurance," he observed that at some bases, construction had been halted midway, as in the case of the "palatial" Churchill hospital, which was virtually empty except for a $1,000 lamp hanging over the intended site of an operating table.

Yet MacDonald's evaluation of the airfields' commercial potential was pessimistic. Citing the remarks of an American colonel, that the "sole possible use" was for "defence or attack against the enemies of the North American peoples," MacDonald also questioned their military value because of the high maintenance costs involved. Already, he observed, there were signs of serious deterioration owing to lack of American expertise in Arctic construction. In his opinion, which verged on cynicism, "the Americans have added to the schools of White Whales, families of White Bears and thousands of White Foxes which are the commonest inhabitants of those regions, a fine little herd of White Elephants." Since Canada had paid $32 million to protect her sovereign rights to the northeastern bases, he concluded that "if the whole undertaking turns out to be a series of colossal errors, the Canadians are literally going to pay for the Americans' mistakes."[22]

MacDonald's secretary, O. L. Williams, added his own report, which contained factual evidence of "over-building" at each site. While the larger bases were equipped to handle a thousand aircraft a month, in the summer of 1944 only two or three planes were landing each week. Similarly, Churchill had been built to house 1,500, with only 150 on location at the time of the visit; Frobisher and Chimo could have accommodated 800 and 700 respectively, with the current population running between 80 and 150. With the exception of Goose Bay, which had separate Canadian and American commands, all bases were totally under USAAF control (see Appendix D).[23]

MacDonald's emphasis on defence potential was particularly significant, considering Churchill's agreement with Roosevelt in May 1943, to the continued postwar use of American air bases built on British territory.[24] Already, there was an uneasiness that Britain might be tempted to barter Commonwealth bases for privileges in commercial aviation should Canada agree to a "unified consensus of the empire." MacDonald's interest did nothing to allay those fears. Thus, before negotiations on the future of civil aviation began in earnest, it was singularly important that the wartime air bases be secured against American expectation of peacetime control.

Discussions on the process of transfer continued on through 1944, both formally and informally. To some extent, the existence of the government-owned Trans-Canada Airlines (TCA) not only facilitated negotiations by diminishing the influence of private interests in the Canadian decision-making process, but it also provided an easier transition from military to civilian aviation. Plans were already under way to transfer excess RCAF facilities and equipment to the control of either the Department of Transport or TCA.[25] On the other hand, Canada's government-owned airline seriously complicated Washington's plans for a continental air policy based on an integrated system.

As a member of the Canadian negotiating team at the preliminary meetings of the International Conference on Civil Aviation, Escott Reid reported that the Americans were continuing their fight for "commercial air supremacy in order to increase the war potential of the United States and oppose a Canadian or other proposal that encouraged establishment of an effective international authority over air transport." Most Americans, he claimed, believed their country should "be made powerful enough to overcome any possible combination of enemies" and that the two World Wars had occurred because "the United States was too weak, not that the world order was too weak."[26] As a result, he felt that Washington was more interested in increasing economic and military power than in creating strong international regulatory bodies.

Given the fact that Adolf Berle, described by John Holmes as "the anti-imperialist imperialist, *genus Americanus,*" was in charge of American civil aviation, it was expected that there would be stiff resistance to effective international control. Berle was not an annexationist, but he represented a sort of messianic continentalism in his conviction that military and economic integration of the two countries was inevitable. He also assumed that the United States would have access to the northern air bases. Not surprisingly, Canada's draft proposal was rejected at the final meetings held at Chicago in November 1944, as were those of Britain and the United States. However, the final compromise agreement did provide for an international organization to establish and oversee regulations. More importantly, although freedom of transit over the airways of member states was assured, the Americans did not obtain the unconditional right to pick up and discharge passengers and freight en route, and Canada was assured the right of sovereign control over all commercial air bases on Canadian soil.[27] The question still unresolved was whether the Arctic air bases would ever be used for civilian aviation or whether Washington would claim rights of access for the purpose of continental defence by unilateral declaration of the Monroe Doctrine.

III

With Ottawa's attention already so closely focused on the north because of sovereignty concerns, there was little difficulty in arousing interest in some of the domestic issues, especially those related to social welfare aspects of the planned reconstruction programme. In the final years of the war, there were increasing demands from the private sector for a redirection of government policies and administration in the north. They received enthusiastic support from younger reform-minded civil servants and equally strong opposition from the conservative old guard.

Raleigh Parkin was one of the key figures responsible for generating outside concern and protest. After introducing the idea of a comprehensive Arctic study to the Canadian Institute of International Affairs, he then contacted various influential people in Ottawa and the United States to ensure government co-operation and financial support. On his list of "key people to be kept informed" were Malcolm MacDonald, Robert Beattie, Hugh Keenleyside, Diamond Jenness, Arnold Heeney, Brooke Claxton, Group Captain William F. Hanna, and his brother-in-law, J. M. Macdonnell, all of whom he considered "influential in shaping Canadian policy in the north over the next few years." Not surprisingly, Parkin also noted that "the most active and constructive thinking" seemed to be going on amongst officials in departments other than Mines and Resources.[28]

In hopes of finding additional financial support for the CIIA research project, he wrote to both Joseph Willets, director of social sciences for the Rockefeller Foundation, and Walter S. Rogers of the Institute of Current World Affairs. Recurrent themes in Parkin's correspondence were government neglect, Canadians' lack of knowledge about their own Arctic regions, and the underdevelopment of northern resources. He also pointed to a new awareness "that our north country was not a closed barrier but on the contrary, the front door to this continent," and he warned that "Canadians must concern themselves with these implications in both internal and external policy-making."[29]

After CIIA had approved the Arctic study, Parkin became intrigued by another idea inspired by Trevor Lloyd, a proposal for an "Information Centre on Northern Canada." Only weeks after the geographer left for Dartmouth, Parkin suggested to Malcolm MacDonald that a Canadian Arctic research institute might be of value "to ensure a supply of intelligent, trained young men, competent to deal with the sort of problems related to the Arctic areas."[30] Over the succeeding months, this concept was discussed with a number of individuals who were equally troubled by the government's apparent indifference. In Parkin's own words'

The fact is that one thing led to another as persons exchanged ideas; then they talked with other nearby friends. . . . Whatever its limitations, the group that thus came together had the considerable merit of including individuals who knew what they were talking about and what they were trying to do. Most of them had a real knowledge of the North and its problems and some form of responsible relationship to that area. All, without exception, were determined to do something in their private capacity to overcome the neglect of the North.[31]

While most had first-hand knowledge from scientific work or travel, others were involved in branches of government which dealt in some manner with northern affairs. They were convinced that a Canadian polar institute would provide an effective means "to arouse government and people to some sense of urgency regarding the significance of the north."[32] Personal discussions led to informal meetings as the concept of an Arctic research centre gained increasing support in the broader community.

The original planning committee consisted of Parkin, Beattie, Hanna, Jenness, Lloyd, and A. E. Porsild. The first formal meeting was held in Ottawa on 31 March 1944 to discuss a proposal by Lincoln Washburn, who was actively involved in Arctic research for the United States Army Air Force. It was his suggestion that interested Canadians and Americans should join forces to organize an "International Polar Institute." Despite some reservations about the "possible political motives behind United States interest in northern Canada," the planning group agreed that the idea ought to be pursued. The minutes of the Ottawa meeting outlined the basic objectives of the Canadian participants:

> For some years to come in Canada, it will be necessary to stimulate popular interest in the North, and to focus the attentions of government and other agencies on administrative as well as scientific problems. Universities should be encouraged to open departments or expand them to include new studies relative to the North. The welfare of Indians and Eskimos alone is of considerable importance and there is urgent need of disinterested research work concerning them. Canadian research projects will need to be encouraged and financial help obtained; young Canadians intending to follow northern careers will require guidance and support.[33]

Subsequent planning meetings were held in New York that May, and in Montreal the following September. In addition to the original Ottawa group, other Canadians present at these sessions included Hugh Keenleyside, Arnold Heeney, Charles Camsell, Robert Beattie, Colonel Patrick Baird of the Canadian Army, Robert Boyle and Robert Newton representing the National Research Council, J. Tuzo Wilson of National Defence Headquarters, and J. J. O'Neill, dean of engineering at McGill University. The key Americans involved were Lincoln Washburn, Laurence Gould, and Richard Flint, all of the Arctic section of the Arctic, Desert and Tropic Information Centre

(ADTIC) of the USAAF; Ernest Hopkins, then president of Dartmouth College; Walter Rogers of the Institute of Current World Affairs; and Vilhjalmur Stefansson (see Appendix B).[34]

The advantages of a North American organization which would also include the United States, Newfoundland, and Greenland were strictly pragmatic. Apart from financial viability, there were other factors to be considered, such as the scientific tradition of co-operation, the large volume of research to be undertaken, and the access to existing data compiled by American military scientists. Parkin also pointed out that the situation in 1944 was unique. "One country, Canada, held sovereignty over a major portion of the world's arctic areas," and a large number of American scientists wanted to continue on work started during the war.[35] At the request of those present at the Ottawa meeting, Keenleyside and Flint drew up a draft constitution for the next meeting planned for Montreal, the city chosen for the institute's headquarters because of its proximity to the north and the special interests of McGill University.[36]

The selection of Canadian founding members reflected Parkin's aim to ensure future government support. In contrast to the American membership, which was primarily a matter of individual interest, "in Canada the AINA was created with the full awareness and participation of senior government officials." The objectives of the Canadians and Americans also differed. The former were "concerned with the political, administrative, social and economic aspects of problems in their own North, whereas the American scientists were quite naturally primarily concerned... with problems of scientific research."[37] Of additional note, a large majority of the Canadian founders were also active in the Canadian Institute of International Affairs.[38]

The Arctic Institute of North American (AINA) was founded in the fall of 1944 and later incorporated by an act of Parliament in Canada and under the laws of New York State. Lincoln Washburn became the first permanent director, and in 1947 Trevor Lloyd was appointed editor of the institute's official publication, *Arctic*. During the formative years, financial support came from a variety of public and private sources: the Hudson's Bay Company, Banting Fund, Carnegie Corporation, Northwest Territories Council, United States Office of Naval Research, National Science Council, National Research Council, and a number of private companies.[39]

Although others also played a major part, Raleigh Parkin was generally regarded as the founder because of his key role in the initial planning and organization.[40] In later years, Parkin recalled that ever since his days at Oxford, he had always been "involved in creating or helping to create organizations of one sort or another, organizations which will do something about something specific." He described his role as one "which always involved me getting other people involved who would, so to speak, carry the load, be the front people, people who would carry the thing through by their special knowledge."[41] Not only was Parkin successful in persuading others to become involved, he was prudent in his choice of men. In a letter to Walter Rogers, he explained that Hugh Keenleyside's support was crucial to any plans to change government policy in the north, partly because of his influential position, but also because he was the only "really constructive personality in Canadian Government circles who understands the problems we are faced with."[42] In this case, Parkin was exceptionally prophetic. Within a few years, Keenleyside would move into a position where he was directly responsible for introducing innovative policies and programmes in the northern territories.

From its beginning, the Arctic Institute's contribution to the study of northern Canada was substantial in terms of encouraging extensive scientific research, collecting and disseminating information on all aspects of polar regions, and generating both popular and professional interest through the institute's journal and other publications. The Canadian government, in particular, gained direct benefit from the research undertaken at the request of various civilian and military agencies. Ironically, this all came about through the efforts of a man who never once visited the Arctic. More importantly, although the AINA established a permanent base for polar research in North America, it also represented yet another tie binding Canada and the United States more closely together in northern-related activities.

IV

In addition to the Arctic Institute's research, other privately funded studies covered social, political, and economic issues of the north. On one occasion, Parkin's persuasive talents were at work without his knowledge or intent. His letter to the director of the Rockefeller Foundation outlining the necessity for extensive Arctic research was forwarded to the Canadian Social Science Research Council (CSSRC) for "opinion and advice."[43] As a consequence, the CSSRC received a $10,000 grant from the Rockefeller Foundation to undertake "a preliminary survey" of problems in Canada's more northerly regions. As stated, the council's objective was "to stimulate a wider interest among Canadians in the whole region" and at the same time examine "the problems of long-run development."[44] Preliminary reports appeared in the *Canadian Journal of Economics and Political Science* over the winter of 1944–45, and a total of eleven studies were later compiled and published in *The New North-West*, edited by C. A. Dawson.

Unknown to the participants, the scope and depth of the CSSRC survey was limited by the degree of co-operation provided by the northern administration. In a confidential memo, a junior member of the Northwest Territories and Yukon Affairs Bureau wrote to Parkin concerning the deputy commissioner's reaction to the proposed project, reporting that "Mr. G. [Gibson] doesn't seem greatly concerned over the whole Council, saying that it was just some hair-brained people wanting to spend more money looking into something that doesn't concern them." Later Gibson was reported to have expressed concern that the studies might include Ungava, since "it was an area in which native conditions were bad and they weren't proud of it and didn't particularly think that anyone from Ontario should be nosing around there."[45] Significantly, the CSSRC scientists did not undertake any field trips in the eastern Arctic. Yet in spite of Gibson's resentment of outside interference, there were some branches of government that proved more sympathetic. The Indian Affairs Branch, particularly, offered full cooperation and welcomed medical and socio-economic studies of "a number of key points in the north."[46]

The first two articles to appear in print dealt with native education and health services. In the "Foreword," Harold Innis, as president of the CSSRC, wrote that "the urgency of problems will be evident in the recommendations," and he called for immediate government intervention.[47] By far the most critical of government neglect was Dr. G. J. Wherrett's report on health conditions in the Mackenzie District. Rejecting the excuse of limited funds, he argued that "it was high time that the Department formulated a health policy founded on the needs of the people." Taking special note of the high incidence of tuberculosis among the Indian population, he listed a number of recommendations towards providing extensive and intensive health care: more qualified doctors, nursing stations, emergency plane service, TB surveys, dental care, and a full-time resident doctor.[48] Andrew Moore's "Survey of Education in the Mackenzie District" was also critical. Referring to the fact that no new ordinances related to education had been passed since 1905, he called for a complete overhaul of the existing school system and the appointment of a director of education for both white and native schools. Additional recommendations included sweeping changes in the curriculum to meet the specific needs of the native population, upgrading of teachers' qualifications, and construction of new and improved facilities. Furthermore, Moore strongly advocated an end to the mission school system.[49]

Despite the urgency of the recommendations and the support of the influential research council, they had no immediate effect on the territorial government. Both studies were noted as "received" in the minutes of the Northwest Territories Council and simply deferred for later discussion.[50] Moreover, expenditures by the territorial government on health and education actually declined from 1944 to 1946 despite overall budget increases for the administration that more than quadrupled over the two years, from approximately

$400,000 to over $1.8 million. Educational grants dropped by over $1,000 over the same period, and hospital services decreased by over $10,000 since the new Department of Health and National Welfare had assumed responsibility for Inuit services. There were no pronounced changes in government policy, and it was not until 1946 that a school inspector was finally appointed for the Mackenzie District.[51]

Other topics covered in the CSSRC survey included agriculture, transportation, settlement, mining, and the fur trade, which were all assessed in terms of potential economic development. In contrast to the studies on health and education, a report on the territorial government by C. C. Lingard lacked any constructive criticism, aside from noting that "officials" blamed budget limitations as the "principle reason for delays of the past ten or fifteen years in instituting more progressive and far-reaching administrative programmes in the Northland." Lingard pointedly qualified his findings with the explanation that most of his information had been supplied by the Department of Mines and Resources, and he did predict that "a significant change" would be required in government administration.[52] While relatively ineffective in bringing about any immediate change, the "Arctic Survey" did make an important contribution in the longer term by creating a stimulus for further study and providing the basis for a number of new programmes instituted in later years.

Whereas the CSSRC had commissioned a variety of experts to complete their studies, Trevor Lloyd attempted to cover singlehandedly a larger geographical area and an even broader range of topics in his assignment for the Canadian Institute of International Affairs. The process of research, however, proved to be a major challenge and source of continual frustration. Even with the co-operation and support of such senior men in government as Heeney, Keenleyside, and Claxton, Lloyd was often thwarted in his attempts to gain access to primary resource material.[53] When he approached the deputy commissioner for permission to accompany the Eastern Arctic Patrol, he was told that "no one had ever been allowed into the north to secure material for writing" without agreeing first to submit their work for department approval prior to publication. Similarly, he was refused access to government files on the grounds that they were written with the understanding that their confidentiality would be respected, and that many reports could only be comprehended by those "who have gained an understanding of these problems over a period of years."[54] According to Lloyd, Gibson told him "that it didn't matter to him whether the Prime Minister had authorized the study"; he would not be allowed to see the departmental files nor talk to anyone in the department, because of a previous incident when Richard Finnie had gone through the files and subsequently written a book criticizing the government.[55]

Undaunted, Lloyd managed to keep in touch with the bureau's activities through junior members who were in sympathy with his cause. One of them later recalled that "I knew that he was using the information to exert political pressure, and I had no objections because there was a great deal of inertia among government personnel which was undoubtedly delaying orderly development and assistance to the natives."[56] Lloyd also managed a trip to Labrador, Ungava, and Baffin Island in the spring of 1943 with the aid of the Canadian Institute of International Affairs, the Wartime Information Board, and the United States Army Air Force, but without the prior knowledge or approval of the northern administration.[57] Inevitably, his persistent efforts and public criticism alienated the more conservative members of the administration, who up until then had successfully hidden the problems inherent in government policy and programmes from public view.

Others were also apprehensive of his Arctic research, particularly the Hudson's Bay Company general manager, Philip Chester. In a letter to the CIIA research director, Chester strongly urged that the project be curtailed or terminated because it touched on "controversial matters" which "should not be discussed."[58] Although the final version of Lloyd's study was somewhat complimentary to the Hudson's Bay Company, he did point to injustices arising from trader rivalry which he felt might be overcome by a publicly owned monopoly of the fur trade.[59] Raleigh Parkin was not the least surprised by this lack of co-operation, which he perceived as an attitude which "often develops when a situation has been left too long untouched by the light of public information or public opinion."[60] Lloyd, on the other hand, saw the situation in terms of personality and power. In his view, the deputy commissioner had controlled the northern administration for many years with the assistance of a few loyal oldtime civil servants.[61] Regardless of reasons, those reluctant to change would have to be convinced otherwise, or some means would have to be found to diminish their power.

Prior to its completion, portions of Lloyd's study were distributed to the appropriate government officials for their comments, a less than subtle method of alerting key individuals to problems in hopes of gaining influential support in Ottawa. Then finally in December 1946, the full manuscript of over a thousand pages was submitted to the CIIA research director.[62] Titled "The Geography and Administration of Northern Canada," it dealt with every conceivable aspect of the north, including its history, strategic significance, the implications of military activities, the sovereignty issue, climate, geography, settlement and land use, transportation, administration, native welfare, resource potential, plans for economic development, health services and education. Lloyd was particularly suspicious of the motives and strategy employed by the Americans to gain rights to Canadian territory, and he warned that there "was a real possibility that Canadian Arctic sovereignty may become nominal unless some positive stand is made in the face of this

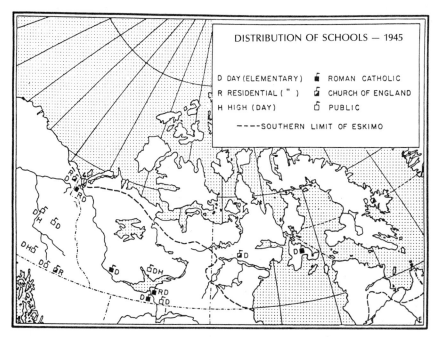

Figure 15 Schools in the Yukon and NWT, 1945 (from Trevor Lloyd, *The Geography and Administration of Northern Canada,* chapter 7)

constant pressure from the south."[63]

Reflecting the concerns of a more socially conscious generation of scholars, a sizable portion of the study was devoted to the status and welfare of the indigenous peoples, which Lloyd considered deplorable. Referring to his experience as acting vice-consul in Greenland in 1944, he emphasized the need for better educational programmes and special training to facilitate native adaptation to Euro-Canadian values and technology. Practical training for new economic opportunities was critically important, argued Lloyd, not simply "the smattering of English and syllabics intermixed with half-understood religious precepts, but an adequate system of schooling attuned to their needs." He visualized a Canadian north where the indigenous peoples would fully participate in the economic and governmental process:

> [The aborigine] is the logical choice as a spearhead of settlement in northern marginal areas not yet adequately populated. Already adapted to a rather uncompromising physical environment, "wise to the ways of the woods," the native, armed with the academic and technical education and skills of the white man, becomes a valuable national asset rather than a pauperized remnant of a race that is passing away.

But he also recognized that "to adopt such a long-term plan would require radical changes in the present relationship between native and trader, and would demand a completely new approach from teachers and administrators."[64] It was a seemingly impossible objective in the mid-1940s.

In summarizing the findings of his research, Lloyd recommended far greater government expenditure and intervention in all aspects of northern affairs. His radical blueprint for the future included a drastic overhaul of the administration through such measures as constitutional reform; a resident commissioner responsible to a special ministry; a legislature composed of elected and appointed members; the extension of territorial boundaries to include the northern regions of the provinces; and the creation of a capital city in Churchill with smaller units of regional government divided on the basis of climate, land forms, and ethnicity.[65] Lloyd fully recognized that his ideas would be considered "stupidly visionary," but he vehemently argued that "the armchair explorers of Wellington Street have had things their way for a very long time and they must be prepared to consider quite new ideas, even rather surprising ones."[66] As predicted, the overall plan proved far too drastic for Ottawa, although some of the more modest proposals related to health and education were adopted almost immediately.

Lloyd's study was likely one of the more controversial projects sponsored by the Canadian Institute of International Affairs. Although it was never published, it accomplished the aims of its author and the institute by drawing public and government attention to the many problems existing in the north. From 1943 through to 1948, a number of articles on the north appeared in the CIIA's *International Journal* by such authors as Lloyd, W. L. Morton, Griffith Taylor, and Maxwell J. Dunbar. Lloyd also wrote two pamphlets on the Canadian Arctic for the institute's "Behind the Headlines" series as well as numerous other articles appearing in popular and academic journals. Over this same period, the CIIA sponsored lectures and study groups at branches throughout Canada focusing on the problems and opportunities arising out of the wartime activities in the north. Among the speakers were Major-General W. W. Foster, O. M. Solandt, J. Tuzo Wilson, and, of course, Lloyd, who himself gave a total of seventeen lectures. While on a speaking tour that stretched from Halifax to Vancouver, he also carried the message to the general public through radio and press interviews.[67] The degree to which the CIIA influenced government and public opinion is difficult to measure or define, but the elitist organization unquestionably provided an effective vehicle for promoting interest and debate on the north among senior bureaucrats, politicians, academics, and businessmen.

The Department of Mines and Resources, however, deftly ignored the more critical reports of privately funded research by declaring that it was in the midst of its own major study. In this respect, the North Pacific Planning

Project (NPPP) became the proverbial "royal commission" for the department, providing the illusion of serious effort to resolve problems related to the two territories. Initially the northern administration had enthusiastically welcomed the project, since it appeared that the Americans intended to provide the major portion of the manpower and funds required to put together a study of potential economic development. Camsell's responsibility thus seemed relatively minor, the simple collection of data from various departments and agencies involved in northern affairs.

In November 1943, a progress report was presented to the Joint Economic Committees at a two-day session. Although Camsell was present, the discussion was led by co-director James Rettie and focused on six key areas: postwar use of the Alaska Highway; sharing of the Canol pipeline and Mackenzie oil production; integration of Pacific shipping; co-operation in commercial aviation; the removal of tariffs; and measures to end the disputes over fishing rights. Also mentioned briefly in the report was the possibility of shared use of hydro-electric power with specific reference to the resource potential of the Columbia and Peace Rivers. On the whole, comments of the American members of the committee were enthusiastic. Canadian chairman W. A. Mackintosh, however, recommended that the Joint Economic Committees "should be more solidly based in the Department of State and External Affairs."[68]

Then in February 1944, the American section of the North Pacific Planning Project put forward a more specific proposal. Claiming that the Pacific northwest could not afford competitive air services, a report was submitted which suggested the creation of a joint Anglo-American-Canadian privately or publicly owned airline.[69] Although there is no record of a Canadian response, it was undoubtedly unacceptable considering Ottawa's expectations for its fledgling Trans-Canada Airlines. However, the timing suggests that it was more than coincidence that Mackenzie King announced the dissolution of the Joint Economic Committees on 14 March 1944, only weeks after the submission of the planning project's report. The official reason for disbanding the committees was that they were redundant owing to the establishment of other joint agencies to deal with economic co-ordination. Later, in reply to a request for an update to be included in a preliminary report, Charles Camsell advised the American director of the North Pacific Planning Project in May 1944 that joint participation was no longer advisable following dissolution of the committees and that any plans for further international collaboration would be subject to the agreement of the State Department and External Affairs. Failing to gain support from the appropriate government agencies, the American section was disbanded owing to "lack of funds."[70]

At this time, Camsell announced that his department would continue an evaluation of the region following the same outline proposed by the now defunct joint project. To obtain sufficient data to assess economic potential, field studies were conducted on the development possibilities of agriculture, fisheries, forestry, mining, and wildlife resources. In addition, there were specialized investigations including topographical, geodetic, hydrographic, hydrometric, and boundary surveys.[71] Despite the appearance of activity, no interim reports were submitted, and it was several years before a final report was published. Significantly, the study focused on future development potential with no provision in the draft outline for examination of administrative or political structures. Nor were there any further suggestions of economic integration with Alaska or Washington state.

By contrast, both the CIIA and the CSSRC studies provided new creative ideas on how the north might be governed. The majority of the recommendations involved increased federal investment and intervention which could only be justified by consent of the electorate. For this reason, public support was particularly crucial to force Ottawa to undertake a more active role in northern affairs. Government interest in the north remained relatively high during the last years of the war, but the major focus of the attention was still on sovereignty. More public pressure would be necessary to shift the emphasis of concern from external to domestic issues.

Many of the early articles and books were optimistic about future potential, with many references to a romanticized frontier concept: the "opening of the northern frontier," "the land of opportunity," "a new era," and a "new north." This was particularly evident in Trevor Lloyd's writings, which described Canadians as longing to complete the nation-building that began a century before, claiming that they were "born pioneers but for twenty years they have lacked a frontier to work on and to plan for. The new frontier, the last Canadian frontier, is the North."[72] Other articles echoed the same rhetoric.

The frontier theme was also adopted by Charles Camsell in an article first published in June 1944. The deputy minister again wrote of the "new North" and described its geographical significance "as the crossroads of the great inter-continental air routes of the future." In addition to geopolitical importance and resource potential, he defined the "lure of the North" as "something inherent in the human heart and the human soul which responds to the appeal of the wilderness." In a manner reminiscent of late nineteenth-century Canadian nationalists, he wrote of destiny and empires: "Just as the map of Canada has for a century been unrolled westward, so now it is northward that 'the tide of the Empire takes its way.' The same racial stock which has carried the flag around the world will also carry it to the farthest north, and we may be sure that they and their sons and daughters will write a record of achievement not unworthy of the races from which they sprang."[73] Although the article was reportedly ghost-written by a junior member of his department,[74] this fact does not diminish the popularity of the message. Over the next year, the article was repeated in the form of a speech in Vancouver, Winnipeg, Toronto, and London, England. Twice published, first in the *Beaver* and then in the *Canadian Geographical Journal*, the paper was awarded the R. B. Bennett Empire Prize by the Royal Society.

A number of books on the north appeared during this period. With a few exceptions, most were written by Americans, but they promoted a similar romantic image of frontier development although they were related more to Alaska and a continental vision. The titles alone reflect the mysticism, promise and excitement now attached to the region: *Romance of the Alaskan Highway, Alaska and the Canadian Northwest: Our New Frontier, Northwest of the World, Alaska Comes of Age, War Discovers Alaska*, and *Within the Circle: Portrait of the Arctic*. The message spilled over into American newspapers and popular journals. In 1944, the United States media tended to focus on the unexploited oil fields and potential settlement with an enthusiasm not dissimilar to the "Manifest Destiny" fervour of the previous century. In describing the United States weather stations, one author wrote that "our first little outposts undoubtedly will expand and grow until we have developed full-fledged airway-navigation points like lighthouses around the polar sea."[75]

At roughly the same time, both Canadians and Americans turned to film to counter possible adverse publicity attending the Truman Commission. In December 1943, the National Film Board, as part of the "Canada at War" series narrated by Lorne Greene, produced a black-and-white movie on the Alaska Highway and Canol projects. Titled "Look to the North," the half-hour feature film minimized the dominant American presence, highlighted the "joint co-operation" aspect, and particularly stressed the opportunities provided for the postwar development. By contrast, "The Alaska Highway" and "Canol," produced by Richard Finnie with approval from the United States government, were full-length technicoloured extravaganzas, complete with philharmonic background music. These latter two films stressed the heroic adventures of the American Army and civilian engineers in their attempts to protect their country from the enemy, with several references to the military co-operation of American's friendly neighbour.[76] When viewed together, the differences in motives prompting the productions were unmistakable. The National Film Board wanted Canadians to view the defence projects in terms of peacetime opportunities; the Finnie films glorified the American efforts to defeat the enemy.

On the whole, the Canadian press was more factual and cautious in their predictions, particularly after negotiations were underway to settle compensation for American investment in the northwest. The Wartime Information Board still issued press releases, most of them now quite perfunctory, describing current mining production, new air routes, or the general progress of the Alaska Highway, but with specific emphasis on Canadian participation.[77] Even Camsell's article warned that any great population growth would only come from extensive mineral development and therefore be less dramatic than some believed. By 1945, government reports reflected increasing scepticism about rapid frontier development. As a result, those advocating extensive changes in administration and increased government expenditure experienced more difficulty in generating and sustaining public support.

Lester Pearson's article "Canada Looks 'Down North,'" published in December 1945, again referred to the "unexplored frontier, luring the pathfinder into the unknown," but, more significantly, it also reintroduced the issue of security as a government responsibility. While maintaining that the Canadian Arctic was "no country for weaklings and its economic development will test the finest qualities of the men of the North," Pearson concluded with an ominous prediction:

> It is for the Great Powers to decide, by their policies and their plans, whether that development can be conducted in an atmosphere of friendly cooperation between all the Arctic nations, and with a resultant benefit to all, or whether the Northern Hemisphere is to become an area of national rivalries, fears and ambitions. Canada will certainly do its best to ensure the former, for to no country would the consequences of the alternative be more disastrous. In 1946 there is no isolation—even in the Arctic ice.

He noted that Canada was "conscious of the limitations on her own ability to translate these peaceful desires into realities" and that the future would depend on "the ability of the Great Powers, and of all other powers, to work together within the United Nations." He also called for co-operation between the Arctic countries to advance research and development of the polar regions.[78] Perhaps more than others, Pearson's article recognized the importance of combining foreign policy objectives with domestic ones.

V

Another individual who had considerable influence on government perceptions of the north during the latter years of World War II was Major-General W. W. Foster, the special commissioner for defence projects in northwest Canada. In practice, he provided an effective link between the policy-makers in Ottawa and the domestic scene in the northwest, with his added advantage of being directly involved in the ongoing activities of the American military. Foster also filled the void created by a detached and conservative Department of Mines and Resources. Although he was part of officialdom since he reported directly to the Cabinet War Committee, Foster had no vested interests to protect, no axe to grind. His role as adviser was temporary, not integrated into the military structure, and his viewpoints were generally in harmony with the cause of the northern reformers. In turn, their efforts lent support to his recommendations. He was more closely connected with the most influential supporters in government: Heeney, to whom he reported, and Keenleyside, who was the son of a close friend. There were no direct links between Foster and the Arctic lobbyists, but he shared their belief that the future of Canada lay in the responsible development of the north. As such he can be considered a devout northern nationalist.

Foster's dual mandate caused him to consider both external and domestic factors. The conflicts were many, but like Trevor Lloyd, the special commissioner believed that satisfactory solutions could not be implemented without a drastic change in the northern administration. "The present system of government," he reported, "is now inadequate to the situation, and would not appear adequate for the provision of social, economic and other public services upon a parity with other portions of the Dominion." To plan constitutional and administrative changes necessary for "adequate government," Foster proposed that a committee be appointed to study the problem and advise Ottawa "upon a comprehensive form of administration"[79] (see Appendix E).

The major resistance to this proposal came from the deputy minister of mines and resources, a fact of little surprise since the department had become the target of increasing criticism from other government agencies over the past year. The previous December, Keenleyside had reported need for improvement in Canada's northern administration, saying it compared poorly to the performance of other countries with polar regions.[80] Then a few months later, W. E. D. Halliday of the Privy Council Office also suggested major changes in both the council and the Northwest Territories and Yukon Bureau. Referring to "gossip and so forth" concerning problems in the Department of Mines and Resources, Halliday claimed that Camsell should be pleased to accept a recommendation which implied that "the war brought about changes which required a re-examination of the north."[81] In a private letter to the deputy minister prior to formal submission of his recommendation on 30 April 1944, Foster pointed out that his advisement was prompted by "comments in the press and by individuals" demanding new government services in the north.[82]

As expected, Camsell was indignant and suggested that Foster had gone "a bit far afield in interpreting his duties as Special Commissioner." In his view, the population increase in the Mackenzie District was only temporary. Thus he rejected any need for electoral representation on the grounds that "with only a few hundred voters and many of them with little more than the educational status of an Indian, parliamentary representation has not appeared to be warranted." Replying to the irate deputy minister, Heeney defended Foster, claiming the special commissioner had not implied any adverse reflection on the present administration, but that "it was inevitable that any person in his position was bound to have given serious thought to the future, and reach some conclusions as to the federal government's continuing responsibilities in administration of the Northwest."

Rather unexpectedly, Keenleyside appeared to come to Camsell's support, perhaps in hopes of mediating an apparently unresolvable impasse. He agreed that Foster's "knowledge of the Northwest Territories, being limited in time and space, is not sufficient to justify the acceptance of his Recommendation." Referring to his own proposal for "a review of current administrative policies," he suggested that such an investigation was the responsibility of the Northwest Territories Council. Keenleyside concluded with the reminder that he had also proposed "a Royal Commission be appointed to examine the whole question of policy involved in the administration of the Canadian North," and in this event, "it was worth considering the advisability of nominating General Foster."[83] The attempt to soothe ruffled feathers succeeded.

Following a private meeting attended by Heeney, Keenleyside, and Camsell, it was agreed that Foster's recommendation should go before the Cabinet War Committee with the suggestion that it be referred for consideration to the minister of mines and resources. Camsell also agreed to ask for the resignation of three council members to allow for the appointment of representatives from the northern communities. The "reformed" council would then consider what steps should follow.[84] Heeney informed Foster of the decision, expressing his hopes that a reconstituted council would initiate "constructive action." In a separate personal letter, he expressed his pleasure that Foster had submitted the recommendation, "for the government must, before long, face these basic problems, although I do not anticipate any early result." In reply, Foster argued that it would have "seemed wiser to approach the problem de novo rather than point out existing difficulties."[85] It was clearly evident that the veteran of two World Wars had little patience with the diplomatic compromises required to keep the political machine running smoothly in Ottawa.

Despite its referral to the Department of Mines and Resources, the issue was freely discussed by other departments that year. A number of officials offered suggestions: the minister of national defence for air fully supported Foster's proposal; a member of External Affairs' legal division advised against any civil servant having power over the north, stating that such responsibility should rest with a lieutenant-governor; another member of External Affairs rejected the appointment of council members with vested interests, suggesting instead independent experts in professional fields; a Mines and Resources official suggested splitting the department in two, with one deputy minister solely in charge of administration of the two territories; Foster proposed the division of the Northwest Territories in two, with administration headquarters at Fort Smith and Churchill, as well as the transfer of the Yukon capital from Dawson to Whitehorse; and Charles Camsell called for constitutional reorganization along the lines of "colonial administrations familiar throughout the Empire."[86] With the exception of Camsell, there was a general consensus that at least partial representative government should be granted to the Mackenzie District.

Keenleyside still believed that the present structures could be modified to meet the new demands, but he insisted that there must be a substantially increased budget. In July 1944, he proposed that

> rather than leave the developments of the north to somewhat haphazard inclinations of the many departments which have had a hand in it, we should seek to bring together the control of activities in that region under the supervision of a responsible authority, namely the Northwest Territories Council. Other Governmental Departments can be used as agencies by the Council, but the coordination of plans and the direction of their execution should be the Council's responsibility.[87]

Keenleyside was a centralist and an interventionist, but his objective in advocating that full authority be vested in the Northwest Territories Council might also have been related to his membership in that body. Confident of his own ability and ideas, he thought it logical and expedient to effect reform from within the existing system. Significantly, his proposal in July 1944 did in fact form the basis of Ottawa's new approach to northern affairs after 1947.

Most administrative and constitutional changes suggested in 1944 attempted to diminish or divert the existing power of the Department of Mines and Resources, but they offered little real advance towards more responsible government. All saw tight federal control as imperative.

VI

Meanwhile Foster attempted to institute reforms on an ad hoc basis. The need for increased health and educational facilities along the Alaska Highway became urgent by the summer of 1944. As part of postwar planning, Foster had hoped to attract men with families to the construction camps as a means of establishing a more permanent labour force for highway maintenance. But without schools and health services, reaching this objective was impossible. In September, both Foster and Keenleyside attended a special committee meeting of the Joint Defence Construction Projects Panel, which was set up to consider the problems of inadequate services and facilities. There, it was agreed that representatives from the Department of Labour and the Department of Pensions and Health would study the situation along with the special commissioner.[88]

Although British Columbia and Alberta agreed to provide some form of assistance, the Yukon Council was particularly reluctant to approve additional funds for health services. Up until that time, United States medical officers provided health care for all those employed on the defence projects, and Jeckell maintained that the Yukon Council could not afford to assume this responsibility when the Americans withdrew. Moreover, he argued that if the territorial government provided travelling doctors and nurses along the Alaska Highway, the remote areas of the Yukon would demand similar services. He pushed the financial issue to its limit when he suggested that if RCAF medical officers were granted permits to render emergency aid to Yukon residents, it might be appropriate to charge fees which "should be paid to the Receiver General of Canada to be credited to the account of the Yukon." The council even refused an offer by the Canadian North West Air Command to allow their dental and medical officers to treat civilians in the Yukon, on the excuse that it would require an amendment to the Yukon Act.[89]

In terms of education the provincial governments proved especially cooperative, with Alberta and British Columbia agreeing to provide teachers for settlements along their respective portions of the highway. Controller Jeckell, however, flatly rejected such proposals on the grounds that the existing population did not warrant the expenditure unless the federal government was willing to pay the full cost. Instead, he suggested that correspondence courses would be quite adequate. Jeckell also recommended that families should be charged for this service; otherwise, "if the Government makes the course free, that much less consideration will be given to getting the full value out of it by the parents."[90]

In a letter marked "most secret," the frustrated Foster reminded Heeney that the problem of supplying adequate services was part of the reason he had called for changes in the administration of the northern territories. He pointed out that "a great deal of anxiety is being displayed as to the future arrangements for medical attention, workmen's compensation, schools and other facilities at points along the Alaska Highway, airfields, and the Canol Project" and that many families who had been encouraged to come north had already moved out because of the lack of services.[91] No doubt the lack of co-operation on the part of the Dawson-based council was a major factor influencing his recommendation that the seat of government be moved to Whitehorse. On the other hand, the Department of Mines and Resources appeared equally guilty in supporting the self-interests of the Yukon Council members. By contrast, along the provincial portions of the highway it was reported that "the settlement of families had stabilized employment and increased efficiency."[92] Yet despite a number of protest meetings held by Yukon residents, Jeckell steadfastly refused to consider the issue, and the matter was still unresolved when the war came to an end.[93]

A similar problem arose in the Northwest Territories, where American medical officers at the airfields and weather stations were likewise providing emergency treatment for local residents. Despite Keenleyside's warning of "the inadvisability from a national standpoint of relying on the United States," the territorial council showed no interest in assuming responsibility for continuation of the services. Noting the unsatisfactory state of Inuit and Indian health, Keenleyside then proposed that the council sponsor extensive independent studies on the medical and educational needs as a first step towards "radical and fundamental reform."[94] This recommendation was approved in April 1944, but no effort was made to follow it through.[95]

In spite of repeated attempts, neither Keenleyside nor Foster was successful in convincing Ottawa of the immediate necessity for increased social services to the territories. In November 1944, Keenleyside formally resigned from the Northwest Territories Council as a result of his appointment as Canadian ambassador to Mexico. The following April, Foster requested release from his duties in order to accept a position with the British Columbia Power Commission. Heeney informed the prime minister that although the departure of the special commissioner had not been anticipated, Foster had accomplished his principal mandate of establishing proper relationships with the United States armed forces and that the unofficial role of adviser was of lesser importance now that American activities in the north had declined sharply.[96] By March 1945, there were fewer than two thousand Americans employed in the Canadian northwest.[97] Roy Gibson's request that the Department of Mines and Resources assume the duties of the special commissioner was denied, and after being filled by a temporary replacement for a year, the office was finally disbanded in March 1946. In the absence of war and with only 456 Americans remaining in the region,[98] there was no apparent need for further liaison.

Keenleyside's personal motives and ideals are particularly important in comprehending the course of his career over the next few years. In January 1943, President Edgar J. Tarr had offered him the position of executive director of the Canadian Institute of International Affairs. Keenleyside refused for two reasons. In the first place, he reminded Tarr that his "political and economic views are pretty well to the left" and would be resented by those who were asked to contribute substantial sums to support the institute. Secondly, he was reluctant to leave External Affairs:

> Any weakening of the liberal element in the Service might have definite repercussions in Government policy—and not only in foreign affairs. It would be a cause for real regret if we ever get a truly *liberal* or *socialist* government in Canada to have that Government hamstrung... by a Foreign Service in which reaction had triumphed. I do not suggest that External Affairs is in that condition nor that there is any immediate danger of it occurring. But Dr. Skelton is gone and those of us who espouse his ideals cannot maintain his traditions if we are not on the job.[99]

For the most part, Keenleyside believed that as a civil servant he would "probably have more influence on causes of concern from outside rather than within the actual party system." In the fall of 1944, he turned down an offer to become president of the University of Manitoba and accepted instead the ambassadorial post. Hoping for a coalition of the CCF and left-wing Liberals, he was interested in running for Parliament with the thought that his diplomatic experience would make him a likely candidate for the position of secretary of state for external affairs.[100] The Liberal win in 1945 ended these political ambitions.

By the end of the war, it was apparent that studies and publicity were not sufficient to bring about hoped-for financial support and drastic structural changes in the northern administration and government. The question of security arising from a potential threat by the Soviets, on the other hand, temporarily assisted the cause of the northern promoters. As John Holmes pointed out, "the small band of Canadian arcticians who had pleaded the cause of the north without success over the years now had the powerful argument of security."[101] In order to sustain interest and concern, both government and the public required more stimulation than that provided by reports of development potential or the unsatisfactory conditions of the native population. Even more important than national security would be the renewed concern about the effects of co-operative defence on Arctic sovereignty.

7

Sovereignty, Stewardship, or Security, 1945–1947

> The United States military men refer, whether nervously or menacingly, to the "undefended roof of North America" and claim the right to return *en masse* to the Canadian Northland which they left so recently. The North is "in the News" and much that is not in the news is in the secret despatch boxes.
>
> Trevor Lloyd, 1946

With the dawning of the nuclear age, domestic and international considerations became intertwined in a complex debate over the future of Canada's Arctic. The euphoria and optimism which had accompanied the Allied victories at the end of the European war quickly turned to sober reflection after the bombing of Hiroshima and Nagasaki. World co-operation was no longer an idealistic goal; it was now a necessity. At the same time, Canada's undefended north attained greater geopolitical importance as animosity grew between the United States and the Soviet Union. Pressure for renewal of the joint defence agreement with the United States soon followed, and with it arose once more the question of Arctic sovereignty. Coinciding with external influences was the introduction of nationwide social welfare measures which indirectly increased government involvement in northern affairs. A number of postwar reconstruction programmes were also a contributing factor to the accelerated growth of federal investment in the territories. While it was conceded that a different approach to governing the north would be required to adapt to the changes brought about by the war years, the direction was still unclear.

I

With the prospect of new joint defence projects multiplying throughout the Arctic, it was feared that once again the "new north" might acquire a decided American presence. The only alternative was decisive federal action to establish recognition of its effective jurisdiction. This premise explains the repeated references to "national purpose" and "preservation of sovereignty" as a means of justifying proposed social reforms and economic planning in the territories. From this perspective, the underlying objectives of a northern domestic policy were closely related to, and in a sense contingent upon, the issue of sovereignty. In the immediate postwar years, the potential threat to national security was of serious concern, but still of a lesser priority than northern sovereignty.

As the war neared its end, most countries looked to the proposed United Nations as an instrument of peace. Canada's active participation in the preliminary negotiations denoted a significant change in foreign policy compared to the prewar years when Mackenzie King deliberately avoided direct involvement in world affairs. The "neo-internationalists" led by St. Laurent and Pearson successfully countered former fears of commitment with the argument that more power could be gained and more influence exerted through collective action. Moreover, they believed that Canada was capable of playing a constructive functional role in world politics as a leader of the middle powers.

The country emerged from World War II with new respect and status, partially achieved through military contributions, but also related to the temporary absence of competition arising from the disarray in Europe. In F. H. Soward's opinion, "Canada moved nearer to the head of the class because some of the boys were in quarantine."[2] Yet, the bombing of Hiroshima and Nagasaki had a paradoxical effect on Canada's power and autonomy. On the one hand, because of its uranium resources and participation in nuclear research, Canada gained immediate acceptance as "one of three atomic powers."[3] But the very factors which added to the nation's status at the same time contributed to its vulnerability because of her geographical location between the two opposing superpowers that emerged in the postwar world. The defection of Igor Gouzenko in September 1945 and his report of a Russian espionage network in North America increased suspicions of Soviet intentions, so much so that Mackenzie King speculated that "if there is another war, it will come against America by way of Canada from Russia."[4]

Others were equally concerned and began to view the possession of uranium as a potential liability. External Affairs member C. A. S. Ritchie argued that because Canada was a lesser power, "her possession of uranium is perhaps more likely to expose her to embarrassment and difficulties."[5] In the worst scenario, Canada would be particularly vulnerable to an enemy attack should a race to develop atomic weapons polarize politics between the east and west. Yet Canada did not have the finances, technical expertise, or manpower to defend her northern border adequately. Moreover, the greater prestige in international affairs did little to diminish the military dependency on the United States that had escalated during the war years. Thus, Ottawa directed all efforts towards promoting international co-operation and, as a first priority, control of atomic energy through the United Nations. To achieve this goal, it was critical that both the United States and the Soviet Union remained active participants in the world forum, despite the limitations created by the veto in the Security Council.

For similar reasons, Pearson and St. Laurent sought international co-operation in the development of the Arctic regions. Pearson particularly emphasized the need for close collaboration of the five Arctic nations in polar research and development projects. He first proposed the idea in an article appearing in the winter 1945–46 edition of *Foreign Affairs* and raised it again in a speech to a New York audience that February. Expanding the concept, St. Laurent called for "cooperative measures within the United Nations for development of economic and communications resources of the northern territories."[6] These efforts proved futile. Apart from Soviet lack of interest, public disclosure of the Gouzenko affair in March 1946 had the effect of hardening American opinion against any free exchange of scientific information.

Even before the war ended, the military chiefs of staff of both countries had declared that adequate defence of northern Canada was crucial to the security of North America and could only be accomplished jointly. The implied alternative was that if required to do so, the United States would undertake this responsibility independently by right of the Monroe Doctrine. Although fears of American intentions are often dismissed as unjustified, this contingency plan was indeed a part of American defence policy. As outlined in an USAAF intelligence report, "if the American Government had good reason to believe that invasion or occupation of the Canadian Arctic by a foreign nation were imminent, it would be justified in taking suitable counter measures, with or without Dominion consent." The report did emphasize, however, that such action would be politically unwise unless the situation was critical.[7] (See appendix G.)

The prospect of shared responsibility for security of the Canadian north also resurrected the sensitive question of Arctic sovereignty. In John Holmes's words, "the Arctic frontier posed squarely for Canadians the double edge of defence policy. They had to defend themselves on another plane against their defenders."[8] But he also claimed that there was no conscious policy favouring continentalism, that "history did not make the United States and Canada friends; it made them natural antagonists and they remained antagonists from the eighteenth to the twentieth century. It took the Germans and then the Russians to make them allies."[9] From this perspective, one could argue that it was merely circumstances in Europe and Asia that forced Ottawa to accept continental defence, rather than any natural affinity.

The demands on Canadian diplomats were unprecedented during the late war and early postwar period, with seemingly formidable challenges if Canada was to maintain its posture as an independent nation. To one observer, dealing with the British was akin to a fencing match, but with the Americans it was a "new and exhilarating game of one-upmanship and teammanship."[10] The stakes, however, were high, and emotions were often strained. As a consequence, attitudes towards the Americans fluctuated, yet the British Foreign Office caused equal frustration with its imperial mind-set. During the war years, Malcolm MacDonald had successfully played the role of mediator by constantly warning London of Canada's sensitivity to lack of consultation and heavy-handedness, while at the same time soothing the ruffled feathers caused by inappropriate British remarks and actions. Even then, there appeared to be increasing tension: the British believing Canadians were oversensitive and petty, the Canadians viewing the British as arrogant, demanding, and presumptuous. Thus, it was no great surprise in the spring of 1944 that Canada refused to make a commitment to a proposed imperial defence alliance.[11] By the end of the war, it was too late. American courtship of the Canadian military was in full swing, and Ottawa could not afford to be considered a junior partner in any imperial defence scheme if diplomatic negotiations on continental defence were to be conducted on a bilateral plane.[12] Once again Canada was the source of Anglo-American rivalry, although Ottawa hoped to gain some flexibility and independence in the process. Ultimately, geopolitical considerations won out over traditional loyalties.

In the postwar period, the traditional fear of American encroachment increased and decreased in an inverse relationship to the perceived threat of Soviet aggression. When the need for security against an alien aggressor became paramount, the objective to guarantee sovereign rights was superseded, a pattern which had precedent in the war years. And as northern sovereignty declined as a priority, so did efforts to promote northern development. As Trevor Lloyd reported in 1947, "it is now clear to all that the future of the north is inextricably bound up with Canada's foreign relations."[13] As a result, there emerged three distinct components to Canada's northern policy: two external, relating to the issues of security and sovereignty, and one internal, the desire to assert effective governance. The aims of the latter generally complemented sovereignty objectives, but both would inevitably collide with American defence plans.

II

During the immediate postwar period, the internal and external components of northern policy were still quite distinct. Domestic policy, which was influenced in part by considerations of sovereignty, was also governed by a number of other factors. Increased population in the northern territories demanded more social services, which in turn required changes in administrative structures, a vast increase in federal expenditure, and unprecedented government intervention. The call for a new approach to northern government also corresponded to the mood of the country. According to a Wartime Information Board survey, two out of three Canadians desired more government economic planning and increased social services.[14] Public support for increased territorial expenditures was greatly facilitated by enthusiastic media coverage, but the commitment to take positive action came from the "intellectual elite" within government.

The first major impetus to reform was provided by the new social welfare programmes promoted in the 1945 election campaign. As parliamentary secretary to the prime minister, Brooke Claxton was assigned the task of investigating the costs, benefits, and means of introducing the various pension, health, and family allowance schemes.[15] His subsequent appointment as the first minister of national health and welfare in October 1945 allowed him to participate actively in adapting the reforms to the needs of the northern territories. It was at his insistence that the same benefits provided to non-native Canadians should be equally available to the indigenous people, especially those in the more remote regions where the need was the greatest.

Respected by most of his peers as an ambitious, hardworking politician, Claxton was described by Mackenzie King as "a reformer and real intellectual," and by C. D. Howe as a tactician whose "mind operates on a lofty plane."[16] The *Monetary Times* on 1 September 1943 characterized him as belonging to "that group in Canada's parliament known as the intelligentsia" and as having "earned the reputation of being the foremost internationalist in Ottawa." Raleigh Parkin, who considered him a "best friend" claimed that he had "a wide interest in international affairs and a broad progressive view towards all Canadian questions."[17] Heeney admired "his immense vitality, his knowledge of, and concern for, all areas of public affairs."[18] Although Claxton's interest in the north was likely aroused through discussion with close friends and associates, Parkin and Heeney in particular, his commitment to rectifying the problems encountered by the native peoples was in keeping with his personal convictions and social idealism.

If Canadians at large believed that the federal government should assume more responsibility for the health and welfare of the nation, nowhere was the need greater than in the remote regions of the territories (see figure 16). Before the creation of the new ministry, both Keenleyside and Foster had urged immediate government action to provide increased medical care, a plea fully supported by the various privately funded studies. Others also called for changes; a few were firmly opposed. In the fall of 1944, the Anglican Church

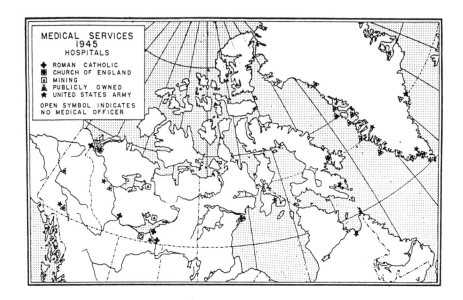

Figure 16 Hospital Services in the Yukon and NWT, 1945 (from Trevor Lloyd, *The Geography and Administration of Northern Canada,* chapter 6)

denounced Ottawa's handling of native health care and suggested that all hospitals should be operated by the government.[19] About the same time, the CSSRC report on health services in the Mackenzie Valley was distributed and discussed in Ottawa, giving rise to speculation of imminent reorganization of territorial medical services.[20] The rumours prompted a formal protest by the Indian Affairs Branch to the Prime Minister's Office opposing any suggestion of transferring the responsibility for Indian welfare to another department. Similarly concerned about outside intervention, the Catholic Church also submitted a petition defending their role as guardians of native health and education. As noted by Jack Pickersgill in a memo to the prime minister, the whole question of northern health care was becoming a "touchy subject," which could be discussed more freely once jurisdiction was removed from the Department of Mines and Resources.[21]

Reorganization finally took place on 12 October 1945, at which time the responsibility for medical care, hospitalization, and welfare programmes for all Inuit and Indians was transferred to the new ministry of National Health and Welfare. In a speech delivered a fortnight later, Claxton announced with enthusiasm that "there never has been a time when people are so keenly interested in seeing that the benefits hitherto available only in certain places and to certain people shall be available to everyone everywhere."[22] A report in the *Ottawa Journal* on 19 November 1945 described the transfer as indicative of "the emergence of a growing social consciousness" among Canadians. Certainly Claxton's own concern for the native population in Canada encompassed far more than medical considerations. At a later hearing of the Special Joint Committee of the Senate and House of Commons appointed to examine and consider the Indian Act, he took a strong stand in favour of providing all Indians with the "full opportunity for economic development" and "the attainment of an adequate educational standard."[23]

As a matter of first priority, Claxton attempted to regularize the distribution of family allowances among the Indians and Inuit of the northern territories. Because of the need to correlate payments with an accurate census, the RCMP were given the task of registration, with the Bureau of the Northwest Territories and Yukon Affairs responsible for the actual distribution of payments. "White" northerners would receive cash payments, but the allowances for the indigenous peoples were to be paid in specified goods that would be of direct benefit to the children. This policy was justified on the grounds that "the geographical, sociological and economic conditions prevailing in the far north prohibited the issue of this allowance in the form of cash or cheques."[24] In the Yukon, however, there was confusion as to whether the mixed bloods should receive cash or goods in kind. It was eventually established that cash payment would be granted to those "living the life of Whites," whereas specified goods were to be distributed among the "Nomads." No payment would be made for children attending residential schools.[25] These regulations might be considered both racist and paternalistic, but the distribution of family allowances among the northern natives was only a first step in the overall objective to offer benefits and services in the north equal to those available in the south.

Important advances were also made in the expansion of medical services. Once granted the jurisdiction, Claxton quickly set about initiating new programmes and improved facilities for native health in the north: extensive TB surveys, increased nursing aid, training for native assistants, improved hospital facilities, and new studies into special conditions related to the north.[26] When Claxton announced the proposal to build new government-owned hospitals, as expected, the only opposition came from the Catholic Church, which feared the loss of federal subsidies it needed to operate its missions. Although they were not critical of the new initiative, the reaction of the northern administration was quite predictable. In a somewhat apologetic letter to Dr. Brock Chisholm, the new deputy minister of national health and welfare in March 1946, Roy Gibson claimed that his administration had attempted to provide adequate services but was thwarted by insufficient funds during the Depression and war years. His recommendations for greater government assistance and the extensive list of urgently needed facilities might have signified a sudden change of heart, had he not concluded the report with a reminder that the proposed increased expenditures would now be the responsibility of another department.[27]

Aside from increased health care and welfare assistance, other northern policy reforms were considered, but few were implemented. Some concern was expressed for the future role of the Inuit in the anticipated development of the "new north," with most of the discussion centring in and around the Privy Council Office. A report on possible postwar use of airports was sent to Arnold Heeney, proposing the utilization of the wartime air bases as scientific and social study centres. It was argued that an Inuk was fully capable of participating in the development of the eastern Arctic, but as a first step "it will be necessary for him to receive education in those fields which will best enable him to fit into a new world order."[28] The proposal was received with interest, but no action was forthcoming.

The problem of the increasing destitution among the Inuit of the eastern Arctic was also a topic of frequent debate. Relief payments were not generous, and they were granted only to those who were unable to hunt or whose families could not provide aid.[29] The family allowances provided some relief, but other forms of assistance would be required to prevent annihilation of the Inuit through disease and social disruption. The cyclic and declining fur trade offered little security for their future. Yet despite thoughtful discussion, there was no apparent consensus on what would be an appropriate economic base for twentieth-century Inuit society.

III

Prior to the 1945 election, T. A. Crerar retired as minister of mines and resources. Replacing him was James Glen, former Speaker of the House and fellow westerner from Winnipeg. If the northern promoters had anticipated new progressive ideas and leadership, they were profoundly disappointed. Initially, Glen's rhetorical speeches were almost identical to those of his deputy minister, Charles Camsell. The recurrent theme was one of northern exploitation for southern benefit. In his home constituency, Glen announced support for the expansion of northern resource industries as a means of increasing the nation's exports and creating new markets for southern manufacturers. He also spoke of a "northern empire."

> We also have our own interests to serve in the development of great areas like the Canadian Northwest, in providing employment for returning veterans and displaced war workers, and in combating inflation. The Dominion Government is fully seized of the import of what is transpiring. In my

own administrative sphere every measure necessary will be taken to further the speedy and orderly development of the treasures of our northern empire.[30]

Some of the phrases so closely resembled those in Camsell's articles published in 1944 and 1946, that one might suspect either that they were written by the deputy minister or that they both employed the same speech writer. Presumably Glen was attempting to appeal to a southern audience, but the new minister appeared profoundly out of step with the more socially conscious intellectuals in the civil service.

The objectives of the department's policies were clearly reflected in the allocation of the budget increases from 1945 to 1947. Capital expenditures by the northern administration grew by over $1.5 million as part of the government's overall reconstruction programme. The funds were applied to public works, construction of administration buildings, and assistance to the Canadian-owned mining industry. Significantly, no new educational or medical facilities were included in the appropriations.[31] New developments announced by Glen included approval of the Snare River Hydro Project to supply the Yellowknife gold mines, a survey to investigate the commercial potential of the fishery industry, agreement to proceed with all-weather construction on the Grimshaw–Hay River winter road, and creation of a Forest and Wildlife Protection Service in the Mackenzie District, primarily aimed at the prevention and control of forest fires.[32] Despite the increase in funds, the department had adopted the traditional approach to northern development by providing government support for private industries. In economic terms, the programme was sound. For those advocating drastic changes in northern policy, there was little to celebrate.

The North Pacific Planning Project, which was to have given new direction to development of the northwest, was finally completed in 1947, with no mention of Canadian-American integration in the final report. The one small section devoted to the native population included recommendations for improved health and education facilities, but other than a reference to employment opportunities, the social aspects covered by the study were extremely superficial. The focus was unquestionably on economic and settlement potential, with specific attention to the areas adjacent to the Alaska Highway and the Canol pipeline. The major emphasis centred on the mining industry and related services such as the development of waterpower resources, improved road and water transportation facilities, and the expansion of civilian aviation. Other industries included fisheries, agriculture, and forestry. Glaring in their omission were the lack of criticism of the existing administration or any suggestions of constitutional changes required to accommodate future growth and development.[33]

The thrust of the report certainly showed Camsell's influence, but his direct involvement in the publication appeared negligible. The "Foreword" acknowledged that the investigations had been planned by his assistant, R. K. Odell, and that the published report titled *Canada's New Northwest* had been written by M. W. Maxwell, an industrial engineer employed by Canadian National Railways.[34] Of curious note were the two short paragraphs on native education in the conclusion that appear strangely uncharacteristic of a deputy minister who had ignored the problem for over ten years and refused to admit the Métis connection in his own family. Referring to the fact that the existing system fostered ambitions "to adopt the white man's manners and customs," which ultimately created frustration and the "loss of the dignity of race and the native pride," the report went on to describe plans for the future.

> The educational system in the northern territories that are under Dominion administration is being reviewed with a view to the establishment of suitable, specially equipped schools under direct Government control with a curriculum better suited to the practical needs of the native population. This plan is primarily directed to the preservation and development of the native culture to the end that these Canadians of the Northland, proud of their race and ancestry, no longer wards of the State, may become upstanding citizens of the Dominion of Canada.[35]

These two atypical paragraphs suggest the fine hand of the new deputy minister, appointed in January 1947, whose first objective upon assuming office was to improve native education. Camsell retired at the age of seventy and began to write his memoirs. Published eight years later, *Son of the North* focuses entirely on stories of his youth and his explorations with the Geological Survey. Only in the last five pages is there a very perfunctory description of his twenty-eight-odd years as deputy minister. Significantly, there is no mention of his involvement in the North Pacific Planning Project that was to provide guidelines for the future development of the "New Northwest."[36] Considering the enthusiastic promotion of the study and the supposed effort that was put into compiling the research, the published version certainly failed to meet expectations.

IV

The question of constitutional changes in northern government was raised again in January 1946, this time by the prime minister himself. King's sudden personal interest in the subject may have been prompted by a letter re-

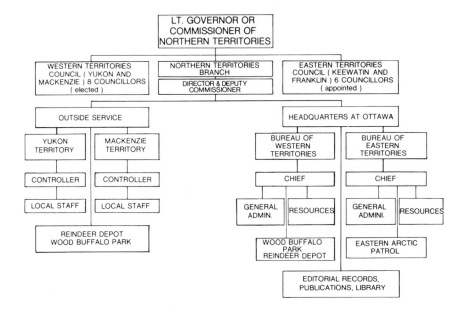

Figure 17 Camsell's Plan for Territorial Government, 1946 (from NAC, RG 2/18, vol. 57, file A-25-3 [pt. 1])

ceived from the Labour Progressive party of Yellowknife. The preamble included a particularly emotional plea:

> In 1827 [*sic* 1837] your Great-Grandfather [*sic* Grandfather] led an uprising because of the fact there was taxation without representation. We in 1945 are crusading for the same principles fought for by our Fathers of Confederation. . . . Should we forget that principle for which your Great-Grandfather fought, and remain in a status of virtual dictatorship when we know that we are eligible for representation under Canadian Democracy, if not under its constitution? Therefore, we press for rapid legislation to bring about representation in the Federal House.[37]

The Mackenzie District did in fact receive representation in Parliament in 1947, but Yellowknife's demand for a fully elected local trustee board was deferred.

For whatever reason, Mackenzie King chose to bypass the minister responsible and consult directly with his deputy concerning possible restructuring of the territorial government. In response, Camsell provided an outline of suggested constitutional and administrative reforms (see figure 17). One fundamental change was the designation of an appointed lieutenant-governor or commissioner to preside over two new territorial councils, one elected and one appointed, but there was no recommendation that increased authority be granted to the councils. The new "Western Territories Council" would be comprised of eight elected members from the Yukon and the Mackenzie District. The "Eastern Territories Council" would have six appointed members representing the Keewatin and Franklin Districts. A deputy commissioner would remain in charge of the civil servants, employed locally or in Ottawa. Admittedly, the proposed structure would have eliminated the pressure of departmental responsibilities that plagued Camsell and his deputy, but it did little to advance self-government in the territories. The Mackenzie District would be incorporated into the existing Yukon political structure but with separate local administrations which still came under direct control from Ottawa.[38] Six months earlier, Camsell had written the prime minister requesting "early" retirement from the responsibilities of deputy minister, yet expressing the wish to remain on as commissioner of the Northwest Territories since, in his opinion, there was "no one capable in the Department" to assume the position. Someone must have convinced him otherwise, for when he submitted his proposal he cited ill health and requested full retirement from government service.[39]

On 1 March 1946, James Glen submitted a formal document to Cabinet, with two alternative proposals. One incorporated most of Camsell's suggestions; the other gave the Mackenzie District the "same government as the Yukon," with the remaining territory governed by the existing Northwest Territories Council. These councils would still be under the jurisdiction of an appointed lieutenant-governor or commissioner, who would not sit on the Yukon or Mackenzie councils, but who would have the right to approve or reject bills passed by them. Significantly, there was still no separation of legislative and administrative functions, and the federal government still retained full authority over the natural resources of the entire north. Glen rejected any increase in the Yukon council's legislative authority, for the stated reason that there simply had been "no demand in the Yukon for greater autonomy." Given Yellowknife's agitation for more self-government, the choice of Fort Smith or Fort Simpson as proposed sites for the Mackenzie administrative unit and seat of government seemed somewhat retaliatory.[40]

There were a number of other proposals. W. E. D. Halliday, now assistant secretary to the Privy Council Office, questioned the legality of a lieutenant-governor having administrative powers and the lack of a residency requirement for the appointed deputy commissioner. As an alternative, he suggested the appointment of a "resident minister," who, as in the British system, would sit in Parliament but not as a member of the Cabinet. The acting special commissioner opposed any attempt to integrate the Yukon and Mackenzie District because of the diversity of geography, interests, and composition of their respective populations.[41] In April, Meredith Glassco of the Privy Council Office submitted an historical analysis on the evolution of government in the Northwest Territories, claiming that "the government of the Northwest Territories provides a clear example of the negation of the federal theory and the principle of the separation of powers." He ended his report on a derisive note, stating that "though we profess democracy, and claim that Canada is a democratic country, the government of the Northwest Territories, far from being responsible or representative in character, is decidedly autocratic."[42]

After further study and debate, the proposed constitutional changes were again discussed by Cabinet on 21 March 1946, but the question was once more deferred.[43] The major flaws in the existing system were duly recognized as was the need for a major overhaul of the constitution, but lack of consensus created a stalemate. Furthermore, there was no known candidate at the time with the leadership qualities required to direct and implement new policies. The subsequent constitutional changes in 1946 were minimal: a slightly expanded Yellowknife Trustee board with its chairman and the majority of members still appointed, and the addition to the Northwest Territories Council of a local resident to be selected at the discretion of the minister of mines and resources. While offering token representation, these changes did not advance responsible government or reform the administration. In fact, local pressure for more self-government seemed singularly ineffective in altering Ottawa's determination to maintain tight control over a region of potential value to the south.

In the immediate postwar years, the consequences of the increasing external influences on Ottawa's northern policy became clearer. Internationally related matters such as military, trade, judicial, economic, communication, or transportation issues were now directly influenced by decisions of the Privy Council Office, External Affairs, and ultimately the Cabinet. Sometimes "recommendations" were brought to the council for approval; other times the council was merely consulted and then notified of Ottawa's decision. Despite the new token representation, the federal government began to exert greater overall control through direct intervention and investment. Ironically, it was quite similar to the strategy used by the United States during the war in expectation of rights and advantages, and similarly justified in traditionally imperialist terms: necessity, benevolence, and the "white man's burden." Ottawa, however, possessed the constitutional right.

The arguments advanced for increased federal intervention in the north were logical and compelling, but often quite contradictory. Maxwell Dunbar claimed that some Canadians "revel in a dream of the romantic north, read books about it and hear lectures," while others took "the pessimistic view that northern Canada will never amount to anything, romantic or not."[44] There were equally conflicting objectives and priorities among those departments involved. As a consequence, there was no unified effort to promote development. On the civilian front, those who proposed agricultural development or secondary industry were at cross-purposes with the new transportation companies which sought to increase the importation of southern produce and manufactured goods.[45] Even the military were divided on priority of need. The Army requested ground research stations; the Air Force demanded more meteorological studies, radar, and weather stations to support the new air routes; the Navy and the Coast Guard wanted icebreakers. A more direct conflict was apparent between the military and civilian departments. When J. Tuzo Wilson of National Defence Headquarters requested permission to build permanent scientific stations in the Arctic with the co-operation of the National Research Council,[46] the deputy commissioner rejected the idea out of hand, claiming that the Department of Mines and Resources was already conducting scientific studies. In a memo to his superior, Gibson defended his decision on the grounds that the future economy depended on mining development; thus, it was important "to make it known as quickly as possible that aside from this possibility, there is little opportunity for the accommodation and sustenance of additional population in these areas."[47] There seemed to be only two issues capable of neutralizing opposing interests: the old shibboleth of "Arctic sovereignty," which had served to arouse Ottawa from frequent bouts of lethargy in the past, and the more recent concern for national security. In 1946, both demanded priority attention.

V

Despite the belief that the agreements of 1944 had successfully deterred American plans to pursue postwar advantages in the north, the problem was far from resolved. As early as April 1944, Major-General Maurice Pope, who sat on the Permanent Joint Board on Defence, warned that there would be pressure to renew the wartime Cooperative Defence Plan, ABC 22. While he believed that some agreement was necessary, he also argued that "what we have to fear most is a lack of confidence in the United States as to our security, rather than enemy action."[48] Although Pope may have been motivated by hopes of preventing major demobilization of the armed forces at the end of the war, the statement was both perceptive and accurate.

In May 1944, the Working Committee on Post War Hostilities Problems met to devise a plan for Canada's future defence policy. From a military perspective, the world had changed dramatically since the outset of the war. Not only was Canada's northern boundary now vulnerable to attack, but the proposed development of commercial air routes passing over Canada to connect the United States to Europe and Asia also provided access routes for an enemy attack against the United States.[49] In February 1945, the working committee submitted a final draft of a position paper to the Cabinet War Committee that dealt with possible postwar defence relationships with the United States. The basic concept of joint co-operation was approved in principle that July, after External Affairs recommended peacetime extension of mutual defence as long as all military facilities in Canada and Newfoundland were effectively under Ottawa's control.[50] At that time, there was still optimism that dependency on the American military would gradually diminish as the newly created United Nations assumed its role as guardian of world peace. Unfortunately, security problems increased rather than decreased as the postwar scene unfolded to reveal the Soviet Union and the United States as the major competitors for economic, military, and ideological dominance. As a result, Washington began to exert even greater pressure for continental integration of military forces.

Quite apart from the issue of joint defence, the question of continued economic integration was also raised before the end of the war. At the request of "free trader" Will Clayton,[51] the United States ambassador, Ray Atherton, requested an extension of the Hyde Park principle into the postwar period. Knowing full well that the prime minister, the under-secretary of state, and other key officials were in San Francisco for the United Nations negotiations, Atherton requested an immediate reply from those left in charge in Ottawa. Although C. D. Howe advised the prime minister by telegram, he did not wait for approval but verbally gave official assent to the extension, which provided for similar reciprocal arrangements into the postwar period. The wording clearly stated that Canada would be considered "as within the domestic area."[52] Compared to the consequences of the original pact in 1941, however, the impact was minimal. As stated by one observer, "without a common enemy, the raison d'etre of 'integration' vanished. If there was to be an integrated continental economy in peacetime, it would have to be on the basis of a new philosophy for which neither side was prepared in 1945."[53] Furthermore, there was less advantage for the United States now that Canada's deficit in its trade balance was steadily increasing.[54]

The uranium issue also resurfaced in relation to proposals for a peacetime extension of the Quebec Agreement. The high-level meetings held in Washington from 8–17 November 1945 produced two documents: a public declaration and private minute. The former, known as the Washington Declaration and signed by Truman, Attlee, and King, announced their intentions to share knowledge of atomic energy for peaceful purposes with the commitment to prevent the use of nuclear fission for destructive purposes. It also called for the creation of a commission under the United Nations to control and monitor the application of atomic energy. Canada was directly involved with the discussions and drafting of the declaration, but it was intentionally excluded from negotiations leading to the second document, which extended the mandate of the Combined Policy Committee for the joint control and accumulation of uranium production. The slightly revised agreement was entirely the work of British and American delegates led by Sir John Anderson and General Groves. At these meetings, the only representation of Canadian interests was indirectly through Malcolm MacDonald. It had been agreed that C. J. Mackenzie might sit in on some of the discussions, but when it was finally considered appropriate, the document had been finalized and already signed by Anderson and Groves. When Howe was handed the agreement for his signature, he refused to do so without further study and discussion with Mackenzie King. At that point, it was reported by a member of the British delegation that it was abundantly clear to Howe that they did "not attach enormous importance to a Canadian signature."[55] Once Canada's uranium had been secured and the Belgian Congo mine reopened, the junior partner in the tripartite agreement was expected to be seen and not heard.

The fall of 1945 saw increasing pressure from both Britain and the United States for Canada's agreement to participate in either an imperial or continental defence alliance. Another one of Malcolm MacDonald's infamous reports alerted the Dominions Office and the British minister of defence to American attempts to "secure certain defensive arrangements with Canada." From a lengthy conversation with Air Marshal Robert Leckie, MacDonald discovered that United States Ambassador Ray Atherton and the deputy chief of staff of the USAAF had called an informal meeting to discuss how the defence of North America could be "treated as a unified whole" that included an enticing offer to supply the RCAF with whatever aircraft and supplies they might need. Similar offers were suggested by General Guy Henry at sessions of the Permanent Joint Board on Defence and by junior officials at social events held at the United States embassy. Leckie believed that the ideas were not simply those of the officers, but "a plan by which the U.S. would in effect absorb Canada for purposes of defence," both conceived and pressed by "very high authorities in Washington"[56] (see appendix D).

The British chiefs of staff and defence minister were duly alarmed, particularly in light of Canada's continued refusal to commit to an imperial defence alliance. Recognizing Canada's primary importance in any such plan, the ministry of defence recommended placing "all our cards on the table with the Canadian government" to convince them that their participation in a Commonwealth defence scheme was crucial to Britain's security.[57] Agreement was not forthcoming, and in June 1946 Clement Attlee finally conceded the logic of Mackenzie King's argument "that collaboration between the U.K. and Canada on military matters would have to take into account the necessity for close collaboration between the U.S. and Canada."[58] When negotiating with the Americans, Ottawa reversed the argument by declaring that any agreement on continental defence would have to take into consideration responsibilities to the Commonwealth. In retrospect, it would seem to be more than simply a delaying tactic; rather, it was a determined attempt to maintain optimum independence and power in negotiating a defence agreement with the Americans.

The Permanent Joint Board on Defence continued to advise on proposed plans for North American defence. Arnold Heeney's attempts to decrease the military representation on the board failed against firm opposition by the American military representatives supported by Jack Hickerson and Graham Parsons of the State Department.[59] Subsequently, the appointment of General A. G. L. McNaughton to succeed Colonel O. M. Biggar as the Canadian chairman delighted officials in the State Department, who believed he was "very pro-U.S."[60] but it greatly troubled Malcolm MacDonald, who saw his attitude as more "unfriendliness towards the War Office."[61] When overseas, McNaughton had been so antagonistic towards the British military that he was reported to have prompted a retort from Eisenhower, "Remember General, we are fighting the Germans, not the British."[62] Over time, however, McNaughton proved to be a formidable negotiator and defender of his country's interests.[63] This was particularly crucial for Canada because of the extremely powerful role of the PJBD during the postwar period, so much so that United States military historian Colonel S. W. Dzuiban contended that at times it extended beyond the function of an advisory committee to become synonymous with an "executive agency."[64]

McNaughton's first challenge after assuming the chairmanship was to parry the American proposal for complete uniformity of dress, equipment, and training of the two armed forces. He agreed that there were advantages in having standardized equipment and training procedures, but only on the condition that Britain and other Commonwealth members agreed.[65] According to Arthur Schlesinger, Jr., President Truman's proposal to extend military standardization throughout the hemisphere was directed towards the goal of "ultimately producing an inter-American army under the United States generalship," a goal that was shared by senior members of the Army Air Force and the State Department.[66] In the short term, the plan was thwarted by McNaughton's insistence that since Canada was a Commonwealth country, standardization would have to include Britain and others. Skilful negotiations would be required to retain any degree of independence and control in the proposed joint defence plans.

Meanwhile, pressure was building from another quarter. On 21 March 1945, Senator Owen Brewster from Maine introduced a bill in the Senate to authorize the construction of joint Canadian-American weather stations throughout the entire Arctic. The plan was reported to have originated in the United States Weather Bureau and apparently had the approval of Canada's Inter-departmental Meteorological Committee.[67] The bill, which received final approval by Congress on 12 February 1946, authorized the weather bureau to "take such actions as may be necessary in the development of an international basic meteorological reporting network in the Arctic region of the Western hemisphere, including the establishment, operation, and maintenance of such reporting stations in cooperation with... foreign countries." Although the proposal appeared to have originated from the civilian agency, the government's *Editorial Research Reports* noted that the weather stations were "coordinate with Washington's plans for joint defence in the Arctic."[68] As events unfolded, Ottawa would finally agree to construction of the weather stations as a military necessity, but it was to the advantage of both countries that the project be carried out for civilian purposes to avoid condemnation by Congress, Parliament, and the world at large (see figure 18).

In some circles, it was thought that the secret code name for the weather station project was "Arctops," although American military historians suggest that the term was coined from 'arctic topography' and included the weather stations as part of a broader objective encompassing all aspects of Arctic research.[69] Both explanations contain truth.

The actual "Arctops Project" was designed during the early war years at the Massachusetts Institute of Technology for the Research Board for National Security and included the weather stations as an integral component of an extensive Arctic research programme carried out at bases located at Fort Chimo, Frobisher, and Padloping Island, in Canada, and Sondre Stromfjiord and Angmassalik in Greenland. The code names were Crystal 1, Crystal 2, Crystal 3, Bluie West 8, and Bluie East 2 respectively. This research was conducted by the USAAF beginning in 1941 and was the basis upon which the plans for a massive network of weather and radio communication stations were proposed first in 1942 and again in 1946. The initiative came from the American Air Force, but the U.S. Weather Bureau provided an effective civilian cover after the war. A later report by the director of intelligence for the United States Army described the meteorological posts as integral to a joint intelligence plan to collect comprehensive information on the Arctic regions and their potential resources. Aside from weather observations, there would be extensive mapping and aerial photography, experimentation with communications and radar technology, and scientific studies into Arctic conditions and resources.[70]

On 7 November 1945, the Permanent Joint Board on Defence met to con-

Arctic Region Now Dotted
With Nations' Weather Stations

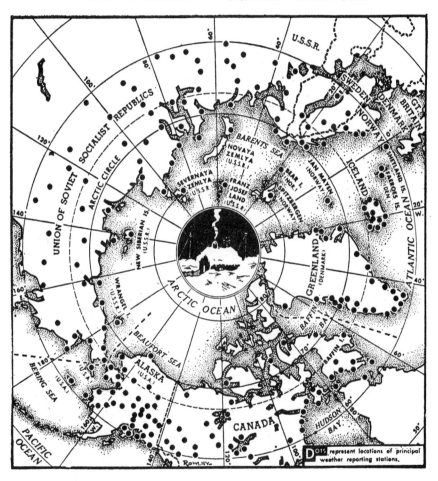

Figure 18 Weather Stations in the Circumpolar North, *Globe and Mail*, 5 January 1946. Many Canadian stations were set up simply to observe and record weather data and were often operated by the RCMP or trading post staff. Those built by the Americans during the war had additional air communications and radar equipment. Those proposed in 1946 were estimated to cost $200,000 each.

sider specific proposals put forward by the secretaries of the United States Army and Navy for the security of Alaska, Canada, Labrador, Newfoundland, and the northern portion of the United States. It is significant to note that "joint co-operation" did not mean participation in American plans for defence of the remainder of the continent. At that time, the Cabinet Defence Committee agreed to proceed with further planning discussions based on the need for more precise details of the American plans.[71] In January of the next year, a memo from the PJBD describing the measures and general principles to be incorporated into the new "Joint Security Plan" was presented to Cabinet. Instead of the expected working paper on procedures, the proposal took "the form of a basic security pact and contained a statement of fundamental military obligations." Arnold Heeney cautioned against the speed with which the plans were taking shape and recommended "that appropriate steps be taken to defer action by the two governments on the Board's recommendations, on the grounds that in their present form they are inappropriate and premature." Heeney also reiterated that any joint security plan must be considered in relation to Canada's commitments to the Commonwealth and the United Nations.[72]

In the spring of 1946, the Americans put forward numerous requests for extension of the wartime projects and the initiation of new schemes which included a new chain of Loran stations, more reconnaissance flights and naval operations, expansion and continued operation of the Arctic airfields, and additional weather stations.[73] Ottawa's response was increasingly more cautious. Then in May, the Canadian secretary of the PJBD passed on the disconcerting news that the Air Coordinating Committee had just announced its intent to probe unexplored regions of the Arctic Archipelago in hopes of finding undiscovered islands to claim for air bases.[74] Tired and frustrated, the prime minister again voiced serious doubts about American intentions. At a cabinet meeting on 9 May 1946, he warned that "the long range policy of the Americans is to absorb Canada. They would seek to get this hemisphere as completely one as possible. They are already in one way or another building up military strength in the North of Canada. . . . It might be inevitable for us to have to submit to it."[75] King's suspicions were further heightened when he received a letter from his acting minister of national defence, informing him that the Americans had no intentions of withdrawing from Goose Bay, Fort Chimo, and Frobisher Bay as previously agreed and that it appeared likely that they would ask for additional air bases.[76]

On the recommendation of the Chiefs of Staff Committee, the responsibility for negotiating mutual defence plans was removed from the PJBD by the creation of the Canada–United States Military Cooperation Committee (MCC), which was composed primarily of the board's military members. This move eliminated A. G. L. McNaughton from the process, but according to documents now available, it did not restrict involvement of the State Department. During this period, the American secretary of the PJBD was in possession of unusually detailed information which included documents describing the composition and organization of the Canadian armed forces; details of all command units, size, location, and equipment inventory; as well as in-depth assessments of communications, research, and training establishments. He had also received photo surveys of the Canadian north, maps of air bases and weather stations, details of projects, including bacteriological warfare investigations, and a map entitled "Plan for Post War RCAF, 1 March 1946" that was marked "secret" and listed the purpose and troop posting at every airdrome across Canada. Related correspondence indicated that the American secretary also had inside knowledge of the committee's progress and that he relayed that information to his superiors.[77]

At the first meeting held in May 1946, the Military Cooperation Committee approved two significant documents prepared by the American military strategists. The first outlined the necessity of a joint defence plan; the second detailed a proposed security scheme, which included an extensive radar system across northern Canada, an expanded network of air bases, interceptor aircraft, and anti-aircraft defences. Phase II proposed setting up a "Combined Air Defence Headquarters with operational control of all continental air defense forces."[78] The plan was much more extensive than any of the wartime projects and ultimately involved much greater expenditure and manpower. Moreover, it was designed to be permanent.

Not unexpectedly, the proposal aroused strong opposition in Ottawa. The Cabinet Defence Committee rejected the Basic Security Plan as having too much of a bilateral emphasis and at the same time announced deferral of an American request to begin the weather station programme with a base on Melville Island.[79] The latter decision suggests that Ottawa may have been aware that Melville Island was listed in United States intelligence reports as a possible choice for takeover within the legal rights of international law because it was uninhabited and not part of any routine RCMP patrol.[80] Both decisions were strongly supported by the Canadian media. In the *Financial Post* of 29 July 1946, "Ottawa Scotches U.S. Plan to Man Weather Bases in the Canadian Arctic" described how an American expedition had proceeded without any prior approval from Ottawa and was waiting to leave Boston Harbor with ships fully loaded, when news was received that permission had been denied. Equally critical of American pressure was an article denouncing the proposed security measures, "Canada Another Belgium in U.S. Air Bases Proposal."[81] References to a "Maginot Line" and comparison to Belgium in World War II were repeated in newspapers and speeches throughout the summer and fall.

Meanwhile, Ottawa appeared to be playing for time. Although the principle of mutual defence appeared inevitable from a geopolitical perspective, the specific proposals demanded an enormous financial expenditure as well as a permanent commitment and dependency. Cabinet had hoped to defer consideration of the Basic Security Plan for a year in an effort to slow the American momentum,[82] but the United States military continued to push ahead with their plans. After erecting a new weather station in Greenland, they requested the reopening of the facilities at Mingan, Fort Chimo, Frobisher, Cape Harrison, and Mecatina. In most cases, the military were on site before approval had been granted.[83] Similarly, preparations for the winter training of troops at Churchill were well underway before plans for the joint services experimental station were submitted to the PJBD.[84]

The question of Arctic sovereignty was not taken lightly, especially in light of the reported search for undiscovered islands in the Archipelago. The legal division of External Affairs advised against any public assertion of claims lest it imply doubts as to their validity, a position which was endorsed emphatically by Hume Wrong.[85] From the Department of National Defence, General D.C. Spry's assessment was equally alarming.

> In the case of the Canadian Arctic, definite sovereignty is asserted in the right of Canada, over all known land masses and islands within the "Canadian Sector" of the Arctic. However these claims are largely based either on contiguity to continental Canada, or on original discovery and exploration, (principally by British explorers). Due to the desolate nature of the areas in question, these claims have little support on the grounds of effective occupation, settlement or development. Thus, while Canada's claims to sovereignty over these regions have not heretofore been seriously challenged, they are at the best somewhat tenuous and weak.[86]

A number of ideas on how to reinforce Canadian claims were advanced, ranging from Norman Robertson's recommendation to increase the number of RCMP posts in the remote areas[87] to Pearson's suggestion that Washington might agree to recognize the sector theory in return for Canada's approval of the security plan.[88] None carried any guarantee of success. Although general agreements had not prevented American encroachment in the past, the only apparent solution in 1946 was to try to work out some sort of accord which included American recognition of Canadian sovereignty.

V

The Canadian strategy of deferment met with only partial success. Realizing that pressure tactics were not accomplishing the desired results, the

American military began reassessing their needs and alternatives. Canadian consent was crucial to overall American defence strategy, which also included establishing a large offensive unit at Goose Bay as well as in Alaska and northern Greenland. If they were unable to obtain rights from Denmark, it would be "necessary to ask for joint base rights in Baffin Island or other northern Canadian territory." The USAAF also planned to use the three wartime staging routes and believed that the resulting traffic would "probably be sufficiently heavy to require small detachments of the AAF at certain Canadian air fields along the routes in question." Equally important was the provision of supportive services such as weather stations, radio communications and radar detection. In an internal document sent to Graham Parsons of the State Department, now American secretary of the PJBD, Major General Henry outlined these considerations as well as the fears responsible for Canadian resistance: unaffordable costs, loss of sovereignty, anticipated adverse public opinion, conflicting loyalties to the Commonwealth, and the prospect of becoming another Belgium. In Henry's view, "Canadian public opinion must be convinced of a potential threat before the Dominion Government will feel fully justified in carrying out this new, and from a Canadian viewpoint, revolutionary policy." He also suggested that the new strategy should concentrate on an agreement in principle in expectation that the details could be worked out later.[89] Once again, as in the case of the Alaska Highway, the American military planners believed that Ottawa would continue to resist the proposed plans unless sovereignty was guaranteed and a real crisis existed. To do so, the State Department elected to call upon the under-secretary of state and the president of the United States for assistance.

Thus, on 1 October 1946, Dean Acheson wrote to Truman apprising him of the problem and requesting that he set up a meeting with Mackenzie King to see if he could overcome the impasse. A second memo on 26 October clearly mapped out the strategy for the president. Noting that the prime minister was "reluctant to make any decision until events have made it imperative," Acheson suggested that Truman give reassurances that both he and the "non-military authorities" would guard against any "over-extension of military planning." He also reminded him of Canadian fears related to their sovereign rights, the exorbitant costs, and the belief that "Canada might ultimately have to withdraw from the British Commonwealth." In the latter regard, it was hoped that the recent Anglo-American agreement to discuss standardization of equipment would help appease the pro-British factions in Ottawa. Attached to the memo was an "Oral Message" for Truman to hand to the Canadian prime minister (see Appendix F).[90]

Meanwhile, the Canadian ambassador to the United States also briefed the prime minister, with the caution that "some of the proposals are clearly not for public consumption." Hume Wrong's account was much more detailed than Acheson's, but it also included the political implications and Ottawa's strategy to date. Stating that cost was a major factor, he claimed that by allowing the United States to assume a major portion of the costs, Canada would gain security protection which would otherwise be unaffordable. This would only be acceptable if all operations remained under Canadian control and sovereign rights were guaranteed. In terms of process, Wrong clearly saw the PJBD as the best "medium for recording joint decisions," thus avoiding any formal declarations which would require official registration under the terms of the United Nations charter. For the same reason, he warned that it was important to "emphasize the training uses of northern air fields rather than their utility as defence bases" to avoid provoking a potential enemy to take retaliatory measures. He also claimed there was no intention to approve a detailed plan, but it was hoped that an agreement in principle would allow greater access to United States defence plans than the current "piece-meal approach."[91]

On 28 October 1946, the president and the prime minister met at the White House to discuss Arctic defence, both well aware of the other's position. Claiming that a plan of military co-operation was urgent in the face of "the unsettled world," Truman offered assurances that the United States would assume "an equitable portion of the cost," that Canada's relationship in the Commonwealth would be recognized, and that any arrangement would be in accord with the principles of the United Nations. A significant comment which was not recorded in Canadian documents was Truman's suggestion that "the projected air bases in Canada could be established under the cloak of civil aviation, but in such a manner that they could rapidly be taken over for military purposes."[92] This reference explains in part the rationale behind the "civilian" weather station proposal in terms of the Americans' long-term objectives. According to St. Laurent, who was named secretary of state for external affairs in September 1946, the Americans eventually hoped to acquire "a total of 46 airfields in Canadian territory, each capable of handling one or more fighter and reconnaissance squadrons," as well as associated weather stations and radar systems.[93]

That same fall, several incidents occurred in Britain that seriously offended the Canadian prime minister and members of External Affairs. Without prior consultation or notice, a white paper on "Central Organization for Defence" was published and distributed which implied Canadian consent to participate in an imperial defence alliance. Then, despite Attlee's concurrence that Canada could not commit to a formal Commonwealth security pact because of the necessity for some form of agreement with the United States, Mackenzie King received a telegram from the British prime minister urging an early reply on Canada's participation in the "imperial defence plan." Similar assumptions were made publicly by British politicians and picked up by the press, creating untold embarrassment to Canadian diplomats who were in the process of negotiating a defence agreement with the United States.[94] A personal apology was forthcoming, but by then the decision to co-operate in the continental defence plan had been made.[95]

The consequences of Malcolm MacDonald's departure from Canada at the beginning of the new year were now clear. Aside from the loss of an unusually adept mediator, there was no longer anyone closely attuned to happenings in Ottawa. Apparently, senior British officials were unaware of the details or seriousness of the ongoing Canadian-American negotiations until the first part of November.[96] Without reliable information and no one to play the role of conciliator, London was caught behind the starting gate when the race had almost finished.

Following a special meeting with the Chiefs of Staff Committee and senior officials in London, Prime Minister Attlee sent an urgent telegram to Foreign Secretary Ernest Bevin who was in New York at the time, requesting that he meet with St. Laurent to try and delay any agreement on Canadian-American defence. In Attlee's opinion, "the proposal was one in which the United States would be the sole beneficiary," and it would adversely affect Canadian autonomy in foreign policy. He also expressed concern that other Commonwealth countries might seek similar guarantees from the Americans, that a military alliance would only serve to provoke the Soviets, and that it would destroy confidence in the United Nations.[97] During the discussions held on 12 November 1946, Bevin urged St. Laurent to consider tripartite discussions in hopes of finding a compromise more suitable to Commonwealth objectives. Considering Ottawa's past experience with "tripartite" negotiations, it was probably the worst advice Bevin could have given. There was also a touch of *déjà vu* in the foreign secretary's caution regarding "the importance to Canada and ourselves of not rebuffing American advances."[98]

From outward appearances, British attempts to stall the process seemed to accelerate it. On the same day and with apparent resignation, Norman Robertson advised the prime minister that the Soviet threat could no longer be discounted and that the United Nations was not in a position to preserve peace as long as the USSR retained a veto in the Security Council. In conclusion, he suggested that any plans for national security would require cooperation "primarily I think, with the United States of America."[99] The next day, the Cabinet Defence Committee recommended acceptance of the PJBD's 35th Recommendation which outlined the "principles of cooperation between the Armed Forces of the United States and Canada." The full Cabinet discussed the proposal over the next two days, and while agreeing to the principle of co-operative defence, it deferred approval of the detailed air defence plans pending further discussion at the diplomatic level.[100]

Cabinet's hesitation in approving the "Air Annex" arose out of serious differences of opinion voiced by senior members of the Canadian military. Air Marshal Leckie, in particular, profoundly disagreed with the Canadian chairman of the Military Cooperation Committee, Air Vice Marshal Curtis with regards to the need for such great expenditures. Also at issue were the plans to make Goose Bay a major offensive base and concern that the Americans were exaggerating the Soviet threat.[101] Confusing the matter further were the different procedures of approval employed by the two governments. As Major General Guy Henry of the War Department explained at the 21 November meeting;

> we take up the position that the military draw up the appreciation, then the plan to implement it, and it is only after the military appreciation and plan have been approved by the joint Chiefs of Staff that the matter is submitted to the President for approval. The Canadians, on the contrary, take the position that a detailed military appreciation is not an adequate basis upon which the Canadian Government can take a decision. It needs first an appreciation of the political situation, after which the military situation could be assessed and a decision finally reached.[102]

In accordance with the strategy recommended in the late summer, Henry went on to suggest that if there was agreement on the appreciation, then they "could go slowly, review it annually and speed it up or slow it down as the international situation seems to indicate."[103] Although historian J. T. Jockel has provided a well-substantiated argument that the American joint chiefs of staff were unaware of the detailed Arctic defence plans,[104] the procedure appeared to be within normal limits. Those responsible for military planning in the United States were given a relatively free rein before submission of their plans to the joint chiefs, who would then forward them for government approval. Certainly the State Department was kept informed of the full details through the PJBD secretary, Graham Parsons, and his close communications with the director or deputy director of the Office of European Affairs and Atherton, the United States ambassador to Canada.[105]

Fully aware of Ottawa's sensitivity to the political and financial consequences of the plans, Henry notified Major General Lauris Norstad, Director of the Plans and Operations Division of the War Department General Staff, of Ottawa's request for written documents supporting the "probable potentialities of the USSR" and justifying the United States military proposal to station "combat air forces at Goose Bay in time of peace." Norstad was also asked to forward the "Air Annex" to the appropriate senior officers for approval in principle. Significantly, it was stated that the military support documents were to be "coordinated with Mr. J. Graham Parsons, who was handling the political aspects for the State Department."[106] Meanwhile, despite Cabinet's request that joint defence planning be halted until the conclusion of diplomatic discussions, Pearson and Heeney agreed that the Military Cooperation Committee could continue working on existing plans.[107]

At this point, the focus of negotiations had changed from its former military emphasis to the political concerns expressed by Cabinet. The Americans were well aware of the potential problems, however, and were prepared in advance.[108] Their inside information appeared to derive mainly from the PJBD meetings, but on at least one occasion, Air Vice Marshall Curtis reported directly to State Department's Graham Parsons on the substance of discussions at a Cabinet meeting, with direct reference to those who opposed the security plan and suggestions on how their arguments might be countered.[109] As a consequence, there were ready answers and reassurances for most major concerns. Questions which the Americans wished to avoid were either diverted or deferred as in the case of Arctic sovereignty. Pearson had placed the issue on the agenda for the first meeting, but the Americans perceived it as a ploy "to obtain acceptance of the 'Sector Principle'" and circumvented debate by declaring it was "not the proper place to discuss the possible claims of other countries to territories in the Canadian Arctic."[110] The major actors in the discussions were Pearson and Heeney for the Canadians, with Atherton, Parsons, and Henry providing the mainstay for the Americans. At the concluding meetings held at the Chateau Laurier on 16–17 December, there were additional representatives from the Canadian chiefs of staff and from the American Departments of War and State (see Appendix F).[111]

There was general concurrence that certain items in the plan should be implemented immediately; others would follow as the situation required. Those of immediate priority included extensive research programmes with particular attention to radar technology, the maintenance of certain vital airfields, completion of air surveys, specialized military training schools, continuation of the mapping programme, as well as construction of new Arctic meteorological and low frequency communications (Loran) stations. At Canada's specific request, these were all to take place under civilian cover. In support of "civilianization," there were three pages of justification in the Canadian working papers distributed to the American delegates. To avoid the question of possible conflict with the United Nations charter and possible adverse reaction from the Soviets, it was agreed that the public announcement would be discreet and general, referring only to an agreement in principle. For the same reason, all approvals would follow the same procedure as in the past, simply by "an exchange of letters between Canadian and United States sections of the Permanent Joint Board which would notify acceptance by their respective governments."[112] Cabinet had already given approval to the appreciation recommended by the Permanent Joint Board on Defence. The only question still undecided was the timing of the public announcement. The sub-

Figure 19 Media Reaction to Joint Defence Plans, *P M Sunday,* 22 December 1946

stance, conditions, and differing objectives would all have decisive but vary-
ing impacts on the direction and priorities in the new northern policies that
developed over the next few years.

Canada's hesitation to support the detailed security plan was leaked to the
press and resulted in adverse media coverage as illustrated in the article by
Canadian journalist Leslie Roberts that appeared in New York's *PM Sunday*
on 22 December 1946. Considering the agreement was already concluded,
the headlines "Canada Fears U.S. Militarism More Than Soviet Expansionism" must have sparked at least a moment of conscience among the privileged inner circle of Ottawa's decision-makers (see figure 19). Not surprisingly, more rigid censorship related to military planning and activities
would be forthcoming.[113]

Once the decision had been made, there were considerable second thoughts related to its effect on northern sovereignty. In a report submitted on 11 February, a Canadian defence research officer warned that "United States policy has been consistent with a stand of non-recognition of claims of unoccupied territory."

It is particularly important that the most northerly islands be occupied. These have no Eskimo population so the establishment of police, trading and missionary posts serve no useful purpose as in the more southerly islands. Establishment of at least three main scientific stations in the northern islands, from which smaller parties could operate, would be of great value as well as proving occupation. The scope of investigations would include other branches of geophysics besides meteorology.[114]

The report also reiterated the now familiar warning that "until occupation of the whole Canadian Sector is established, it is to Canada's interest to postpone international dispute over the validity of the sector principle." Implied in the overall analysis was the fact that, if guaranteed Canadian control, the proposed weather stations might indirectly provide a means of ensuring sovereign claims to the uninhabited Arctic islands.

Unknown to Ottawa, USAAF Intelligence had already studied the possibility of taking possession of the unoccupied islands of Melville, Prince Patrick, and Grant Land, on the legal premise that "sovereignty cannot be claimed without a degree of effective occupation, colonization and use." The decision was not to proceed at that time because of the political implications.

The breach in Canadian-American relations might be sufficiently wide to put an end to all possibility of continued political and military cooperation between the two countries, and would probably be a greater blow to the American security system than a failure to obtain Arctic bases. A rupture between Canada and the United States would, furthermore, have unfavorable repercussions upon the relationship between Great Britain and the United States, and might alienate from this country lesser Powers who would otherwise have been willing to lend it support in case of hostilities.

The report, however, went on to qualify this position by stating that the United States would not "be compelled to remain idle if it seemed probable that penetration of this area was threatened by a potential enemy." Although Washington had decided not to challenge Canadian claims at that time, they certainly had not discarded the idea should the situation worsen.[115]

In January 1947, Cabinet approved a three-year plan to take over operation of the United States weather stations in northeastern Canada. At the same time, however, nine new Arctic stations were planned for construction. By agreement, a Canadian was to be in charge and the costs of permanent installations were to be assumed by Ottawa. The Americans were responsible for the actual construction, provision of transportation, equipment, and half the personnel.[116] Plans were well under way before public announcement of the agreement, and as in the past, the Americans still launched projects without permission. In one instance, the *New York Tribune* ran the headline, "Army Will Send More Troops to Base in Canada," with an article describing plans to send at least five hundred to Fort Churchill. Approval had not been granted as is indicated in the comments written on a State Department memo describing the article: "Tip the Gen'l off—tell him the story is out. (This may be quite awkward since we do not yet have permission to get these troops etc. in there.)"[117]

On 12 February 1947, Canada and the United States made a joint declaration affirming mutual co-operation in the defence of North America. For official purposes, the statement was merely an expression of diplomatic accord on the need for joint security plans. All specific projects were to be submitted for individual approval.[118] In his announcement to Parliament, Mackenzie King again emphasized that there was no formal treaty or pact; nor would there be "Maginot lines of large scale defence projects." Taking Truman's suggestion to heart, the prime minister defined the northern programme as "primarily a civilian one to which contributions are made by the armed forces."[119]

As expected, the Soviet Union was not fooled. The official newspaper *Izvestiya* claimed that "the intensive efforts of the United States military circles to transform Canada into an advance United States base for imperialist expansion have at last been successful." On 6 March 1947, *Pravda* added Britain to the list of conspirators. By virtue of "London's silence," it was deduced that Canada was merely "a connecting link between the United States of America and the British Empire."[120] For many in the United States, however, the nature of the agreement was an unexpected turn of events, as was described by James Reston of the *New York Times*:

> it should be added that the agreement admittedly is somewhat different from what some of our leading soldiers were talking about early last summer. . . the generals in Washington, particularly some of the Air generals, were talking somewhat casually about the necessity of immediate protection of "our Arctic frontier." Certain ambitious plans were drafted at that time. . . . These proposals were even the subject of a letter from President Truman to Prime Minister W. L. Mackenzie King, which embarrassed the latter with his Anglophiles and his Yankeephobes.[121]

If the chiefs of staff had hoped for endorsement from the American people, they were disappointed. But they had moved Ottawa to make the initial step. From there it would be a gradual process. Although Canadian sovereignty was acknowledged and to be respected, the official announcement stated that "no treaty, executive agreement or contractual obligation had been entered into" and that "all cooperative arrangements will be without impairment of the control of either country over all activities in its territories."[122]

The phraseology of the agreement seemed to satisfy potential dissenters, for no serious debate arose in the House of Commons. A few months later however, the issue of sovereign rights was raised over the proposed Visiting Forces Act, which allowed Americans the right to discipline their own forces for misconduct while on Canadian soil. Both CCF and Progressive Conservative members of Parliament expressed concern that Canada might in the future become little more than a military satellite of the United States. Following an intensive debate, one member expressed the consensus that it was perhaps "better for Canada to have on Canadian territory at this time United States troops, than Russian troops later."[123] It was also agreed that northern sovereignty must be preserved through negotiation of individual agreements and that modifications must be secured in accordance with the more moderate defence plans advocated by Canada. Accommodation was assumed possible because of the symbiotic relationship between needs and dependency. Just as Ottawa feared the United States might take matters into its own hands in the event of emergency, Washington had no wish to remain unprepared in the interim.

By February 1947, the military aspect of northern policy appeared to have been defined, but the issue of administrative or constitutional change was still under debate. Just prior to the official announcement of military cooperation, another decision had been reached. There would be no drastic overhaul of the structural framework of territorial government. Instead, Hugh Keenleyside was recalled from Mexico to replace the retiring Camsell. His mandate would be to bring about reform from within the department and at the same time to formulate and implement a new northern policy to complement the military exigencies dictated by the changing world scheme. The dilemma that had faced Ottawa in June 1946 now appeared to have some promise of solution. Two respected and senior men had moved into key positions: Claxton as minister of national defence and Keenleyside as deputy minister of mines and resources. Both had a keen interest in and sensitivity for the problems of Canada's north, but they had a formidable challenge ahead.

8

New Leadership and New Directions, 1947–1949

> If we are to continue to retain this vast domain of land, sea and ice, we must prove we are conscious of our stewardship.
>
> Hugh L. Keenleyside, 1949

The appointment of Hugh Keenleyside as deputy minister of mines and resources on 15 March 1947 marked a distinct shift in Ottawa's approach to northern government. To most observers, it simply reflected recognition of the north's importance in foreign relations, and certainly, from the viewpoint of External Affairs, it was most wise to have an experienced diplomat at the helm if various military activities were to be kept under "civilian cover." Keenleyside, on the other hand, gave a quite different reason for his appointment, claiming that he personally had requested the posting in the fall of 1946.[1] Whatever the reason, those individuals who had pressured Ottawa to adopt a new northern policy believed they had succeeded, for a founding member of the Arctic Institute who was committed to the concept of a "new north" was now in charge.

The department which had firmly resisted any alteration of its structure or authority would soon experience massive reorganization and new policy directives. Yet changes were inevitable considering the proposed defence plans and the new health and welfare reforms. By 1946 it appeared that Ottawa might consider minor modifications to the structure and form of government. Constitutional change comes slowly in Canada; thus the fact that it was even considered reflected Ottawa's changing attitudes towards the north.

I

As a result of Yellowknife's continued pressure for representation in Parliament, the issue was finally brought forward during the House of Commons debate on redistribution in June 1946.[2] Subsequently, a bill was introduced the following February calling for the expansion of the Yukon electoral riding to include that part of the Mackenzie District lying west of the 109th meridian of west longitude.[3] Strong and persistent opposition to the proposal came from George Black, the sitting member for the Yukon, who supported his cause with petitions signed by residents of both territories. Black argued that shared representation would be unjust to Yukoners and the citizens of the Mackenzie Valley as well.[4] The Liberal member from Grey-Bruce, W. E. Harris, defended the government bill, claiming that the purpose was simply to give a vote to the more than five thousand "white people" in the Northwest Territories and that "as far as we know there is no settlement east of that line."[5] In 1947, the "treatied" Indians and the Inuit did not have the vote, and in the government's view, such a small "white" population did not warrant the creation of a separate constituency. By southern standards, in 1945, the argument was valid. From a northern perspective, the Yukon lost representation proportionally, and the lesser populated Mackenzie Valley was unlikely to gain more than an indirect voice through a Yukon-based member of Parliament. Considering the Yukon's vehement objections, the passage of the bill merely emphasized the futility of minimal representation in the federal government. As expected, the request for an elected Northwest Territories Council was refused. As a compromise, J. G. McNiven, a local mine manager, was appointed to the council on 20 February 1947. Neither measure could be described as an important accomplishment; instead, they signalled Ottawa's unwillingness to make even minor changes. Certainly any major reform would need more aggressive, committed leadership.

Just prior to Keenleyside's appointment, the future composition of the Northwest Territories Council was the subject of serious discussion by Arnold Heeney, Louis St. Laurent, and his newly appointed under-secretary, Lester Pearson, all of whom were chiefly concerned that military and diplomatic interests be adequately represented.[6] At a cabinet meeting on 20 February 1947, the matter was resolved. As commissioner, Keenleyside would chair the meetings, but he would not be designated as a council member. Two members representing Mines and Resources would be asked to retire; the remaining three, Deputy Commissioner R. A. Gibson, Commander S. T. Wood of the RCMP, and R. A. Hoey of Indian Affairs, would retain their seats. Aside from J. G. McNiven, the new appointees included L. C. Audette, a retired naval commander and current legal adviser for External Affairs, and Air Commodore H. B. Godwin of the RCAF, who was also on the Chiefs of Staff Inter-Services Planning Committee. In Heeney's opinion, the new appointments were an absolute necessity "in view of the defence interest in the northwest."[7] Henceforth, the Privy Council Office, the military, and External Affairs would be intimately involved in the domestic affairs of the north. Initially, the military plans and "civilian cover" strategy worked in favour of advancing northern development. Keenleyside's penchant for social reform, however, would result in changes far beyond the expectations and perhaps intent of St. Laurent and the External Affairs Department.

The first Northwest Territories Council meeting chaired by Keenleyside clearly reflected the administrative expertise of the new commissioner. Henceforth, regular sessions were to be held monthly "instead of leaving it to the exigencies of the moment," and for the first time in its history, members of the press were invited to an "open session." In contrast to previous years, the minutes of the meetings were lengthy and detailed, revealing serious, forthright discussion on broader aspects of northern problems. Moreover, changes in policy appeared imminent when the issue of a new Anglican mission school was deferred pending investigation into government takeover of all northern education. As Keenleyside stated in his opening remarks, "the responsibilities of being in charge of the Council were not to be undertaken lightly."[8]

"Special sessions" continued by telephone, but at the next meeting it was made clear that issues of a purely administrative nature would henceforth be dealt with by the Northwest Territories and Yukon Bureau. The council would continue as a legislative and advisory body to assist the commissioner; minor administrative problems were now the direct responsibility of appropriate individuals or departments. This change was an informal attempt to segregate the legislative and administration functions, but it did not in any way diminish council activity. In 1946, only four regular meetings had been held, plus nine "special sessions." Under Keenleyside's direction, the count was ten and seventeen respectively.[9] That first year also marked a major turning point in the development of northern policy, as reflected in the rapid introduction of new programmes; yet the process was not as simple as it appeared.

Recalling the numerous obstacles and frustrations, Keenleyside claimed his initial attempts at reform were simply a matter of "efficiency and expediency." He soon found that resistance to change was not always internal, and he recounted how efforts to institute more government control over native health and education were opposed by the Catholic Church and the local white communities, both of which resented outside interference or regulation; similar problems were encountered by Paul Martin, Claxton's successor in National Health and Welfare. On the other hand, Keenleyside commented favourably on how government co-operation was greatly facilitated by Jack Pickersgill's influence in the Prime Minister's Office.[10]

Keenleyside's expertise in diplomacy would prove to be a decided asset in implementing the necessary policy changes. As one of the new generation of civil servants, he shared their conviction that reform could only be effected by efficient management and direct intervention. Thus when he accepted the appointment, he anticipated that the position of deputy minister "would offer countless fascinating responsibilities and would give me an immediate chance to prove the validity, or otherwise, of my faith in my managerial ability."

> The new post itself would be very much in tune with my increasing desire for constructive and positive activity that could be expected to have a direct bearing on resource development, community welfare, and individual lives. Moreover, it would give much more opportunity for the exercise of authority, for the working out and subsequent execution of plans and projects that could be expected to produce clearly identifiable results. I would have the power to get more things done.[11]

Yet despite his seemingly pragmatic and ambitious approach to career development, it was also an efficient means of attaining his personal goal of social justice in the development of the "northern frontier."

If Keenleyside was perceived as a continentalist because of his active participation in the Hyde Park Agreement, there was no question of where his loyalties lay when he was deputy minister. In referring to northern sovereignty, he declared that "this country has not surrendered and will not surrender the control of its territory or of its activities to any foreign state—no matter how friendly our relations may be. We have not gained independence from London in order to relinquish it to Washington." He went on to warn of "an altogether unhealthy emphasis placed on the military significance of recent developments in the Canadian North."[12] The loss of the nation's autonomy was a high price to pay for security in a time of peace, a concern which formed the crux of the sovereignty debate among the more thoughtful senior statesmen. In this regard, he was not so much "anti-American," as simply a proud Canadian. In 1947 the problem did not seem insurmountable, and Keenleyside set out to build his vision of a "new north."

The first item on the agenda requiring immediate attention was the reorganization of administrative structures. That summer, Keenleyside travelled throughout the territories, seeking advice from local government agents on how to improve efficiency and service.[13] He then discussed tentative proposals with the prime minister as well as C. D. Howe, who was acting minister of mines and resources. The final draft of his plans was sent to Arnold Heeney with the note, "here it is at last." In his estimation, the proposed reorganization would save the department $80,000 a year, a rather paltry sum compared to the dramatic budget increases he would submit over the next two years.[14]

Within a month the plan was approved and implemented, setting a pattern of speed and efficiency for the introduction of many changes and new projects over the next three years. Of major importance to northern government was the creation of three divisions within the administration based on regional interests: the Yukon, Mackenzie District, and Arctic. The title of the former bureau was changed to Northwest Territories and Yukon Services, under a renamed Lands and Development Services Branch (see figure 20). Two new divisions were provided in the Indian Affairs Branch for education and welfare services, a new special projects office reported directly to the deputy minister, and all research activities were placed under the new Mines, Forests and Scientific Services Branch. The emphasis on "service" and "development" clearly identified the reorientation of objectives from the former laissez-faire approach.[15]

Of special interest was the new Northwest Territories Power Commission, created in 1948 to initiate and regulate hydro developments such as the Snare River Project near Yellowknife. Originally, the Department of Mines and Resources had started construction on a hydro dam to supply power for Giant Yellowknife Gold Mines Ltd., but the new commission, with authority to formulate regulations independent of parliamentary control, soon expanded power services to the town and other mining operations. Gradually, the commission began to acquire control of the private diesel-generated plants operating in various isolated communities in an effort to provide more efficient service and prevent duplication by competing interests.[16] In 1951, its jurisdiction was extended to include hydro-electric development in the Yukon, and it was eventually renamed the Northwest Canada Power Commission. In contrast to the various provincial power commissions, there was no great political or public demand; the initiative came from the civil service and reflected the objective of the deputy minister to forward planned development.

In 1947, numerous ordinances were introduced in an attempt to bring tighter government control over a wide variety of northern activities. The list was endless, ranging from regulation of archeological exploration to restrictions on chimney construction and, believe it or not, "seduction." Of a more serious nature was the revision of the Northwest Territories Act to bring the territorial judicial system in line with that of the provinces.[17] Other reforms were directed toward social welfare and education.

Significant by virtue of its omission was the lack of any reference to more responsible and representative government in Keenleyside's agenda. When later asked by his minister why there was no progress in this area, he prepared a lengthy document that outlined the history of northern govern-

DEPARTMENT OF MINES AND RESOURCES, 1947

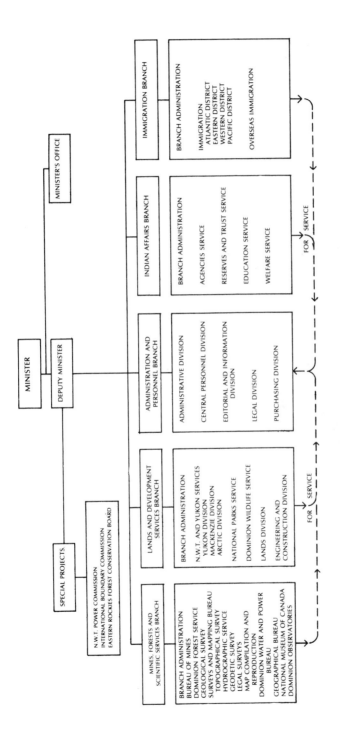

Figure 20 Department of Mines and Resources, 1947 (from *Annual Report of the Department of Mines and Resources*, 1948)

ment in Canada. Referring to the established precedent that "good local government" was the preliminary step to broader responsibility and representation, the commissioner maintained that the problems encountered with the Local Administrative District of Yellowknife had slowed the pace of evolution toward more responsible self-government in the Northwest Territories.[18] As long as the territories were heavily dependent on federal subsidies, he believed that Ottawa had the right to control and direct the allocation of funds. In the Yukon, where there were fewer financial problems and less local agitation for services, there was still insufficient local tax revenue to cover costs. The elected council's answer to the dilemma had been to limit social services, a circumstance that forced the socially conscious deputy minister to seek an alternative solution.

In June 1947, Cabinet was asked to approve a regularized system of federal grants. In return, the Yukon Territorial Council agreed to cease the tax levy on personal incomes and corporations and instead to increase local taxes on gasoline, amusements, and property.[19] The request was temporarily deferred pending plans for administrative changes. This was not a delaying tactic. The next year, J. E. Gibben was appointed commissioner of the Yukon, assuming the duties of the retiring controller, G. A. Jeckell. The tax structure was subsequently remodelled; there was an increase in pay for the councillors; and gradually the territorial administration was expanded to accommodate the increased work load. In 1949, provision was made for the establishment of municipal government, and approval was granted for construction of a road to connect the Dawson capital to the more rapidly growing Whitehorse.[20]

The Alaska Highway had permanently changed the demography of the territory. The population stabilized after the war, and then began to increase again owing to increased mining activity and expanded Canadian military establishments. It soon became evident that Whitehorse would likely be the most populated centre in the Yukon, and the council reluctantly accepted the fact that it would eventually become the seat of government. There was also a growing confidence that increased self-government was imminent, as was expressed in the opening remarks at the second session of council in October 1946: "It was indicated from a perusal of past sessional papers that the business coming before the Council had taken on added importance from year to year with the development of the Territory along provincial lines and the more complex problems of administration arising out of the broader view held by the authorities of the Federal Government and the Yukon toward the development of the North."[21] Political changes evolved relatively slowly in the Yukon compared to the gold rush years, but they were steady. By contrast, the Northwest Territories, especially Yellowknife, presented Keenleyside with a much more volatile situation.

II

The cause of increasing dissension in Yellowknife was inherent in the character and make-up of the community. Initially, the Consolidated Mining and Smelting Company had provided housing, a hospital, and other amenities. With the arrival of competition, however, the company no longer felt responsible for the community as a whole and fully supported the miners' demands for federal grants to finance local improvements. For the most part, the residents of the mining town were rugged, hard-working individuals who expected and demanded the rights of free Canadian citizens. They also had a dynamic leader in Jock McMeekan, editor of the *Yellowknife Blade*, who took great joy in waging "ceaseless and bitter war against Government employees and Government policies."[22] Inevitably, the citizens of Yellowknife were on a collision course with a commissioner intent on enforcing firm central control.

In 1945, the Northwest Territories Council firmly rejected Yellowknife's petition for a fully elected Trustee Board. Instead, two new members, one elected and one appointed, were added to the existing board, a compromise that did not alter its power or character. The appointment of the stipendiary magistrate as chairman only multiplied local resentment. Aside from these two offices, Fred Fraser was also the mining recorder, crown timber agent, chief game officer, dominion lands agent, registrar of titles, veterans' affairs agent, and, in the words of one cynic, "Lord High Everything Else."[23] The tradition of northern autocracy reflected in the powers accorded to the appointed deputy commissioner were duplicated on a smaller scale in Yellowknife. Similarly, the appointment of J. G. McNiven to the territorial council failed to satisfy the demands for more representative government, particularly when he proved ineffective in forwarding the community's interests.

Initially, Keenleyside was sympathetic to Yellowknife's demands. At a closed council session in October 1947, McNiven proposed that the composition of the Trustee Board be changed to allow for an elected majority, that there should be increased local representation on the territorial council, and that at least one council meeting a year be held in Yellowknife. While the latter two proposals were rejected, the motion for an elected majority on the Trustee Board was approved despite Deputy Commissioner Gibson's strong objection that elected members could not be made responsible for debts incurred. Keenleyside, on the other hand, fully supported the move, with the proviso that the chairman of the Trustee Board still be appointed by the council.[24]

The next item on the agenda appeared to alter the commissioner's benevolent attitude considerably. McNiven reported that Yellowknife residents were increasingly concerned that Indians were drifting into the settlement and camping in "white" residential areas. A request was put forward that land on the outskirts be set aside for use by the natives. Council approved the motion, but with stipulations suggested by Keenleyside. Indian Affairs would be responsible for selecting the site and building a community centre; no white resident would be allowed to camp there; and any Indian would be assured the right to buy or lease land elsewhere in the community.[25] The creation of the quasi-reserve may have solved immediate racial tension, but it also alerted the commissioner to racist attitudes in Yellowknife.

Keenleyside was decisive and explicit concerning the authority and responsibility of the territorial council. In reply to Jock McMeekan's severe criticism of the government's failure to respond to the wishes of the Yellowknife community, he described the formal line of authority by which the Northwest Territories was governed. The Department of Mines and Resources did not make policy decisions on its own, Keenleyside asserted, but only provided a link between the commissioner and the government in Ottawa. He then explained in detail the constitutional basis for governance of the territories:

> the Northwest Territories are governed by the Commissioner, the Deputy Commissioner, and five Councillors appointed by the Governor General in Council. The Commissioner in Council has power to make the ordinances for the government of the Territories, under instruction from the Governor General in Council, or the Minister of Mines and Resources, subject to the Act of the Dominion of Parliament applying to the Territories.[26]

To give further definition, Keenleyside provided the disgruntled Yellowknife journalist with a diagram showing the position of the local Trustee Board in the framework of Yellowknife, which affirmed the right of the territorial administration to act independently of the local board (see figure 21). Neither accepted the views of the other, nor did they intend to compromise.

From 1945 through 1949, the federal government had invested large sums of money in the development of Yellowknife: planning a new townsite, building roads, installing a $1.5-million sewage system, as well as educational and health services.[27] Regardless, demands continued for more financial assistance. Relations were further strained when the Trustee Board on occasion bypassed the council and applied directly to the Treasury Board for funds. If granted, the council retaliated by rejecting the offer or reducing the sum approved as "being unreasonable." As a result, Yellowknife exerted even greater pressure for a fully elected Trustee Board, a request that was refused with equal determination by council. Keenleyside later justified this action on the grounds that "the Local Administrative District was continually recommending fairly substantial—and perhaps extravagant—expenditures without being prepared to raise rates or taxes proportionately."[28]

Racial tension in Yellowknife was further heightened by the council's new social policies, which the townspeople believed gave unwarranted preferential treatment to the Indians. The complaints were fed to southern newspapers by McMeekan. In an earlier interview with the *Montreal Gazette*, he claimed that "one thousand Indians have more than twice the area of Scotland as private hunting preserves." McMeekan also claimed that the Northwest Territories had room for 250,000 people; therefore, Ottawa should have been concentrating its efforts on developing mining, agriculture, and oil production.[29] The racial issue finally developed into an open confrontation in November 1949, when Keenleyside accused the local hospital of practising segregation. When the hospital administration refused to change its policy, the commissioner threatened to withdraw federal grants.[30] However, the dispute over discrimination was secondary to the increasing concern for Yellowknife's financial problems.

In the summer of 1949, the Northwest Territories Council set up a three-member commission to investigate the community's financial relationship with the territorial administration. Noting that the federal government had invested over $2.5 million in capital improvements since 1945, the report claimed that Yellowknife had not proved capable of handling its financial affairs. The committee saw the problem as arising from unrealistic expectations of growth, which had resulted in the initiation of projects far beyond the requirements of the community. Believing that Yellowknife would likely remain dependent on federal assistance, it recommended that the request for a fully elected Trustee Board be denied. Furthermore, if the Local Administrative District proved unable to keep "its expenditures within its income," then an administrator should be appointed "to control the financial affairs of the District."[31]

A revised grant system was put into operation with restrictive stipulations. School and hospital subsidies would be increased, but the general grant was now based on the Administrative District's tax assessment. Furthermore, residents were to be charged for the sewer and water system, and the Trustee Board would assume responsibility for the maintenance of roads and any future capital expenditures. At the same time, a modest adjustment was made to the structure of the Trustee Board. As before, there were five elected members and three appointed, but now the chairman would be selected by the trustees rather than appointed by Ottawa.[32] Yellowknife was to enjoy increased representation in local government, but along with democracy, the board now had the burden of financial responsibility.

In the spring of 1950, Keenleyside acceded to pressure exerted by his new minister, Robert Winters, to increase local self-government and submitted additional proposals for reform. He recommended that the Mackenzie District should be set off as a separate territory with a fully elected council, but warned that this must be a gradual process occurring over an extended period of time, and not before the vote was given "to all British subjects over the age of twenty-one resident in the Northwest Territories, whether white, Indian or Eskimo." He justified his position on the grounds that "while there are many people in the Territories who would make excellent and responsible members of the Northwest Territories Council, there are many others who would behave in an irresponsible and partisan manner."[33]

Keenleyside may have appeared autocratic and paternalistic, but his reluctance to introduce more representative and responsible government in the territories was motivated by a desire to protect the disenfranchised from the self-interest and racism exhibited by the agitators in Yellowknife. The deputy minister's attitude towards the indigenous peoples of the north and the role they might play in its future development was one of the more progressive views expressed during this period. Medical services, education, economic opportunities, and welfare assistance were important, he argued, but utmost caution must be entertained in forwarding the process of native adaption to the modern world in order to prevent total loss of their cultural heritage. "The change must be gradual and voluntary. It must be conditioned by a recognition of the values that were developed in the more primitive forms of society. Its inevitability must not be accepted as justification for compulsion or for unnecessary fracturing of native codes, customs and ideals."[34] Like many others, he perceived integration as inevitable, but by his definition, integration meant "amalgamation" not absorption. Only in this way did he believe northern natives could be saved from a life of destitution or eventual annihilation.

The confrontation with the northern mining community may appear insignificant compared to problems occurring on the world scene, but it provided an important insight into the conflict between Keenleyside's idealistic goals and the realities of the north. Ironically, one of the finest tributes paid to him appeared in the Yellowknife *News of the North* after the announcement of his resignation as commissioner of the Northwest Territories:

> Surprising little attention has been paid by any of the newspapers reaching Yellowknife to the recent resignation of Dr. Hugh L. Keenleyside, who goes to the broader field of the United Nations.
>
> Now Yellowknife has disagreed with Dr. Keenleyside on a number of occasions and we feel that sometimes that disagreement was justified.
>
> He has been accused of being a Communist or at least a fellow traveller,

of being a bureaucrat, a dictator, a do-gooder (if that's a bad thing) and many other things.

He may be all those things, but no one can deny he acted, according to his lights, in the interest of the people for whom he was working.

He was devoted to the cause of making the world a better place in which to live and anyone who goes forth in this day and age to fight what he sees as evil is regarded as a gallant Don Quixote, though he may actually be a Sir Galahad.

Perhaps Dr. Keenleyside was a happy combination of the two personalities.[35]

Thirty years later, Keenleyside described the residents of Yellowknife as "rugged individuals," adding with a slight hint of admiration, "and they fought like tigers."[36] Their attitudes and reactions, however, ran counter to the philosophical ideals that motivated his approach to northern government. Although he spoke of the frontier as "a bastion of freedom" and of the north as a permanent frontier, his view of development followed the British tradition of "peace, order, and good government." More importantly, his interpretation of democracy and liberty did not include the American right to local self-government and squatter sovereignty or the right of a Euro-Canadian white minority to rule a non-voting native majority.

III

Of all the new policies and programmes introduced under Keenleyside's leadership, the most dramatic changes occurred in the fields of native education and social welfare services. In addition to increased budget allocations, there was a distinct departure from the former *laissez-faire* attitude which had relegated the major responsibility for native welfare to the missionaries and fur traders. Having first proposed full government control of health and education to the Northwest Territories Council in 1944, Keenleyside now had the opportunity to put his ideas into practice.

Education was the first priority. At the June 1947 council meeting, Keenleyside announced the creation of a Special Education Committee consisting of himself, Deputy Commissioner Roy Gibson, and R. A. Hoey from Indian Affairs. The purpose of the committee was to investigate means of improving education for the Indian and Inuit population and to determine how the non-native population should bear their proportionate share of costs. Despite protests from his deputy commissioner, Keenleyside declared that in the future the federal government would bear the full costs of new schools and payment of teachers' salaries. The Canadian Social Science and Research Council's report on education was distributed to all council members, and the author of the report, Andrew Moore, was sent on the Eastern Arctic Patrol that summer to study the needs of Inuit education.[37]

Following a report by the Special Education Committee in November, a motion was passed by council that made the territorial government responsible for the operation and cost of education until municipal governments became self-supporting. Also approved was the principle of establishing government day schools rather than residential facilities, but to the annoyance of many "white" northerners, they were to serve all children, Euro-Canadian, Métis, Indian and Inuit, irrespective of denomination. To improve the quality of education, a northern living allowance was recommended to attract more experienced teachers, and scholarships were set up to allow capable students to go outside for higher education not available in the north. It was also proposed that the council would assume sole jurisdiction over education in the Northwest Territories after revision of the Indian Act.[38] That event did not occur until 1955, but the policies upon which future northern education would be based were established in November 1947.

Another of Keenleyside's major objectives was to bring about the co-ordination of all departments and agencies actively concerned in northern affairs. His success was readily apparent in the close co-operation between two divisions within his own department, Indian Affairs and the Northwest Territories and Yukon Services. One innovation combined native health and education services into the role of the "welfare teacher." Employed for twelve months of the year, these teachers who were trained in social work were expected to conduct classes, initiate community programmes, provide assistance to distressed individuals or families, and, at the same time, to work closely with local health authorities.[39] The welfare teacher was seen as a partial answer to the problems of social disorientation among the natives and the apparent increase in racial tension in the mixed communities. Racism was particularly prevalent in the mining communities and transportation centres, which tended to attract many transient labourers from the south. It was hoped that through education and integration of social activities, the differences of culture, language, and occupation could be accepted and appreciated. In Keenleyside's belief, "the successful welfare teacher is the symbol of the new day in the Canadian North."[40] Increased adult education was a side benefit of this new programme, which was later expanded to include special radio broadcasts, film showings, and fitness classes.[41]

Although the Indian Affairs Branch was still responsible for the education of the treatied Indian, by 1948 most programmes were effectively integrated, with the northern administration paying for the salaries of all welfare teachers and of those employed at the new government day schools in the Northwest

Territories.[42] As before, financial responsibility for grants paid to mission schools was divided according to the racial origin of the students enrolled. The new schools planned by Indian Affairs were also joint efforts, with sharing of initial and ongoing costs. The Mackenzie District schools were "operated largely as a unit" and inspected regularly by a superintendent of education appointed by the territorial council. In addition, school curriculum was now modelled on that of the Alberta Department of Education "in order that the standing achieved by the pupils may be accepted by educational institutions throughout Canada."[43]

The new government schools were first established in the Mackenzie District in 1948, and the following year in the eastern Arctic and northern Quebec. By 1950, Indian Affairs was operating eight schools in the Northwest Territories, while the territorial government had ten. In addition, there were the existing mission schools, another operated by the Yellowknife School District, and one jointly funded and operated by the government and Eldorado Mining Company at Port Radium. In the Mackenzie District alone, the enrolment increased from 800 pupils in 1947 to 1,247 by December 1950. The missions continued to receive educational grants, supplies, and equipment, but no financial assistance for new construction.[44] A number of new programmes and incentives were also initiated in an attempt to adapt the system to the special needs of the north. In addition to scholarships and tuition grants, a "school of opportunity" was built in Yellowknife to provide higher education for promising students in the Mackenzie District. Manual training programmes were introduced in some schools; other innovations included films, school radio broadcasts, and free correspondence courses.[45] With the government in control, changes occurred rapidly, well ahead of local demand for reform.

By comparison, progress in educational reform was much slower in the Yukon, where responsibility for direction and funding fell upon the shoulders of the elected territorial government. There were no school boards, and a single superintendent was expected to make no more than a yearly visit to each school.[46] In 1943, there were six schools and two residential facilities run by the churches.[47] By 1950, there were all of eleven schools, the three new facilities all being located along the Alaska Highway and built by either the American or Canadian military forces. Teachers' salaries for non-native schools were paid by the Yukon territorial government, while Indian Affairs subsidized the predominantly native schools. Only the school at Teslin was reported to have enrolled both native and white children.[48]

While Keenleyside succeeded in having two welfare teachers placed in Yukon native schools,[49] for the most part, educational facilities and programmes were far inferior to those established in the Northwest Territories during the same period. This fact did not go unnoticed by the teachers them-

selves. A Yukon Council report on education for 1949–50 complained that
teachers were demanding an increase in living allowance and better conditions on a par with those schools run by Indian Affairs in the Northwest Territories.[50] It was not until 1951 that the Yukon government constructed its first
new school since the war years, and it was located in Whitehorse to meet the
needs of the increased white population. Apart from contributions made by
Canadian military forces who were now in charge of maintenance along the
Alaska Highway and adjacent airfields, the greatest advances resulted from
efforts by the Indian Affairs Branch of the Department of Mines and Resources.

Expenditure by Indian Affairs on both welfare and education increased
substantially during Keenleyside's administration, with the year 1948 mark-
ing the turning point, as shown in Table 2.

TABLE 2: Expenditures on Territorial Welfare and Education, Indian Affairs,
1945–49

	Welfare		Education	
Year	Northwest Territories	Yukon	Northwest Territories	Yukon
1944–45	14,829.00	12,597.00	43,811.00	11,632.00
1947–48	24,471.00	14,012.00	55,242.00	15,554.00
1948–49	60,558.00	25,678.00	373,001.00	56,474.00

Source: *Annual Reports* of the Department of Mines and Resources, 1945–49

On a comparative basis, funds allocated to the Yukon and the Northwest Territories in 1948 were significantly higher than the national average (see Table
3), reflecting Ottawa's new commitment to the north and its attempt to remedy the problems created for former neglect. While the indigenous people of
the Northwest Territories would appear to have gained a disproportionate advantage, the picture changes somewhat when population totals are considered. According to the 1941 census, there were 1,701 Indians in the Yukon
compared to 4,334 in the Northwest Territories. Taking this into account,
there was a relatively smaller increase in welfare payments to the Indians of
the Northwest Territories, perhaps owing to the lesser disruptive impact of
the wartime military projects. The estimated 7,700 Inuit were the responsibility of the territorial council and are not included in these expenditures.[51]

TABLE 3: Comparative Increase in Welfare and Education Costs, Indian Affairs, 1948 over 1947

	Welfare (%)	Education%
Northwest Territories	76	575
Yukon	83	264
National average	42	49

Source: Calculated from statements in *Annual Reports* of the Department of Mines and Resources, 1948 and 1949

Although comparable figures are not available for the welfare and education costs borne by the territorial governments, some facts are evident from the general allocation of the funds. Increased expenditures from 1945 to 1947 were primarily a result of the reconstruction programmes instituted by the King government; these included capital outlay for new roads, administration buildings, and navigational aids, as well as the many studies for the North Pacific Planning Project.[52] After 1947, the funds allocated to community social services were proportionately much higher. As stated in the department's *Annual Report* ending March 1950, "Provision for increased public services was the key-note of departmental activities in the Northwest Territories and Yukon."[53] In the fiscal year ending March 1950, the estimated budget of $204,000 for five new schools was a sum comparable to the total administrative expenditure in the Northwest Territories for 1944.[54] Of additional significance was the lack of any increase in spending during the fiscal year 1950–51, primarily a result of events which led to Keenleyside's resignation in September 1950 (see Table 4).

TABLE 4: Expenditures and Revenue of the NWT and Yukon Services, 1945–1951

Year ending 30 March	Northwest Territories		Yukon	
	Revenue	Expenditures	Revenue	Expenditures
1945	223,702.51	407,677.35	78,616.17	48,495.14
1946	321,476.40	926,013.24	87,653.31	66,284.61
1947	429,440.34	1,865,114.43	79,438.55	117,981.83

Northwest Territories and Yukon Combined

Year	Revenue	Expenditures
1948	638,507.97	2,879,046.07
1949	606,507.97	3,242,119.72
1950	781,330.71	4,671,479.43
1951	1,038,346.20	4,686,796.13

Source: *Annual Reports* of the Department of Mines and Resources, and Department of Resources and Development, 1945–50

Since the Northwest Territories Council was directly responsible for the welfare of the Inuit, including those residing in northern Quebec, a good portion of the increased budget was spent on their behalf. For example, in the spring of 1948, Inuit old age allowances were increased to eight dollars a month for those over seventy to bring them into line with those paid by Indian Affairs. A year later, they were increased again. As in the case of Family Allowances, payment was generally issued by traders, missionaries, or medical officers in the form of food and clothing. Similarly, all applications required certification by the RCMP.[55]

The Northwest Territories and Yukon Services were able to co-ordinate the health care services under their jurisdiction with those of National Health and Welfare. Likewise, the director of Indian Health Services provided regular detailed reports to the Northwest Territories Council, advising of progress and problems.[56] One direct result was a lengthy report to the council in the spring of 1949, requesting more assistance for "mixed bloods," who were described as "living on the verge of economic disaster." The recommendations included immediate welfare aid and longer term plans to alleviate feast and famine syndromes: adult education, game and forest conservation, marketing of handicrafts, improved medical transport, construction of a new hospital at Hay River, and a medical health plan.[57] By agreement, the medical officers of National Health and Welfare also supplied services for whites and mixed bloods in some sections of the Northwest Territories.[58]

The tuberculosis surveys continued, and all active cases discovered among the Indians, Inuit, Métis, and indigent whites were transferred to the new Charles Camsell Hospital which opened in Edmonton in 1948.[59] Five new nursing stations were set up in the Mackenzie Valley, at Coppermine, and at Port Harrison. Only one new dispensary was reported built in the Yukon during the same period.[60] With the unofficial censorship policy lifted, reports from the Eastern Arctic Patrol were now much more detailed and critical. In 1950, services offered by the patrol were considerably upgraded, with modern hospital facilities, x-ray equipment, and a sick bay on the new

First meeting of the Permanent Joint Board on Defence in Ottawa, 26 August 1946. *Left to right* are J.D. Hickerson, U.S. secretary; H.L. Keenleyside, Canadian secretary; A/C A.A.L. Cuffe, RCAF; Capt. L.W. Murray, RCN; Brig. K. Stuart, deputy chief of general staff, Canada; O.M. Biggar, Canadian chairman; Fiorello La Guardia, U.S. chairman; Lt.Gen. S.D. Embrick, USAAF; Capt. H.W. Hill, USN; Lt.-Col. J.T. McNarney, USAAF; Commander F.P. Sherman, USN.

Mackenzie King signing Alaska Highway notes of agreement with Pierrepont Moffat, U.S. Minister to Canada, on the left, 18 March 1942.

"Crystal III" weather station and research facilities, built by a USAAF volunteer detachment in October 1941, was photographed from USS *Bear* in 1942. Although there were plans for an adjacent airstrip, the terrain proved unsuitable, and the station was closed after the war.

American fighter planes destined for Alaska, seen here refuelling at White-horse in 1942, were flown from California along the Northwest Staging Route.

The Eldorado Mine at Great Bear Lake, 1943. After closing down in 1940 with ample ore stockpiled, the mine reopened in 1940 to supply uranium for the U.S. atomic research projects.

C.D. Howe, minister of munitions and supply, 1939–1945, was ultimately responsible for the allocation of wartime materials. On learning that Howe was unable to deliver uranium for U.K. atomic research as he had promised, Winston Churchill reportedly declared that Howe had "sold the British Empire down the river."

American soldiers unloading trucks and equipment at Dawson Creek, B.C., for construction of the Alaska Highway, 1942.

Soldiers sparring to keep warm at a construction camp near Fort St. John, B.C., 1942. Bell tents were standard issue for the U.S. Army Corps of Engineers.

"The Trail of '42," a typical stretch of the Alaska Highway prior to its upgrading by the U.S. Department of Public Works.

Official opening ceremonies of the Alaska Highway at Soldier's Summit, Kluane Lake, 20 November 1942. Ian Mackenzie, wearing a flying helmet, represented the government of Canada along with a small detachment of RCMP.

The dominant American presence was noticeable everywhere in the Canadian Northwest, even on signposts such as this one near Watson Lake in the Yukon, 1942.

The small river tugs imported from Missouri by the U.S. Army Corps of Engineers experienced numerous difficulties, as seen here at the end of the Fort Smith Portage in 1942. They also proved grossly inadequate for the stormy waters of Great Slave Lake.

The *Distributor* at Norman Wells, NWT, 1942. Sternwheelers owned by the Northwestern Transportation Company, a subsidiary of the HBC, pushed barges laden with construction material down the Mackenzie River.

A stretch of the Canol Road with the pipeline on the left. There was no effort to elevate or bury the pipe, although trestles were used to carry it over rivers after spring floods took out portions lying on river bottoms.

Aerial view of Camp Canol's lower section on the west bank of the Mackenzie, directly opposite Norman Wells, 1943.

The sign at the entrance to Camp Canol clearly identifies it as a "US Military Reservation."

Abandoned "Nissen" barracks at Camp Canol created an instant ghost town after the pipeline was shut down. At one time the camp housed an estimated 15,000 workers and staff and had the distinction of having a 54-hole washroom facility.

Major-General W.W. Foster, special commissioner for defence projects in the northwest, officially acted only as a liaison. But on instructions from the prime minister, he was also to ensure that the "joint" projects did not constitute a threat to Canadian sovereignty.

Tent camp, oil refinery, and new storage tanks on the east bank of the Mackenzie River, 1942.

government-owned ship, *C. D. Howe*. The cost to the government was reported to be $2 million.[61] As in the case of education, health services in the Northwest Territories expanded in quantity and quality at a rate far exceeding that of the Yukon. The reason for the disparity was never stated, but the Yukon Council's limited budget and reluctance to support programmes shared by the Indian or Métis population were probable factors.

IV

In contrast to earlier development strategy, which concentrated on support for private industry, Keenleyside's administration placed a heavy emphasis on establishing a more diversified and stable economic base for the native peoples, with special attention directed to the Inuit. When the price of white fox fell from a high of $20 a pelt in 1946 to $3.50 in 1949, a study was undertaken to investigate means of encouraging economic recovery of the fur industry. Recommendations included the opening of government stores in areas not supplied by private interests, the possibility of the government taking over all trade and subsidizing food prices, and the suggestion that further studies be made into creating a supplementary industry such as native handicrafts. Within months, the Canadian Handicraft Guild was contacted to aid in the development of an Inuit craft industry. The project began in 1950 and was the genesis of the highly popular Eskimo art enterprises and co-operative stores of the 1980s.[62] Under Keenleyside's direction, extensive "study" was no longer a ploy to defer action but instead a means to initiate it.

In 1948, the Northwest Game Act was amended to transfer legislative power from the Advisory Board on Wildlife Protection, as set out in the original 1917 Act, to the commissioner of the Northwest Territories. By this move, the responsibility for the conservation of wildlife in the region was now delegated to the government branch most directly concerned with the welfare of the northern natives. It was estimated that approximately three-quarters of the land in the Northwest Territories had been previously set aside as game preserves "for the exclusive benefit of native Indians, Eskimos and half-breeds." For a decade, non-natives had been prohibited from hunting in the preserves unless "they had held hunting licenses in the Territories in 1938," and still resided there. Children of these licensees who were "dependent on hunting for their livelihood" were also permitted rights. Regulations concerning seasonal limitations and protected species remained virtually unchanged, but the indigenous peoples were now required to apply for trapping permits. Claims were granted according to traditional trapping lines, and licences for natives were free. The aim was to protect the rights of natives to "their ancestral hunting grounds" and at the same time prevent encroachment by the seasonal influx of outsiders. It was also hoped that by assigning specific hunting limits to each family, the natives would refrain from over-trapping and learn to improve their individual areas.[63] That same year, the Department of Fisheries announced new regulations restricting seal hunting by non-residents and limiting the killing of beluga whales.[64] The reasons for the new regulations were not fully understood by the native population, who perceived the restrictions as a denial of their natural or treaty rights.

A new influx of American forces into the Arctic in 1948 presented serious complications to the Inuit preventive health programme and the longer term plans for an Inuit-based economy. In an attempt to prevent venereal and other diseases, the deputy commissioner dispatched a letter to External Affairs, reminding the department of "previous experience," which had resulted in serious health problems among the natives, and advising "special precautions."[65] Practical preventive measures inevitably promoted segregation and alienation.

The question of government policy on Inuit wage labour was also debated. Construction crews supervised by the United States Armed Forces were already hiring local natives when the Royal Canadian Air Force requested clarification of regulations regarding Inuit employment at the new Arctic air bases and weather stations. Still concerned about the effects of the boom-and-bust cycle of construction projects and the tendency of the Inuit to abandon traditional hunting and trapping practices, the Northwest Territories Council suggested that changes should be made to existing labour regulations to allow for temporary or full employment. As a concession to fur-trade interests, it was agreed that wage rates should be set low in order not to create discontent among Inuit employed elsewhere. It was also recommended that living quarters should be segregated and the Inuit provided with double-walled tents for the winter.[66] Although the designation of separate living quarters was related to health concerns, neither it nor the pegged wage rates did much to provide equal opportunity for the natives. As the military projects began to increase, hopes for gradual adaptation were no longer realistic. Progressive ideas of planned social development held a very low priority compared to national security.

As a result of the policy set down in 1948, a few Inuit were hired at the new weather stations and air bases. At Cambridge Bay and Kittigazuit, for example, an Inuk received sixty dollars per month, paid as a credit note on the Hudson's Bay Company, plus food and segregated housing. There was no special training provided to upgrade skill levels for higher paying jobs. At Fort Chimo, 25 per cent of each Inuit's wages were held back on the instructions of the northern administration "as a credit against the time when he would have to go back to the native way of life."[67] The intent may have been benevolent, but the action was overtly paternalistic and degrading. Further debate on the issue of Inuit employment took place at a meeting of the Arctic Research Advisory Committee of the Defence Research Board. At that time, it was stated that Inuit should "not be enlisted in the service due to their difference in customs and eating habits," but the idea of a long-term training program was discussed at length. There was no final decision on the issue, but it was hoped that the new schools planned for the air bases would enable future specialized training and enlistment of local Inuit.[68]

The federal government's increased interest and activity after 1947 was not focused entirely on native concerns. Development of mining, agriculture, tourism, and other industries was studied with the serious intent of devising both short- and long-term plans and policies. Government approval for immediate proposals required public support, which in turn necessitated substantial publicity. Long-range planning demanded more feasibility studies and research.

The mining industry was still considered basic to economic growth in the north. Mines in the Mayo and Yellowknife regions prospered in the postwar period as a result of greater market demand and a plentiful supply of labour.[69] Mineral production in 1948 showed an increase over a five-year period of 164 per cent in the Yukon and 31 per cent in the Northwest Territories, excluding the value of uranium.[70] Keenleyside submitted requests for further increases in financial support to the Cabinet Committee on Economic and Industrial Development that had replaced the former Committee on Reconstruction.[71] In contrast to the prewar policy of only providing funding for local mining roads, government policy now favoured assistance for transportation facilities to the outside, as in the case of the proposed construction of the Grimshaw-Hay River and Dawson-Whitehorse roads. To provide for more efficient construction in areas of new settlement, Keenleyside also proposed the use of prefabricated housing and standardized building plans designed specifically for the northern climate.[72]

Although many of the deputy minister's ideas were innovative, they were also very costly. Since the increased budgets required parliamentary approval, Keenleyside initiated an intensive promotional campaign to encourage public support. As a first step, an editorial and information service was set up to provide regular news releases on current happenings, both for the media and for interdepartmental use.[73] Government publications and reprints of articles were also a means of providing the public with more complete information on the north. Similarly, in May 1949, a film production was approved to inform Canadians on the progress of the northern health and education reforms. As a caution against creating too much publicity, the Northwest Territories Council was warned that public promotion might have the undesirable side effect of encouraging tourism to a region with few facilities to cater to southern visitors. One suggestion offered was to restrict travel by issuing entry permits only to bona fide scientists, but no action was taken on this proposal.[74]

V

In addition to his general interest in education, Keenleyside was an avid promoter of research and study into all aspects of Canada's north. Scientific exploration prior to 1940 was modest, and it was primarily undertaken by naturalists and the Geological Survey, with little attempt to compile, integrate, and disseminate findings.[75] The justification for more research in the postwar period was based on broader principles. In Keenleyside's view, "if Canadians are to understand the significance of their own northern problems, it is essential that they know more than they commonly do about their Arctic and sub-Arctic regions."[76] Toward this end, he encouraged more independent research by universities and private institutions. But he also believed that government should assume a major part of the responsibility. One of his first actions after taking office was to set up the Geographical Bureau. This proposal, introduced in April 1947, was supported by Arnold Heeney, Brooke Claxton, and C. D. Howe, the acting minister of mines and resources. Despite strong objections from the military establishment that it might conflict with the work of the Joint Intelligence Committee, the Geographical Bureau was formally approved by Cabinet on 5 June 1947.[77] Diamond Jenness was acting chief until Trevor Lloyd took office later that year.[78] This event, in combination with the appointment of Tom Manning as an Arctic adviser to the Defence Research Board, was evidence that the wartime agitators for changes in government policies were now eager to participate in the development of their image of a "new north."

In addition, Keenleyside actively supported northern research within his own department, often jointly with other branches of government. In most cases, the military objective was de-emphasized, if not censored. There were hydrographic surveys and continued geodetic studies, investigations into improved mapping techniques, and legal surveys to determine accurate boundaries. Water power assessments, geological surveys, and topographical mapping provided new data for the expansion of the mining industry. In connection with the territorial administration, there were medical, welfare, and educational studies; soil surveys and farming experiments were carried out in collaboration with the Department of Agriculture; and studies on potential development of commercial fisheries were co-ordinated with the Department of Fisheries. The Geological Survey, the Bureau of Mines, the Natural Museum, the Forest Service, the Dominion Observatory, and the Dominion Wildlife Service were all employed in some aspect of northern research.[79]

As chairman of the Advisory Committee on Arctic Research, Keenleyside wrote to Canadian universities calling for all those interested in any facet of northern studies to contact the National Research Council, the Arctic Institute, the Canadian Geographical Society, or the Defence Research Board. He particularly emphasized the need for more studies and the promising future for experts on the north:

Due to the development of modern methods of transportation and to other causes, there has recently been a noticeable increase in public activity within the Canadian Arctic. It is anticipated that this trend will continue and that there will be considerable public activity in the Northwest Territories, the Yukon and the other northern areas within the next few years. The Northwest Territories Council, the National Research Council, the Advisory Committee on Arctic Research and other bodies interested in this part of the country believed it to be of great importance that this expansion should not be handicapped by lack of qualified personnel of the best type.[80]

To provide further encouragement, Keenleyside proposed that the Northwest Territories Council establish a non-military scientific research station on Baffin Island. Decision in this case was deferred pending further investigation of existing facilities.[81]

Military studies in the north during this period also contributed greatly to the accumulation of knowledge. Although they were required for purposes of planning Arctic security, the "civilian cloak" used to allay public fears also provided greater access to information. A number of expeditions were carried out in the Arctic and sub-Arctic regions by Canadian and United States forces, and experiments at the new research station at Fort Churchill provided new ideas and adaptations for Arctic clothing, equipment, construction material, and transportation vehicles to meet the adverse climatic conditions. Other subjects under investigation covered a broad range from the Navy's marine studies to the examination of the "mosquito, blackfly, bull-dog and other pests."[82] Canada's north had never before been subjected to such extensive and intensive scrutiny.

Interest in northern scientific research reached a new peak in the postwar period, resulting in the creation of yet another private institution calling itself "The Arctic Circle." Formed in December 1947 under the direction of ex-naval officer and scientist Tom Manning, this group was composed mainly of government and military personnel located in Ottawa. The objective was to bring together all those interested in the Arctic and sub-Arctic, to exchange information and discuss plans for future research. In conjunction with the meetings a monthly newsletter, the *Arctic Circular*, was published "to provide concise and accurate information on current activities in the Arctic" and "to assist research by publishing requests for information on particular regions or subjects."[83] These newsletters chronicled a comprehensive record of activities and studies, both public and private, that were conducted in northern Canada during the late forties.

Considering the progress of northern study and research, many people quite naturally assumed that development would follow at a more rapid rate. Moreover, it appeared that Ottawa intended to establish its "order and good government" in advance of such an event. As stated in the *Annual Report* of the Department of Resources and Development, "1949 may be regarded as a year of continuing progress in practically every phase of government activity in the Yukon–Mackenzie River area."[84] Yet, within a year, northern budget allocations and proposed programme expansion were frozen by sudden changes in world politics that were assigned a much higher priority. Defence activities, on the other hand, flourished as the growing intensity of the Cold War shifted the focus on the north from a domestic concern to a military priority.

9

The Military North, 1948–1950

What the Aegean Sea was to classical antiquity, what the Mediterranean was to the Roman world, what the Atlantic Ocean was to the expanding Europe of Renaissance days, the Arctic Ocean is becoming to the world of aircraft and atomic power.

Hugh Llewellyn Keenleyside, 1949

As the Cold War intensified, concerns about the north shifted dramatically; optimism about its future economic development was replaced by fear for its vulnerability should war break out between the United States and the Soviet Union. The influences affecting decisions on northern policy became increasingly complex and often conflicting in purpose. In some respects, the agreement to hide the first phase of northern defence plans under "civilian cover" greatly facilitated the introduction of Keenleyside's social and economic policies, but when the threat of a Soviet-American war moved from "possible" to "probable," and in some minds, "inevitable," the momentum of the northern reforms came to a sudden halt. Increased military activity demanded increased secrecy and as a result, censorship. The potential conflict inherent in the dual northern policy came into full play with the external goal of Arctic defence the apparent victor in the competition for priority.

If the years from 1947 through 1949 might be perceived as a period of progressive reform in domestic northern policy, events of the following year were regressive. Expenditures by the territorial administration remained relatively stable during 1950, but internal revenues rose sharply, reflecting a conscious attempt on Ottawa's part to make the territories more self-supporting. Now, all available funds were needed for the Arctic defence plans in order that Canada could assume an equitable share of the costs. Participation in the continental defence scheme also meant changing traditional military structures and practices to conform to the American system. As the perceived threat to national security increased, concern for northern sovereignty declined in priority. By 1950, Ottawa policy-makers were once again talking of a "new north," but this time, it was a military north.

The challenge facing Ottawa in 1947 was not simply one of national security. When Malcolm MacDonald wrote in 1943 that "delicate and difficult problems exist in the north which will require wise statesmanship for their happy solution,"[1] he anticipated the importance of such issues as native health and welfare, economic planning, and the intricacies of Canadian-American relations. He had not foreseen the emergence of the Soviet Union as a superpower opposing the west, the threat of a nuclear war, or the subsequent conflicts between military and civilian priorities in the north.

The mutual defence agreement allowed for gradual implementation of specific plans towards the full military alliance anticipated by the American planners in 1946. The decision was neither pro-American nor anti-British, but simply one dictated by geography, aviation technology, financial limitations, and the state of international affairs. As General Charles Foulkes, former chairman of the Canadian chiefs of staff, later recalled, "There are no boundaries upstairs, and the most direct air routes to the U.S. major targets were through Canada. Therefore, air defence was to be a joint effort from the start." He went on to emphasize "that the decision for joint air defence was taken in 1946, not 1958, as some of the critics claim when discussing NORAD."[2] The agreement also allowed for piecemeal approval of plans that meant Ottawa could approve, defer, or reject proposals pending ongoing assessment of the situation. Until the Soviet detonation of an atomic test bomb in the summer of 1949, however, the fear of sovereignty loss through dependency on the United States resulted in continued resistance to major commitments. At times, the government appeared to be playing for time in hopes that multilateral alliances would diffuse the polarization of east and west or at least diminish Canada's dependency on the American military.

At the same time, however, the defence agreement resulted in the growth of new infrastructures and processes to deal with long-term planning. The Permanent Joint Board on Defence continued as an advisory and liaison body, but the authority to implement decisions was now divided. In the planning of Arctic defence, External Affairs was responsible for ensuring that the joint ventures did not impinge on Canadian sovereign rights. The chiefs of staff were to provide the necessary forces to maintain Canadian control at the northern bases, and the Department of Transport was assigned the task of training Canadian personnel to assure equal participation at the weather stations. All proposals were discussed by the Permanent Joint Board on Defence, which in turn recommended their approval by the Cabinet Defence Committee. New projects were referred on to Cabinet. Agreement to specific projects were then recorded by a simple exchange of notes between the American and Canadian sections of the board.[3] The "civilianization" policy contributed to the decline of parliamentary control over the decision-making process and it was effective in diverting public criticism, but as had occurred in 1942, the approval procedures and the remote location of the projects allowed them to proliferate without Cabinet's full awareness of the total picture.

While the American military were returning to the Canadian north for the same reasons and through the same process of approval, there were major differences. After 1948, Mackenzie King, who had been so suspicious of American intentions, was no longer prime minister; Malcolm MacDonald had been posted to Malaya/Singapore, then South East Asia; a selective censorship procedure restricted media access to sensitive military activities in the Arctic; and most former critics of American intrusion were now internalized into the government's new northern development programme. After adoption of "civilian cover," Heeney and Pearson's subsequent efforts to hold the military planners in close rein suggested a possible ploy to defer commitment to a more formal binding alliance.[4] Unfortunately, the new generation of civil servants were equally concerned with efficiency and they tended to adopt methods that avoided delays and interference in getting the job done. Thus new procedures and institutions were created to implement the objectives of a few idealists, but without firm "hands on" control, their policies and process were easily adapted to the aims of others.

While King was still prime minister, decisions at Cabinet level were influenced greatly by financial considerations.[5] The shortage of Canadian dollars became acute by the winter of 1947–48 and resulted in serious discussion of a customs union with the United States. Although initially appearing in favour of the plan, the prime minister squashed the proposal in March 1948. By that fall, the situation had improved considerably as a result of import restrictions imposed the previous year and Washington's agreement to allow Marshall Plan recipients to buy Canadian goods. The solution was only temporary, however, and the problem resurfaced in 1949. This time the trade imbalance coincided with demands for increased military budgets to meet increased military commitments. The signing of the North Atlantic Treaty Alliance (NATO) in April 1949 created the potential for further costs.[6] Financial implications had always been a consideration in northern policy, but peacetime demands had never been as heavy as in the late 1940s.

I

The preparatory stage for joint air defence proceeded immediately in the spring of 1947, but for the most part it was publicized as part of overall development of Canada's north. The second phase proved more difficult owing to increased construction and a more permanent military presence. Weather

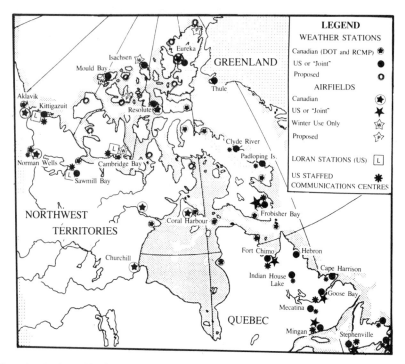

Figure 21 Arctic and Northeastern Weather Stations, Airfields, Loran Stations, and Communications Centres, Summer 1948 (data from NAC, RG 2/18, vol. 57, file A-25-5, 10 August 1948)

stations were considered an integral part of defence plans, not only because they provided information for aircraft in flight, but also because in some cases their airstrips could be used as possible secondary bases if needed. Although plans were to transfer existing stations to the Canadian Department of Transport after the war, it was announced in December 1946 that trained personnel would not be available for several years. As a result, a number of stations in the northeast were still controlled and operated by American military personnel through 1947 and most of the next year; these included Mingan, Fort Chimo, Frobisher, Mecatina, Indian House Lake, Padloping Island, Cape Harrison, and Clyde River. There were no civilian meteorologists at these stations, only military radio operators. The sole involvement of the United States Weather Bureau was in receiving and interpreting data at centres located in the south[7] (see figure 21).

Two of the proposed six new weather stations for the Arctic were built during the summer of 1947, at Eureka Sound on Ellesmere Island and Resolute Bay on Cornwallis Island. By agreement, a Canadian officer was to be in charge of these "joint" stations, but, significantly, there was no arrangement for transfer to full Canadian operation or for Canadian control and operation of the accompanying airstrips. Canada assumed the costs for building the permanent facilities; the Americans were responsible for the actual construction, equipment, and regular supplies. In addition, there were a number of ionospheric and rawinsonde stations scattered at various locations, for the most part manned by American personnel. All provisions for the Arctic airfields and weather stations were supplied by the United States Navy or Air Force, a factor that accentuated the visual image of dependency on the American military to northern residents.[8] To the vast majority of Canadians, on the other hand, these remote projects were more easily publicized as aids to future civil aviation.

The continued control and expansion of existing military airfields was more difficult to explain to the public. In 1948, the United States Air Force still operated the fields at Fort Chimo, Frobisher Bay, and Mingan and had begun repairs and extensions as planned. The Cabinet Defence Committee was aware of the situation, but it had given no formal approval.[9] In light of the Canadianization policy announced in 1944, the situation was confusing to many observers. As reported by Group Captain W. W. Bean, secretary for the Chiefs of Staff Committee, to Arnold Heeney:

Naturally, with its future status in Greenland insecure, the U.S. is interested in consolidating its hold on bases in Canada as they constitute not only intermediate staging points but the second line for defence or offence. . . . It may be that the position is acceptable, but I am not sure that it is fully understood. Neither the Department of Transport nor the Air Force is likely to initiate action to take over and operate these air facilities. The Department of Transport claims that there is insufficient civil aviation involved; the R.C.A.F. has not the resources.

Of particular concern were the airstrips attached to the new Arctic weather stations where Bean claimed Canada was "not exercising any real control," and as a result, "the U.S. will just carry on as they please."[10] The warning was valid; by the summer of 1948, the State Department recorded 211 American officers and enlisted men at the Resolute weather station and had requested approval to expand the airfield at Eureka.[11]

A chain of Arctic Loran stations was also approved by Cabinet in February 1947. Allegedly controlled and operated by the American Air Force only until Canadians were able to supply trained personnel, these low frequency navigational aids were situated at Cambridge Bay on Victoria Island, Sawmill Bay on Great Bear Lake, and Kittigazuit near Aklavik, and they were tied in with others located in Alaska and Greenland. Further stations for the northeastern Arctic were planned for a later date. Officially, their purpose was to assist pilots equipped with Loran receivers in determining their exact mid-flight position. However, the continued operation of a more southerly chain, the construction of additional control monitors, and the regular flight checks by B29 aircraft stationed in Edmonton raised British suspicions. While these were claimed to be simply training tools and a means of checking accuracy, it was noted that they were also recording and measuring signal to noise ratio and that results from these experiments were strictly classified.[12]

While the Loran equipment alone was expensive, the facilities built to house the staff were exceptionally elaborate. At Kittigazuit, there were not only the usual warehouses, workshops, quonset huts, and Jamesway buildings, but also log-sided, three-bedroom bungalows, complete with maple furniture, electrical appliances, and Bendix washers and heated by a central oil-fired steam plant. Additional log buildings were built for a dozen Inuit workers and their families, a mile from the station. Yet despite the air of permanency, the Loran programme was phased out at approximately the same time the Pinetree radar warning system came into effect. Described by the *Montreal Standard* as "white elephants," they were reported to have cost the Canadian and American taxpayers well over $50 million.[13]

In the early postwar period, Canadian military operations in the Arctic increased significantly. In 1946 the RCAF photographed an area covering 402 square miles of the islands and mainland and carried out search and rescue missions and anti-submarine reconnaissance, reportedly "to establish a wide ranging Canadian presence." That same year, the first in a series of army expeditions, Operation Musk-Ox under the command of Lt. Col. Patrick Baird was undertaken to test equipment, air supply, and training techniques over a remote three-thousand-mile route. This venture resulted in the establishment of a scientific station at Baker Lake under the auspices of the government and the Arctic Institute of North America. The Royal Canadian Corps of Signals continued to man a few radio stations, and in 1948 the Royal Canadian Navy employed the new icebreaker *Labrador* in regular Arctic patrols.[14]

Extensive scientific experiments and aerial photography were also carried out by the Americans over a three-year period, and for the most part they were described in terms of civilian benefit. Operation "Polaris" was an air transport service established on a regular basis between Alaska and Iceland, but it had the additional objectives of providing operational experience in the Arctic, study of polar air circulation, assessment of navigational problems, aerial photography, and experimentation with various communications systems. Originally approved in 1946, continuation of the programme was endorsed by the Cabinet Defence Committee in March 1948. Similarly, exercise "Nanook" was part of a United States naval operation, "Task Force 68," conducted in the summers of 1946 and 1947. Although primarily

designed for scientific studies and the training of American military personnel in Arctic conditions, the naval operations also included aerial reconnaissance and expeditions involving landing parties. Although air photography
for purposes of mapping was originally the responsibility of the RCAF, in
April 1948 the Cabinet Defence Committee formally approved an expanded
programme by the United States Air Force.[15]

The most secretive and ambitious experimental operation was located at
Fort Churchill. As approved by Cabinet in September 1946, the base was to
remain under control of the Canadian Army, but facilities would be shared by
both countries for training and scientific experiments. According to the
American military, the long-range plan was "to provide facilities for developing the art of warfare in the Arctic through study, experimentation and
training," and to expand the facilities to accommodate 2,310 personnel by
1952.[16] Ottawa, on the other hand, defined the purpose of the permanent facility in non-military terms: "joint research, experimentation, and tests of
Arctic material and equipment." In their belief, the building programme
would be completed by the summer of 1948 and would provide accommodation for 300 Americans and 515 Canadians.[17] The United States contributed
$350,000 to the cost of construction, which included extensive water and
sanitation systems and a school.[18] No strings were attached to the financial
support, since it was advantageous to the United States to conduct its experiments in a more accessible location than Alaska. Moreover, the U.S. Army
hoped that a joint programme would "further the policy of the two governments towards unification of arms and equipment."[19]

The nature of the experiments and the powers of authority were at times
unclear. In one instance, a request for clearance of a conducted tour "to stifle
speculation by the Press as to experiments being conducted at Churchill"
was forwarded to the War Department. The reply stated that it "preferred no
such tour, but if pressure was coming from the Canadian Press, it would be a
risk, security-wise, to object." Only selected members of the press were to
be included and assurances given that "they will not be shown or told anything of a classified nature."[20] Although never publicized, there were vague
references in internal American documents to weaponry tests and rocket-
launching sites.[21]

Perhaps in partial fulfilment of the objective to establish training schools
with the provision for exchange students, as suggested by the American military planners in 1946, the National Defence College of Canada formally
opened its doors in January 1948. Despite the fierce opposition of the Canadian military establishment, Pearson, Heeney, and Claxton together supported the creation of a senior academic institution to integrate civilian expertise into "the study of war and security problems." Enrolment was open

to military and civilian students from Canada, the United States, and Britain.[22] Originally, it was hoped that the civilian influence would minimize the potential for military dominance and control.

There had always been an element of tension between the various military and civilian branches of government, with each jealously guarding the perimeters of their jurisdiction. Motivated by patriotism and the common goal of defeating the enemy, the "spirit of co-operation" peaked during World War II. In the postwar period, the Ottawa mandarins earnestly endeavoured to build on this trend. Centralization, co-ordination, and unification were their primary objectives, but success was more readily achieved on domestic issues where the traditionalists in the military were least involved. Many senior civil servants and politicians, especially Mackenzie King, tended to mistrust the military, believing that the current generation of officers were trained to think in terms of winning wars abroad, rather than of preserving peace in their own homeland. The nuclear age demanded flexibility and adaptation, traits quite foreign to traditionally conservative military attitudes.[23]

Attempts to reduce the influence of the military began in 1944, when Cabinet approved the creation of a Committee on Research for Defence to study postwar military requirements. The appointment of Dr. O. M. Solandt as director general in December 1945 reflected a further commitment to incorporate civilian participation into military planning. The committee was replaced in October 1946 by the Defence Research Board, whose function as an advisory body paralleled attempts to shift joint defence planning from the military to the diplomatic level. Following the announcement of the joint defence agreement in February 1947, the board's terms of reference were changed once again, providing full power to direct and regulate military research. Solandt was named chairman.[24]

The Defence Research Board's primary focus of concern was the Arctic. As a result, in 1947 the Arctic Research Advisory Committee was set up as a sub-committee, under the chairmanship of Keenleyside. Responsibilities included preparing lists of required research projects, planning the northern research laboratory at Fort Churchill, allocating observers for the American military expeditions in the Arctic, and approving applications of scientists wishing to work in the far north. The committee was also responsible for initiating comprehensive security regulations for the Arctic and partially instrumental in the establishment of the Advisory Committee on Northern Development. Other sub-committees under the Defence Research Board included a Medical Research Panel, an Environmental Protection Service, and a Human Resources Advisory Committee.[25]

Military ascendancy in northern affairs was reflected in the changing perceptions and directives of the Arctic Research Advisory Committee over the next four years. A report in December 1948 noted that Canada's north had not reverted to the prewar state as expected. Population increases were attributed in part to military activities, but they were also related to advances in civil aviation and mining operations at Yellowknife and Great Bear Lake as well as in northern Quebec and Labrador.[26] Two years later, the committee was given new terms of reference and mandate. In addition to advising the Defence Research Board on Arctic matters, the civilian research committee was to ensure that defence interests were taken into account in the research plans of all other agencies. Of greater significance was the fact that members of the committee were now required to take an "oath of secrecy." A report submitted for 1950–51 noted that development of the north was proceeding "far more rapidly than was considered possible before the war, or even during the immediate postwar years" and that the influence of the south was now exerted much more diligently throughout the north.[27]

The creation of the Defence Research Board and its sub-committees was only a part of the overall plan devised by Claxton, Heeney, and Pearson to bring about the integration and eventual unification of the three branches of the armed forces, a step which would also facilitate co-ordination with both the American military system and various civilian agencies of the Canadian government.[28] In February 1947, an amendment to the National Defence Act was introduced that abolished the three ministries representing the Army, Navy, and Air Force and replaced them by a single Department of National Defence. As the new minister of the unified department, Claxton later recalled that the three services "simply would not accept the idea of cooperation and coordination; they were still living in the mood of the war when the sky was the limit and there was little or no civilian control."[29] The appointment in 1948 of former External Affairs member C. M. Drury as deputy minister was seen as a further move to bring about closer co-ordination of military and diplomatic policy objectives. Claxton also attempted to incorporate civilian influence into military planning by adding representatives from the Defence Research Board, the Privy Council Office, External Affairs, Finance, and National Defence to the Chiefs of Staff Committee.[30]

Attempts to curb military influence were also exerted politically. After October 1946, the Cabinet Defence Committee, which had replaced the Cabinet War Committee, was chaired by Mackenzie King rather than his minister of National Defence, for the stated purpose of "effecting saving of the public money."[31] Although budget considerations were paramount to the war-weary and penny-conscious prime minister, the move also served to slow the pace of American defence projects. But it was also a period of improved communications and, at times reluctant co-operation, between military and civilian agencies. As chairman of the Defence Research Board, Solandt was in close consultation with A. G. L. McNaughton, the Canadian chairman of the Per-

manent Board on Defence. Both men encouraged the use of the Arctic Institute of North America for government research.[32] As expected, Solandt, J.
Tuzo Wilson of National Defence Headquarters, and C. J. Mackenzie of the
National Research Council were members of the institute's research committee.[33]

Meanwhile the issue of censorship was debated in an effort to prevent
"sensational stories in the press" that were considered both "embarrassing
to the two Governments and harmful to the joint defence program." In the
belief that undue secrecy promoted intensive probing by the press, the new
policy allowed "simple factual announcements" of joint defence projects in
the initial stage, but only on approval of both governments. No individual department could issue a statement. Instead, all proposed announcements or
publicity had to be channeled through the American section of the Permanent
Joint Board on Defence. Representatives of the State Department and the
United States military would then determine, in consultation with "appropri-
riate Canadian authorities, to what extent, at what time, and by whom the
publicity should be issued."[34] From now on, it appeared that the ultimate control over the nature and degree of publicity rested in the hands of the American State and War Departments.

II

The objective of "civilianizing" the joint defence measures had a number
of serious flaws. While there was a concerted effort to exert more diplomatic
and political control over defence planning, military influence was also in-
filtrating civilian and private agencies. Moreover, although both
McNaughton and Solandt generally supported combining civilian and military efforts where possible, there was an important stipulation. Military
secrecy must remain intact, which indirectly gave the American military ultimate control. This factor alone created insurmountable problems in co-
ordinating domestic northern policies and programmes.

The first indication of serious tension arose when Keenleyside proposed
the creation of a new geographical bureau to compile all the available research data on Canada and other countries. As mentioned in the previous
chapter, the committee of the Joint Intelligence Bureau (JIB) raised serious
objections to the proposed involvement of a civilian agency in collecting
what they considered "strategical information."[35] Heeney stoutly defended
the proposal:

I am fearful lest the old desire to build up within individual services may
result in half-hearted cooperation and consequent loss of efficiency in

every way. For myself I would even be prepared to have the Mines and Resources Bureau collect and collate geographic data from abroad.

Finally, I am quite sure that there will be a good deal more support from the government for the development of a geographic bureau in Mines and Resources than in any comparable development in National Defence. . . . Keenleyside's memorandum may take in too much territory, but this is a fault we can stand for a change.[36]

Even after Cabinet approval in July 1947, the debate continued over the terms of reference for the geographical bureau. Members of the JIB argued that, although they would be willing to make unclassified geographic information available to the civilian agency, it was only proper that they should have first priority on all data collected.[37]

The terms were eventually settled by agreement between Keenleyside, the chiefs of staff, Pearson, and Heeney, with the military appearing to have lost the first round. The bureau was granted the right "to collect, organize and make available all geographic information about Canada for the use of all branches of government."[38] Once the bureau was in operation, however, further conflicts arose over jurisdiction, primarily involving research in northern Canada. One issue at stake was the Defence Research Board's assumption of complete control over the "CANTIS" reports, a "Strategic Intelligence Study of Canada" which involved detailed descriptions of all regions including history, geography, communications, aviation, resources, industry, and trade.[39] As chief of the new bureau, Trevor Lloyd was particularly frustrated by the JIB's refusal to share information which would later appear in the American media. In one case, Lloyd complained that 230 copies of a report on the American "Task Force 68" in the Canadian Arctic were distributed to 177 United States military and civilian agencies and private institutions. Only six copies were sent to the Canadian chiefs of staff and the Joint Intelligence Bureau, which, in turn, refused to forward a copy to the Geographical Bureau. The JIB argued that the information was classified and that only through American authorization could it be released to a Canadian civilian agency.[40]

Keenleyside sought other means to bring about closer co-operation among agencies involved in northern affairs. After a tour of the Mackenzie District in the summer of 1947, he reported an alarming inefficiency in government activities. To overcome this problem, he suggested that the Mackenzie District might be divided into administrative units, with representatives of the territorial administration assigned to each area and having "sufficient authority to coordinate all government activities in this district." It was vital, he argued, that such matters as the construction and transportation needs of each department be co-ordinated for purposes of economy and efficiency.[41]

That fall, the commissioner also considered "strengthening" the composition of the Northwest Territories Council in "preparation for the exercise of a more active and direct part in the management of northern problems." He suggested that the council be composed of the clerk of the Privy Council, the chairman of the Chiefs of Staff Committee, the deputy minister of transport, the commissioner of the RCMP, the member from Yellowknife, and himself. Deputy Commissioner Gibson would become an adviser along with the director of Indian Affairs and the senior legal officer of Mines and Resources.[42] This plan put a much greater emphasis on the military and transportation considerations in policy decisions. When he forwarded his proposals to Heeney, Keenleyside suggested that this revamping of the council might assist the government in dealing with such issues as American control of the Arctic weather stations and lack of interdepartmental co-operation in planning and development.[43]

Along with this proposal, Heeney received numerous other reports expressing serious concern about loss of Canadian control over the northern defence projects. Even the military were now recommending some means of co-ordinating efforts in the north to provide more "effective protection of Canadian sovereignty." Graham Rowley, director of the Joint Intelligence Bureau, pointed to the dependence of American transportation in Arctic waters as a major factor in the loss of Canadian authority, and Group Captain W. W. Bean, secretary of the Chiefs of Staff Committee, warned that Canada was "not exercising any real control" over the new Arctic airfields.[44]

Heeney reacted immediately. After discussion with Keenleyside, he sent a draft outline of a proposed interdepartmental committee to various individuals including Pearson, Claxton, Solandt, McNaughton, and C. P. Edwards, the deputy minister of transport.[45] Although all departments had considerable input into the proposal, Heeney and Keenleyside appear to have been the major architects of the Advisory Committee on Northern Development (ACND).[56] In justifying the new committee, Heeney described the government's northern policy as being "roughly divided into two categories—civil and defence—although in some cases the line of demarcation is difficult to define." He went on to explain that the Northwest Territories Council and "related government departments" were in the process of considering proposals "to eliminate widespread and wasteful duplication in government services, to rationalize techniques of local administration, to improve transportation and communications, to strengthen the local economy, and to extend educational, health and welfare programmes among the population."[47] In contrast to civilian policy, defence measures were approved by the Cabinet Defence Committee with no input from the territorial government or other concerned government departments.

In his formal submission to Cabinet, Heeney asserted that there must be a cohesive decision-making body that could co-ordinate the dual components of northern policy: "The tendency has been for new Arctic projects to be considered separately. No provision has been made for any comprehensive review which would inter-relate all Arctic activities, presenting for the government a composite picture of the Canadian position in the Arctic and joint advice from the responsible departments on the general policies to be adopted." Cabinet approved the creation of the Advisory Committee on Northern Development on 19 January 1948, with the mandate "to advise government on questions of policy relating to civilian and military undertakings in northern Canada and to provide for effective coordination of all government activities in that area."[48] The mandate had a curious similarity to the one given to Major-General William Foster as special commissioner overseeing the wartime defence projects in the northwest. However, the influence of high-level committee consensus was expected to have a much greater impact on political decisions. Equally significant was the fact that it also reported directly through Heeney to the Cabinet, thus enabling the civil servants to continue their firm hold on the political decision-making process. In contrast to Malcolm MacDonald having to bring pressure from the outside in 1943, this time Ottawa on its own initiative was attempting to enforce tighter measures to monitor and control the "joint" military activities.

III

The role played by the Advisory Committee on Northern Development in the late 1940s has been ignored or downplayed by historians for a number of valid reasons, primarily owing to the fact that access to the minutes was restricted as "classified" until 1982. The right of military secrecy, which prevented public disclosure of the committee's activities for twenty-five years, was ironically the cause of an open confrontation between military and civilian members over the question of Canadian sovereignty. Although some co-ordination of activities followed, the tension between the two factions was not particularly conducive to a "spirit of co-operation."

As established in 1948, the committee was chaired by Keenleyside and included among its members: Heeney, clerk of the Privy Council Office; Edwards, deputy minister of transport; Pearson, under-secretary of state for external affairs; Lieutenant-General Foulkes, chief of the general staff; Air Marshall Curtis, chief of air staff; General McNaughton, Canadian chairman of the Permanent Joint Board on Defence; and Solandt, chairman of the Defence Research Board.[49] Heads of other agencies and departments were asked to attend when appropriate. The secretariat was attached to the Privy Council Office, and all recommendations were directed to Cabinet through

Heeney. There were five meetings of the full committee between February 1948 and December 1949; then there was apparently a lapse of three years before the sixth meeting in February 1953. Sub-committees were created to deal with specific issues such as transportation, construction, immigration, and Canadian sovereignty.

In his opening remarks at the first meeting held on 2 February 1948, Keenleyside indicated that a matter of high priority was the protection of Canadian autonomy in northern defence. The minutes of the first session read as follows:

> *The Chairman* described the purpose for which the Committee had been formed and drew attention to the terms of reference, which permitted consideration of any aspect of northern development. It was hoped, accordingly, that overall co-ordination and some comprehensive programme of northern development could be worked out. The defence aspect was important, particularly the relationships with the United States involved. It was apparent that developments in this sphere would be mostly of a joint character and every effort should be made to provide for the maximum possible Canadian effort, particularly in respect of operating personnel. Only in this way could Canada retain control and a reasonable degree of independence.[50]

The chairman also cautioned that since the committee would be "advising on overall policy," it was important that the principals, not their representatives, be in attendance.

Not surprisingly, the first item on the agenda was the lack of co-ordination among the various government departments in the north, most notably in matters of construction and transportation. Despite protests by the invited deputy minister of public works, his department was asked to conduct a survey with a view to consolidation. A transportation sub-committee was also set up to study long-term needs and Canada's ability to meet them. In regards to labour, Keenleyside suggested that all departments consider the employment of native people. According to the minutes, there were no comments on this recommendation.

The last item on the agenda raised a furore. Two memoranda were presented for consideration: "Northern and Arctic Projects," submitted by the Privy Council Office, dated 28 January 1948; and "A Summary of United States Military Activities in Canada," 22 December 1947, compiled by the chief of the Geographical Bureau. The first report itemized the numerous defence projects and the related agreements. In summary, it stated that significantly increased Canadian participation in terms of personnel and transportation would be necessary to ensure control. Trevor Lloyd's report

charged that projects were proceeding without formal approval and that the
American military had returned to the Canadian north in massive numbers.[51]
The reaction was understandably mixed, ranging from expressed "shock"
by Pearson to protests of inaccuracies from the military representatives.
While Heeney claimed that there was no underlying design by the Americans
to carry on activities without Canadian authority or consultation, he did admit that problems arose "from lack of co-ordination in Canada and the failure of departments to keep other interested departments fully informed both
in Ottawa and Washington." Despite Foulkes' attempt to suppress the report
for fear of leakage to the United States, it was decided to allow those present
to review the material and to send a modified version to the Permanent Joint
Board on Defence.[52]

Before the second meeting, Group Captain Bean, now secretary of the
ACND, was requested to prepare a revision of Lloyd's report "incorporating
such additional facts as were subsequently provided by the members of the
Committee." Bean claimed that this was impractical "since a considerable
amount of the information in the original paper was a matter of opinion and
as such could not be revised on a purely factual basis." Instead, he prepared
what appeared to be a summary of the subjects covered in Lloyd's report,
listing authorizations and referring to a few errors. Closer examination
reveals a degree of implied sympathy with the disputed report. Many of the
"authorizations" were actually approved after the submission of Lloyd's report; others were claimed to be "blanket" approvals; some were merely
statements that plans "were reported to and noted by the Cabinet Defence
Committee." Similarly, a single underlined statement in the middle of the
text could be interpreted according to the bias of the reader. With reference to
the unknown details of the various American undertakings, Bean remarked
that *"whether a closer check should be kept on these operations seems to be
a matter of policy decision."*[53] Undoubtedly following the bias of his superiors, Bean's April 1948 report was a definite contrast to his concern about
"lack of control" expressed in the "secret" memo to Heeney only six
months earlier.[54]

At the second meeting held in June 1948, the chief of the Geographical
Bureau was again criticized, both for his "inaccuracies" and for conducting
a study without proper clearance. Keenleyside came to Lloyd's defence, stating that he personally had asked the Geographical Bureau to prepare the report and that any "inaccuracies" resulted from his inability to obtain information from the Joint Intelligence Bureau and other military departments. In
a memorandum submitted to the committee, Keenleyside presented the modified report, which he claimed still revealed problems related to American
disregard for Canadian rights. He argued that difficulties arose "as a result of
loosely worded authorizations and inadequate inter-departmental co-ordina-

tion in Washington and Ottawa." Still concerned about the sovereignty issue, Lester Pearson now urged increased Canadian militarization on the
grounds that Canada's effort in the north must be "on as large a scale as was
practicable in order to minimize dependence on United States assistance."
After lengthy and heated discussion, the secretariat was asked to compile a
list of all United States activities and personnel in Canada for distribution to
committee members, members of the Cabinet Defence Committee and the
Canadian secretary of the Permanent Joint Board on Defence. This suggestion was strongly opposed by the attending chiefs of staff on the grounds of
security regulations. The committee did agree, however, that all efforts must
be made to speed up Canadian takeover of the air bases and weather stations
and that two studies be prepared on northern sovereignty: a factual record by
the Department of Mines and Resources and a theoretical one defining legal
rights by External Affairs.[55]

When a report titled "United States Activity in Canada, Strength Return"
was submitted to the third meeting of the committee, its circulation was restricted at the request of the attending military officers because of "security
reasons," and the details were not reported in the minutes.[56] However, two
hastily prepared reports, one handwritten and both incomplete, were found in
the Privy Council records and the American State Department files, both
revealing omissions and apparent discrepancies. While there appear to have
been well over a thousand United States officers and enlisted men permanently employed in Canada during the summer of 1948, there was a notable
disagreement about where many of these men were located. Nor did the figures include the various military exercises taking place in the Arctic regions.[57]
To an outside observer, it was obvious that neither government had thought
to keep count.

Whether Trevor Lloyd was accurate or had exaggerated is immaterial. His
report was singularly successful in bringing about an immediate and comprehensive review of the projects and their supporting agreements. It would also
be fair to say that it did not improve relations between the military and
civilian branches of government. Unexpectedly, Lloyd announced in June
1948 that he would be returning to Dartmouth University in the fall. No
specific reasons were stated for his departure, although Keenleyside expressed his personal regrets that organizing the new bureau had been so
difficult—"for reasons which were for the most part beyond your control."[58]
The professional relationship between the two men that began in 1943 came
to an end, but the geographer's influence continued, as is evidenced by the
number of social and administrative reforms implemented by Keenleyside
over the next year; many bore a striking resemblance to the recommendations
set forth in Lloyd's Arctic study compiled for the Canadian Institute of International Affairs.[59]

That summer, various sub-committees of the ACND began work on the studies assigned at the general meeting. Thus, while the transportation sub-committee attempted to estimate the requirements of all private and government agencies in freight and passenger transport over a ten-year period, the construction sub-committee began to compile lists of ongoing northern construction.[60] Yet the original objective of the ACND was far from fulfilled. Of serious concern to Heeney during the fall of 1948 was the attitude the committee seemed to be adopting. "It seems to me important that this Committee is in danger of becoming a mere discussion group and a mechanism for the distribution of information. It is of great importance that having collected the information the Committee should act upon it—that is, submit recommendations to Ministers and to Cabinet for the general tightening up of Canadian policies and activities in the North."[61] In Heeney's estimation, one of the primary aims of the ACND was to implement the "government policy of Canadianization" of the north. By now it was evident that while both Pearson and Heeney had been the negotiators for the "civilian cover" policy under "direction of Cabinet," their own efforts in their respective capacities were directed toward protecting Canadian sovereign rights.

Causing further consternation was the continued reluctance of Washington to allow the release of information on the extent and nature of American activities in northern Canada. As Heeney noted with obvious displeasure, "the perennial conflict between the Services and the civilian departments and the ever recurring question of Canadian sovereignty are both raised here."[62] Whether justified or not, the military continued to use the argument of security to preserve their right to operate without criticism from other government agencies. "Co-operation" in their definition did not include sharing their information or discussing their activities.

Unknown to Heeney, a debate over the issue of Canadian access to United States military information had continued unabated for over a year between the State Department and various United States military agencies. At the core of the issue was the interpretation of the PJBD's 34th Recommendation. Signed by President Truman in June 1946, it set out the terms of exchange of information: "Subject to the national policies of the two Governments, there shall be a free and comprehensive exchange of military information in so far as it affects the security of the two countries, the circulation of which shall be subject to restrictions as may be specified by the originating country."[63] Thus according to the United States Army Navy Air Force Coordinating Committee the United States was not required to divulge the number of military personnel or the detailed nature of their activities in Canada. The final word on where the ultimate power of authority resided was presented in a five-page report by Major General E. O'Donnell, USAF, that stated, "The Director of Intelligence, Air Force, was responsible for formulating security policies under which information may be channelled to Canadian authorities."[64]

Coincidentally, Secretary of the Navy James Forrestal arrived in Ottawa in late August on an assigned mission to foster closer relations, to reinforce the commitment to co-operative defence, and to encourage more active participation in the joint defence plans. He was well briefed for the occasion with the suggestion that, next to the prime minister, Claxton was the key individual who would determine how Canada would co-operate. Forrestal was told that Claxton was "distinctly an intellectual" and forewarned that he believed "firmly in Canada's destiny as an independent nation" and not as a "satellite of the United States or the United Kingdom."[65] The Americans had done their homework thoroughly. As a result, there was less likelihood of their offending the more devout Canadian nationalists by false assumptions or inappropriate comments, as was so often the misfortune of the British.

Apparently undaunted by the tension between the military and civilian agencies, Keenleyside persisted in his efforts to co-ordinate the domestic and defence activities in the north with some success. Sharing transportation with the military, for instance, resulted in more efficient and less expensive service to the new schools and nursing stations.[66] Furthermore, the priority attached to sovereignty still worked to the territorial government's advantage. In the case of the request for a new government-owned vessel for the Eastern Arctic Patrol, the matter received "urgent" attention "in order that control of transportation in northern waters should not remain in the hands of U.S. authorities any longer than necessary."[67] As in the past, this argument was still singularly effective in bringing about government action.

While the ACND appeared to be making some headway towards co-ordinating activities in the north, it was evident that military influence on decisions was increasing. Various comments by members suggested that the "fear" of war was being replaced by a sense of "inevitability," and as a result, new sub-committees were created to deal with the probabilities. One was specifically charged with investigating customs and immigration procedures in the event of war, noting that "the U.S. Forces would have to be able to enter as completely armed military units with their own transportation."[68] Other emergency plans were discussed for inclusion in the "War Book." At the third meeting, held in late November 1948, the tone of discussion implied that a crisis was imminent.[69] Although, retrospectively, the intense fear of Soviet aggression may appear unwarranted, it must be remembered that not only were many of the Ottawa decision-makers veterans of World War I, but also a good number had been among those who had misjudged Germany's intentions in the 1930s. This time, they wanted to be prepared in the event they were not able to prevent a third world war.

The fourth meeting of the ACND again reflected the increasing priority given to defence matters. Although a report was submitted on the progress of various departments in furthering "the government's policy of keeping the Canadian Arctic Canadian," there was less concern for the effect of United States military infiltration and more focus on appropriate security measures in the event of war. Not unexpectedly, Keenleyside's proposal for a "Canadian Committee on Arctic Information" to compile the data collected by all agencies was firmly rejected by the military members as "impeding on jurisdiction" over areas already adequately served. The only positive sign of cooperation came from the construction sub-committee, which noted that tests were proceeding on standardized prefabricated units for Arctic conditions and that steps had already been taken to ensure that only one department would be responsible for construction in any given area.[70]

By June 1949, formal security regulations were introduced to divide the Arctic into two regions: Plan A to cover the mainland and Plan B for the relatively unsettled archipelago. In the islands, which now contained several American-built air bases and most of the new weather stations, the regulations were strict. "Classified information" included any details of personnel, equipment, size of runways, the number and class of airplanes, descriptions of buildings in the area, and the nature of stored supplies. In addition, any "reference to service personnel or officials other than those of Canadian nationality" was strictly forbidden. On the more settled mainland, regulations were consistent with existing censorship policies to avoid undue speculation over the intent of military buildup. To avoid rumours, concise announcements of new developments were to minimize their importance.[71] The security scheme appeared comprehensive, but it was not without loopholes. As pointed out at a Northwest Territories Council meeting, while foreigners were required to undergo a security check when applying for a scientific permit, applicants for miners' licences were not subjected to any screening process.[72] Any expansion of services or economic developments were now considered a liability to security.

The fifth meeting of the ACND held on 19 December 1949 was the scene of yet another disagreement, this time between the Department of Transport and the RCAF over responsibility for the Arctic air bases. With more available funds, the Air Force had no intention of allowing a civilian agency to control military bases. On this occasion, Keenleyside was noticeably less involved in the discussion and appeared to exhibit little of the enthusiasm shown at the first session less than two years earlier. It was apparent that the committee's role had become somewhat redundant; military supremacy meant compliance with orders, not engaging in discussion. As a result, although the sub-committees continued to meet, the regular body did not convene again for over three years. By then, the whole face of government had changed as well. St. Laurent was now prime minister; Pearson had moved into the Cabinet as secretary of state for external affairs; Heeney had replaced him as under-secretary; Norman Robertson returned from London to become clerk of the Privy Council; and a new minister, Robert Winters, was responsible for northern affairs.

The international scene had also taken on a distinctive new character. After a year of serious negotiations, the North Atlantic Treaty was signed in April 1949. While the alliance guaranteed an alternative to total reliance on the United States for security, it also required more financing to meet its obligations. As expected, St. Laurent began to loosen the strings on the defence budget. Following the Soviet Union's successful test of its first atomic bomb in late summer, plans were quickly put in motion for construction of the Pinetree radar network extending from Vancouver Island to Newfoundland, with the United States agreeing to provide two-thirds of the cost and the required manpower.[73] After four years of peace, the world was openly and rapidly rearming.

Although there was still a heavy reliance on "paper sovereignty," Ottawa appeared to have retained a surprisingly good measure of control in the Arctic. Canadians were reported to be in charge of at least four of the newest weather stations, and in January 1950, it was announced that the RCAF had officially taken over the air bases at Mingan and Fort Chimo, with only a few Americans remaining on location. Most USAF personnel had departed from the bases at Edmonton, Fort Nelson, and Whitehorse, leaving only a few weather technologists to assist in training the Canadians, and according to plan, the experimental Loran stations on the mainland were phased out as soon as the Pinetree radar system came on stream. Furthermore, the new Eastern Arctic Patrol vessel, the *C.D. Howe*, agreed to supply the Arctic weather stations and thereby reduce dependency on the American navy. The expanded RCAF freight service was similarly decreasing reliance on United States charter and military aircraft.[74] Not one of these events was significant in its own right, but when taken as a whole, Canada appeared to be regaining some semblance of control.

By 1950, only Frobisher Bay remained under American control, and even this foothold would be relinquished once construction on the large modern base was completed at Thule in Greenland. Luckily for both Canada and the United States, Denmark was much more amenable to the presence of a foreign air base on her colonial territory, but they also encountered the consequences of Arctic impulsiveness. A full month and a half before commencing negotiations on the defence agreement, construction had begun on the Thule base.[75] Meanwhile, the U.S. Army and the State Department were fully apprised of Ottawa's "formidable" opposition to the presence of American bases in the Arctic. Studies as far back as 1946 not only attempted to analyze the reasons but also to devise methods to overcome the problem. (see Appendix G).

IV

The year 1949 was also a period of changing priorities in the domestic affairs of the north. In terms of new initiatives, it was described as a year of increased government activity in every phase of development; it was also the last year for new socioeconomic programmes and expanding budgets. Reflecting the new priorities in government policies, Colin Gibson was appointed minister of mines and resources; considering his former experience as secretary of state, minister of national revenue, and minister of national air defence, the implications were obvious.

Much of that year was spent on major reorganization which was to be implemented after the federal election. Thus as expected, on 18 January 1950, Prime Minister St. Laurent announced the creation of three new ministries to replace two: Mines and Resources and Reconstruction and Supply. Northern affairs would now come under the jurisdiction of Resources and Development, but what was perhaps not expected was the appointment of another new minister, this time Robert Winters, a native of the Maritimes. A press release described five branches within the new department, with the chief of the Northern Administration Branch not yet assigned. The obvious candidate, Roy Gibson, had been moved to become director of the new Development Services Branch.[76] Further internal changes occurred later, but the final structuring resulted in a department quite similar to the new Department of Northern Affairs and National Resources created in 1953 (see figures 22 and 23). Significantly though, in 1953 the Advisory Committee on Northern Development was brought out of the closet, and the administrative organizations for the Yukon and Northwest Territories were now divided on the chart and reported directly to the deputy minister.

The appointment of Robert Winters as minister of resources and development heralded a new approach to northern affairs, and one which was distinctly regressive in terms of social reform. A native Maritimer and graduate of the Massachusetts Institute of Technology, Winters was elected in his home riding of Lunenberg after service in World War II. He served as a parliamentary assistant, first with National Revenue and then Transport, before accepting the portfolio of Reconstruction and Supply which he held for just over a year. Winters's background did not provide any special knowledge of northern Canada, but he did have considerable military and mining experience, a fact which casts some doubt on Pickersgill's claim that his appointment was simply the result of St. Laurent's election promise to give him a department "with more substance and scope."[77]

Upon assuming office, Winters was quick to question the constitutional development of the territories. Taking his deputy minister completely by surprise, his initial query was whether he, as minister of resources and develop-

DEPARTMENT OF RESOURCES AND DEVELOPMENT

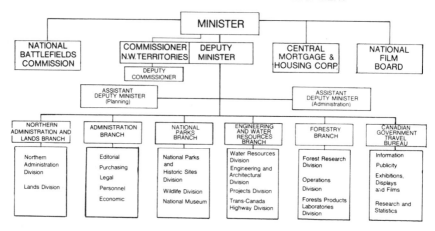

Figure 22 Department of Resources and Development, 1950–51 (from *Annual Report of the Department of Resources and Development*, 1951)

DEPARTMENT OF NORTHERN AFFAIRS AND NATIONAL RESOURCES

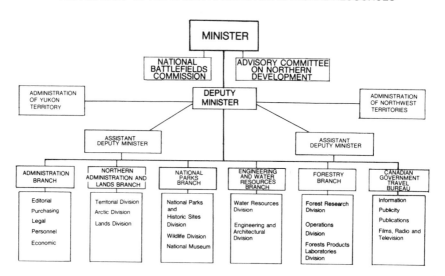

Figure 23 Department of Northern Affairs and National Resources (from *Annual Report of the Department of Northern Affairs and National Resources*, 1954)

ment, could assume the position of commissioner of the Northwest Territories. After consultation with the deputy minister of justice, Keenleyside tactfully reported that such a move was impossible without "very substantial amendments to the statutes."[78] Winters's next query was to ask why the Northwest Territories had not been granted "a more democratic form of government."[79] At this point, it appeared that the agitators in Yellowknife had found their champion.

Noting that earlier proposals to incorporate the Mackenzie District into the Yukon framework "apparently were dropped without decision," Keenleyside wrote down his proposed plan of constitutional development. First, the Northwest Territories Council would be expanded to eight members and include three elected representatives from separate constituencies centred on the Fort Smith–Hay River area, the Yellowknife–Port Radium region, and along the Mackenzie River from Fort Simpson northward. He also reported that although the Indians in the Mackenzie District had voted for the first time in the 1949 election, the Inuit were still not enfranchised under the 1945 Dominions Election Act, a wrong which Keenleyside declared must be addressed immediately. He also recommended that at least one council meeting a year be held in the Mackenzie District.[80] Then, with the question of more representative government still unresolved, Keenleyside left on a temporary leave of absence to head the first United Nations Mission of Technical Assistance in Bolivia.

During his absence, Winters continued to search for a way to place himself in direct authority over the Northwest Territories. When he consulted Acting Deputy Minister C. W. Jackson about bringing the territorial government "under the control of Cabinet," the reply was straightforward. Jackson denounced the idea of a cabinet minister being a commissioner of the Northwest Territories as "a backward step," then described the unethical politics of such a move and the numerous amendments which would be required of the House of Commons Act and the Northwest Territories Act. In his opinion, "the Commissioner is in many respects legally equivalent to a Premier of a province, and the Council of the Northwest Territories is legally equivalent to a legislature of a province," and it was simply "improper that a Premier of a province should be a member of the Federal Cabinet." Jackson also warned that it would be very unwise to raise the issue in the House of Commons.[81] It is not known how many people Winters consulted on the issue, but the replies must have been equally direct.

Throughout the summer, Winters was busily restructuring the financial practices of the administration and the procedures of the council. When Keenleyside returned in mid-August, Gibson forewarned him of the minister's plans. Of critical concern was the proposed attrition policy, which Winters claimed was a firm directive from the Treasury Board.[82] In essence, the new guidelines spelled the end of all plans for new programmes or the expansion of existing ones. Moreover, it now appeared that Winters's strategy was to offset any adverse local reaction to the drastic budget cuts by granting more representative government.[83]

As he neared retirement after years of dedicated service, Roy Gibson's customary deference to his superiors finally gave way. In September 1950, the deputy commissioner wrote directly to Winters outlining his own views on how the Northwest Territories and Yukon should be governed. Rejecting outright the idea that provincial boundaries be extended to include areas of the Yukon and Northwest Territories, he argued that such a move would have a detrimental effect on the Indian population unless there was "a very definite understanding as to the rights of the natives and of those who lead the native life." He also maintained that more elected representation on the council would not improve the quality of government, and pointed out the obvious contradiction in his minister's new policy: the proposal to advance democracy by increasing representation on council, while at the same time restricting council activity to broad policy decisions and leaving all other problems to be dealt with by the administration in Ottawa.[84] Then, after twenty-nine years of faithful service to a north he appears to have never visited, Gibson retired.

On his return from South America, Keenleyside was offered a senior position with the United Nations, a proposal he took under serious consideration.[85] Although it was perhaps inevitable, the timing of his decision was likely influenced greatly by a particularly offensive memo from his minister. Not only did Winters criticize "the administrative techniques presently employed in territorial affairs," but he specifically attacked the "disbursement of territorial funds." He then directed that all ordinances and items for discussion at the Northwest Territories Council meetings must first be presented to him, at which time the final agenda would be "settled by conference" between the two of them. He also outlined his suggestions for "a more democratic form of government," a plan which was essentially a duplication of Keenleyside's earlier proposals, but with the omission of any reference to native franchise reform. In a parting shot, Winters wrote that he would "be glad to discuss necessary amendments to the Act before you prepare my submission to Cabinet."[86] Keenleyside's reply was his letter of resignation, tendered a few days later.

Keenleyside dwelt only briefly on the circumstances of his resignation in his published *Memoirs*. He expressed little regret and, surprisingly, was not critical of his minister. In his opinion, tension was expected considering that Winters was the most conservative minister he had worked for, but he denied "any lack of personal cordiality" between them. In his words, Winters was "a 'strong' minister who liked running his own show without too much concern about the views of subordinates," a trait quite foreign to Keenleyside's previous "less well-informed and more supple ministers." Furthermore, the challenging position at the United Nations offered an opportunity of unlimited scope for the social reformer and "made refusal impossible."[87] In October 1950, he was appointed director general of the Technical Assistance Administration of the United Nations.

Years later, Keenleyside wrote that he always had "to combat a tendency to speak in superlatives and to act beyond necessity."[88] He might have added that he had also learned to walk through adversity with dignity and pride. Even if his vision had been too idealistic to become reality, it still must have been difficult to think that his "northern frontier" and "bastion of freedom" might be turned into a battleground for defensive war games and a chequered map of restricted security zones. Yet he fully understood the inherent risks in his profession as he explained in a lecture delivered at the University of British Columbia. Quoting a passage written by Heeney, he described the mandate of a public servant:

Decision is the prerogative of the minister. But that does not mean that the civil servant must have no opinion. Any civil servant worth his salt must draw conclusions from the facts. You cannot expect a man of training, talent and character to work upon problems of public concern without his reaching conclusions. Furthermore such a man is bound to indicate his conclusions to his superiors. He will be bound, in all honesty, to recommend courses of action. He will warn against one line, urge the wisdom of another. . . . But the expert must stick to his last. He must appreciate the limitations of his office. He must appreciate the limitations of his own expert knowledge. He has neither the experience, nor the special kind of wisdom—let alone the authority—to govern.[89]

Keenleyside had performed by the rules of the book, but he knew his limitations and handed over the responsibility for Canada's "new north" to those with a "special kind of wisdom" and the "authority to govern." The United Nations would be served well by the turn of events.

V

The northern territories, meanwhile, were suffering from a very "unhealthy" state of affairs owing to their strategic location in the Cold War. The ascendancy of military influence was first apparent in the new composition of the Department of Resources and Development. Following Keenleyside's resignation, the former vice-president of Central Mortgage and Housing, Major-General Hugh A. Young, was appointed as deputy minister and commissioner of the Northwest Territories.[90] A native of Winnipeg and veteran of two World Wars, Young's two years in the sub-Arctic with the Royal Canadian Corps of Signals seem to have qualified him for the post.[91] Other new faces appeared in senior administrative positions. Another veteran of World War II, Colonel F. A. Cunningham, was appointed deputy commissioner, while the former director of the Lands Division, G. E. B. Sinclair, was transferred to head the northern administration unit.[92] Essentially, Winters had installed his own team and, in doing so, had dispersed the former power structure that had resisted his initial attempts to take charge.

The legacy of Winters' "democratic reforms" might be better described as autocracy in disguise. For example, while Bill 189 amending the Northwest Territories Act allowed for three elected members on the council, it also gave the commissioner the authority to decide who should be allowed to vote.[93] As a result, the Inuit were refused the right to vote in territorial elections, despite the fact that they had been granted the federal franchise on 30 June 1950. Whereas Keenleyside had withheld elected representation to protect the disenfranchised natives, Winters legislated a denial of Inuit rights to participate in the territorial government.[94]

The elected representatives to the Northwest Territories Council soon discovered the limitations of their hard won "self-government," and protests arose over the procedures, especially in relation to the new ruling that members' bills must be presented six weeks in advance of a meeting. As the member from Yellowknife pointed out, there was not time upon receiving notification of the meeting to prepare any substantive submission. The "democratic" character of the new territorial government was further revealed when a bill was presented to extend the period of time for disallowance by the commissioner-in-council of any by-law passed by Yellowknife's Trustee Board, a measure considered essential to accommodate plans to hold the council sessions only twice a year.[95] The elected Yukon government was also granted increased representation in 1951, adding two more members to make a total of five. Yet here as well, there was no significant increase in responsibility.

The meetings of the Northwest Territories Council changed dramatically under Commissioner Young, with the recorded minutes reading somewhat like an agenda: short, without explanation or detail, and unbelievably dull.[96] After local protest against the proposal to limit the sessions to twice a year, it was decided that meetings would be held quarterly. But priorities had also changed, and the emphasis was clearly on financial cut-backs. Means to increase revenue were also explored, such as the proposals to institute a poll tax on males between twenty and sixty-five years of age not residing in the Mackenzie District, and a tax of six cents a gallon on gasoline to help pay for increased costs of road construction.[97] Furthermore, the attrition policy was astonishingly successful in both the Yukon and Northwest Territories. While total expenditures by the northern administration for the year ending March 1951 rose by only $15,000 over the previous year, revenues had increased by over $250,000. On the negative side, the same *Annual Report* showed no new programmes or projects under consideration in the foreseeable future. In terms of political changes, it was also apparent that increased representation would not be accompanied by further responsibility until the two Territories could prove greater self-sufficiency.

The irony of the situation would become clearer in time: the costly interventionist policy, designed and promoted by well-meaning southerners for the perceived benefit of northerners, was now regarded as just cause for their continued dependency. For northern affairs, the philosophical idealism of the late forties had been replaced by more urgent military and financial considerations, and the intellectual concept of a "new north" would be destined to remain simply a vision—a promise unfulfilled.

10

Patterns and Priorities

> The pendulum of historical judgement on events and conditions,
> on their nature and causes, customarily swings from one conclu-
> sion to the opposite extreme.
>
> Lester B. Pearson, 1974

From a historical perspective, the interventionist northern policies established in the 1940s were an abrupt departure from the somewhat laissez-faire
approach of the previous decade. Yet despite the rapidity with which the
change took place, the process involved in policy decisions was extremely
complex owing to the interplay of diverse internal and external influences.
The result was the emergence of the oft-times confusing and contradictory set
of policies by which the territorial north has been governed. In addition to the
traditional patterns of government response to potential resource wealth and
perceived threats to northern sovereignty, a number of new priorities surfaced in the 1940s that would have a direct effect on the future of the northern
territories. Their relationship to the more traditional factors that shaped policy decisions in the past suggests a continuity of fundamental objectives with
only a moderate divergence in approach.

To date, there has been little attempt to examine the origins of northern
policy in the terms of how the decision-making process was affected by the
various influences and how those factors interrelated to diminish or gain in
importance. Most northern historiography has dwelt on the exploration and
discovery themes, on economic growth and political development, or on the
various aspects of northern society. As a result, the significance of Canadian-
American relations and the military impact have been understated, and the
"civilian cover" policy virtually ignored.[1] The secrecy involved in the
civilianization strategy was equally effective in reinforcing the somewhat
confused and mildly distorted view of northern history. Most oldtime northerners seemed quite unconcerned about the presence of increasing numbers

of military men in the postwar period, perhaps already accustomed to peacetime involvement with the RCAF activities in the 1930s; the media were moderately restricted by the cost of Arctic travel and by the peacetime censorship policies invoked in the late 1940s. Well hidden from southern vision lay the new airfields and radar warning systems, the military exercises and Arctic survival experiments, the weather stations, and the surveillance teams. Thus the initial adoption of a "civilian cover" policy offered a means to delay and moderate possible adverse public reaction until such time as the idea of a jointly occupied military north had been accepted as fact.

At the same time, however, there were also demands for new policy directions in the domestic affairs of the north: for structural reorganization of the administration and an overall plan for development, by the younger efficiency-minded civil servants; for constitutional changes and increased government services comparable to those available in the south, by newcomers to the north; and for improved health and educational opportunities for the indigenous peoples, by the more social-conscious southerners. Yet regardless of the rationale or the process required to initiate major action, the ultimate decisions were made directly or indirectly at the highest level, and they were weighed carefully in terms of the shifting priorities attached to sovereignty and national security. If prewar policy had been directed towards maximum sovereignty at minimal expense, the postwar dilemma centred on how to maintain adequate security with minimal loss of sovereignty.

From the time of Confederation to World War II, there had been periodic bursts of government interest and activity in the north, primarily in reaction to real or perceived American threats to Canadian jurisdiction in the remote regions of the territories. Most often, these challenges were associated with some form of resource exploitation such as whaling, mining, or oil production. Ottawa's response tended to follow a distinct pattern of first setting up adequate institutions to represent authority and maintain law and order, then providing financial assistance to private interests who indirectly reinforced sovereign rights, and, when appropriate, making an official declaration of its claims. During the war and early postwar years, however, the perceived threats to national security and subsequent dependence on the United States military seriously complicated the issue. Understandably, when the possibility of an enemy attack increased, concern for sovereignty diminished, but it was increasingly apparent that former methods of dealing with perceived challenges were no longer effective once the challenger and ally were one and the same.

Government response after MacDonald's startling report in 1943 was initially comparable to previous patterns, especially the appointment of a special commissioner, the repayment for the costs of wartime construction, the re-examination of the legal position, and the promotion of future economic advantages in hopes of encouraging private enterprise. Had the Japanese threat of attack been an isolated incident, the future of Canada's north might have been quite different. As it happened, however, the realities of the post-war geopolitical situation suggested an even greater danger might be on the horizon. The possibility of Soviet aggression, combined with the uranium fields on the shores of Great Bear Lake and the advances in aviation technology firmly entrenched the wartime significance of the region. With Canada now lying inconveniently between the two opposing superpowers, Ottawa again faced the dilemma of being dependent upon a traditional adversary to defend against a potential one. The painful process of assessing the various options began in earnest.

Balancing the alternatives in the sovereignty or security debate required wisdom, diplomacy, and a sensitivity to the longer-term implications that did not come easily to the election-conscious politicians. Describing the limits of a diplomat's authority, John Holmes wrote of the need for compromise and moderation. "Discretion in diplomacy is not incompatible with boldness of initiative in foreign policy or even with dramatic moves in international politics. The discretion is in the calculation of the issues at stake and the forces which can be mustered. Above all it lies in the recognition of contradiction and the acceptance of paradox."[2] Without denying the principles of democracy, Holmes also argued that diplomatic responsibility must rest on a few "highly educated and well informed elite" to avoid emotional overreaction by a less informed general public.[3] In this context, Canadians' longstanding sensitivity to matters adversely affecting their northern lands appear to justify extra caution.

Traditionally, Canada has been a non-militaristic and non-aggressive nation, and there is no reason to suggest that the senior politicians and diplomats of the 1940s were otherwise motivated. The fear that the next war might be a nuclear one and fought on Canadian soil or even the consequences of being unprepared for such an eventuality, weighed heavily on the shoulders of senior statesmen. Doubtless, they would not have conceived Truman's idea of "civilian cover" to be deceptive or in excess of their executive power, but merely the assumption of invested authority towards preventing a third World War. In this context, the policy was likely considered a right and honourable example of "the end justifying the means."

A more serious problem arises from the precedent established, rather than the action itself. The strategy may well have been *bona fide* and the intentions of the men, honourable, but there are inherent dangers in continuing confidentiality. The subtle circumvention of democratic rights may not have warranted criticism during the volatile atmosphere of the postwar years, but doing so for the expediency of avoiding public criticism raises the question of political ethics. Indirectly, this issue would ultimately affect northern policy decisions and process in the years to come.

The other reasons advanced for "civilian cover" were of equal, if not of greater importance. Concern about possibly inciting criticism for contravening the United Nations Charter and the fear of precipitating a Soviet response to perceived American aggression were particularly critical for a middle power the size of Canada. On the other hand, Washington's assumption that Ottawa was concerned about becoming estranged from the Commonwealth was probably less of a real concern, but it seemed to be an effective bargaining tool in negotiating a less binding commitment and better terms. The underlying strategy behind the compromise solution appeared to follow a similar pattern to that of the Ogdensburg Agreement in 1940. In this instance, however, an agreement in principle still allowed active participation in the planning of North American defence, but with seemingly more flexibility to reject proposals than in an official alliance. Besides, the provision that each project must be approved individually was expected to safeguard against unauthorized activities by continual review of their necessity. As had occurred during the war, the "paper guarantees" did not always translate into practice, and in the late 1940s, the proliferation of activities again concealed the overall dimension of American involvement. Although the wartime Permanent Joint Board on Defence became truly "permanent" in 1947, it was perceived to have been granted more official permanency when institutionalized with the NORAD agreement in 1958.

In addition to the PJBD, a number of civilian co-ordinating institutions also survived into peacetime, with many retaining the basic infrastructure set down in 1909 with the creation of the International Joint Commission. In essence, the precedent for negotiated agreement was already in place; World War II simply accelerated and expanded the process by which the two countries were quickly moving towards an executive confederal-styled relationship. The procedures and tensions involved in the negotiations for the Auto Pact, the Distant Early Warning System, the Columbia River Treaty, or, more recently, the free trade agreement and attempts to resolve sovereign claims to the Northwest Passage were vaguely similar to those involved in Canada's federal-provincial relations and remarkably so in the debates on resource-sharing and access to the Arctic lands and water, which appeared to be Canada's key bargaining chips in negotiations. The question which should concern Canadians is whether the country is moving from a *de facto* North American binational confederation, less formalized than the European Economic Community, towards an unofficial co-operative federal-style association. If so, the consequences affecting the future of Canada's north are indeterminable. In the 1940s, ironically, only Mackenzie King, Malcolm Mac-

Donald, and a number of private citizens appeared seriously concerned; others did not anticipate the degree to which Canada's military and economic autonomy would erode over the succeeding decades.

The sovereignty debate is ongoing, whether it is related to the legal rights in Arctic waters or the more insidious loss of control through American economic investment in northern resources. Similarly, the question of joint defence in the Arctic continues to make the front pages. Ever since the Alaska Boundary decision in 1903, the long-term strategy has been to avoid public challenges that might lead to an adverse decision by the International Court of Justice and instead to seek consensus through binational or international negotiation or by a unilateral declaration based on principles likely to gain international acceptance. A more recent example of this sequence was the voyage of the SS *Manhattan* in 1969, and again in 1970, followed by Pierre Elliott Trudeau's unilateral declaration of the Arctic Waters Pollution Prevention Act. Active participation in multilateral negotiations came later at the Law of the Sea Conferences. A similar pattern came after the voyage of the SS *Polar Sea*, when baseline boundary limits were drawn around the Arctic Archipelago and then followed by attempts to negotiate American acceptance of Canadian sovereignty over the Northwest Passage. Reminiscent of prewar strategies, Prime Minister Brian Mulroney then announced the construction of a new icebreaker, ostensibly to show a presence of authority. An overt challenge usually resulted in an immediate response; a less direct threat was dealt with by more subtle, cautious means. Yet the inherent paradoxes now seem greater, especially when one considers that Ottawa is currently planning to increase its military strength by acquiring a submarine fleet primarily for reasons of asserting Arctic sovereignty rather than protection against an enemy invasion. The two issues appear to have been melded into one.

For the most part, patterns of government response to northern issues have had a distinct exploitive character, justified as being in the "national interest" and consistent with various hinterland/metropolis theses. The origins of many policies are rooted in the events of the 1940s, with concerns for the environment and aboriginal rights only recently added to the list. Even here, southern priorities have continued to provide the primary motivation behind new policy directions and the speed with which they have been set down and implemented.

In the postwar years, the impossibility of solving the "sovereignty or security" question on a permanent basis became readily apparent. The key was to build upon agreements and institutions which offered the optimum of flexibility. Yet the perceived security crisis in 1950 revealed the degree to which the "sovereignty reinforcing" civilian activities were directly counterproductive to plans for Arctic defence. Moreover, the costs of economic development and social programmes competed directly for funds needed to support the escalating costs of the joint defence plans. There is a crucial lesson here, for fundamentally at stake was the more important question of whether the territories of the future would become a civilian or military north, Canadian or American. The decision then was a compromise: optimum security with minimal, but perceived unavoidable loss of sovereignty.

Quite apart from the complicated international influences affecting northern policy decisions, there were internal pressures which followed more closely the traditional patterns of government response. In a manner somewhat reminiscent of the nineteenth-century experience in the Canadian west, the economic growth and settlement patterns in the territories were shaped largely by policies in the 1940s. Despite the general similarities to early prairie settlement, there were also major differences dictated by time and place. There were airways instead of railways; weather stations and flying fields in place of train stations; miners instead of farmers; and the Department of Mines and Resources rather than the Department of the Interior. The fear of American encroachment on sovereignty was also present, but in a much different form. And there were other distinct differences: a more genuine concern for the welfare of the native people as opposed to the goal of simply acquiring their land through treaties; the threats to national security and the hurried military decisions about the location of air routes and highways; and the fact that the inhospitable land could not sustain any sizable population or agricultural production. Economic value was not measured in bushels of wheat, but in ounces of gold and barrels of oil. Nor did the frontier roll back as the white settlers arrived; instead, it developed pockets of company towns and military bases amid vast wilderness lands where Indians and Inuit still roamed, free from the limitations set by reservations. Circumstances also encouraged acceptance of a sizable American presence, but in the 1940s, they were temporary residents, not prospective Canadian citizens. Just as the history of the northern territories does not fit the traditional mold of Canadian growth and development, the military aspect was not compatible with the romantic vision held by many Canadians.

The "new north" promoted in the 1940s was a dream growing out of optimistic Canadian nationalism, forcing Ottawa to abandon its former apathetic approach in favour of aggressive intervention. Geography prevented planned settlement as was the case of the west, yet there was need for much more than just a presence of authority to counter the American military presence. In some respects, Ottawa's attempts to cope with the problem were trial and error, a result of being faced with a dilemma that had no precedent. At the same time, however, the policies cannot be explained solely in terms of geographical, social, economic, and international pressures. The actual process of policy-making, the resistance encountered, the personalities and idealism of the people involved, and the force of public opinion all constituted major influences on the ultimate nature and degree of government involvement.

Government action rarely occurs without public pressure. Attempts to sustain the burst of government activity in the 1920s failed, partly owing to a growing belief that the region was of little importance to the south. During the postwar years, however, awareness of the Arctic's new strategic significance was paralleled by an overall increase in social consciousness and the expectation of greater government responsibility for the welfare of the Canadian people. Likewise, the nature of government involvement was a reflection of the aims and methods of a more progressive outlook in Ottawa, and those who promoted change in northern government were inevitably centralists and interventionists. Their belief that a "new north" would increase Canada's importance as a world power was in complete accord with the aims and perceptions of the internationalists.

The expectation that development of the northern frontier would strengthen the nation's role in world affairs also had a curious precedent in the past. The imperial federationists in the 1890s envisaged Canada as a major power in a restructured British Empire. As a prerequisite, settlement of the western prairies was crucial to economic growth and autonomy. Immigration, trade, and transportation policies were also designed to strengthen the nation against threat of United States expansion. Thus the proposed Imperial Federation was perceived as a means of recognizing Canadian autonomy in hopes of reducing American influence.[4] The same rationale was used by the internationalists of the 1940s to justify active participation in the United Nations and the North Atlantic Treaty Organization. Both generations of nationalists saw planned frontier development as protection against possible American encroachment or domination. The involvement of Sir George Robert Parkin in the Imperial Federation movement and that of his son George Raleigh Parkin as a key mover behind the northern nationalists of the 1940s were perhaps more ironic than symbolic, but the similar elitist intellectual thrust in their arguments was undeniable.

Of greater significance was the similarity of the conviction that Canada's future in the 1940s lay in responsible development of the north, just as ordered settlement of the west had been seen as crucial to the building of a a strong and independent nation. Both objectives demanded extensive financial involvement by a strong centralist and interventionist federal government. The aim of "peace, order and good government" in western settlement was also inherent in the northern policy set down in the late 1940s, and although the planned social benefits for northern natives reflected more progressive attitudes, they were equally paternalistic. Unquestionably, there was a distinct element of empire-building in the goals of the northern nationalists as illustrated in their emotional plea to Canadians to envision an "unexplored frontier luring the pathfinder into the unknown,"[5] or the "map of Canada unrolling northwards"[6] with "visionary men hurrying the Northwest forward to its new destiny."[7] A particularly eloquent version was expressed in the conclusion of Keenleyside's speech to McMaster University in May 1949: "The North has been referred to as the frontier. But the frontier is more than a geographical area; it is a way of life, a habit of mind. As such it plays a most significant role in the national life. . . . In Canada the frontier has persisted longest in the North. Here indeed is a true frontier and one that will never be fully conquered. . . . The frontier is a bastion of freedom, and the North is a permanent frontier."[8] In his view, the Canadian frontier was to remain open, never fully conquered. Subconsciously perhaps, he may have been expressing the somewhat schizoid hopes and beliefs of many Canadians, that the north will inevitably be "developed" yet still retain its mythical romantic influence on the Canadian identity.

Just as the promise of frontier development and the more nebulous "myth of the north" retained their ability to inspire, perceived challenges to Canada's Arctic sovereignty continued to be a catalyst arousing concern. In the 1940s, the reasons were more complex, and the fears not as easily dispelled. Even before receiving final payment for the facilities they had constructed during the war, Washington again was proposing northern defence projects of a magnitude that went far beyond Canada's technological or financial capabilities. Earlier rumours that Washington planned to investigate the ownership of all Arctic islands[9] appeared to be borne out in 1946 with a report that the United States Air Force had begun searching for undiscovered islands to claim as American territory.[10] Fears that Washington might act independently if Canada refused to co-operate required more careful consideration of the options.

The price Washington was asked to pay for Canada's peacetime co-operation was, by all accounts, unexpectedly high. Not only would the U.S. taxpayer be required to pay the major share of costs for the new defence facilities built on foreign soil, but the American military, although mainly responsible for their operation, would often have Canadian officers nominally in control. Washington also agreed to recognize Canadian sovereignty at all the bases, and even then they only had an informal agreement which required, where possible, concealment of the initial stages under the guise of civilian activities. Thus it happened that in contrast to the situation in Greenland, the Caribbean, and elsewhere throughout the postwar world, there would be no United States military bases on Canadian soil.

In the eyes of the Canadian public, on the other hand, Ottawa had adopted an aggressive approach to northern affairs primarily to encourage economic growth and reinforce sovereignty. Understandably, the new policies would require strong central control with minimal regard for an expansion of local representation or more responsible government, a side effect which only later gave rise to severe criticism of Ottawa's colonial attitude in the territories. Federal intervention in all aspects of territorial affairs reached an unprecedented high by the end of the decade, with the result that Ottawa had become the largest single employer in the northern territories. Yet such a dramatic increase in government involvement necessitated an equally dramatic increase in expenditure—far out of proportion to the rise of local revenues or population increase.[11] To justify sustaining such a financial burden, there would be need of a continuing sovereignty crisis of greater priority than perceived threats of enemy attack.

Even so, such a sizable government investment would not have been possible without the approval of southern taxpayers. Towards this end, the "northern nationalists" played a key role in bringing the problems of the territories to the attention of all Canadians. Their enthusiasm was infectious and spread to a number of politicians and bureaucrats who were in a position to influence policy and administrative changes. The call for reform came not from northern residents, but from southerners who came to know the north through their various fields of endeavour.

New policies also brought to light the inherent conflicts involved in northern development. The problems of territories were diverse and interdependent, with the solution of one often in discord with another; inevitably the visions of nation-building were forced to come to terms with northern realities. This divisiveness concerned all aspects of politics: internal tension between traditional conservative thought and the reform-minded intellectuals, intergovernmental jealousies between the civilian and military agencies, and competition between Britain and the United States over Canada's future military allegiance. The latter was further complicated by each country's internal differences and conflicting purposes. All served to create temporary shifts in the priority attached to various domestic and externally related policies.

In December 1941, the issue of security was a new problem superimposed on traditional concerns about the north, and further complicated in 1945 when atomic warfare necessitated a reconsideration of priorities. The old fears of British paternalism and American imperialism were looked at differently in the new nuclear age, and the new peacetime commitments would not have "the end of the war" as a defined point of termination or renegotiation. Instead, the Cold War escalated the implementation of the defence plans until they finally brought a halt to the momentum of territorial development. Still faced with the prospect of adverse public opinion in 1950, St. Laurent demanded more promises of secrecy. Apprised of Ottawa's reluctance to engage in further consideration of future defence projects for fear of a leak to the press and disclosure to the public, Washington promised that "the United States authorities concerned will make every effort to avoid disclosures of information which will prove embarrassing to the Canadian government."[12] Eventually, Canadian attempts to maintain the image of joint participation began to frustrate the Americans, prompting one officer to complain that "when the U.S. has 95 per cent of the sites to be protected and 95 per cent of the equipment, why should we consider a joint commander with Canada. All we need is permission to station forces in Canada."[13] American intentions had changed little since the war.

A strategy similar to that used in 1947 to divert public attention from the build-up of military activities was again employed by St. Laurent in 1953. Claiming that Ottawa had previously governed its north in a "fit of absence of mind,"[14] St. Laurent announced the creation of a new Department of Northern Affairs and National Resources. One could argue that the "absence of mind" was perhaps St. Laurent's own because of the similarity in structure and function to that created by Keenleyside in 1950; it was primarily the name and the key players that had changed. As well, it seems more than coincidental that this announcement was in juxtaposition with the signing of an agreement for the new Distant Early Warning (DEW) radar system and tentative plans to convert several additional Arctic airfields into offensive bases. This pattern of coincidence might also raise speculation over the timing of Diefenbaker's "northern vision" and the signing of the NORAD agreement. Similarly, there would seem to be a distinct correlation between publicity of increased government involvement and the planned expansion of joint military activities.

The focus on security by the late 1940s marked the beginning of yet another phase of policy changes for the territories. The image of a "frontier of destiny" was transformed into a nightmarish undefended wilderness. As Michael Young reported in *Saturday Night*, 13 October 1951, the western Arctic was "not exactly a soft under-belly, rather a big toe an enemy can stand on while he slugs you." Even Claxton, the minister of national defence, admitted to the House of Commons that "while the risk of even a diversionary raid or diversionary attack was slight indeed three years ago, it is an actual possibility now."[15] Now, such concern about a possible Soviet attack on the United States by way of Canada seems grossly exaggerated, but in 1950 the fear was real and widespread. Yet the growth of the military north was not without its injurious effects on northern residents. Despite the social reforms instituted between 1947 and 1949, success in the short term did not ensure that the long-term objectives would remain the same, particularly with regards to the social and economic programmes designed to encourage more gradual adaptation of the indigenous peoples to modern technology and the white mans' standards of living. With the renewed military activities after 1950, the Inuit were exposed again to the advanced technology and faster pace of the white man's world, but there were only limited opportunities to share in the activities since there had been no provision for teaching the technical skills required for permanent employment at the defence installations. In a sense, "civilization" arrived too quickly and before the planned reforms could repair the neglect of a former era. Some programmes, which were intended to make the Inuit and Indians independent citizens, capable of full participation in development of the north, only succeeded in transferring their former dependency on the fur traders and missions to the federal government.

White communities suffered a similar fate. Construction and transportation needs of the new settlements were costly and required advanced technology to adapt to the harsh conditions. Moreover, the influx of government administrators and workers resulted in demands for northern living allowances, tax exemptions, fringe benefits, and basic services to make life in the north comparable to that in the south. What had begun as a simple inducement to attract better qualified teachers to the native schools soon escalated into what some called "the plague of the north."[16] Ironically, the rapid growth of white settlements actually served to increase the need for federal financial assistance, creating a dependency not envisioned in the image of a new frontier, the "bastion of freedom." Thus, the price paid by white northerners for more government involvement in social and economic development was a loss of independence.

Despite the non-fulfilment of long-term goals, the accomplishments of the northern nationalists in the 1940s helped force an end to Ottawa's former apathetic approach to northern government and encouraged public awareness of their social responsibility for the native population. As we approach the last decade of the twentieth century, Canada will require equally enthusiastic northern nationalists to maintain its sovereignty over the vast Arctic lands and waters. The alternative to binational control perhaps may be found in Mikhail Gorbachev's suggestion of scientific co-operation and proposals for a demilitarized Arctic or in the Inuit Circumpolar Conference's concept of a third order of government.

In the Canadian experience, concern for northern sovereignty has been a manifestation of nationalism, as was the American tendency to dominate or encroach on the rights of neighbouring independent nations. As pointed out by Joseph S. Nye, Jr., professor of political science at Harvard University, "the transnational world of North America is not a post-nationalist world." In his analogy, "the eagle may soar; beavers build dams."[17]

The territorial north has many images and many interpretations of its history. From whatever perspective—military, economic, political or social— the 1940s marked a significant turning point in the direction of government policy. The circumstances and events affecting the issues of sovereignty, stewardship, and security were as numerous as they were diverse, but the crucial policy decisions were made by a few individuals as influenced by world affairs, public opinion, and their own personal convictions. All believed in the future of their country and that the key to that future was the image of a "new north," a Canadian north free from American domination and secure against enemy attack—a "true north, strong and free." Sadly, the present has not entirely lived up to their dreams and expectations.

The questions of Arctic sovereignty versus national security are still raised and still unresolved. Yet only a few are aware that the debate originated from commitments made in a railway car at Ogdensburg, New York, in the summer of 1940 and cemented at the Chateau Laurier Hotel in Ottawa in December 1946. Canada's north did indeed undergo dramatic changes which had an enormous impact on the lives of most northerners and on the minds and economy of southerners. But more importantly, the "new north" acquired a military emphasis which would have serious and enduring implications—including the perpetuation of the sovereignty or security debate.

Appendices

APPENDIX A

Cabinet Changes circa 1940–50

Prime Minister
W. L. M. King   November 1935–1948
L. S. St. Laurent   November 1948–June 1957

Secretary of State for External Affairs
W. L. M. King   September 1935–1946
L. S. St. Laurent   September 1946–September 1948
L. B. Pearson   September 1948–June 1957

Minister of Mines and Resources
T. A. Crerar   April 1936–April 1945
J. A. Glen   April 1945–June 1948
J. A. MacKinnon   June 1948–March 1949
Colin W. G. Gibson   April 1949–January 1950

Minister of Resources and Development
R. H. Winters   January 1950–September 1953
J. Lesage   September 1953–December 1953

Minister of Northern Affairs and National Resources
J. Lesage   December 1953–June 1957

Minister of National Defence
N. McL. Rogers   September 1939–June 1940
C. G. Power   June 1940–July 1940 (Acting)
J. L. Ralston   July 1940–November 1944
A. G. L. McNaughton   November 1944–August 1945
D. C. Abbott   August 1945–December 1946
B. Claxton   December 1946–June 1954

Minister of National Defence for Air
C. G. Power   May 1940–November 1944
A. L. MacDonald   November 1944–January 1945 (Acting)
C. W. G. Gibson   January 1945–March 1945 (Acting)
C. W. G. Gibson   March 1945–December 1945 (Office disbanded)

Minister of National Health and Welfare
B. Claxton   November 1944–December 1946
P. J. Martin   December 1946–June 1957

Changes in the Civil Service circa 1940–50

Clerk of the Privy Council
A. D. P. Heeney   March 1940–March 1949
N. A. Robertson   March 1949–June 1952
J. Pickersgill   June 1952–June 1953

Under-Secretary of State for External Affairs
O. D. Skelton   April 1925–January 1941
N. A. Robertson   January 1941–December 1946
L. B. Pearson   December 1946–September 1948
E. M. Reid   September 1948–March 1949 (Acting)
A. D. P. Heeney   March 1949–December 1951

Deputy Minister of Mines and Resources
Chas. Camsell   1936–January 1947
H. L. Keenleyside   January 1947–January 1950

Deputy Minister of Resources and Development
H. L. Keenleyside   January 1950–October 1950
H. A. Young   October 1950–February 1953
R. G. Robertson   February 1953–December 1953
                           (Department renamed as of January 1954)

APPENDIX B

Founding Members of the Arctic Institute of North America

Note: Charter members are considered to be those present at any of the three preparatory meetings (31 March 1944 in Ottawa; 13 May 1944 in New York; 8 September 1944 in Montreal), or elected to the first board of governors.

Founders   *Occupation in 1944–1945*
Baird, Patrick D.   colonel, Canadian Army
Bajkov, A.   U.S. scientist in private employ
Beattie, J. Robert   director of the Bank of Canada

Bélanger, Henri	Canadian land surveyor
Bill, E. Gordon	dean of faculty, Dartmouth College
Boggs, Samuel W.	geographer with the Department of State
Boyle, R. W.	National Research Council of Canada
Camsell, Charles	deputy minister of Mines and Resources
Carlson, William S.	United States Army Air Force
Chester, Philip A.	general manager, Hudson's Bay Company
Collins, Henry B.	anthropologist with the Smithsonian Institution
Deason, Hilary D.	zoologist with the Department of the Interior
Flint, Richard F.	United States Army Air Force
Gould, Laurence M.	United States Army Air Force
Gushue, Raymond	lawyer and, in 1944, chairman of Fishery Products Committee, International Emergency Food Council, Washington
Hanna, William F.	R.C.A.F., a member of the Permanent Joint Board on Defence
Heeney, Arold	clerk of the Privy Council
Hopkins, Ernest	president, Dartmouth College
Jenness, Diamond	chief anthropologist, National Museum of Canada
Joerg, W. L. G.	geographer, National Archives, Washington
Keenleyside, Hugh L.	assistant under-secretary of state for External Affairs
Lloyd, Trevor	Dartmouth College and acting vice-consul for Canada in Greenland
Mackenzie, C. J.	president, National Research Council of Canada
MacMillan, Donald B.	American explorer
Newton, Robert	member of the National Research Council of Canada and president of the University of Alberta
O'Neill, John J.	dean of Engineering, McGill University
Parkin, G. Raleigh	assistant treasurer, Sun Life Assurance Company of Canada
Patterson, G. A.	Hydrographic Office, Washington
Porsild, A. Erling	chief botanist, National Museum of Canada
Porsild, Morten	botanist, Danish Arctic Research Station, Greenland
Rogers, Walter S.	director, Institute of Current World Affairs
Smith, Philip S.	with the U.S. Geological Survey
Stefansson, Vilhjalmur	Arctic explorer and author
Washburn, Albert	United States Army and Air Force
Weaver, John D.	geographer, Hydrographic Office, Washington
Wilson, J. Tuzo	director, Operational Research, National Defence Headquarters
Wright, John K.	American Geographical Society
Wynne-Edwards, V. C.	zoologist, McGill University

APPENDIX C

Opening of the Alaska Highway
by Captain Richard L. Neuberger

[A personal account of the ceremonies written by the aide to General O'Connor, USAAF.]

The ceremony opening the Alcan International Military Highway has come and gone and now the road is in actual operation. The first trucks have arrived in Fairbanks. Appropriately enough, the first vehicle ever driven overland from the interior of North America to Alaska was piloted by a pair of enlisted soldiers, a corporal from Chicago and a private from Minneapolis. This was at the direct order of General O'Connor, who felt that enlisted men should share in the culminating event of the construction of the road. . . .

It was a ceremony international in character. Your friend Bob Bartlett (Governor of Alaska) led a representative delegation from Juneau. The Honourable Ian Mackenzie of the Canadian Cabinet headed an outstanding delegation from Ottawa, General George R. Pearkes represented Canada's armed forces. In 1914, Pearkes was a constable in the Royal Mounted at Whitehorse. He told me that some of the territory he drove over en route to the ceremony he once patrolled on horseback in a scarlet tunic. When the first World War broke out, Constable Pearkes resigned from the Mounted and enlisted in the Canadian Army. He won the Victoria Cross for valour and now commands the Pacific Command of his country.

Just as the construction of the Highway demonstrated the ingenuity of our soldiers and workers on a large scale, the ceremony opening the Highway demonstrated the ingenuity on a much smaller scale.

We had no printing press, yet programs seemed indispensable. What to do? Mimeographing was too colourless and drab. The blueprinting machine on the Public Roads Administration finally was pressed into service. Jean Ewen, PRA design engineer, made some excellent Arctic drawings. Gay Pinkstaff, PRA photographer, ran off the copies. The result was a program which many people thought was not only printed but actually engraved!

It was quite a task to find distinctive food, because supply difficulties in the wilderness are enormous, as you know. We finally relied on nature's larder. Major Dick Lucknow, whom you may remember as one of the men who helped to build the Alaskan Railroad, sent out hunting parties. The result was moose meat, mountain sheep steaks and a thinned-out black bear. We gave all the groceries local names, vis. "Dawson Creek Crackers," "Fairbanks Cheese," and "Slims River Salad." The "Slims River Salad" turned out to be lettuce and hot-house tomatoes, and we never succeeded in convincing any of our guests that the lettuce and tomatoes were picked right outside at 40 degrees below.

Where to hold the ceremony? This problem was a stickler for a month. Finally Col. T.W. Essig made a trip over the road. He selected Soldiers' Summit. This is a stretch of highway 1,500 feet above the wide swath of Kluane Lake. Above the road, dark crags tower. Below, the lake is spread out like a vast inland sea. The setting symbolizes the vastness which the Highway penetrates. Kluane Lake is approximately 100 miles east of the Alaska-Yukon International boundary.

The participants in the dedication ceremony, accompanied by newspaper correspondents and photographers, drove from Whitehorse to Kluane Lake on a day that the temperature crowded 15 below. Many feet, tender from the luxuries of civilization, were chilled by the time the new spruce barracks of Kluane were reached. Everyone slept that night dormitory style. The blue-printed programs were given out and privates traded autographs with colonels. A Negro soldier asked General O'Connor for his autograph, and the General climbed out of his sleeping bag, put on his spectacles, and signed the soldier's program. "That's the epitome of democracy, isn't it?" Bob Bartlett asked Ian Mackenzie, as they watched.

When we went to bed, all of us were slightly apprehensive over the fact that neither General Pearkes nor General Ganong of Canada's 8th Division had arrived. They had been delayed by bad flying weather, but were expected later. I think I went to sleep about 10 o'clock. Some time later I was awakened by a gentle padding on the lumber floor. I cautiously peeked out of a corner of the bag. General O'Connor, in his long underwear, with his fur cap on his head and his parka thrown around his shoulders, was tip-toeing to the door. He threw it open and a lusty "Halloo there!" came through.

The red hat bands and lapels of British general officers appeared in the darkened portal and in walked Generals Pearkes and Ganong. I lay there in my sleeping bag and struggled between comfort and duty. Could I stay in bed while he welcomed our late-comers? Soon from near by another shape of underwear emerged. It was Col. K. B. Bush, our chief of staff. He and General O'Connor, looking like union-suit advertisements, were convoying the Canadian generals to their bunks. My conscious overcame my drowsy laziness and I got up and added my size 42 underwear to the scene. "you chaps look quite nifty in those," said Lieut. Bob Sails, the aide to General Pearkes. This was British politeness at its kindest.

In the morning the ceremony was held. It was an event full of colour, drama and significance. Colonel Bush's hands became blue as he took off his gloves to read the statements received from yourself and many other distinguished men in public life. A long file of Royal Mounties stood at attention in their scarlet coats and leather boots. Their feet must have been as cold as anvils, but they stood as straight and rigid as signal poles. "Discipline and tradition account for that," said Colonel Bush, and Inspector William Brennan, commanding the Mounties in the Yukon Territory, nodded his assent.

All the speakers stressed the historic importance of what was taking place. Bob Bartlett presented an Alaskan Flag sent by the Fairbanks chapter of the Daughters of the American Revolution, whose head is Mrs. Donald MacDonald. Colonel Bush described Donald MacDonald as a pioneer advocate of a land route to Alaska, and Bartlett said that the people of Alaska wanted their flag to grace the headquarters of the Northwest Service Command. Ian Mackenzie spoke most eloquently for Canada and brought an inspiring message from Prime Minister King.

The ceremony moved toward a natural climax. At its end Mackenzie and Bartlett were given a pair of scissors. These scissors had been especially engraved in Alaskan gold by William Osborne, pioneer resident of Juneau. Fittingly, Mr. Osborne's daughter is Mrs.

Joe Crosson, the wife of the Arctic aviator who has saved so many lives. Mackenzie took one blade of the scissors, Bartlett the other. The crowd became tense. Then the blades closed and the red, white and blue ribbon across the road was severed. In the cold and gloom of the Arctic morning an American Army band played "God Save the King." Then, the strains of "The Star-Spangled Banner" filled the snowy air.

As the basalt cliffs flung back the last strains of the music, a great cheer went up from the crowd. I hurried from General O'Connor's side and struggled to save the ribbon for posterity. The first truck bound for Fairbanks rolled forward as the band played "The Maple Leaf Forever" and "Washington Post." At the wheel of this truck were two American Army enlisted men selected personally by General O'Connor—Corporal Otto Gronke of Chicago and Private Bob Howe of Minneapolis.

The General had declared that rank and file soldiers, who did so much to construct the road, were to be given genuine representation at the ceremony. The ribbon was held by four enlisted men: Corporal Refines Simms, Jr., of Philadelphia and Private Alfred Jalufka of Kennedy, Texas, representing the Whitehorse sector, and Master Sergeant Andrew E. Doyle of Philadelphia and Corporal John T. Reilly of Detroit, representing the Fort St. John sector. Sims and Reilly are Negroes, symbols of the coloured troops whose toil has played a material part in the 1,630-mile undertaking.

After the ceremony, lunch was served in the barracks. The smell of spruce pitch and wood grain was still in the air. Boughs hung from the ceiling. The crimson tunics of the Mounties mingled with the somber khaki of their American allies. We ate moose meat and mountain sheep. The band played Johann Strauss's "Tales From the Vienna Woods" and "The Blue Danube," lilting memories of a land which may soon be free. It was like some scene from a Graustarkian operetta. Inspector Grennan swayed his head to the gay waltzes, and so did the American mess sergeant who hurried along the tables seeing to it that no one's plate was empty.

It was an episode which will not soon be forgotten by those who participated in it. My own vivid memory of it is the playing of our national anthem by the band at Soldier's Summit. As the music faded away and I looked around me at the stern faces of the American soldiers and at the grim countenances of the Mounties, I felt sure that in such a scene as this lay the future of the United Nations—that in the ability of us all, Canadian, Americans and Alaskans, white and black, civilian and soldier, to fuse together our efforts in such a project as the Alcan Highway rests the hope of free peoples throughout the earth.

Source. NAC, Special Commissioner's Reports, RG 36/7, vol. 48, file "Press Releases"

APPENDIX D

*Reports to London Office by Malcolm
Macdonald, High Commissioner to Canada,
1941–45*

Document 1

[Excerpts from a report, on the subject of Anglo-Canadian Relations, to the Dominions Office (ca. March 1941]

I have had three long private talks over the luncheon and dinner table with Mr. Mackenzie King since I arrived. Some of the conversation has consisted of a mutual exchange of anecdotes, personal reminiscences and philosophic comments on politics and politicians which had better not be put "on the record," but it has illustrated a shrewd and humorous outlook on men and affairs which is an attractive part of the Prime Minister's character, and one of the weapons in his armoury which has enabled him to survive with good health and excellent temper a long life of political vicissitudes. . . .

There may be much to criticise in the Canadian Government's slowness in the early part of the war in coming to grips with the tasks involved; and there is still lacking here the urge which would come from the bombing of Ottawa, Montreal and a few other Canadian cities. But there is a growing consciousness that these grim experiences will only be denied to them if victory is denied to Hitler in Britain. Such reflections have stirred Mr. Mackenzie King and his colleagues into much greater energy. A deep natural affection for the Old Country for its own sake, and a proud admiration for the resistance of the people of Britain are also of course sharp spurs to action.

Another factor is now making Mr. Mackenzie King change the attitude of caution amounting to timidity and reticence amounting to dumbness which has sometimes characterized him. The efforts of the United States as an arsenal of democracy are receiving immense publicity, and seem to be completely eclipsing the valuable efforts of Canada in the sight of the overseas public. This tendency seems to be encouraged in Washington itself, where Canada's war effort is, I gather, being spoken of in terms of sarcasm which can only be compared with the sarcasm which I have heard used by our sailors who have to go to sea in the fifty destroyers which the United States presented to Britain. This sneering is very unjust to Canada, for such contributions as the Empire Air Training Scheme and the provision of dollars by Canada, not to mention the sacrifice of many young Canadian lives, are very great. Incidentally, it would be very helpful if orators in Britain who readily praise the aid that is to come to us from the United States would at the same time remember to mention that this grand young North American neighbour of the U.S.A., which is blood of our blood and flesh of our flesh, is giving aid which, in relation to the size and wealth of his population, is at least as great. But of course Mr. Mackenzie King is himself primarily to blame for the world's imperfect knowledge of Canada's effort. Until recently there has been no serious attempt by the Ottawa Government to make its extent known, and the Prime Minister in person has constantly frowned upon anything in the nature of "propaganda." He is modifying his attitude to this question. He is alarmed at the impression being created in so many quarters that the United States is the only workshop in this all important North American arsenal of democracy. He is unleashing the dogs of propaganda, and intends himself to lead the pact. One of the proposals that he wishes to make to the President when he meets him this week at Warm Springs is that he (the Prime Minister) should come to the United States and make a speech about Canada's war effort.

He has spoken much in our talks of his intimate conversations with the President. There is no doubt that these two get on very well together, and that Mr. Roosevelt confides a great deal to his fellow alumnus of Harvard when they meet. Not only their chats together at the fireside in the President's home, but also their telephone conversations in the hearing of subordinates appear to be conducted without any conventional official restraints or any respect for individual persons. . . . He has sought the Prime Minister's advice on some of his own Washington problems, and sometimes acted on his suggestions as to solutions. No doubt all these conversations are on record in some appropriate place, and I need not repeat their gist here.

The pleasant relationship which exists between these two statesmen "buddies" is illustrated by the story, which Mr. Mackenzie King told me with a merry twinkle in his eyes, of the beginning of their talks a year or more ago on North American defence. There is a large swimming pool at the President's house in Warm Springs, in which Mr. Roosevelt spends much time, for the buoyancy of the water seems to give a little life to his paralyzed limbs. The two friends were both up to the neck in the pool one day when Mr. Roosevelt remarked "Mackenzie, what are you and I going to do about the defence of the North American Continent?" The conversation then continued for two hours whilst the President and Prime Minister ("both of us," explained the latter to me, "stark naked except for little belly bands") basked in the sunny waters, and by the time that they had finished their bath they had also laid the foundations of the United States-Canadian agreement for military co-operation in the defence of this end of their Continent.

This friendship is not only charming but fruitful, and can be of much value to us. There may be some danger that Mr. Mackenzie King will be inclined to associate Canada too closely as a North American country with the United States as distinct from the United Kingdom. But I doubt whether he will really push this process further than is in any case inevitable. He has expressed to me more than once his relief that there is no body of opinion in the Dominion in favour of joining the United States. Loyalty to the British Commonwealth is, I believe, paramount in his mind as it is in the minds of his fellow countrymen.

This week he is going on another visit to the President, when he hopes to hear revelations of Mr. Roosevelt's intentions about United States participation in the war. I have ventured to wish him good bathing.

Source. PRO, London. Premier 4/44/10.

Document 2

[Report to the Dominions Office on the Hyde Park Agreement, 24 April 1941, on the subject of the Hyde Park Agreement.]

Office of the High Commissioner
for the United Kingdom,
Ottawa

Most Secret, Personal [handwritten]

24th April, 1941.

Dear Bobbety, [handwritten]

This is just to keep you posted about developments here which may be of interest to you. I expect you are a bit exercised about the long term political effects of these comings and goings between Mackenzie King and Roosevelt, though their results from the immediate point of view of waging the war are excellent and to be warmly commended. My own reflections on all these developments can be stated quite briefly as follows. It is natural and inevitable that Canada and the United States should come closer and closer together, on account of their geographical situation; it is to the general advantage of the English-speaking peoples and of the world that they should do so; nevertheless it is undesirable that the effect of this should be any weakening of British sentiment in Canada, and of her links with the British Commonwealth; the real danger of this comes from the propinquity of a small nation of eleven million people with an enormously powerful nation of 130 million, whose ideas and culture keep slopping over every day into Canada, this process must be countered by the deliberate keeping alive of British ideas and culture through visits of Canadians to Britain and some of the best British citizens to Canada; at present this work is being done by the magnificent fortitude and heroism of the whole British people, which makes Canadians prouder than they have ever been before to be a member of the Commonwealth.

Yours ever,
M. M.

The Right Hon. Viscount Cranborne,
Secretary of State for Dominion Affairs,
London.

* * *

[EXCERPTS]

I had a talk with Mr. Mackenzie King yesterday afternoon on his return from his week-end visit to President Roosevelt at Hyde Park.

He told me the story of his conversations, first with Mr. Morgenthau and then with Mr. Roosevelt, which ended in what the Prime Minister keeps inviting future historians to call the Declaration of Hyde Park. When I think somewhat irreverently of all the declarations which have been made by one person to another under the trees in that Hyde Park which comes first into the mind of a Londoner, I feel that the new pronouncement is in some ways quite in keeping with those others. This is a declaration of love between Canada and the United States, and the bachelor Prime Minister who acted as proxy for the Dominion which is already married into the family of the British Commonwealth, is as proud and smiling as any infatuated swain.

The Declaration contains the announcement of a quite handsome exchange of dowries between the two parties, which is a valuable contribution to the problems of war production and dollar exchanges here. The text of it is in London, so I need not expand upon its terms. Its substance was first discussed by Mr. Mackenzie King with Mr. Morgenthau; between that conversation and his Sabbath meeting with the President, Mr. King got his colleague Mr. Howe and some of his advisers who were in Washington to draft the statement, and Mr. King took this in his pocket for the talk with the President. In the course of their talk he produced it; Mr. Roosevelt went through it paragraph by paragraph and accepted it; Mr. King read it then and there to Mr. Morgenthau, who approved; a number of copies were promptly typed, and Mr. King asked the President whether he proposed that they should formally append their signatures to the document. Mr. Roosevelt said they need not bother to do that, but took out his pen and scrawled on the top copy "Done by Mackenzie and F. D. R. on a lovely sunny day at Hyde Park." So the famous Declaration was born.

Each of the principal partners in this love affair seems to have played his part with skill. One result is a considerable strengthening of Mr. King's reputation as a Statesman in Canada, where this latest achievement is deservedly greeted by the press and the public as something of a triumph. Though this development undoubtedly marks a further step in the close drawing together of Canada and the United States, it will not mean any loosening of the tie of devoted loyalty binding Canada to the United Kingdom. In all parts of the Dominion this sentiment is now intense and exceedingly warm. A "rapprochement" between the two North American countries is natural and inevitable, and is at present entirely consistent with the other relationship between the Dominion and the British Commonwealth. I see no particular reason why this situation should alter to the disadvantage of the Commonwealth. It is just one important part of that process which Mr. Churchill described as the affairs of Britain and the United States getting somewhat mixed up together. But what the more distant future may bring is still inscrutable. . . .

Ottawa
24th April, 1941.

Source. University of Durham, England, MacDonald Papers, 14/4/2-5.

Document 3

Printed for the War Cabinet. October 1942

SECRET
W.P. (42) 465   Copy No. 9
October 13, 1942

WAR CABINET

REPORT ON A VISIT TO NORTH-WEST CANADA AND ALASKA

Memorandum by the Secretary of State for Dominion Affairs

I think the attached despatch from the United Kingdom High Commissioner at Ottawa, reporting on a visit he recently made to the North-Western Provinces of Canada and Alaska, will be of interest to my colleagues.

C. R. A.

Dominions Office, October 13, 1942

Office of the High Commissioner
for the United Kingdom
Ottawa, September 4, 1942

(No. 508. Secret.)

Sir,

I have the honour to inform you that I have recently returned from a northern journey. My companions were Mr. T. A. Crerar and Dr. Charles Camsell (the Minister and Deputy-Minister of Mines and Resources respectively) and Mr. Ian Maclennan of this Office. We made the trip in an amphibian aeroplane and in three weeks travelled some 8,700 miles. We landed in various places in Northern Alberta, Northern British Columbia, the furthest point alighted 120 miles north of the Arctic Circle, at Aklavik. Generally speaking, this vast area is a land in which the virgin forest still reigns undisturbed over plains and mountains. Its spruce and poplar trees crowd to the edges of thousands of lakes and along the banks of many rivers. It is populated by millions of moose, caribou, wolves, bears and other fur-bearing animals, but only by small scattered communities of human beings.

2. We had two main purposes in making this journey. The first was to inspect the progress of the Alaska Highway and other works now being undertaken in Canada for the military defence of Alaska and Western Canada. There are three such main efforts. The first is the building of the Highway itself, the second is the construction of a chain of airfields along a similar route, and the third is the development of oil production at Norman Wells (on the banks of the Mackenzie River), with the laying of a pipe-line to transport this fuel

to Alaska. The American authorities are responsible for the building of the Highway, Canadian contractors are constructing the airfields, the Canadian officers of the Imperial Oil Company are charged with the production of oil at Normal Wells, and the American army is undertaking the laying of the oil pipe-line. Some Americans are also surveying the terrain for a railway to Alaska, but this a more remote project.

3. Our second purpose in going north was to meet the white settlers, Indians, Eskimos and half-breeds in those outlandish places, and to have a look at the conditions and prospects of fur-trading, mining and other activities there.

The Alaska Highway

4. The Alaska Highway is to run for some 1,500 miles from Dawson Creek (the terminal of the Northern Alberta Railway) through the passes and along the valleys of the Rocky Mountains to Fairbanks in Alaska. I need not enlarge upon the difficulties of a piece of construction which bids fair to be the greatest bit of road-making yet attempted by man. I will simply state that those difficulties have a way of disappearing before American imagination, boldness and mechanical resource. Whilst you look at it the road grows by leaps and bounds before your eyes. We motored along some miles of it and flew along some hundreds of miles of it. It is being constructed in a series of pieces, each of which stretches through the forest until it joins with the next-door bits. The Americans are being unnecessarily extravagant and making some mistakes. It does not matter. They are driving the road through. They have mobilised great herds of the most modern construction vehicles, which are worthy associates of the moose, bears and other wild creatures who are also sometimes to be seen careering amongst the trees. But the newcomers are much more powerful than those old-timers. There is, for instance, the bull-dozer. I was told that each bull-dozer along the Highway can clear each day a strip of ground seven miles long through the dense forest. There are many of these pugnacious creatures continuously on the job, for work on the Highway proceeds without interruption day and night. First the pioneer road is cleared, and after it follows the more finished gravel road. The Americans expect to complete the 1,500 miles of pioneer road and long patches of the gravelled road before winter freezes construction this year. They expect to complete the whole gravel road next year. Along the entire route the cleared ground will be 36 feet wide with a gravelled strip 24 feet wide running along its centre. There is some talk of hard-surfacing the road later, but no decision about this has been taken.

The Airfields

5. The chain of airfields (which does not coincide everywhere with the route of the Highway) is also being rapidly made. We landed on all of the fields save one, and looked upon that one from the air. Some of them are close to existing settlements or Hudson Bay Company forts, whilst others are being cut straight out of the untamed bush. There are seven airfields between Edmonton and Fairbanks inclusive, and in addition landing strips are now being put down every hundred miles. All of them are to have 5,000-feet runways, and in some cases runways of nearly 7,000 feet are being constructed. On them also work

proceeds without interruption day and night. I slept two nights in a sleeping-bag on one of the fields, and was often woken by the rumble and crash of the grading-machines in action.

6. Already a considerable traffic is making gigantic hops-skips-and-jumps along this air route northwards. Fighter and bomber aircraft and huge transport planes speed in a steady stream to Alaska. The transports are carrying men and materials. It is strange to meet them in the forest. One day I watched one of these creatures alight on a runway amidst the surrounding trees, open its door and eject a couple of jeeps. It was easy to imagine that one was really watching a prehistoric monster giving birth to twins.

7. R.C.A.F. administrative staffs are to be in charge of all the Canadian airfields but the groundcrews to service aircraft passing through will be provided by the United States Army Air Corps. I beg the Air Ministry to keep a close eye on this important air route. Unless I am mistaken it will be the simplest, speediest and busiest airway from the Americas to the Orient in the future. And the air route which the Americans are now planning across Canada and through Hudson Bay, Greenland and Iceland to Europe will have similar prospects in the opposite direction. The Agreement between Canada and the United States provides that after the war the Alaska Highway, the airfields across Northern Canada and the other defence works shall all revert in unqualified ownership to the Dominion. But I confess that I do not trust all the responsible authorities amongst our American allies, and I saw enough in the north-west to give me an unpleasant feeling that they will seek to use their power after the war to gain control of these vital air-routes. Mr. Crerar and I have communicated our opinions on this to members of the Canadian Government. It is primarily for them to defend British interests in Canada, but I trust that in Britain we shall be alert to stimulate and support them in any efforts that may be needed.

Oil

8. At present the oil for Alaska has to travel from distant places to the American Pacific seaboard, then up the coast by ship to Skagway, across the mountains by rail to Whitehorse and thence by road to its destination in Alaska. The route is long and vulnerable to a daring enemy. There is a much closer potential source of oil supply a few hundred miles away from Whitehorse, at Norman Wells in the Mackenzie flats. The main obstacle is the barrier of the Rocky Mountains lying between Whitehorse and Norman Wells. But the engineers on the job exclaim: "To hell with the Rocky Mountains!"

9. Oil was being produced from a single well at Norman before the war started. It is a fuel of excellent quality. So now the production is being stepped-up as rapidly as possible. The production figure originally aimed at by the authors of the scheme was 3,000 barrels a day, and they roughly estimated that perhaps as many as 30 wells would be required to achieve that figure. But already some half-dozen wells have been developed to the production stage, and their capacity has exceeded expectation. Some of them have not been properly tested and have had to be "capped" for the time being, because neither the pipeline to carry the oil away nor adequate tankage to store it at Norman Wells have yet been provided. But the evidence seems to show that most if not all of these wells will produce three or four or even more hundred barrels of oil a day. Therefore many authorities at Norman now consider that much fewer than 30 wells will attain 3,000 barrels a day, and

that a much larger production can be comfortably achieved if necessary. Other authorities, however, still speak more cautiously of the future.

10. The production side of the business is therefore proceeding satisfactorily so far. The erection of a pipe-line to convey the oil to Alaska has not made the same good progress. At the best of times the problem of conveying from Edmonton to Norman Wells about 1,200 miles away the immense length of 4-inch pipe and all the other equipment required to accomplish the task is difficult. These supplies cover the first 300 miles of the journey by rail. But after that there is neither rail nor road. The customary route is by boat down the Athabaska River, across a small space of Lake Athabaska, down the Slave River, across a large stretch of Great Slave Lake and along the Mackenzie river to Normal Wells. some of the freight can be carried in aircraft, and adequate air transport is now being developed. But this cannot carry the heavier loads.

11. The first difficulty on the waterways was lack of sufficient boats. The Americans, however, have now built the boats. The second difficulty was more formidable. It was Great Slave Lake. This is one of the most treacherous water passages in the world. The lake is broad, shallow and exposed, and when the wind blows straight at it from the Arctic its choppy waves are the grave of any unwary craft. They have been an obstacle to explorers and voyagers from the days of Sir Alexander Mackenzie onwards, and are proving no more amenable to exasperated American engineers to-day. Six precious bull-dozers and some other vehicles are already nestling in the mud at the bottom of the lake, and their loss has been a serious deterrent to the American attempt to hustle the northern lakes and forests. Colonel Wyman, the experienced American officer who is in charge of the laying of the pipe-line, told me that he would "rather bring the stuff across the Pacific Ocean than across Great Slave Lake." He ought to know, because until six months ago he was constructing the line of military airfields across the ocean from the United States of America to Australia.

12. The third difficulty in the way of transport this year has been created by forest fires. This has been a remarkably dry season in the north, so fires galore are raging. Consequently, a thick pall of smoke, as dense as a bad fog, has hung over the whole country between Edmonton and Great Slave Lake week after week, at a time when air and river transport is usually very active. For long periods every aeroplane in the place has been grounded, and small craft like scows have been tied up. The pipe and much other important equipment got stranded hundreds of miles south of where it was needed.

13. However, these difficulties are being overcome as quickly as possible. But the proposal to start the actual laying of the pipe-line this year has been abandoned. The surveying of the best route over the plain and across the Rocky Mountains is proceeding, but the laying of the pipes is now postponed until the ice and snow have loosed their grip on the land next spring. Those responsible hope to complete the work before another winter can intervene.

14. Some well-qualified judges doubt whether the Americans' present plan will ever work effectively. They think it would be wiser not to take the pipe-line due west from Norman Wells and across the Rockies to Whitehorse, but to lead it in a north-westerly direction from its starting-point, keeping it in the lower country east of the mountains until it can outflank their northern tip and continue over easy ground to Fairbanks in Alaska,

giving Whitehorse a miss. This would be a longer but more practicable route, the sceptics say.

15. But the Americans and the experienced Canadian who is their chief surveyor are determined to make a direct assault upon the Rockies, seeking out the mountain passes. Even by this route the pipe-line will be about 500 miles long. It will cross three distinct mountain ranges, climbing from 200 feet above sea level at Norman Wells to about 4,500 feet at the highest point of its journey. The temperature in those parts may fall as low as 50° or 60° below zero in the winter. But laboratory tests show that the oil continues to flow at a temperature of 70° below zero. So there is no need to sink the pipe-line underground; it will be built over the surface of the ground and covered with earth and moss, which, in any case, is a good insulator against cold.

16. Certain minor difficulties are inevitably associated with all these works. Generally, the qualities of ability and tact in the American officers in charge of their sections of the undertakings are impressive, the conduct of their troops (including battalions of negroes) has been good, and relations between them and the Canadian authorities are excellent. But some of the Americans throw their weight about in an unfortunate manner, and the fact that the pay of American civilian workers on these projects is about double that of the Canadian is also perhaps storing up friction between them for the future. The customary troubles connected with wine and women (though not yet noticeably with song) are now invading the north, and setting a few posers for the Yukon and North-West Territories authorities. Another severe difficulty is mosquitoes. Nature is sending her air-squadrons to attempt to defeat the violation of her virgin wilderness. Some of the insects are of a devilish size. I was told of an occasion when one of them alighted on the runway of an airfield and was filled up with eighty-seven gallons of petrol before the airman realised it was a mosquito and not a bomber. But none of these various difficulties are being allowed to hamper the progress of the vital defence works.

17. The figures in all the above paragraphs were given me by high American or Canadian officers engaged on the undertakings. I presume that they are correct.

Redskins, Trappers, Eskimos, & c.

18. We had many interesting and entertaining experiences amongst the regular inhabitants of the north, with which I need not trouble you. But it will gratify you to know how eagerly these remote people are following the fortunes of the war. For example, many of the white trappers and some of the better-off Indians and Eskimos possess portable wireless sets. When they disappear into the northern forests, the Barren Lands or the Arctic islands for the long winter months of trapping they take these prized instruments with them so that they may keep in touch with events in the outside world. It is strange to think of these men, often living in solitude amidst the ice and snow with only their dog-teams as companions, travelling along their trap-lines to secure their catch of fox, marten, mink and other fur-bearing animals — and tuning-in their wireless sets each day to catch also the latest news from the distant war fronts.

19. These sturdy men are eager to play their part in the world-wide struggle of Liberty against Tyranny. Usually the white traders and trappers are too old to make any contribu-

tion other than taxes. These they pay with enthusiasm! Some of them make good money. Thus, we spent one day some seventy miles north of the Arctic Circle in the small summer settlement of half-a-dozen white trappers and traders. One or two of them had already departed for the season's work on their trap-lines, but the others had lingered to greet us. Most of these six men had immigrated into Canada as young prospectors, had taken part in the Gold Rush to the Klondyke in '98 and had been trading or trapping in the Arctic ever since. They are a cosmopolitan company of old boys—an Englishman (from Yorkshire), a Canadian, an American, a Norwegian, a Dane and a Pole, whilst the married men amongst them had Indian wives and their children are half-breeds. This year those half-dozen citizens paid the Canadian Government more than $3,000 in income tax, and their eyes sparkle with pleasure as they speak of that contribution to the undoing of Hitler.

20. The Indians and Eskimos do not pay income tax. But many of them also do their bit. For example, we stayed two days in the Indian village of Old Crow on the banks of the Porcupine River in the Arctic, a redskin community containing only 150 inhabitants counting every man, woman and child. A year ago their chief turned up one afternoon at the local Royal Canadian Mounted Police post and handed the corporal in charge $393. The villagers had spontaneously collected this, and asked that it should be sent across the continent and the ocean as a gift to London children who had been orphaned in air raids. Since that gift they have collected close to another $500 for other war charities.

Fruits of the Soil

21. We watched the gold dredges at work in Bonanza and other creeks on the Klondyke. The company expect to produce about $2,500,000 worth of gold this year, but their operations look like being restricted thereafter by shortage of labour. Gold-mining operations at Yellowknife, on the shore of Great Slave Lake, are being steadily reduced for the same reason. Tungsten is being found there in various places, and is being sought elsewhere in the north, but it has not yet been discovered in worth-while quantities. At Great Bear Lake we saw the radium miners hard at work.

22. On our way north, crossing more than a thousand miles of prairie from Eastern Manitoba to the Peace River country, we saw the largest crop of golden corn that has ever been grown in Canada being harvested. The experts in Winnipeg are still expecting a yield of 550 million bushels. The Granary of Democracy is filled to bursting-point.

I have, &c.

Malcolm MacDonald

Source. PRO, London, War Cabinet Documents, 1942.

Document 4
["Notes on Developments in North-Western Canada" with covering letter to Clement Attlee]

Office of the High Commissioner
for the United Kingdom
Earnscliffe, Ottawa.

7th April, 1943.

Dear Atlee,

I enclose a Note which I have written for the War Committee of the Canadian Cabinet about the development works taking place in North-Western Canada. It is, as it says, a "personal, informal and frank note on the subject." I fear that it may be impertinent, not to say unconstitutional, for a High Commissioner to send such a Note to the Canadian Government, but the situation in the North-West is so disturbing that I felt something had to be done. And as a matter of fact the Prime Minister and his colleagues seem to have welcomed my move.

The situation is pretty alarming. I have set it down as tactfully as I could in the Note, and have probably understated rather than overstated the case. I felt so concerned when I got back from Edmonton that I discussed my impressions immediately with Mackenzie King. He asked me to talk to one or two of his principal colleagues in the same strain, and I did. Afterwards he put the subject of the North-Western developments on the agenda of the War Committee of the Cabinet which Eden and I attended, and invited me to express my views at the meeting. I have also talked over the situation with Norman Robertson and other senior officials. The result is that the Government is now fully aware of what is happening, and I hope that they will take vigorous action. They were already beginning to feel very uneasy before my recent trip. Mackenzie King encouraged me to write the enclosed Note for their further consideration.

In a further talk which I had with him to-day, Mr. Mackenzie King indicated that the Government would probably adopt something in the nature of the suggestions which I have made in the Note. I should like to say that Mr. Costley-White of the Dominions Office, who came north with me, was an invaluable colleague on the trip. His powers of shrewd observation and quick summing up of a situation were a great help, and some of the most fruitful ideas in my Note originated with him.

The Note itself really gives you a general picture of what is happening, and I need not add to it on the political side. I would only say that on the picturesque side, the trip was interesting and enjoyable. We got as far as Coppermine on Coronation Gulf, which is part of the Arctic Sea, and paid our respects both to the small white community and the Eskimo families there. From there we went across to Norman Wells in the Mackenzie Valley. I had to fly south from the Wells in order to get back to Ottawa on time and so missed Aklavik. But Mr. Costley-White went there to look at the developments in that region and returned to Edmonton two days later.

I am most grateful to you for letting me go on this trip, which I feel may have been of

some real help to Canadian interests in particular and to British interests in general.
I am sending a copy of the Note privately to Lord Halifax for his information.

Yours ever,

(Sgd.) MALCOLM MACDONALD

The Right Hon.
Clement R. Attlee, M.P.,
Secretary of State for Dominion Affairs.

* * *

MALCOLM MACDONALD TO W. L. M. K.
[above written by hand—M. M.]

SECRET AND PERSONAL
NOTE ON DEVELOPMENTS IN NORTH-WESTERN CANADA

I have recently returned from a second visit to the Canadian North-West to see the development works being accomplished there. They leave two major impressions on a casual
visitor. First, they are colossal, and their significance may be very far-reaching indeed.
Second, the Americans are doing the greater part of the planning and execution of these
works, and at present at any rate the Canadian authorities have too little influence on the
shaping of these important affairs in Canadian territory. The situation even seems so disturbing that I venture to write this personal, informal and frank note on the subject.

There can be no question of the Canadian Government's wisdom in giving every encouragement to these enterprises. The development works are to be wholeheartedly welcomed. They will open up the North-West a generation sooner than would otherwise have
been the case, and will add immensely and immediately to Canada's importance in world
affairs. Moreover, the Canadian Government have been right in agreeing to the Americans doing much of the work. When so much of Canada's energy was being thrown into
other parts of the war effort it was beyond her power to achieve some of these additional
works quickly, and from the point of view of the military defence of North America they
had to be accomplished without delay. Again, the Canadian Government have been right
in announcing that the work as a whole should be an act of co-operation between the
American Government and the Canadian Government working as partners together. They
have been right also in insisting that after the war the Americans should withdraw from the
work except insofar as the Canadian authorities might be willing for them to continue, and
that every part of the development works which remained on Canadian soil then should
belong in undisputed ownership to Canada.

So the Canadian authorities have nothing to reproach themselves with on the general
policy. On the contrary they have acted with foresight, broad-mindedness and courage.
Where things seem to have "slipped" is in the practical carrying out of the third principle
of policy outlined in the above paragraph. In theory the Canadian and American Governments are co-operating as equal partners in the work. But in practice the American author-

ities have gained increasing control of what is done, how it is done and where it is done, whilst the Canadian authorities' influence on events is comparatively small. There are explanations for this. Circumstances have been extremely difficult for the Canadian authorities. For one thing, they have thrown so much of their best personnel into organizing Canada's tremendous war effort at many other even more urgent points that they have so far not been able to spare enough good men to make their influence sufficiently felt in these perhaps rather remote North-Western developments. For another thing, on the Americans' side difficulties have been greatly increased for the Canadians by the fact that the State Department through whom the Canadian Government quite properly deal with the American Government has been largely ignored by the American Army and other authorities carrying out the works on the spot in the North-West.

But whatever may be the reason for what is happening, the facts of the situation are clear and disturbing.

II

I need not give a list of the works being accomplished or projected. When Mr. Crerar, Dr. Camsell and I visited the North-West last August there were four principal undertakings, that the Canadian and American authorities truly divided responsibility for them. These were the building of the Alaska Highway, the creation of a chain of airfields from Edmonton to Fairbanks, the production of oil at Norman Wells and the laying of a pipeline to convey the oil from Norman Wells to Whitehorse. American authorities were responsible for the carrying out of the first and fourth of these works whilst Canadian authorities were responsible for achieving the second and third. The first three were proceeding with remarkable speed and efficiency. The fourth was making disappointing progress owing to American miscalculations about the ease of transport in the Mackenzie country.

Generally speaking—though there were signs that matters might develop unfortunately—the situation from the point of view of the preservation of Canadian interests was reasonably satisfactory in August. It is since then that there has been a serious deterioration. The following are some of the developments which alter the general picture:

1. Last August it was assumed that the chain of airfields then being built by the Canadians from Edmonton to Fairbanks along the general route of the Alaska Highway would provide, in war and peace, the principal air way from America to Asia. Since then the opinion of the American and Canadian experts in those parts seems to have changed. Of course, that opinion may swing back again. But at present it holds that, although the route through the mountains may always be important as an alternative flying route, for reasons that I need not go into a new chain of airfields from Edmonton down the Athabaska, the Slave and the Mackenzie valleys and thence across northern Yukon Territory to Fairbanks will be the more important. This air route is now being built solely by the Americans. They settle exactly where the airfields shall be; they decide where the auxiliary works shall be placed; they are building the airfields; and they are providing the equipment and administrative staffs. These new airfields are magnificent, all of them with 5,000 feet runways and some of them with runways already stretching 7,000 feet.

2. Just as the Americans have built the Alaska Highway partly as a feeder to the earlier chain of airfields, so they have now begun to build roads partly to serve this air route down the river valleys of Alberta and the North-West Territories. The world was astonished when the Americans built the Alaska Highway 1,600 miles long. But now already they are at work, and far advanced, on the construction of nearly 2,000 miles of other roads further east, from Grimshaw to Norman Wells, Fort Smith to Alexandra Falls, Fort Nelson to Willow Lake and Fort Norman to Whitehorse. The Americans are solely responsible for this roadbuilding, and the decision as to when, where and how the roads shall be brought into existence rests mainly with them. No doubt they have yet other plans for the not distant future.

3. It is perhaps easy to overstate the danger of so much initiative and decision belonging to our American allies. Admittedly it is highly important from the point of view of the vigorous prosecution of the war that these roads and air routes should be built forthwith, and they will in any case be of immense value to Canada after the war. But it is surely unfortunate that the Canadian authorities have little real say as to, for example, the exact placing of these airfields and the exact route of these roads on Canadian soil. The Americans decide these things according to what they consider American interests. They pay no particular heed to this or that Canadian national or local interest. This aspect of the matter assumes even greater importance when one realises fully the considerations which the American Army, and the other American interests working with them, have in mind in all their efforts in the North-West. Responsible American officers will tell you frankly in confidence that in addition to building works to be of value in this war, they are designing those works also to be of particular value for (a) commercial aviation and transport after the war and (b) waging war against the Russians in the next world crisis.

4. With the same considerations in view the Americans are pushing ahead with many other development works, such as the building of oil pipelines (there are already three such projects besides the Norman Wells–Whitehorse one), the improvement of navigation on the Athabaska, Slave and Mackenzie Rivers, the extension of railroad facilities, etc. In some of these matters they engage in only a minimum of consultation with Canadian authorities.

5. There has been a very encouraging expansion of oil production at Norman Wells during recent months. The Americans are very alive to this and to the possibility that further prospecting may reveal an oil field of considerable importance in the Mackenzie valley. American oil interests are watching the situation closely, and if developments look good they will seek to gain control there. Canadian oil interests do not seem so alert to the possibilities. I was told at Norman Wells that no senior representative of the Imperial Oil Company has visited the place for a long time past.

6. The American Army are sedulously collecting all the information that they can about the Canadian North-West. For example, their aeroplanes are flying widely over the territory photographing it. I doubt whether they recognise any limits to what they can do if they want to do it. All the information that they collect goes to the War Department in Washington. Does it come likewise to Ottawa? I doubt whether all of it does. In fact the American authorities probably now know much more about this part of Canada than the Canadian authorities do, which is a most undesirable state of affairs.

7. Do the Americans intend to surrender all control over the works which they have es-

tablished after the war? There can be no question at all of the good faith of the American Administration in supporting the agreements which they have made with the Canadian Government. But certainly many influential American individuals who have had a hand in these developments in the North-West have no serious thought that the interests which they represent shall withdraw. American money, energy and labour have been spent on an immense scale whilst the Canadians have had comparatively little to do with some of the most important undertakings. One can imagine some of these people stirring up quite an unpleasant agitation in Congress circles to force the hands of the Administration, if they feel so disposed.

These are some of the worrying elements in the present situation. From them may flow other unfortunate consequences. For example, the political effect in Western Canada of these developments may be significant. Wherever you travel north of Edmonton there are large numbers of American military officers, troops and airmen and civilian workmen and representatives of American business and finance. Everywhere these Americans are talking eagerly about the development of the North-West, and their words are being translated into deeds. The American Army calls itself "the Army of Occupation." Much of this annoys the Canadian citizens of the territory, yet they cannot help realising that it is largely the Americans who *are* now opening up their country. The Canadian counterparts of the Americans who swarm through the country are conspicuous by their comparative absence. The inhabitants of those regions are beginning to say that it seems that the Americans are more awake to the importance of the Canadian North-West than are the Canadian authorities. This state of affairs tends to play into the hands of those Western Canadians who are inclined to assert that the West receives little sympathy and help from Eastern Canada, and that its destiny lies in incorporation with the United States of America.

III

The centre from which these various activities are generally directed is Edmonton. Some other places have also assumed a new importance, such as Whitehorse, which is the headquarters of the American builders of the Alaska Highway, but the growth of Edmonton under American stimulus in connection with these North-Western developments has been most remarkable. The Americans fill a large part of the MacDonald Hotel, they have taken over completely many other pre-existing buildings, and I am told that their Army and civilian organisations have caused the erection of eighty or ninety new buildings in the city during the last four months alone.

They have recognised the importance of the work by stationing a whole Army division in the region. Their local organisation runs to one General, eight Colonels, other high ranking officers and an assortment of civilian business executives presiding over military and civil departments established to examine, check and approve of field investigations, construction works, aerial reconnaissance, aerial photography, camouflage, public relations, postal service, legal matters, contracts, labour relations and various other branches of activity staffed by about 13,000 military and civil employees.

The regular Canadian organization in Edmonton on the other hand consists of one man. He is Mr. Leonard E. Drummond, who is a consulting mining engineer and the secretary of the Alberta Chamber of Mines. He acts as a representative of the Department of Mines and Resources, but is not strictly speaking a Canadian servant. Even his correspondence on behalf of the Canadian Government with the American authorities about all those works is conducted on either his Chamber of Mines or his private notepaper. I must say at once that I doubt whether any better choice could have been made as the semi-official representative of the Canadian Government. Mr. Drummond has an excellent knowledge of North-Western Canada and he is keen, industrious and tactful. His defence of Canadian interests is stout, and at the same time his relations with the Americans are excellent. American military and civilian officers alike speak in high terms of his wise and helpful advice. The extent to which he has been able to keep in touch with their multifarious activities is remarkable. But as often as not, as is inevitable in the circumstances, he only learns about these activities after they have happened, instead of being brought into consultation, as should invariably be the case, before decisions and actions are taken. He works from one small room in Chamber of Mines office, and I believe his staff consists of one stenographer.

In addition the Department of Mines and Resources has other representatives in smaller centres in the North-West. The Commissioner for the Yukon in Dawson City and such men as Dr. Urquhart at Fort Smith and Dr. Livingstone at Aklavik in the North-West Territories are admirable representatives of the Federal Government. They are doing excellent work as local Canadian advisers and liaison officers to the Americans in their respective districts. But they have other duties also to perform for the Department, and I expect (though I do not know) that they have insufficient staffs under them to achieve satisfactorily the many new tasks which fall to them as a result of the new developments.

Besides these permanent representatives of the Canadian Government, individual departments in Ottawa send officers to Edmonton or elsewhere in the area for 'ad hoc' discussions with the American authorities on particular questions.

These arrangements clearly do not any longer measure up to the situation. One should not exaggerate the extent to which the Canadian authorities have lost their influence over events. The Departments concerned in Ottawa have sought to keep a keen eye on every development, and the Americans may have had to secure their authority in general terms for every project. This control from Ottawa might have worked reasonably satisfactorily if the control on the American side had remained in Washington. But, as has already been said, the dynamic American authorities in Edmonton and elsewhere in the North-West have tended to ignore Washington. At any rate, the War Department has ignored the State Department. And in any case Washington and Ottawa could only deal satisfactorily with the general principles of development policy. Speed required that much of the important detailed work should be settled in Edmonton. The Americans feel handicapped by the inadequacy of the Canadian organisation on the spot there. I understand from one of them that some time ago they offered to finance a considerable increase in Mr. Drummond's staff and office accommodation! Quite apart from other considerations, the effect of this state of affairs on the Americans' opinion of Canadian government is not good.

I am not qualified to propose the remedies. My visits to the North-West have been too superficial for me to claim any real grasp of the problems. Nor am I sufficiently acquainted with the difficulties of Canadian administration in war-time, and anyway it is no business of mine. But perhaps it would help those who read this Note if I risk censure by making some positive suggestions, however impractical or inappropriate they may turn out to be, so that they have something to "get their teeth into." In that spirit I throw out the following tentative suggestions:

1. Someone in the nature of a special Commissioner should be appointed to represent the Canadian Government and be at the head of its organization in Edmonton dealing, under the general supervision of the Government at Ottawa, with all questions of war-time development in North-Western Canada.

2. He should be assisted by a "general staff" living and working in Edmonton. On it should sit appropriate senior officers of all the Government Departments concerned (Department of External Affairs, Department of Mines and Resources, Department of Transport, Defence Department, Air Ministry, etc.). They should have an adequate complement of juniors, clerks, stenographers, etc.

3. This staff should be sufficiently large to allow some of its members to travel from time to time through the North-West, maintaining contact with the work in the field.

4. They should be housed in office quarters in Edmonton sufficiently imposing to impress everyone with the presence and authority of the Canadian Government.

5. They should be given appropriate powers. Their two main duties would be:
(a) to guard Canadian interests as such in all matters connected with the developments. They would naturally co-ordinate the efforts of all the Canadian Departments concerned.
(b) to act as a co-operative partner organisation with the American organisation. Real consultation and co-operation between the Canadians and Americans before decisions and action are taken should be organised in every department of the work.

6. The staffs of the Government's representatives in the Yukon and the North-West Territories should, if necessary, be increased. It might also be found desirable to appoint local representatives in some places where they do not at present exist.

These suggestions deal only with organisation. Other suggestions concerning other aspects of the situation naturally leap into one's mind. But I am very conscious that my observation of these affairs has been too cursory to make me in any way a reliable judge, and I repeat that I mention even the above suggestions diffidently on that account. This leads me to the one proposal which I do make with confidence. It is that two or three really good men should be appointed at once to proceed to Edmonton and the North-West forthwith as an official Commission to enquire into the situation and make recommendations to the Government. For obvious reasons their appointment should be rather informal and should be attended by no publicity.

I would only add that I expect some of the authorities concerned will find mistakes of fact or of emphasis in this Note. I have not consulted them on these matters because this is in no sense a formal or official document. When I started out for the North-West I did not expect to find myself writing this Note, and so did not collect information with a view to its production. However, I submit it with all its imperfections, for I believe that the general picture which it presents is true.

M. M.

6th April, 1943.

Source. PRO, London. FO 954/48/100660. Notes also in NAC, King Papers, MG26 J4, 304/3282.

Document 5

Report on tour of the American-built Airfields in the Eastern Arctic

OFFICE OF THE HIGH COMMISSIONER
FOR THE UNITED KINGDOM
Earnscliffe,
Ottawa

29th August, 1944

No. 496
SECRET AND CONFIDENTIAL

My Lord,

I have the honour to report that I have recently returned from a flying tour of the air-bases built by the American Army Air Force in the Eastern Arctic. The Canadian Government are about to purchase these airfields, all of which are on Canadian soil. They therefore sent a party of R.C.A.F. and civilian experts to inspect them. Mr. O. L. Williams and I accompanied the party.

2. Starting from Ottawa we flew first to Winnipeg. Thence we visited the bases at The Pas and Churchill in northern Manitoba, near Coral Harbour on Southampton Island, Frobisher Bay on Baffin Island, Chimo in Ungava, Goose Bay in Labrador, and Mingen and Seven Islands on the Gulf of St. Lawrence. After that we returned to Ottawa.

3. Except for The Pas (which was built by the Canadians to American specifications), Goose Bay (which was built and is partly operated by the Canadians) and Seven Islands (which was built and is wholly operated by the Canadians) all these airfields were built and are being operated by the Americans. Some of them are mother stations for smaller establishments in the region, where meteorological and/or wireless units function. The Churchill base, for example, has such offspring at Cape Churchill and Eskimo Point on the west shore of Hudson Bay, whilst that at Frobisher Bay has given birth to triplets parked in different regions of Baffin Island. Unfortunately we could not visit any of these minor stations. They are not equipped with landing strips for wheeled aircraft, and so can only be visited by machines on floats in summer and on skis in winter. We are flying in a Dakota on wheels.

4. In the course of our tour we had many glimpses into the customary life of north-eastern Canada. We saw Hudson Bay Company posts, religious Missions, Royal Canadian Mounted Police stations, Eskimo summer camps and Indian villages. Much about these simple, lonely and heroic communities is fascinating. But I should not divert your

attention from more urgent business by tales of them since they are not likely to require the official concern of the Dominions Office.

5. But you may be interested to read something about the air-bases. They are striking examples of the American nation's magnificent impertinence, imaginativeness, energy, mechanical skill and extravagance. I do not use the word "impertinence" only because, I understand, their Army authorities started these works on Canadian territory without properly informing or consulting the Canadian Government. It is also because they treated with similar indifference the obstacles which Nature—whose sovereignty in the Arctic is even more supreme than that of the Canadian Government—put in their way.

6. The results are remarkable. Let me give as an example the Americans' achievement at the most northerly of their main air-bases, in Frobisher Bay on Baffin Island. Frobisher Bay is a long arm of the sea reaching about sixty miles from Hudson Strait into the interior of the Island. Its shores are naked rocks, rising in many places precipitously from the water's edge to a height of over 1,000 feet. A vast ice-field sprawls across many of the heights, and from its edge glaciers slip slowly into the sea. The shore line is jagged and indented by numerous fjords. We visited the place in the middle of August. Even then a great fleet of ice-bergs floated on the broad calm waters of the Bay.

7. The airfield lies at the head of the Bay, where a river runs into the sea. A considerable patch of gravel and sand has collected there. On this two runways have been constructed, about 70 feet above sea level. The rocky hills in the vicinity stand back a little way from the airfield, and here they do not rise to more than 400 feet above the sea. We were told that any possible danger to aircraft was reduced by the fact that during 98% of the time the prevailing wind allows landings and departures to take place on a 6,000 feet runway which stretches along the river valley and is approached from the open bay at one end and across reasonably low ground at the other.

8. Prior to the Americans' arrival this place was utterly desolate. The nearest Hudson Bay Company post was a hundred miles away. Occasionally a few passing Eskimo families used an island off-shore as a summer fishing camp. The only regular visitors were seagulls, ravens and seals.

9. Here the Americans have built what is in effect a small town. The present population is about 100 officers and men, but there is accommodation for eight times that number. I stayed in the Commanding Officer's house, which is like a glorified boarding-house. It has several guest rooms, a "bathroom" with three wash-basins and a shower, all plentifully supplied with running hot and cold water, and a lounge with a well-stocked bar above which stands the proud inscription "The only circular bar in the Friendly Arctic." The rooms are well and comfortably furnished. Their panelled walls are decorated with a striking collection of pictures of the Arctic dressed in its white winter frock and of pin-up girls dressed in practically nothing at all. The lounge contains a small library of books. Its inmates keep in touch with the rest of the Earth by means of a fine wireless set which reports perfectly everything that London, New York, Moscow, Berlin, Tokyo and any other large centre speaks or croons to the world.

10. Besides the runways, an operations building, a hangar, a workshop and the other appurtenances of a modern aerodrome, there are various establishments in the station. These include barracks, mess-rooms and kitchens; a twenty-five bed hospital with a completely up-to-date operating-room, X-ray department and dentist's quarters; a shop and

coffee-house; a theatre furnished for film shows, the legitimate drama and concerts; a laundry, a barber's shop and Turkish bath-house. Each of these is equipped with everything necessary to perform to the full its proper functions. The shop, for instance, provides, amongst a lavish display of other goods, every item of food or drink that a "super" ice-cream machine and soda-fountain respectively can concoct. A new programme of films is shown in the theatre three times a week. Sometimes the latest feature films from Hollywood can be seen in the Arctic wastes before they are seen in New York or Chicago. The principal defect in the air-base is the lack of feminine society. The legend that on Southampton Island and Baffin Island there is "a girl behind every tree" is literally true, as the doughboys sadly perceive when they first behold the tree-less landscapes. But even the gentle sex appears occasionally, when touring companies of actors and actresses drop in to spend an evening entertaining the boys in the Arctic.

11. Shooting and trapping on land are forbidden to white men on Baffin Island. These activities are reserved for the Eskimos, for whom they may be a matter of life or death. But the air-base is well furnished with motor-boats and fishing rods for those who like to take part in the excellent char-fishing there. The Americans will also take you on seal hunts in the winter and spring, with harpoons or rifles according to your taste. The dog-sleighing during the nine months of snow is excellent. The air-base owns kennels with about fifty well-born and bred Canadian, Alaskan and Siberian huskies. At the same season the skiing is good.

12. I can highly recommend the food and drink provided in the Mess at Frobisher Bay. Three meals are served each day, with soups, eggs, pork, poultry, meats, vegetables, sweets, etc., both lavish in quantity and enjoyable in quality. It is the same at Churchill, Southampton Island and the other air-bases. The Americans have certainly made the Arctic—where travellers used to live skimpily, when they did not positively starve, on such seal meat and fish as they could find—realise that there is a war on.

13. These airfields were of course built for strategic purposes. What precise strategic objects they might serve was anybody's guess. If the Axis Power had overwhelmed Britain, one arm of their attack on North America might have swung down through the Arctic. In that case these airfields would no doubt have been important defence outposts. They might have been involved in bloody military actions. Alternatively, if fighting in the German war was confined to Europe, there seems to have been an idea in somebody's head that the airfields might be used for evacuating and treating wounded American soldiers from the fronts. In either of these cases ample accommodation and equipment for treating casualties would be required. Hence, the large, magnificently equipped hospitals and laundries which are generally amongst the principal features of the airfields.

14. But undoubtedly the primary use of the bases was to be as stepping stones for aircraft making the gigantic hop-skip-and-jump from North American factories across the Atlantic to the European fronts. The chain of airfields through Northwestern Canada to Alaska (on which I reported in my despatch No. 608 of September 4th, 1942.) has been extremely valuable for a similar service to the Pacific and Russian fronts. But, as it turns out, these Eastern Arctic airfields have in practice served no such purpose. A more southerly route, through Goose Bay, has proved more convenient and speedy. So the establishments at The Pas, Churchill, Southampton Island, Frobisher Bay and Chimo have been

useless. They have been in every sense of the words left out in the cold.

15. They have proved a colossal piece of over-insurance, which of course has its part in a world war on which the future of human civilisation hangs. Their barracks are only half-filled, their hangars are bare and their hospitals are uninhabited, except for the odd Eskimo who finds his or her way here and a few American soldiers suffering from complaints which they might have got anywhere. The bases' prospective uselessness was recognized by the American authorities before the work was completed. It was stopped at that point. At Churchill, for example, the palatial hospital has not a single item of medical or surgical equipment, except a $1,000 lamp stuck in the ceiling above the empty space where an operating table should have been. And on most of the airfields the third side of the proposed triangle of runways has been left unfinished.

16. Whether the airfields will serve any greater purpose in peace-time is, to say the most, problematical. Some of the hospital beds and equipment may come in useful as aids to the present sparsely scattered medical service for the 300 more or less regular white inhabitants and the 6,000 Eskimos who inhabit the Eastern Arctic. A runway here or there may come in handy once in a blue moon for aircraft concerned with such minor economic developments as may be possible in the Hudson Bay region and the Arctic regular air route of the future. But the runways and their expensive attachments are more likely to fall quickly into desuetude and gradually into decay. I rather think that the Americans have added to the schools of White Whales, families of White Bears and thousands of White Foxes which are the commonest inhabitants of those regions a fine little herd of White Elephants.

17. Of course, in case of another war they may still prove to have strategic importance for defence or attack against the enemies of the North American peoples. The American Colonel who is in command of the American Army Air Force in Central Canada, and who accompanied us on our tour, expressed the opinion that this was their sole possible use. The Canadian Government may well consider it worthwhile maintaining them in some shape for this purpose. That is a decision which they will have to take in due course in the light of all the relevant facts. The survey party which I accompanied was charged with gathering as many of those facts concerning the airfields themselves as possible. Some even of these facts, are disappointing. It seems that the American engineers responsible for the construction work were always inexperienced and sometime ill-advised about construction requirements in the Arctic. Some of the runways already betray a tendency to sag and even collapse. Some of the buildings show signs of falling apart. They may need much expensive adaptation to the rigours of Arctic existence. The Canadian experts in our party shook their heads sorrowfully at this bold but fleeting work.

18. However, for reasons of sovereignty and high policy, the Canadian Government have decided that they should acquire from the Americans all the permanent installations and equipment which they have created on these airfields. I understand that the purchase price is to be the American costs of production translated into Canadian terms. If the whole undertaking turns out to be a series of colossal errors, the Canadians are literally going to pay for the Americans' mistakes.

19. I enclose an admirable memorandum prepared by Mr. O. L. Williams recapitulating briefly the salient facts about this Northeastern air route, together with some docu-

ments concerning the Canadian-American agreement about its future disposal. From these it will be seen that the bill which the Canadians will pay for the bases totals up to nearly $32,000,000.

> I have the honour to be,
> My Lord,
> Your Lordship's more obedient
> humble servant

The Right Honourable Viscount Cranborne,
Secretary of State for Dominion Affairs, London.

* * *

ORIGIN AND DEVELOPMENT OF THE NORTHEAST STAGING ROUTE

At a time when the production of aircraft in North America was expected to undergo its greatest expansion plans were laid for the construction of alternative air routes from Canada to Europe which would relieve the Newfoundland base at Gander of a pressure of air traffic with which it was expected to be quite unable to cope. Accordingly, in the summer of 1941 a survey was made in Labrador leading to the discovery of an ideal site at Goose Bay upon which work was begun immediately and completed by the winter. It was contemplated that from Goose Bay it would be possible to ferry short-range aircraft to Europe via the intermediate bases at that time being constructed in Greenland and Iceland.

2. A year later in June, 1942, the Permanent Joint Board on Defence of the U.S.A. and Canada approved the immediate construction of a more northerly route through Hudson Bay and the Eastern Arctic in a chain of bases extending from Winnipeg through Le Pas, Churchill, Southampton Island and Frobisher Bay in Baffin Island. In conjunction with this, a supplementary route through Northern Quebec via Fort Chimo on Ungava Bay was to link up at Frobisher Bay with the main northern route. These two routes in their turn connected with the Greenland and Iceland hops.

3. The Northeast Staging Route as a whole was thus designed to ferry all types of aircraft from North America to the European theatre of war. It will be seen that strategically the base at Goose Bay occupied the key position in that it constituted an alternative both to Gander for long-range aircraft and to the northern route for short-range aircraft.

4. With the exception of the airfields at Le Pas and Goose all the bases in the Northeast Staging Route were built by the U.S. Army Air Force. The other two were built by the Canadian Department of Transport to U.S. specifications. All are operated at present by the U.S. Air Force with the exception of Goose which is under separate Canadian and United States commands. The U.S. command of the whole chain of bases itself falls into two sections. Le Pas, Churchill and Southampton Island operate under the command of the U.S. Army Air Force in Central Canada, while Frobisher Bay, Chimo and the American part of Goose Bay come under the northeast wing of the Eastern Division of the U.S. Army Air Force.

5. As may well be imagined, the construction of each of these bases presented formidable difficulties. The country lying to the north of northern Manitoba, Ontario and Quebec

is underlain throughout its length and breadth by the rock of the Pre-Cambrian shield. Between irregular outcrops of this rock the top soil consists either of sand or, further north where the forest ceases of spongy muskeg several feet deep with here and there deposits of sand or gravel. The winter covering of ice and snow which, owing to the extreme temperatures, makes construction impossible in any other season but the summer, turns during the spring into an impenetrable morass of swamps and lakes. At Le Pas in northern Manitoba the engineers had to select a spot which was relatively free from swamp and, having cleared the forest, to remove quantities of rock and boulder which obstructed the runways. In Churchill they had to remove several feet of muskeg over a wide area and fill it with crushed rock before laying the top surface. On Southampton Island large outcrops of gravel between areas of muskeg provided a wider choice of site but a great deal of draining and levelling was necessary. In Frobisher Bay the engineers built on sand as also at Fort Chimo, where the forests had also to be cleared and much levelling was required. In every case, as might be expected, the cost of constructing the runways alone formed a significant proportion of the total cost of the base. Signs are not wanting that the construction was so hurried as to be detrimental to the durability of the runways and to their powers of resistance to the rigorous winter.

6. The following supplementary details of the U.S. operated bases are given for the sake of completeness:

The Pas

Latitude	50° 58′
Longitude	100° 06′
Altitude	886 feet above sea level
Runways	Two asphalt runways
	6300′ × 200′
	4200′ × 200′
Hangar	One 200′ × 120′
Fuel Storage Tanks	Two 1000 gallons each.

Churchill

Latitude	58° 45′
Longitude	45° 05′
Altitude	100 feet above sea level
Runways	One concrete runway
	6000′ × 200′
Hangars	One 120′ × 100′
Fuel Storage Tanks	In drums. Bulk fuel storage in Churchill town.

Southampton Island (Coral Harbour)

Latitude	64° 11′
Longitude	63° 1′
Altitude	210 feet above sea level

Runways	One asphalt runway
	6000' × 200'
	One gravel runway 5000' × 200'
Hangars	One 80' × 120'
Fuel Storage	6,300 gallons.

Frobisher Bay, Baffin Island

Latitude	63° 44'
Longitude	68° 24'
Altitude	96 feet above sea level
Runways	One asphalt runway 6000' × 150'
	One gravel runway (construction discontinued) 5000' × 150'
Hangars	One 200' × 120'
Fuel Storage	Drums.

Fort Chimo

Latitude	58° 06'
Longitude	68° 25'
Altitude	121 feet above sea level
Runways	Two (asphalt) 5,400' × 150' and 6,000' × 200'
Hangars	One 120' x 200'
Fuel Storage	Drums.

Mention should be made of an emergency air base at Mingan in the lower Gulf of St. Lawrence built and operated by the U. S. A. A. F. which is used as an alternative to Goose Bay on the rare occasions when the latter is not open to traffic. Brief particulars of this base are as follows:

Latitude	50° 17'
Longitude	64° 09'
Altitude	71 feet above sea level
Runways	Two 5000' x 150'
Hangars	One 82' x 120' (nose hangar)
Fuel Storage	3,500 gallons.

7. The U.S. Government doubtless had long term considerations in mind when they decided to press forward the building of these bases. But from the point of view of its wartime utility the northern branch of the Northeast Staging route has not lived up to expectation. For this there are several reasons. In the first place the base at Goose Bay was found to enjoy incomparably superior weather conditions to any other in that area. It remains open to aircraft on the average 95% of the year. On the other hand in Hudson Bay and the Arctic islands fogs develop rapidly over the whole area during the summer months which render the use of all the bases there most uncertain, while in the winter the snowfall, although not particularly heavy, is subject to constant blizzards and drifts. Another

factor which contributed to the failure of this route was the unexpected development on a large scale of the South Atlantic route which became possible with the liberation of North Africa. This greatly relieved the strain on Gander and Goose and enabled them to cope with all the traffic available. It is a sad spectacle, although perhaps an unavoidable misfortune of war that these finely constructed and equipped bases designed to handle as much as a thousand aircraft a month have never been used for more than two or three aircraft a week which fly up regularly but mainly with supplies for the local bases.

8. As an illustration of the situation described above the following statistics of personnel on the bases may be given:

The Pas
Full complement   450 persons
Present   7 officers, 143 men

Churchill
Full complement   1500 persons
Present   12 officers, 138 men

Southampton Island
Full complement   500 persons
Present   8 officers, 77 men, 30 civilians

Frobisher Bay
Full complement   800 persons
Present   9 officers, 71 men and a few civilians

Fort Chimo
Full complement   700 persons
Present   8 officers, 87 men, 60 civilians

Mingan
Full complement   250 persons
Present   12 officers, 118 men

9. With the approach of the end of the war in Europe the Canadian and United States Governments recently decided to come to an agreement in regard to the disposal of these bases, as well as of those along the Northwest Staging Route. On the 1st August 1944 Mr. Mackenzie King announced that such an agreement had been signed and that it provided for the transfer to the Canadian Government of all immovable defence installations at the bases within one year after the cessation of hostilities. At the same time, the Canadian Government was to reimburse the United States Government in full the sums expended in the construction of the route, subject only to a reduction in respect of expenditures by the United States not resulting in equipment of permanent value. Payments thus agreed upon amounted to $31,631,310 U.S. and may be summarised as follows:

The Pas	$ 415,000
Churchill	$ 6,206,800
Southampton Island	$ 5,318,870
Frobisher Bay	$ 6,833,190
Fort Chimo	$ 8,686,470
Goose Bay	$ 543,000
Mingan	$ 3,627,980
Total	$ 31,631,310

A copy of Mr. Mackenzie King's statement and of the agreement and appendix thereto is attached to this memorandum.

O. L. W.

Source: University of Durham, England. MacDonald Papers 14/4/107-16.

Document 6

[Report on American pressure for a postwar continental defence alliance]

1085 1
Top Secret

1st October, 1945

Dear Secretary of State,
As mentioned in my official telegram No. 1853 of the 6th September, I have it in mind to address you officially on the subject of Imperial defence in the post-war period and we are collecting certain material bearing on this. I hope also to have a chance of private discussions with those concerned on this side.

Meanwhile, however, I feel that I should report to you the substance of a long private discussion which I had recently with the Chief of the Air Staff here. I enclose a fairly full note of this. You will see that the situation is not altogether satisfactory in that there is some danger of United States embarking upon a competition with us to secure certain defensive arrangements with Canada and particularly in the matter of homogeneity of equipment.

We have a good deal of independent evidence to substantiate what Air Marshall Leckie says as regards the special efforts which the United States authorities seem to be making in this direction. I had indeed to admit this to Leckie. I feel clear that many of the junior officers in the United States Embassy have received instructions to forward the same policy as is being proposed to the Canadians by more responsible authorities like the Ambassador and the Generals to whom Leckie had referred. It is significant in any case that the United States Embassy had no less than nine naval and military attachés and these officers, often assisted by their, on the whole, attractive wives, make a point of entertaining lavishly important members of the younger generation of Canadian service representatives. I have reason to know that the conversation at these gatherings frequently turns upon the question of the advantages which Canada would gain if she were to join wholly with the United States in matters of defence. Canadians are asked why Canada still relies so much on United Kingdom types of aircraft, army equipment, spare parts, etc. and are given authoritative assurances that if they wish to acquire the best United States weapons these would be forthcoming on very advantageous terms.

It is of course natural that the United States should be strongly represented in Canada. They were the first diplomatic mission here in 1928, the post being established shortly before this Office was first started. But I cannot help thinking that it is our responsibility to you to watch any tendency of the kind to which I have referred rather closely, whether it is in the field of defence or in any other field, e. g. political or economic. In line with this for instance it is to be remarked that United States maintain a very large consular corps in this country with some twenty-one different posts throughout Canada, practically all of which are headed by a career officer.

What I have said and what Leckie said to me is, I feel, a very strong endorsement of the suggestion made in my telegram under reference that the senior officers of the naval, army and air force missions here should be definitely attached to the High Commissioner as his service advisers. In their present capacity merely as the respective heads of temporary and largely technical missions sent here for war purposes they are in no proper position to provide the necessary balance for this very strong military representation of the United States. And the time as I see it to make these appointments is now, while we have senior officers available who have established good relations with the Canadians and whose appointment as advisers to the High Commissioner would thus be much more likely to escape without criticism or comment than if we waited until the service missions had come to an end. I hope, therefore, that I may be shortly receiving permission to take the matter up with the Canadian authorities on the lines I suggested. I realise of course that the matter is one for each of the service departments but I believe that the case is a strong one which should carry conviction with them.

Yours sincerely,
Malcolm MacDonald

The Rt. Hon. Viscount Addison
Secretary of State for Dominion Affairs,
London

* * *

TOP SECRET   *NOTE*

2nd October, 1945

1. In the course of a discussion which I had with him on the 12th September, the Chief of the Air Staff said that there were certain influences at work in the higher councils of the Canadian Government which were likely to affect the question of co-operation in defence

matters between Canada and the U.K. One of these was the attitude of General McNaughton on his return from Britain, which was in a mood of unfriendliness towards the War Office. This was leading him to favour co-operation with the U.S. rather than with the U.K. in military matters and it was primarily his decision that the Canadian military forces should co-operate with the U.S. forces in Stage II of the war, acquiring U.S. equipment and becoming virtually units in the U.S. contingent. A/M Leckie had only just managed to defeat a similar proposal by Gen. McNaughton, then Minister of National Defence, in relation to the R.C.A.F. A good deal of support had been obtained in the Cabinet by the Minister but the Chief of the Air Staff had been able to enlist Mr. Ilsley's aid and had pointed out that the proposal would mean that the R.C.A.F. would have to abandon all their present aircraft and use U.S. aircraft, spare parts and equipment of all kinds. This would result in a great deal of unnecessary waste in an expenditure of $700,000,000 on new equipment. Mr. Ilsley had told the Cabinet that this was not only unnecessary but impossible and the Cabinet had thus agreed to the R.C.A.F. co-operating with the R.A.F. in the proposed "Tiger" force. A/M Leckie feared that Gen. McNaughton's accession to the chairmanship of the Joint Defence Board would put him in a position to push his policy further in post-war matters.

2. The other influence being strongly pressed in favour of co-operation between Canada and the U.S. at the expense of co-operation between Canada and the U.K. came from Washington. He told me that about two months ago the U.S. Ambassador, Mr. Ray Atherton, had suddenly sent for him. This had never happened before and was of course most unorthodox. The Ambassador received him with his customary courtesy and charm, but A/M Leckie felt that he was even more courteous and charming than usual. With him was Major General Walsh, General Arnold's deputy as Chief of Staff of the American Army Air Force. Mr. Atherton started by saying that Gen. Walsh had come to Ottawa especially to see A/M Leckie and he made some general remarks about Canadian-American co-operation. General Walsh then took up the tale. He said that the defence of the Americas was now one problem and should be treated as a unified system. This was the case now between the U.S. and the Central and South American Republics. This system was only incomplete because Canada was not thoroughly in it. He realized that Canada was a large country with a small population. They could not produce or afford the equipment which they required for their adequate defence. But they should not worry about that. The R.C.A.F., for example, could get any aircraft and other supplies that they wanted from the U.S. The U.S. Authorities would give them every facility and every consideration. In fact, if Canada wished to secure her aircraft, etc. from the U.S. their orders would be given absolutely top priority. Those responsible in Washington would see that Canada got what she wanted even if others had to go without.

3. A/M Leckie said that exactly the same line had been taken by General Henry, a representative of the American Army, at a recent discussion on the Joint Defence Board. After arguing that the defence of North America should be treated as a unit, he urged that the Canadian Army should be equipped throughout with the same equipment as the American Army. He indicated that the Americans would give every facility for the securing of this equipment from the U.S.A.

4. A/M Leckie went on to say that General Henry's proposals had been referred after-

wards to various departments concerned, including the Department of External Affairs. Some inter-departmental discussions had taken place. Some people in the National Defence Department were inclined to support the General's proposals. But Mr. Hume Wrong, for the Department of External Affairs, had opposed them. He argued that it would be a good thing if the equipment of the Canadian Army and the American Army were standardized to the same patterns but only if the U.K. Army adopted the same standards. In fact he urged that all three armies should work towards using common equipment, but only on that condition should the Canadians agree. A/M Leckie said that he himself had taken the same line.

5. General Henry's proposals had therefore, at any rate for the time being, not been accepted. But he was apprehensive that the movement away from co-operation with the U.K. and towards co-operation with the U.S. would be reinforced as time went on unless active and vigorous steps were taken to pursue the policy of all three countries working towards the same standards. He was particularly uneasy about General McNaughton's influence on the Joint Defence Board. He was convinced, moreover, that the ideas put forward by Major General Walsh and General Henry were not expressed on the initiative of those officers themselves, or even of their immediate service superiors in their department. He believed that a plan by which the U.S. would in effect absorb Canada for purposes of defence was deliberately conceived by "very high authorities" in Washington and was being pressed at their instigation.

JG.   M. M.

APPENDIX E

Thirty-Third Recommendation:
30 April 1944
Administration of the Yukon and North West Territories

1. The provision of transportation and ancillary facilities, as a result of war time construction projects, has created widespread interest in the potential development of these areas, and already resulted in extensive development.
2. The population has greatly increased and upon the termination of hostilities large scale additions may be anticipated.
3. These new conditions affect the existing mining, fur trading and other industries as well as the situation in respect to the Indian and Eskimo peoples.
4. The present system of government designed for vast areas with an extremely limited population is now inadequate to the situation, and would appear not adaptable for the provision of social, economic and other public services upon a parity with other portions of the Dominion.
5. It appears that these conditions require consideration being given to:
(i) Parliamentary representation which is at present confined to the Yukon Territory.

(ii) Local administration.
(ii) Co-ordination of services with those of adjoining provinces.
(iv) Supervising authority with direct responsibility to the Government of Arctic.

IT IS THEREFORE RECOMMENDED that
No. 33. A committee be appointed to survey the situation above outlined in all its aspects, including the constitutional one; such committee being empowered to obtain information from all available sources within or without the Government, and submit a report to the Government of Canada with a recommendation upon a comprehensive form of administration.

W. W. Foster,
Major General,

Special Commissioner.

Source. NAC, RG 36/7, vol. 5, File "11th Report."

APPENDIX F

Documents Related to Mutual Defence Discussions, August–December 1946

* * *

Document 1

U.S. Discussion Papers on Canadian American Relations

CANADA   UNITED STATES
PERMANENT JOINT BOARD ON DEFENSE
WASHINGTON 25 DC
(TOP SECRET—COPY)   28 August 1946

MEMORANDUM:

SUBJECT: United States–Canadian Relations

DISCUSSION:
1. What is known as the Joint Canadian–United States Military Cooperation Committee is engaged in drawing up the Joint Canadian–United States Security Plan for the security of the North American Continent.
    a. This plan is based on a joint appreciation of the ability of any potential enemy to in-

flict damage on the vital centers of Canada and/or the United States. It has been considered that our plans must envision readiness for major enemy capabilities five years hence. This damage is visualized as being produced by aerial bombardment or by various other types of aerial guided missiles or other new weapon attack, employing atom bomb warheads.

b. The joint plan will be not only a war plan but will cover the peacetime cooperation between the Armed Forces of Canada and the United States. However, much of the peacetime cooperation that the United States desired to implement in the way of training and other activities presents many difficulties due to lack of legal authorization unless the "Inter-American Military Cooperation Act" is passed at the coming session of Congress.

c. This joint security plan, if carried out, will greatly change Canada's postwar military, as well as foreign, policy in regard to its relationship with the United States. It also represents a considerable departure from traditional concepts of Dominion cooperation only within the Empire.

2. All the above produces both political and financial problems for the Canadian Government, and Canadian public opinion must be convinced of a potential threat before the Dominion Government will feel fully justified in carrying out this new and, from the Canadian viewpoint, revolutionary policy.

3. In drawing up the Joint Security Plan the Canadians demanded the mission of providing for the security of Canadian and Newfoundland territory assisted by the United States. A first glance at the proposed United States and Canadian Air Annexes to this plan indicates that a disproportionate burden is placed on the Canadian taxpayer. Such a conclusion disregards the facts that the plan is a purely *defensive plan* and that the scope of the air defense annexes is limited to Canada, the United States and Newfoundland. Actually, other United States contributions to the security of North America not included in the plan but of great importance are:

a. Defensive deployments, not only in Alaska, Greenland, Iceland and the Azores, but world-wide, aimed at maintaining strategic frontiers at a maximum distance from vital areas in North America.

b. Our Strategic Air Force deployed throughout the world in an offensive-defense mission for speedy retaliatory strikes at the sources of attacks and vital enemy installations. If these deployments and the expenses connected therewith were presented to the Canadian authorities as an additional expenditure by the United States for the security of the North American continent over and above that shown in the United States Air Annex to the Joint Security Plan, it would show that Canada is not accepting an undue proportion of the financial burden for the security of this Continent.

4. At present, the United States armed forces have the continuing right of air transit, until revoked by either Government, between the United States and Alaska and the United States and Newfoundland, but no other clearly defined rights on Canadian or Labrador soil. The Joint Security Plan does not envision the permanent deployment of United States tactical troops in Canada or Labrador during peacetime, with the exception of Goose Bay Airfield where we are now attempting to obtain long term rights. However, to support our

deployments to Alaska and hoped for deployments to Greenland and Iceland, we must have peacetime transit privileges over the Northwest Staging Route, the Harmon Field–Goose Bay route and the Mingan–Fort Chimo–Frobisher Bay–Greenland route. Also, our traffic over these routes will probably be sufficiently heavy to require small detachments of the AAF at certain Canadian airfields along the route in question.

5. Strategically, we wish to push our Air Forces as far out on the perimeter as practicable. Harmon Field, Newfoundland, is too close in and too contracted to be strategically well situated. To avoid some of this congestion we would like to put tactical units into Goose Bay and if we should fail to obtain base rights in Greenland there is a possibility that the United States will feel it necessary to ask for joint base rights in Baffin Island or other Northern Canadian territory. Any of these actions on the part of the United States would be as advantageous for the security of Canada as for that of the United States proper.

6. All of us who are dealing with the Canadian problem feel that individuals in the Canadian Government, and the Canadian armed forces and Canadian public must come to believe and accept the above general picture in order to assist that Government in embarking upon this entirely new military policy of such close cooperation with the United States and the expenditure of funds connected therewith. Our friends in Canada feel sure of the ultimate success of the joint cooperation program but they summarize the opposition, in brief, as follows:

a. *Politics*: The opposition of certain politically minded Ministers who are ignorant of, if not indifferent to, defense considerations. This is a serious but probably temporary difficulty; these same individuals being afraid that cooperation with the United States is either anti-British or dangerous to Canadian sovereignty.

b. *Finances*: This is a difficult one. Construction of an early warning system and interceptor fields would be very expensive. Opposition on financial grounds is stronger because of ever-present reluctance to accept too much from the United States as a gift for fear of later unwelcome involvements.

c. *Russia*: Most of the Cabinet Ministers realize that Russian reaction to cooperation with the United States is inevitable and must be shrugged off, but, nevertheless, Canada is a small country and the Belgium parallel is rather unpleasant to face.

RECOMMENDATIONS

7. That in talking with important Canadian officials the general picture as indicated above be explained to them with particular stress laid on the following:

a. The ability of a potential enemy to threaten, by aerial attack over Canadian territory, the vital areas of Canada and the United States in five years or less.

b. That the contemplated military expenditure to be made by the United States in Alaska, Greenland, Iceland and thruout the world in general, and its deployment of troops to these areas will be as much for the security of Canada as the United States and should, therefore, be looked upon by Canadians in this joint light.

c. That to support the United States forces in Alaska and Greenland the United States will need the continuing authority for transit of aircraft across Canadian territory. Also, that this traffic will be sufficiently heavy to require small United States servicing detachments at certain Canadian airfields.

d. That the United States desires to obtain rights to station operational troops at Goose Bay, Labrador, not only for strategic reasons, but also for joint training with Canadian troops and for experience in operations in that general territory.

e. When conditions permit, the United States will welcome joint training and exercises with Canadian troops in the United States, Alaska or Newfoundland.

f. That the United States wishes in every way to respect Canadian sovereignty.

8. That the War Department begin now its efforts to secure the early passage of the "Inter-American Military Cooperation Act" at the coming session of Congress. Although little stress has been placed on the Canadian–United States aspect of this bill, its enactment is necessary in order to place postwar cooperation between the Canadian and United States armed forces on a secure legal basis.

GUY V. HENRY
Major General, U.S. Army
Senior U.S. Army Member

Source: National Archives, State Department Records, RG 59, PJBD Series, vol. 10, file "Correspondence—1946."

Document 2

Instructions to the President
on the Subject of Joint Defence

October 26, 1946

TOP SECRET

MEMORANDUM FOR THE PRESIDENT

Subject: Joint Defense Measures with Canada

When Prime Minister MacKenzie [*sic*] King of Canada calls on you on October 28 at 2:30 p.m. it is hoped that you will emphasize that you consider that the time has now come for the basic decisions in this field to be made by yourself and the Prime Minister. The Permanent Joint Board on Defense and the planning authorities in our respective Armed Services have defined the problem and made recommendations but it is now up to the statesmen of both countries to direct the carrying out of joint defense measures with minimum disturbance to the two peoples and maximum advancement of world security through the United States.

The foregoing is suggested as the highlight of your conversation because Mr. King is reluctant to reach any decision until events have made it imperative to do so. We understand, moreover, that some in authority in Canada think that our military sometimes proposes more extensive plans than are necessary. It will be doubly helpful, therefore, to assure Mr. King that our non-military authorities are convinced that the program is necessary and also that you and they are watching to prevent any over-extension of military plans.

The former Canadian Ambassador, Mr. Pearson, with whom you talked recently, has remarked to Ambassador Atherton in Ottawa that it would also be helpful if you wished to provide Mr. King with some written document on this problem. Accordingly, there is attached a memorandum which you may wish to hand to him. The last part of the memorandum sets forth the three matters on which we want Canadian approval.

These problems which we now ask Mr. King himself to decide are the most important problems currently before the Canadian Government. The following quotation from my memorandum to you of October 1 suggests why this is so:

> In view of Canada's traditional close association with the United Kingdom, the shift to an even closer association with the United States armed forces is a matter of great moment in Canada and one which involves considerable political risk for the present Government. Some Canadians fear we would encroach on their sovereignty and some fear that Canada might ultimately have to withdraw from the British Commonwealth.

Now that General Eisenhower and Field Marshal Montgomery have discussed standardization and the United States and British Navies have agreed to continue to make their facilities reciprocally available, it should be somewhat easier for Mr. King to approve similar steps proposed in the 35th Recommendation of the Joint Defense Board.

Outside the joint defense field we do not have any particular questions to raise. We do not know if Mr. King has any. Our relations with Canada continue to be excellent. We have, however, been disappointed by the Anglo-Canadian wheat agreement, a long-term bulk purchase deal, which we consider to be somewhat at variance with our proposals for liberalizing trade. On the other hand, the Canadians are troubled about our customs administration which they consider to be unduly restrictive in its effect on Canadian exports.

Mr. King's Government has lost three by-elections over the past few weeks but, while his majority in Parliament is narrow, the opposition groups are split. One of the by-elections was fought and lost on the issue of the Anglo-Canadian wheat deal.

Dean Acheson
Acting Secretary

Attachment:
Memorandum.

Source: National Archives, RG 59, PJBD Series, vol. 10, file "Correspondence—1946."

Excerpts from Typed "Oral Message" Handed to Prime Minister King following Discussion with President Truman, 28 October 1946

TOP SECRET OCT. 28/46 [annotated]

ORAL MESSAGE

The Government of the United States is grateful to the Government of Canada for the favorable consideration which the latter has given to proposals relating to joint defense. . . .

Although many problems remain for future determination, the United States Government believes for the reasons set forth in this memorandum that decisions by the Canadian Government on the following existing problems would be timely and would enhance the security of the Canadian and American people:

1. Further Canadian endorsement of joint planning now in progress would assure the United States authorities of continuing Canadian cooperation and an adequate measure of joint action between Alaska on the west and Greenland on the east.

2. Approval of the 35th Recommendation of the Permanent Joint Board on Defense would help to define the relations between the armed forces of Canada and the United States and would provide authoritative guidance as to the nature and limits of the collaboration desired by both Governments.

3. It is hoped that the Canadian Government, with Newfoundland concurrence, will permit the stationing of certain United States Army Air Force units at the Canadian 99-year leased base at Goose Bay, Labrador. Reciprocally, (as soon as the present congestion can be relieved), the United States authorities will be agreeable to a similar arrangement at United States bases in Newfoundland proper. While remaining an important feature of the defenses of the northeastern approaches to the continent, these latter bases are, however, too close to Canada and the United States to provide adequate protection against ultra-modern high speed aerial attack. Moreover, they do not afford as would Goose Bay, a highly favorable situation for the acquisition by United States and Canadian Air Force units of the experience of training together under cold weather conditions, of testing northern equipment and of coordinating their respective methods and tactics. Finally, arrangements of this kind at Goose Bay and other bases would be consistent with the joint responsibilities which the two Governments have discharged in the past for the defense of Newfoundland.

In conclusion, the United States Government reiterates that it has been gratified by the cooperative attitude of the Canadian Government and by the informality, frankness and mutual trust which have prevailed during discussions of the delicate and momentous problems of joint defense. It believes that final decisions, not only on the three points just mentioned, but also on others in this field can be reached without necessity of any more formal documentation than has been customary since establishment of the Permanent Joint Board on Defense in 1940. There is no doubt that public opinion firmly supports effective collaboration with Canada and, in the view of the United States Government, this is a strong and satisfactory basis for joint action.

Source: NAC, RG 2/18, vol. 74, file D-19-2.

Document 3

Excerpts* from Canadian "Working Papers for Use in Discussions with the United States"—6 December 1946

* * *

TOP SECRET
NO. 11

CONTENTS

*1. Background and Purposes.
 2. Political Appreciation.
*3. Civilian Operations in Support of Defence Projects.
 4. Publication and Registration of November 20 Recommendation.
 5. Sharing of Defence Costs.
 6. Position of United Kingdom in Relation to Canada–U.S. Defence Planning.
 7. Goose Bay.

TOP SECRET
December 6, 1946.
No. 11.

[1] BACKGROUND AND PURPOSES
It might be helpful to the United States authorities to have a brief summary of the background leading up to the discussions which are planned and a statement as to the purposes of those discussions.

  The Joint Appreciation prepared by the Military Cooperation Committee was considered some time ago by the Cabinet Defence Committee. Without making any decision for the time being on the soundness of this Appreciation, the Cabinet Defence Committee authorized its use as a planning document to serve as the basis for continued joint defence

The Rt. Hon. Malcolm MacDonald, U.K. High Commissioner to Canada (left) is seen here with the Hon. Herbert Morrison, Home Office, London (centre) and Prime Minister Mackenzie King, circa 1945.

Mackenzie King and Winston Churchill stand behind Franklin D. Roosevelt and Lord Athlone for a formal photograph at the 1943 Quebec Conference. At a "top secret" session, Roosevelt and Churchill signed a nuclear policy agreement to co-ordinate research.

Raleigh Parkin is described as the unofficial founder of the Arctic Institute of North America. Despite his enthusiasm, he never set foot in the Arctic.

The first meeting of the Board of Governors of the Arctic Institute, Montreal, 19 January 1945. *left to right:* Philip Chester, Raleigh Parkin, R.F. Flint, E.M. Hopkins, Hugh Keenleyside, Charles Camsell, Hugh Collins, Laurence Gould, Walter Rogers.

Trevor Lloyd took leave from Dartmouth College to take on various northern-related assignments for the Canadian government between 1943 and 1948.

Brooke Claxton, minister of national health and welfare, with W.A. Mackintosh at the United Nations Economic and Social Council, May 1944. Mackintosh was Canadian chairman of the Joint Economic Council during the war years.

CANADA

Appearing tired and distraught at the 1946 Paris Peace Conference are the four individuals primarily responsible for Canadian foreign policy in the immediate postwar years: Norman Robertson, undersecretary of state for external affairs; Mackenzie King; Brooke Claxton, soon to become minister of national defence; A.D.P. Heeney, clerk of the Privy Council and secretary to the Cabinet.

The chief delegates to the "Washington Declaration" meeting, November 1945. Seated *left* to *right:* Clement Attlee, Harry S. Truman, and Mackenzie King. Standing: Vannevar Bush, T.L. Rowan, Rep. Charles A. Eaton, Sen. Brian McMahon, Canadian Ambassador Lester Pearson, Secretary of State James Byrnes, and Rep. Sol Bloom.

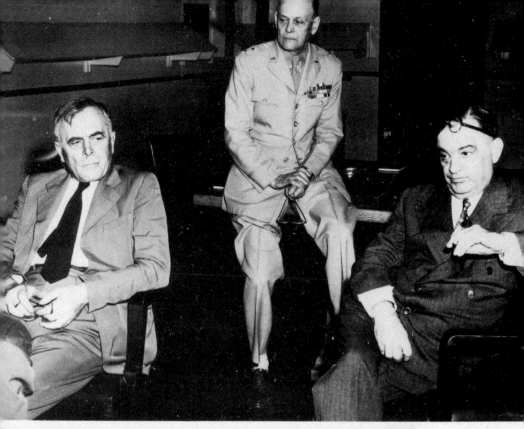

The Permanent Joint Board on Defence was the crucial liaison body for peacetime defence plans. Seated on the left is Canadian Chairman Maj.-Gen. A.F.L. McNaughton with the U.S. Chairman Fiorello La Guardia. The senior and most influential military representative, Maj.-Gen. Guy Henry, looks on from behind.

A.D.P. Heeney, soon to be appointed under-secretary with Lester Pearson, the new secretary of state for external affairs, January 1949.

Louis St. Laurent at the National Liberal Convention in Ottawa, 6 August 1948. St. Laurent campaigned for the leadership on a platform promising peace and security and led the party to a solid victory in the June 1949 election.

SECURITY

At the height of the perceived security crisis brought on by the Korean War in September 1950, Brooke Claxton is pictured with Lester Pearson.

The "business section" of Yellowknife in 1945. Though there were several companies involved in gold production, the high costs of services fell on the federal government.

Married quarters for the RCAF station at Watson Lake, 1950. As Canadian troops gradually replaced the U.S. soldiers along the Alaska Highway, their presence took on a more permanent appearance.

The experimental research station at Fort Churchill, Manitoba, shown here in 1951, was used for training Canadian and American forces in the techniques of Arctic warfare.

An aerial view of
Whitehorse, August
1948, showing the
airport on the plateau
behind. The town
eventually replaced
Dawson City as the
capital of the Yukon.

The Bell helicopter
from the Eastern Arc-
tic Patrol's new ship,
the CGS *C.D. Howe*,
symbolized the antici-
pated "New North."

planning with the United States. This planning took the form of the preparation by joint sub-committees of appendices to a draft basic security plan and has been progressing satisfactorily. Recently, following discussions between the Prime Minister and the President, the Government undertook to review the situation and for the first time gave collective consideration to the Joint Appreciation. Impressed with the extreme importance of the political considerations which are involved, they felt it desirable that discussions should be held with the United States on the official—and later possibly on the political—level before any formal decision was taken with respect to the Appreciation. It should be noted that there has been no rejection of the Appreciation, which is largely a military document, but rather a desire to secure more information on the political and over-all strategic aspects of the situation than has so far been made available.

The purpose of the forthcoming discussions, insofar as the Canadian Government is concerned, can be stated briefly as follows:

(1) To consider, on the official level, and without commitment on either side, the political aspects of potential threats to North American security and on the political implications of various steps that might be taken to meet those potential threats.

(2) To obtain the views of the United States as to what military and naval steps, on a global basis, they regard as essential or desirable for the maintenance of security.

(3) To consider whether any inter-Governmental agreement, or other document, is required in which the two Governments might record their decision to co-operate in the defence of North America, and, if so, what should be the form and substance of such agreement.

(4) To enable the officials concerned to make reports to their respective Governments which might be useful in connection with any discussions on a higher political level which might later take place.

. . . .

[3] CIVILIAN OPERATIONS IN SUPPORT OF DEFENCE PROJECTS

1. It can be accepted that if plans for northern defence are approved by the Governments of Canada and the United States and those plans call for any defence activities in northern Canada, the spotlight of public attention will be focussed on the North. Irrespective of the details of those plans, it is certain that they will call for the expenditure of money and the carrying out of activities in the North. It would clearly be impossible to maintain complete secrecy about such a programme even if secrecy were desirable. Activities undertaken in the North will therefore, to some extent at least, require public explanation and justification by Governments. Not only must public opinion in Canada and the United States be considered; the reaction, favourable or unfavourable, in other parts of the world must also be taken into account.

2. The simplest and most direct course of action would be to state unequivocally but unsensationally that certain defence activities were regarded as necessary in order to insure the security of the continent against the possibility of future air attack over the Pole from Europe or Asia. However, it must be recognized that such a statement would attract criticism both in North America and abroad. From the Soviet world would come vigorous and insistent charges of aggressive imperialism hurled with characteristic disregard for the facts, although similar objections would undoubtedly be raised at whatever Canada and

the United States might do even if it were only the accumulation of harmless weather data. On the North American continent there might well be uneasiness among sections of the public either because of a feeling that menacing gestures were being made at the Soviet Union (which might be regarded as immoral or merely inexpedient), or because a lack of faith in the United States was being shown, or perhaps because of unwillingness to face the expensive facts of the unsettled world in which we live.

3. If a straightforward programme of defence preparations is likely to encounter public opposition to any considerable extent, it appears important to examine the degree to which our objectives can be reached through a programme of civil operations. It might well be possible to place the minimum of emphasis on preparations for defence and to stress the civil benefits that can be anticipated from improving our knowledge of northern conditions and making the resources of those regions more available for general use.

4. There are certain defence activities for which little or no civil justification could be found. To take a particularly obvious example, it would be difficult to offer a convincing argument that a radar interceptor installation was designed to open up the North for development. On the other hand, there are a number of activities for which civilian justification can more plausibly be found and they happen to be those which, under any probable order of priorities, would be carried out within the next few years and before it would become necessary to develop exclusively military installations. Examples:

(a) Mapping and photography of large areas in the North.

(b) Establishment of weather stations.

(c) Establishment of Loran stations and other aids to civil air navigation.

(d) Operation, extension and construction of airfields.

5. There is also an intermediate category of projects which, while undertaken by the armed forces primarily for their own benefit, do provide valuable by-products in the way of knowledge that is useful for civilian purposes. In this category could be listed such things as tests by the armed forces of fuels and lubricants, transport, clothing and other materials.

6. There are certain difficulties in the way of conducting activities on a civilian basis. One of the first to be encountered is that the armed forces frequently have men and equipment available while the civil departments do not. Take, for example, the matter of air transport. Practically every project that might be undertaken in the North (e. g. air photography, weather stations and Loran stations) requires a considerable amount of this. The armed forces are in a position to supply it and because of the lack of any air transport organization operated by a civil department, the only alternative would seem to be the chartering of planes from a civil air operator. Again, in the matter of air photography and mapping, only the armed forces are properly equipped to do it, although in Canada this is the normal peacetime responsibility of the R.C.A.F. Thus there is an initial inclination to assign responsibilities to the armed forces which is not lessened by the reluctance of civil departments to include in their estimates funds which are to be spent for purposes connected with defence. Moreover, the sharing of costs might be made more difficult. Steps in this direction could be taken only as the result of decisions reached by governments on high policy grounds. As far as the United States is concerned, there may be even greater difficulties than in Canada because of the greater measure of autonomy possessed by government departments. It would be interesting to obtain United States views on what would

happen if the Canadian Government were prepared to approve a project sponsored by the War or Navy department (say, the Loran programme) on condition that it were done on a civilian basis. It seems probable that the United States armed forces might find it difficult to turn the job over to a civil agency such as the Civil Aeronautics Administration.

7. In presenting any programme to the public it would clearly be impossible to explain and justify measures for joint (or, for that matter, individual) defence in the North on the ground that the whole programme was primarily an aid to civil development. Such a claim, far from allaying criticism, would invite it. Therefore, it seems desirable to state at a fairly early date that as a routine matter Canada and the United States, like all other nations, are examining their capabilities for defence. They have found gaps in their knowledge of the North which, while unimportant hitherto, are now of more concern because of recent technological advances. They have accordingly decided to fill those gaps and, in addition to conduct certain tests and experiments.

8. Having said this, it would be possible to go on and point to the fact that Canada needs this information in any event if we are to assist in developing the North. Therefore a programme is being undertaken which is only partly military and the results of which will be of general benefit. As this is a mixed programme involving both the armed forces and civil departments, each is being called upon to contribute accordingly to the most economical use of money and equipment. Thus, the preparatory stages might be assigned as follows on the Canadian side:

(a) *Air photography and mapping.*
    R.C.A.F. and Mines and Resources (as now contemplated)
(b) *Weather stations.*
    Department of Transport (as now contemplated)
(c) *Loran programme.*
    Department of Transport (instead of the R.C.A.F. as has been suggested.)
(d) *Operation, extension or construction [of] airfields.*
    Department of Transport (their normal function).

It could be explained that, in general, the R.C.A.F. would assist with air transport where this was required. Mention could also be made of the intermediate category (tests of clothing, equipment, etc.) where the armed forces would undertake experiments which were necessary to improve their knowledge of northern conditions, but where the benefits would be of general civilian value.

9. As suggested earlier in this paper, it will probably be found in discussions with the United States that they would have difficulty in transferring activities from the War and Navy Departments to civil departments. The weather station programme is the only one discussed so far that brings in a civil department. It would be well, however, to examine with the United States representatives the advantages of the approach outlined in this paper and in particular the possibility of putting the Loran programme under civilian auspices.

Source: NA, RG 59, PJBD series, vol. 2, file "Basic Papers."

Document 4

American Notes on Defence Meetings

TOP SECRET

MEMORANDUM OF CANADIAN–UNITED STATES DEFENSE
CONVERSATIONS HELD IN OTTAWA IN SUITE "E"
CHATEAU LAURIER HOTEL, December 16 and 17, 1946

Present:

CANADIAN	AMERICAN
Mr. L.B. Pearson, Undersecretary of State for External Affairs	Ambassador Atherton
	Major-General Henry
Mr. Arnold Heeney, Clerk of the Privy Council	Brig.-Gen. Lincoln
	Rear-Admiral Carey Jones
Mr. R.M. Macdonnell, Department of External Affairs	Capt. Anderson
	Col. Van Devanter
Mr. Evan Gill, Cabinet Secretariat	Mr. J.G. Parsons, Dept. of State
Major-General Mann, Vice Chief of the General Staff	Mr. George Kennan, Dept. of State
Commodore de Wolf	
A/V/Marshal Curtis	Mr. Edward A. Dow, Jr., American Embassy, Ottawa
Mr. Mitchell Sharp, Department of Finance	

I. GENERAL CONCEPT OF THE SITUATION

A. *Political*

Mr. Pearson opened the meeting by referring to the working papers which had been prepared and circulated by the Canadians and by summarizing the first section, which dealt with the background and purposes of the meetings. He said that he thought the main point to be borne in mind was that the Canadian Cabinet had neither accepted nor rejected the Joint Appreciation prepared by the Military Cooperation Committee but desired to have the latest American views on the political and military aspects of potential threats to North American security and the steps regarded as essential to meet the situation.

Ambassador Atherton said that the Canadian memorandum was a most able document and in effect fully covered a number of the points which he had in mind, among which were that home security must be our first thought and that it is now necessary for us to consider not the probability of action on the part of a potential enemy but its possibility. It was clear that any enemy must endeavor to paralyze North American industrial production and if such an effort were made the reaction of our two peoples might be psychologically most important. In this connection there would be serious interference with the morale of the people and there was the possibility of sabotage. In so far as concerned the timing of our defense measures, this could be either accelerated or decelerated in the light of any situation which might be found to exist. Finally, Mr. Atherton reviewed briefly the sequence of events beginning in 1934 when Mr. Baldwin had said, "The Rhine is our frontier," at which time, however, the British Government did not even begin to take any adequate precautions. In 1935 an Anglo-German Naval agreement was signed in clear violation of the Treaty of Versailles and against the wishes of France. In 1937 a United States Government suggestion for the stockpiling of strategic raw materials was rejected by the British. Only in March 1939 was the first public announcement made in England of the intention to re-arm and only in 1940 was full armament commenced in Britain or, for that matter, in the United States. The Ambassador said that he hoped that this sorry sequence would never be repeated. In those years action was not taken because of fear of the reaction of the potential enemy. This should not occur again and with specific reference to the present problem it should be borne in mind that Russia had never hesitated to boast of her development of the Arctic and it seemed unnecessary for us to approach the problem of possible Russian reaction to our own Northern defense plans with undue hesitancy.

Mr. Pearson said that he did not feel that our basic appreciation of the situation should be changed because of such apparent fluctuations in Soviet policy as had recently been witnessed at the General Assembly meeting in New York.

Mr. Kennan agreed that Soviet policy does not change basically, its elements always remaining the same. It was virtually certain that the Russians were not planning a direct attack but there was always the danger of a Russian misunderstanding or miscalculation of the situation which might lead to an outbreak of hostilities which did not form part of any long range plan. Mr. Kennen felt that our best policy was to "contain" Russian expansionism for so long a time that it would have to modify itself. This would require the utmost firmness and patience.

Mr. Kennan said that although once a decision had been made by the Kremlin there was no one in the Soviet Government or the Communist Party who could ever criticize it, yet there was a relatively moderate element in the Kremlin and we could best encourage the moderates by a policy of firmness rather than vacillation. In other words, we should place the moderates in a position to point out to Stalin the extent of our strength and the dangers of an aggressive Soviet policy. At the same time the extremist element in the Kremlin must not be given ammunition for arguments that we were attempting provocation. This could be exploited by the extremists who were certainly not above giving deliberately false information to Stalin. A firm and patient policy of "containment" pursued by us over a period of 10 or 15 years might well result in a frustration which would in itself lead to a period of peaceful policy on the part of Moscow.

Mr. Heeney indicated that in connection with Mr. Kennan's last point, the Cabinet must be convinced that planning itself would not be provocative. At present the Cabinet was anxious to have as much civilian "cover" for defense projects as possible.

B. Military

General Lincoln said that peace-time planning was much more difficult than war-time planning but that the technique of strategy remained basically the same, starting with the estimate and proceeding through the capabilities of the potential enemy. This was a purely military approach but there was also the political intention to be considered. Russian expansion could no doubt be to some extent controlled by our military posture and here there were two "musts";

(1) We should continue to maintain those of our capabilities apparent to the world.

(2) We should maintain the capability to undertake offensive action in case war comes. If our "military posture" remained strong in this way we might overcome many difficulties.

Finally, said General Lincoln, the North American continent would inevitably take a certain amount of punishment in case of war. We could not secure total protection and must be prepared to take calculated risks.

Mr. Pearson mentioned that the United Kingdom might feel some concern lest North American defense be over emphasized to the detriment of overseas potential.

Mr. Atherton emphasized at this point that it was not being suggested that anything in the nature of a Maginot Line should be created in the north but that it would seem apparent that Canada and the United States could not go to anyone's assistance either in the Middle East or elsewhere unless the Arctic were secure. The voter in the United States at least would make this politically impossible.

General Henry, agreeing with *General Lincoln* that there was no rigidity about our plans, added that one must appreciate the position of the Canadian Government on these questions. In his view there was no serious threat of war within five or six years. The interceptor plan, for example was being broken down into stages. If they were all carried out at once it would be very expensive but what is being planned for the next three or four years should prove no great drain on the Canadian treasury and at the end of that time a new appreciation of the situation would certainly be made.

Mr. Pearson pointed out that the entire problem was of far greater internal political importance in Canada than in the United States.

General Lincoln said that there was no border-line between the offensive and defensive in total warfare of the future and victory could only be obtained by the offensive. There would be constant fluctuations in the estimate of the situation and we must maintain flexibility in planning and avoid rigidity in thinking, particularly with respect to the time element. For the present, he said, the United States considered the present appreciation to be basic and sound but the entire situation was subject to periodic, probably annual, re-estimate.

Captain Anderson said that there was a two-and-one-quarter to four-year time lag in creating adequate security measures and the main point we should strive for was to try to minimize this time lag. He fully agreed that the whole plan was subject to new review and re-estimate.

General Henry referred to paragraphs 2, 22, 23, 25 and 26 of the Outline of the Basic Security plan. He stressed that the potential enemy would have additional initial capabilities by 1950 but that in the short-term future his capabilities were more or less limited, a fact of which we must take advantage. With respect to the December 11 memorandum by the Military Cooperation Committee, General Henry stressed paragraphs 1, 3, 4 and 5 (a and c). For long-range planning, therefore, the Committee recommended,

(1) prompt initiation of an accelerated research program with emphasis on radar research;
(2) maintenance of certain vital existing airfields;
(3) immediate accomplishment of air surveys;
(4) establishment of appropriate training schools with provision for exchange of students;
(5) continuation of present RCAF mapping program;
(6) gradual development of weather coverage of the Arctic;
(7) initiation of Loran program.

It was *agreed* that there was no substantial difference between the viewpoint of the Canadian and United States representatives as to the objectives of the Soviet Union and as to the effect on Soviet foreign policy of joint North American defense measures.

II. "CIVILIANIZING" OF DEFENSE PROJECTS

The Canadians expressed the view that there were advantages in providing a civilian "cover" for at least some of the defense projects in their early stages, radar warning research, mapping and weather coverage being mentioned. The U.S. side felt that this was primarily a Canadian problem but that such "cover" could probably be provided in certain cases, although it would tend to complicate the problem in most fields.

It was *agreed* that there might be advantages to carrying out certain of the earlier parts of the projected program under civilian auspices and that whenever this was practicable the U.S. would co-operate to that end.

III. SHARING OF COSTS

There was some general discussion under this heading as to the desirability formulating a definite policy on cost-sharing at present, *Mr. Sharp* urging the exploring of the possibility of an agreed principle and *Mr. Parsons* stating that the U.S. State Department felt that this might be difficult and premature at the moment. During discussion, it was pointed out that radar and other research offered no real problem inasmuch as both countries were working on parallel but purely national lines and that a considerable problem would arise with regard, for example, to the maintenance of such airfields as might be intended for heavy bombers. The Canadians indicated that they might wish to follow the policy of providing land and buildings at their expenses.

It was *agreed* that while no definite principles should be set down at present as regards cost-sharing, annual programs for joint plans should be examined jointly by the appropriate financial authorities of both countries and that they should make joint recommendations on the allocation of expenses as between governments. It was suggested that a "Joint Finance Committee" could appropriately be set up for this purpose.

IV. GOOSE BAY

Colonel Van Devanter read from a prepared statement, the substance of which was that the most probable route of approach to North America included Iceland, Greenland and the line Newfoundland–Labrador–Eastern Canada, the latter portion of which was only about 1200 miles from the main continental industrial centers. Goose Bay was considered to be the only suitable base for very heavy bombardment groups and in fact could be said to be the most important all-round strategic air base in the western hemisphere.

During the ensuing discussion *Mr. Pearson* and *Mr. Heeney* referred to the desirability for political reasons of emphasizing the training side of the Goose Bay project, although *Mr. Parsons* pointed out that Goose Bay was intended for offensive purposes. He added that it was a "facility in being" and there were evident advantages to be derived from this fact.

Mr. Pearson said that regardless of the general question of how far the U.K. should be brought into the Canadian-American discussions it would be essential to discuss the disposition of Goose Bay with the U.K., as Canada was only a limited lessee there.

It was *agreed* that there was urgency with respect to the basing of a VHB group at Goose Bay and that a very preliminary discussion should be held immediately in Ottawa between certain of those present at the meeting and the United Kingdom High Commissioner to Canada.

V. PUBLICATION AND REGISTRATION OF JOINT DEFENSE BOARD'S
RECOMMENDATION OF NOVEMBER 20, 1946

Several of the Canadians present, including *Mr. Pearson*, stated that as soon as Parliament reconvened it was almost inevitable that questions would be asked of the Government concerning the status of joint defense planning and in any event the Government would certainly have to reply to such questions during examination in Parliamentary Committee of the Defense Budget estimates. It was possible that publication of the November 20 Recommendation might tend to ward off detailed questions and in other ways minimize publicity which it was impossible to avoid entirely. At the same time there were of course disadvantages in publication.

Mr. Parsons said that the United States State Department would prefer on the whole that there should be no publication either of the Recommendation or of its substance although the department recognized the Canadian Government's difficulties.

Various suggestions were made by several present, including one that publication of any statement should be accompanied by an emphasis on the provisos to the original 35th Recommendation of the Board, while *Ambassador Atherton* suggested that the solution might be a statement not quoting the Recommendation textually but containing something close to it. A copy might be sent for information purposes to the Secretariat of the United Nations.

It was *agreed* that it would be preferable not to publish the Recommendation itself if only because any suggestion of making a practice of publishing Recommendations might seriously hamper their drafting. There was general *agreement* in favor of the issuance of an agreed statement containing the substance of the Recommendation, referring to past defense cooperation arising naturally from the Ogdensburg Declaration and to the UN relationship. A copy of the statement would then be sent to the United Nations Secretariat. It was *agreed* that it would be unnecessary to register any such statement formally with UN.

With respect to the formalization of the two Governments' decisions to cooperate in the defense of North America it was *agreed* that this might best be accomplished by following the normal procedure of an exchange of letters between the Canadian and United States sections of the Permanent Joint Board which would notify acceptance by their respective governments of the Recommendation of November 20.

VI. POSITION OF UK IN CONNECTION WITH CANADIAN-US DEFENSE PLANS

Mr. Pearson invited the attention of those present in this connection to the Canadian memorandum of December 6 on the subject and emphasized paragraph 6 thereof which states that in the recent conversations between the Prime Minister and President Truman, it was agreed that it was to the interests of both the United States and Canada that the U.K. Government be kept informed of Canadian–United States joint planning. Mr. Pearson said that the United States representatives on the Joint Board apparently had no objection to informing the U.K. in general terms of what was being done but that details should be transmitted only in matters in which cooperation with the U.K. was essential.

It was brought out in the discussion that information transmitted to the U.K. would normally be passed on to various Dominion governments, although it seemed probable that if the U.K. were asked not to transmit information on any specific subject she would not do so.

It was *agreed* that no effort should be made at present to arrive at any formal or hard and fast agreement on the subject of informing the U.K. but that the policy should normally be followed of keeping the U.K. informed in general terms and not in detail, except in those matters in which U.K. cooperation was essential.

Conclusion of Meeting. Before the meeting concluded certain of the American representatives stated that in connection with questions which had arisen during the meeting concerning the existence of a geographical limit to which the Russian expansionist policy could be permitted to proceed, the United States Government did have in mind certain specific limits but although they could be expressed geographically they should not be considered on a purely geographical basis since ethical considerations also entered the matter. It was pointed out, for example, that in the case of the entry of troops into certain areas it would be necessary to consider whether this was or was not being done in contradiction to the wishes of the nation affected.

It was decided that a few of those present would remain behind after the meeting in order to discuss with Sir Alexander Clutterbuck, United Kingdom High Commissioner to Canada, the question of Goose Bay in a preliminary manner in view of the unusual opportunity offered by the presence in Ottawa of several of those concerned with the problem.

> Edward A. Dow, Jr.
> Second Secretary of Embassy

EAD/rb
TOP SECRET

Source: NA, RG 59, PJBD series, vol. 2, file "Basic Papers."

APPENDIX G

USAAF Study on Problems of Joint Defense in the Arctic

SECRET

Office of the PC/S Intelligence, USAAF, 29 October 1946

PROBLEMS OF CANADIAN-UNITED STATES COOPERATION IN THE ARCTIC

I THE PROBLEM

The physical facts of geographical juxtaposition and joint occupation of the North American continent have at all times carried the implication that the defense of Canada and the defense of the United States cannot be artificially divorced. Recent technological developments rendering the Canadian Arctic vulnerable to attack and thereby exposing both Canada and the United States to the threat of invasion and aerial assault across the northernmost reaches of the continent have greatly heightened the compulsion to regard the defense of the two countries as a single problem. The need to provide adequate safeguards for the protection of the Canadian Arctic is equally imperative for Canada and the United States. Since neither nation can undertake this project without the assistance of the other, the situation clearly dictates a program of joint planning and continuous interstate cooperation.

The possibility that American bases in Greenland may prove politically untenable within the foreseeable future lends urgency to the need for the development of the military potentialities of the Canadian Arctic. The loss of North Atlantic bases occupied by American forces during the war would deprive this country of an advanced Arctic bridgehead, that could, if necessary, be utilized for offensive strategy, and would simultaneously weaken the defensive position of the Canadian Arctic. The United States would be compelled to develop a substitute area in which experimentation with the conditions of Arctic warfare, weather and meteorological observations could be fully exploited. Since the Canadian Arctic, Grant Land, and Ellesmere Island in particular, are the only regions which may be considered as possible replacements for the Greenland bases, Canadian willingness to permit American participation in the military development of the polar areas is essential to the success of any program for the defense of the United States.

Nevertheless, although many of Canada's ranking military advisors acknowledge this interdependence, a formidable section of Canadian opinion is either hesitant toward or openly opposed to the idea of active participation by the United States in military projects involving Canada's Arctic or sub-Arctic territory in time of peace. This hesitancy has already delayed joint military ventures in the past; inevitably it will delay them in the future, possibly with results fatal to hemispheric defense. If it is generally accepted that the

United States will not again be allowed a period of grace in which to prepare itself for another war, it is an obvious corollary that steps should be taken immediately and continuingly to remove every obstacle lying in the way of Canadian-United States military cooperation. In view of the present sensitive attitude of sections of the Canadian electorate toward joint action, the reasons for that opposition must be analyzed, and Canadian prejudice overcome at the earliest possible moment. It is the purpose of this estimate first to examine the sources of this antagonism, and secondly, to recommend means by which it may be eradicated or at least neutralized.

II THE SITUATION

If the roots of the Dominion's unwillingness to associate itself closely with the United States are to be fully understood, it must be remembered that the much-heralded friendship between the two peoples has concealed a considerable amount of less advertised friction, particularly on the Canadian side. The frequent annexationist scares during the nineteenth century and the frontier adjustments which Canada feels were made at her expense have left a mark which even today it is not easy to eradicate. The occurrences, together with systematic attempts to foster anti-Americanism by certain Canadian business interests seeking to establish an economic empire independent of New York, produced a striking hostility toward the United States that until 1930 showed no signs of abatement. British ties were artificially emphasized in order to widen the gulf between the Dominion and its southern neighbor, and the focal point of the slowly developing Canadian nationalism became the alleged necessity of saving the country from the acquisitiveness of the United States.

Opposition to closer ties with the United States traditionally has been centered in South Central Ontario, and especially in Toronto, which was originally settled by pro-British refugees from the United States at the time of the American revolutionary war. In this area the United Empire loyalist tradition and British imperial connections are still sufficiently strong to engender unyielding antagonism toward any scheme providing for a closer defensive union between Canada and America which might conceivably lessen the cohesion between the Dominion and Great Britain. In the past, French Quebec has constituted another obstacle to closer cooperation with America. Peopled almost entirely by Roman Catholics, Quebec's foreign allegiance is to the Vatican rather than to France. Intense resentment of Great Britain and English Canada crystallized into isolationism and anti-Anglo-Americanism. During the last war these attitudes assumed the form of persistent efforts to restrict Canada's aid to the Allies and to safeguard the right of French Canadians to refrain from participation in the nation's war effort. Fear that Canada's closer integration in the North American framework might spell encroachment upon its cultural and religious rights has impelled Quebec to resist collaboration with the United States and Latin-America. As late as June 1941 the magazine *L'ACTION NATIONALE* felt it necessary to devote an entire issue to the presentation of objections against Canada's annexation to the

United States. There are some qualified observers, however, who believe that the attitude of the French Canadians is now undergoing modification in this respect. The hostility between Rome and Moscow has been productive of a greater affinity between Quebec and the Anglo-American bloc than that which has hitherto existed and the potentialities of closer cultural links with Catholic Latin America has engendered a friendlier attitude toward inter-American cooperation on the part of French Canada.

With the exception of the strongly pro-British elements in South Central Ontario, and possibly French Quebec, the Canadian attitude toward close cooperation with the United States has undergone a profound change since the outbreak of the second world war. The crisis facing England in the summer of 1940 did more than any other single event to bind Canada to the United States. In that period the Dominion came to realize that within the near future she might be forced to provide for her own defense with whatever help could be secured from the remainder of the Western Hemisphere. Canada, while continuing to render all possible aid to the mother country, at that time virtually abandoned the British Commonwealth pattern of defense in favor of a reorientation in terms of North American regional unity. Canada's economic as well as her military dependence upon the United States became much more pronounced than had formerly been the case: time-honored Canadian hostility to the Americans was tempered by the common danger.

Foremost among the determinants of Canadian policy toward the United States requests for installations in the Arctic Archipelago is the sentiment of national pride, which may be analyzed into three components. The first is the belief that the existence of areas under foreign control within the Canadian borders would constitute a violation of Canada's sovereignty and a breach of its territorial integrity. It is sometimes thought that accession to the current American proposals may place the Dominion so far in the power of the United States that further and more extensive requests of the same nature would be impossible to refuse. In the second place, those groups which have most actively sought to foster the growth of a distinct Canadian nationalism predict that the Dominion may easily become little more than a satellite of the United States unless a firm stand against "American encroachments" is assumed. Since Canada must in any case permanently occupy the position of the weaker partner in relation to America, it is feared that cooperation with the United States in matters of foreign policy and defense will in actuality spell Canadian acceptance of her neighbor's dictates to a degree which will void the Dominion's independence as far as external affairs are concerned. Within the last few years Canadian publications have not infrequently carried statements conveying the impression that American imperialism seeks to include Canada as the forty-ninth state. There is a danger that American requests for bases in the Canadian Arctic may produce a renaissance of the annexationist fears that for so long troubled the Dominion's relations with the United States. Canada's general anxiety concerning the possible long-range consequences of United States military activity upon her territory is sharpened by the specific fear, voiced loudly in some quarters even though it may fail to command widespread credence, that United States activity in the Arctic Archipelago may culminate in annexation of a portion of those undeveloped territories to which the Dominion has already laid claim.

Another major obstacle to the further integration of Canadian and American defense systems is the widespread belief in Canada that closer union with the United States must entail a loosening of the bonds connecting the Dominion with Great Britain and with the other Commonwealth nations. With the exception of French-speaking groups, most Canadians feel that their primary loyalty is to the British Commonwealth, and they hesitate to participate in a secondary alliance. It is significant that Southern Ontario, which feels itself more closely wedded to England than any other section of the country, is the region most opposed to broadening the scope of the present Canadian-United States relationship. The Dominion's traditional attachment to Great Britain has a particularly adverse effect upon that phase of cooperation with the United States which involves the standardization of Canadian and American weapons, industrial equipment and military organization, because in these cases affiliation with the American system necessarily entails an abridgement of Empire unity in matters pertaining to defense.

Also affecting the Canadian Government's attitude toward joint defense of the Arctic is the fear of causing a further deterioration in Canadian–Russian relations by intensifying Soviet suspicions that Canada and the United States are preparing the American Arctic as an offensive bridgehead for possible aerial and land attacks upon the USSR. The Soviet press in publicizing the American maneuvers of Canadian and American experimental task forces has already stated that the scientific mission which these expeditions fulfilled is merely an attempt to screen the fact that they are in reality the prelude to major strategic operations directed against the Soviet Union.* The Government may also take into consideration the increased possibility that Canada would be an object of attack in the hypothetical Russian–United States conflict if a network of American military installations was actually functioning on Canadian soil. Regardless of its will, the Dominion would find it impossible to maintain neutrality were the United States to utilize Canada's territory as a base of operations against an enemy state.

Before recommendations can be made as to the course United States policy should take to neutralize this sensitiveness of Canadian national pride, one further issue requires clarification: whether the United States, either by pleading military necessity, or by establishing a legal claim to one or more Arctic areas, could justify undertaking a program of polar defense without the consent of Canada. In view of Canada's apparent reluctance to cooperate with us to the extent we now consider necessary, in view of Denmark's manifest intent to free Greenland sooner or later from American occupancy, and in view of the deterioration of the international picture towards the sharply-divided Eastern and Western axes, it is necessary to ascertain what authority the United States could invoke if it were faced with the decision of whether or not to occupy and control polar regions generally conceded to be part of the Dominion.

*Canadian circles, also, have expressed concern that military activity in the Arctic might interfere with the development of its natural resources.

Sovereignty over uninhabited areas may be acquired by agreement on the part of the interested power, by effective occupation, by contiguity, and, recently, by the application of the sector theory.* Although Canada has never published an official international declaration laying claim to the American Archipelago directly north of its borders, its actions, nevertheless, make it clear that such a claim is maintained both on the ground of the sector principle and on the basis of actual exploration and occupation. In the eyes of Canadian law, the Dominion entertains perfect jurisdiction: it has been exercised by the Canadian Parliament in the passage of legislation applying directly to the whole of the Canadian Arctic. The United States has neither recognized nor denied the validity of the Canadian claim, although it has always been clear that Canadian activities in the Arctic were not upon a scale enabling the Dominion to meet the rigid standards which the American Government has steadfastly maintained were a prerequisite to the assumption of sovereignty over uninhabited areas. As far as is known, no other countries have acknowledged the existence of Canadian sovereignty over the entire American Arctic, although Norway, while expressly denying the validity of the sector theory, recognized that the Sverdrup Islands were Dominion possessions. It is probable, however, that the Soviet Union would readily recognize Canadian sovereignty over the entire region, since the USSR is itself wholly committed to the sector theory. Great Britain, too, would almost certainly support the Dominion's claim.

Canada could base its claim to the American Arctic upon three principal grounds. First of all, the Dominion could invoke the sector doctrine. That theory, however, is not considered to form a part of the law of nations, and it is unlikely that this plea would be sufficient to establish Canadian sovereignty in the eyes of an international tribunal. Secondly, Canada might rely upon the provisions of the 1867 Treaty, by which Russia ceded Alaska to the United States, as proof that the American Government had committed itself to the sector principle as the basis for division of polar lands. That treaty fixes the western boundary between Russia and the United States as a line on the meridian of 164° "jusqu'à ce qu'elle se perde dans la Mer Glacial," in the English text "without limitation," thus seeming to imply the allocation of unexplored and uninhabited Arctic territories according to the sector tenet. American authorities, however, are confident that these words would not be construed as binding the United States to approval of the sector system.

Canada's most important legal defense of its sovereignty over the American Arctic would almost certainly be grounded upon the actual exploration, occupation, and administration that have been undertaken in that area on behalf of the Dominion Government. The Canadian Parliament has passed certain laws which are technically in force throughout the entire Arctic region. In 1925, an amendment to the Northwest Territories Act was passed providing that all persons desiring to enter the Canadian Arctic must obtain permits from the Government, and this law was supplemented by a 1926 Order-in-Council. Since that time the Government has promulgated other legislation and administrative rules bearing

*For a detailed discussion of these four principles see "Report on the Arctic," Part I, published by the Office of the AC/S, Intelligence, Hq., ATLD-ATC, June, 1946.

upon the polar territories. Until the present war, however, when with the collaboration of the United States, the development of the Canadian Arctic was greatly accelerated, actual Canadian exploration and occupation of the regions in question, particularly the East Arctic, has been meagre and sporadic. In the 20's, small police detachments were established at Port Burwell, Lake Harbor (Baffin Island), Pangnirtung (Baffin Island), Craig Harbor (Southeastern Ellesmere Island) and at Bache Peninsula (Eastern Ellesmere Island). The stations at Bache Peninsula and at Craig Harbor were subsequently abandoned. RCMP patrols through the southern portion of Baffin Island, Axel Heiberg, a segment of Ellesmere Island, Amund Ringnes, Ellef Ringnes, a small sector of Borden Island's coastline, the lower portion of Melville Island, Bathurst Island and Devon Island. Although Canadian-sponsored exploring parties have passed through or by Grant Land, Prince Patrick Island and Banks Island, these areas have remained virtually untouched insofar as the establishment of local administrative agencies or the maintenance of a regular patrolling system are concerned.

It may be said with considerable certainty that the United States could find little legal justification for the unilateral occupation of areas in whose general vicinity the Dominion Government has established police posts with authority to enforce Canadian law. Although Canada's claim to have effectively occupied regions annually patrolled by the RCMP but not equipped with permanent stations is less surely grounded, it now seems probable that an international tribunal would accept even this slight activity as sufficient to fix sovereignty. It follows, therefore, that the United States would be excluded from operations in Ellesmere Island, Baffin Island, Axel Heiberg, Ellef Ringnes, Amund Ringnes, Borden Island, Melville Island, Bathurst Island and Devon Island unless Canadian approval were previously secured.

Prince Patrick Island, Banks Island, and Grant Land remain as the only locations which the American Government could occupy with the hope of making a legal defense of its action. Canada would attempt to support its claim to these areas on two counts. First it might endeavor to maintain that according to the doctrine of contiguity, Canada, exercising sovereignty over the Northwest Territories and the major part of the Arctic Archipelago, automatically held title to all islands adjacent to the mainland and forming a part of the Archipelago which it controls, although a particular island might remain entirely unoccupied. It is not likely that the Canadian case would be sustained on this ground, since recent decisions of international tribunals have tended to deny *in toto* the validity of the contiguity principle.

Secondly, the Dominion would probably claim that the passage of legislation by its Parliament which theoretically applied to the islands in question was sufficient evidence of the exercise of state authority to enable Canada to claim these territories as its exclusive possessions. It is difficult to determine in advance the decision that would be reached by an international court in this instance. Until recently, the orthodox interpretation of international territorial laws demanded a more extensive display of governmental authority than that afforded by the mere promulgation of legislation that could under no circumstances be enforced. In 1933, however, the permanent Court of International Justice conceded that Denmark held undisputed title to all of Greenland, principally because of the existence of similar legislative enactments, although Danish authorities were able to enforce the law only in a fraction of the land.

In the light of the latter decision, we are forced to conclude that the Canadian claim to sovereignty over the entire American Arctic would be sustained by an international judicial body. In any case, however, the United States could present a fairly well documented legal defense in support of any action its Government desired to take in Melville Island, Prince Patrick Island, and Grant Land, particularly since the American Government has consistently maintained that sovereignty cannot be claimed without a degree of effective occupation, colonization and use that until the present has not been achieved in the Canadian Arctic.

It should not be overlooked, however, that any action on the part of the United States which could be interpreted as an usurpation of Canadian territorial rights would be followed by political consequences so grave that, except in the case of a very serious emergency, they could scarcely be justified even in terms of short-run expediency. The breach in Canadian-American relations might be sufficiently wide to put an end to all possibility of continued political and military cooperation between the two countries, and would probably be a greater blow to the American security system than a failure to obtain Arctic bases. A rupture between Canada and the United States would, furthermore, have unfavorable repercussions upon the relationship between Great Britain and the United States, and might alienate from this country lesser Powers who would otherwise have been willing to lend it support in case of hostilities.

Although the United States may be unable or unwilling to invalidate the Canadian title to the islands of the American Arctic, it does not follow that this country would be compelled to remain idle if it seemed probable that penetration of this area was threatened by a potential enemy. The right of self-protection, a keystone of present-day international law, permits a state to take any measures it may deem necessary in order to preserve its existence, even though these may extend beyond its territorial limits.*

If the American Government had good reason to believe that invasion or occupation of the Canadian Arctic by a foreign nation were imminent, it would be justified in taking suitable counter measures, with or without Dominion consent, on the grounds that the security of the United States was directly endangered. Occupation of Canadian territory by American forces, however, could be justified only for the duration of the immediate

---

*Elihu Root writes, "It is well understood that the exercise of the right of self-protection may, and frequently does, extend in the effect beyond the limits of the territorial jurisdiction of the state exercising it. . . . The most common exercise of the right of self-protection outside a state's own territory and in time of peace is the interposition of objection to the occupation of territory or points of strategic, military, or maritime advantage." He also refers to "the right of every sovereign state to protect itself by preventing a condition of affairs in which it will be too late to protect itself." Reference is also made to *"REPORT ON THE ARCTIC,"* pages 24 ff, published by the Office of the AC/S, Intelligence, Hq., Atlantic Division, ATC.

danger and would in no way entitle this country to challenge Canadian sovereignty over the region in question.

III RECOMMENDATIONS

Since the weight of opinion, then, points inevitably to the conclusion that the United States could not, except in the event of indisputable emergency, undertake a program of polar defense without Canadian consent, it remains to suggest methods by which Canada's pronounced national sensitivity regarding her territorial integrity and independence can be overcome. The following recommendations are made:

a. First, and most important, the United States should make it unequivocably clear that this country entertains no possessive design upon the polar territories to which Canada lays claim. To this end, any agreement providing for joint military exploitation and defense of the Arctic should be accompanied by an official recognition on the part of the United States that Canadian sovereignty extends over the entire American Arctic excluding only the Alaska sector. Although the Canadian claim to these territories has never been specifically contested by this government, neither has it ever received formal recognition, and Canada's occupation of the region has as yet failed to meet the rigid standards that the United States has traditionally set for the promulgation of a sovereignty claim over uninhabited areas. A declaration of this nature, therefore, might assuage Canadian anxiety that the United States will use occupation of the Arctic by its military forces as an instrument to set up an opposing sovereignty claim of its own over those areas.

b. Since Canada will undoubtedly find itself unable to bear exclusive financial responsibility for an extensive Arctic program, the United States Government should offer to share the burden upon an equitable basis. Under no circumstances, however, should this Government attempt to finance the entire amount of the expenditure itself, since many sectors of Canadian opinion appear to interpret the presence of United States-financed projects on Canadian territory as equivalent to annexation of the areas in question.

c. The arrangement providing for joint Canadian and American action to secure the defense of the North should make it perfectly clear that the Dominion retains unimpaired sovereignty over all areas in which United States personnel and equipment are utilized. While the agreement should legally entitle the United States, at least for a stated period of time, to full use of the facilities which will be developed as a result of the coordinated activities of the two states, it should also guarantee Canada's eventual right to make whatever disposition of these installations it may desire.

d. The United States should give full assurance that the presence of American military forces will in no way interfere with the peaceful development of Arctic resources and industrial potential by Canadian nationals. On the contrary, it should be pointed out that the construction of a defensive network throughout the Canadian North will involve the building of a communications and weather systems which would be of great assistance to a program of industrial development, and invaluable especially to civil aviation.

A program for joint defense of the Arctic conceived along these general lines would probably eliminate the major psychological obstacles presently restraining Canadian public opinion from full cooperation with the United States. It would assure the Dominion that the presence of American forces on its territory would not threaten Canadian independence. It would provide a means of lessening the economic strain imposed by the construction of a northern defensive network. There is the further consideration that Soviet suspicion concerning American activities in the Arctic might be more effectively countered were Canada itself to take the initiative in that region than if the Dominion permitted the United States to embark alone upon an Arctic military program.

Because of the political, military, and sentimental ties connecting Canada with England, it will prove impossible for the United States to enter into partnership with the Dominion without at the same time drawing into an even closer association with Great Britain. It has already been pointed out that Canada's fear that full cooperation with the United States might alienate her from the British Commonwealth is one of the factors causing the Dominion Government to be hesitant about current American overtures. British sanction of the North American defense arrangements is a necessary preliminary to Canadian consent and cooperation. Now it has become apparent that Great Britain, Canada, and the United States are in general agreement concerning the fundamental objectives of their respective foreign policies. Cooperation has already made material progress, but until the present it has been organized almost entirely upon a bipartite basis. There is no reason why the three countries should not now maintain direct consultation and planning upon a tripartite basis concerning political and military problems in which they all have an interest.* Eventually, an arrangement paralleling this triple relationship may be worked out for other Dominions, Australia and New Zealand, for example, which possess a legitimate security interest in areas where the United States desires to retain a foothold. In effect, this scheme would involve the creation of several regional defense groupings in which the United States and Great Britain would both participate. It is to be remembered that American consent to a system of multilateral control for the Pacific bases would have favourable repercussions upon the Canadian scene. If Great Britain and Canada are convinced that the United States is, in effect, a participant in the system of Commonwealth defense, they are far more likely to satisfy American wishes in regard to military rights in the Canadian Arctic than they would be if they believed the interests of this country were not coincident with their own. It is quite possible that under these circumstances Great Britain would actively favor even more extensive forms of Canadian-American cooperation than those entailed by the Arctic project. Realizing that the total scheme of Anglo-American defense requires especially close relations between the two North American states, Great Britain might withdraw her present objections to the further integration of the Dominion's military establishment into that of the United States. With Britain's consent, it would be possible to secure Canadian military collaboration with the United States on a

---

*The basis for cooperation might be expanded to include Newfoundland, at least in a limited capacity, if that country chooses independence or dominion status in its forthcoming plebiscite.

scale that otherwise would almost certainly have been condemned by large sections of Dominion public opinion.

The United States should work toward the ultimate objective of a hemisphere-wide defense arrangement with provision for interchangeability of weapons, coordination of military establishments, reciprocal use of air and naval bases and a common obligation to aid any American state that becomes the object of foreign attack. There is no compelling reason why Canada should not participate. For the present, however, there is no need to force Canada in advance of its will into a formal military agreement with Pan-America. The immediate need is the achievement of full Canadian–United States cooperation. That cooperation, in the final analysis, must stem from an assurance to Canada that the United States has no intention, now or in the future, of claiming sovereignty over any section of the Canadian Arctic.

Fort Totten, Long Island
29 October 1946

Source: NA, RG 59, PJBD series, vol. 10, file "Correspondence—1946."

Notes

ABBREVIATIONS

DCER   *Documents on Canadian External Relations* (Ottawa: Department of External Affairs)
DEA   Department of External Affairs, Historical Records Division, Ottawa
FRUS   *Foreign Relations of the United States* (Washington: Department of State)
LC   Library of Congress, Washington
NA   National Archives, Washington
NAC   National Archives of Canada
PRO   Public Records Office, London
PWNHC   Prince of Wales Northern Heritage Centre, Yellowknife, NWT
YTA   Yukon Archives, Whitehorse, YT

NOTES TO THE PREFACE

1 Franklyn Griffiths, *Politics of the Northwest Passage* (Montreal: McGill-Queen's University Press 1987), and John Honderich, *Arctic Imperative: Is Canada Losing the North?* (Toronto: University of Toronto Press 1987).
2 Louis-Edmond Hamelin, *Canadian Nordicity: It's Your North Too* (Montreal: Harvest House 1978), 4.
3 William Wonders, "Conclusion," in *The North*, ed. W. Wonders (Toronto: University of Toronto Press 1972), 146.

NOTES TO CHAPTER ONE

Epigraph: Trevor Lloyd, *Frontier of Destiny: The Canadian Arctic*, Behind the Headlines Series (Toronto: Canadian Institute of International Affairs 1946), 2.

1 See pamphlets by Alexander Morris, *Nova Britannia* (Montreal 1858) and *The Hudson's Bay and Pacific Territories* (Montreal 1859).
2 Doug Owram, *Promise of Eden: The Canadian Expansionist Movement and the Idea of the West, 1858–1900* (Toronto: University of Toronto Press 1980); also Carl Berger, *The Sense of Power: Studies in the Ideas of Canadian Imperialism, 1867–1914* (Toronto: University of Toronto Press 1970).
3 Christian Morissonneau, *La Terre promise: Le Mythe du nord québécois* (Montreal: Cahiers du Québec, Hurtubise 1978), 25. Morissonneau describes the myth of the

north in French-Canadian identity as a literary theme and a territorial promise, *une espérance*, "un mythe consolateur qui réfère au mythe originel: un mythe function-nel qui a pu apaiser l'angoisse collective, temperer une crise grave de l'histoire d'un peuple" (175). This thesis has been criticized by many French-Canadian academics as being too presumptive; they believe that the myth was merely part of the mid-19th century colonization promotion encouraged by an elite faction of the Catholic church and not a view held by the majority of French-speaking québécois.

4 R. G. Haliburton, *Men of the North and Their Place in History* (Montreal 1869).

5 Quoted in Gordon W. Smith, *Territorial Sovereignty in the Canadian North: A Historical Outline of the Problem*, Report for the Department of Northern Affairs and National Resources (Ottawa: Queen's Printer 1963), 5. See also A. E. Millard, *Southern Baffin Island* (Ottawa 1930), 9, and Trevor Lloyd, "The Geography and Administration of Northern Canada," unpublished manuscript, Canadian Institute of International Affairs, 1947, chapter 1: 9.

6 Great Britain, Imperial Order-in-Council, dated 31 July 1880, the Court at Osborne House, Isle of Wight.

7 Canada, Dominion Order-in-Council, P.C. 1839, 23 September 1982.

8 Smith, *Territorial Sovereignty*, 6.

9 Kenneth J. Rea, *The Political Economy of the Canadian North* (Toronto: University of Toronto Press 1968), 8.

10 Charles R. Tuttle, *Our Northland: Being a Full Account of the Canadian North-West and Hudson's Bay Route* (Toronto: C. Blackett Robinson 1885), 111. This gilt-edged, leather-bound volume of over 550 pages also contains a complete assessment of the resources, the proposed railway, and Canada's place in an imperial federation. See also Owram, *Promise of Eden*, especially 181–86.

11 Morris Zaslow, *The Opening of the Canadian North* (Toronto: McClelland and Stewart 1971), 78–80.

12 Ibid., 97–99; also Lewis Green, *The Boundary Hunters: Surveying the 141st Meridian and the Alaska Panhandle* (Vancouver: University of British Columbia Press 1982), 54–63.

13 W. R. Morrison, "Showing the Flag: The Mounted Police and Canadian Sovereignty in the Western Arctic 1903–1924," paper presented to the Annual Meeting of the Canadian Historical Association (Vancouver, June 1983).

14 Alan Cooke, "A Gift Outright: The Exploration of the Canadian Arctic Islands after 1880," in *A Century of Canada's Arctic Islands, 1880–1980*, ed. Morris Zaslow (Ottawa: The Royal Society of Canada 1981), 54–55. Also Zaslow, *Opening the Canadian North*, 259.

15 Green, *The Boundary Hunters*, 66–72.

16 Ibid., 63–74. Also see David R. Morrison, *The Politics of the Yukon Territory 1890–1909* (Toronto: University of Toronto Press 1968), 19, 48, and 88.

17 Morrison, *Politics of the Yukon*, 4–6.

18 D. J. Hall, *Clifford Sifton: Volume II, The Lonely Eminence, 1901–1929* (Vancouver: University of British Columbia Press 1985), 124–25.

19 Yukon Territorial Archives, Whitehorse, Yukon (hereafter YTA), Central Registry Files of the Yukon Government, YRG 1, "Introduction."

20 Hall, *Clifford Sifton*, 2: 125–26; also Robert Page, *Northern Development: The Canadian Dilemma* (Toronto: McClelland and Stewart 1986), 13.

21 Hall, *Clifford Sifton*, 2: 123–24.

22 Ibid., 2: 124–26, 224, and 233.

23 Ibid., 126.

24 Zaslow, *Opening the Canadian North*, 260–64.
25 Diamond Jenness, *Eskimo Administration II: Canada*, Technical Paper No. 15 (Montreal: Arctic Institute of North America 1964), 20. Jenness was born in Wellington, New Zealand, in 1886. He spent his graduate years at Oxford and came to Canada in 1913 as a participant in the Canadian Arctic Expedition. He lived for a year with the Inuit as a member of the hunting party that was separated from the ill-fated *Karluk*. Jenness joined the National Museum of Canada in 1920 and was appointed chief anthropologist six years later. During World War II, he served as Deputy Director of Special Intelligence for the Royal Canadian Air Force. A respected authority on northern aborigines, he wrote a number of articles and books on the Canadian Inuit and Indians, including the classic, *Indians of Canada*, first published in 1932 by the National Museum of Canada.
26 William R. Morrison, *Showing the Flag: The Mounted Police and Canadian Sovereignty in the North, 1894–1925* (Vancouver: University of British Columbia Press 1985), 72–86.
27 Ibid., 92–94.
28 Yolande Dorion-Robitaille, *Captain J. E. Bernier's Contribution to Canadian Sovereignty in the Arctic* (Ottawa: Indian and Northern Affairs 1978), 46.
29 Ibid., 54 and 66.
30 Richard Finnie, "Joseph Elzear Bernier (1852–1934)," *Arctic* 39 (September 1986): 272.
31 Numerous articles deal with the legality of Canadian claims in terms of international law: Maxwell Cohen, "The Arctic and the National Interest," *International Journal* 26 (Winter 1970–1971): 58; Trevor Lloyd, "'Some International Aspects of Arctic Canada," *International Journal* 25 (Autumn 1970): 413; L. C. Green, "Canada and Arctic Sovereignty," *Canadian Bar Review* 43 (December 1970): 742–43; and House of Commons, "Foundation of Canada's Sovereignty over the Arctic Region," a study prepared by the Research Branch of the Library of Parliament (Ottawa: May 1969): 11–12. The view that the exercise of authority was the essence of sovereignty was later confirmed in 1931, when the International Court of Justice in the Hague ruled that occupation superseded claims of discovery or contiguity. Although the sector theory has been referred to on many occasions and is certainly the basis upon which Canadian maps were drawn, it has never been asserted as a formal claim. Repudiated by both the United States and Norway, it is still considered unlikely to be judged valid under international law.
32 Zaslow, *Opening of the Canadian North*, 266–68.
33 Dorion-Robitaille, *Bernier's Contribution*, 92.
34 Richard J. Diubaldo, *Stefansson and the Canadian Arctic* (Montreal: McGill-Queen's University Press 1978), 64.
35 Morris Zaslow, "Administering the Arctic Islands 1880–1940: Policemen, Missionaries, Fur Traders," in *A Century of Canada's Arctic Islands*, ed. Zaslow, 64.
36 Diubaldo, *Stefansson*, 161–86, and 209.
37 William R. Hunt, *Stef: A Biography of Vilhjalmur Stefansson, Canadian Arctic Explorer* (Vancouver: Stef: University of British Columbia Press 1986). In contrast to Diubaldo, the American historian presents a more favourable account of Stefansson.
38 Canada, Department of the Interior, *Estimates* (Ottawa, 1905–1920), and Canada, *Report of the Commissioner of the Royal North West Mounted Police* (Ottawa, 1918).
39 Zaslow, "Administering the Islands," 64–66.
40 National Archives of Canada (hereafter NAC), Northern Affairs Records, RG 85,

vol. 347, file 100, "Application for Reclassification of the Northwest Territories and Yukon Branch." See also *Annual Report of the Department of the Interior* (Ottawa, 31 March 1922), Appendix A.

41 Morrison, *Showing the Flag*, 163–68.

42 D. L. McKeand, "The Annual Eastern Arctic Patrol," *Canadian Geographical Journal* 16 (June 1938): 37–38.

43 National Museum of Man, *The Athapaskans: Strangers of the North* (Ottawa: National Museum of Canada 1974), 39.

44 K. R. Greenaway and Moira Dunbar, "Aviation in the Arctic Islands," in *A Century of Canada's Arctic Islands*, ed. Morris Zaslow, 79–83. Also John Swettenham, *McNaughton, Volume I* (Toronto: Ryerson Press 1969), 213ff.; Moira Dunbar and Keith Greenaway, *Arctic Canada from the Air* (Ottawa: Defence Research Board 1956), 403–5; and W. A. B. Douglas, *The Creation of a National Air Force, Volume II* (Toronto: University of Toronto Press 1986), 65–118.

45 Swettenham, *McNaughton*, 1: 220.

46 Canada, House of Commons, *Debates 1930* (Ottawa: King's Printer 1931), 867. See also NAC, RG 85, vol. 347, file 100, "Application for Reclassification of the Northwest Territories and Yukon Branch."

47 David Judd, "Seventy-five Years of Resource Administration in Northern Canada," *Polar Record* 14 (1969): 798.

48 David Breen, "Anglo-American Rivalry and the Evolution of Canadian Petroleum Policy to 1939," *Canadian Historical Review* 62 (September 1981): 297–303.

49 F. B. Fingland, "Administrative and Constitutional Changes in Arctic Territories: Canada," in *The Arctic Frontier*, ed. R. St. J. MacDonald (Toronto: University of Toronto Press 1966), 137.

50 Morris Zaslow, "A Prelude to Self-Government: The Northwest Territories, 1905–1940," in *The Canadian Northwest and Its Potentialities*, ed. Frank Underhill (Toronto: University of Toronto Press 1959), 92.

51 Zaslow, "Administering," 67–69.

52 NAC, RG 85, vol. 347, file 100, "Report of the Northern Advisory Board," and file 200-2, "Minutes of the Northern Advisory Board."

53 Jenness, *Eskimo Administration II*, 31–33.

54 Ibid., 32. See also Richard Diubaldo, "The Absurd Little Mouse: When Eskimos Became Indians," *Journal of Canadian Studies* 16 (Summer 1981): 34.

55 O. S. Finnie, "Land of the Midnight Sun," *Natural History* 28 (1928): 366.

56 Richard Finnie, *Canada Moves North*, 2d ed. (Toronto: Macmillan 1947), 31–37 and 64–65; and Jenness, *Eskimo Administration II*, 48.

57 Jenness, *Eskimo Administration II*, 33.

58 Morrison, *Showing the Flag*, 179–80.

59 Richard Diubaldo, *The Government of Canada and the Inuit, 1900–1967* (Ottawa: Indian and Northern Affairs 1985), 53–57.

60 Finnie, *Canada Moves North*, 68.

61 Jenness, *Eskimo Administration II*, 48.

62 Dudley Copeland, *Livingstone of the Arctic* (Lancaster, Ontario: Canadian Century Publishers 1978), 104, 109. Also René Fumoleau, *As Long As This Land Shall Last* (Toronto: McClelland and Stewart 1973), 267.

63 Jenness, *Eskimo Administration II*, 50.

64 Roderick Nash, *Wilderness and the American Mind* (New Haven: Yale University Press 1982), 67–69, and 281–82.

65 John Wadland, *Man in Nature and the Progressive Era* (New York: Arno Press

1981); and T. D. MacLulich, "Reading the Land: The Wilderness Tradition in Canadian Letters," *Journal of Canadian Studies* 20 (Summer 1985): 29.

NOTES TO CHAPTER TWO

Epigraph: NAC, Raleigh Parkin Papers, MG 30 D 77 (hereafter Parkin Papers), vol. 24, file "Manning," Tom Manning to Parkin, 10 June 1941.

1 Doug Owram, *The Government Generation: Canadian Intellectuals and the State, 1900–1945* (Toronto: Oxford University Press 1986), chapters 7–10.
2 J. L. Granatstein, *The Ottawa Men: The Civil Service Mandarins 1935–1957* (Toronto: Oxford University Press 1982), 2.
3 John Holmes, *The Shaping of Peace: Canada and the Search for World Order*, vol. 1 (Toronto: University of Toronto Press 1979), 15.
4 Granatstein, *The Ottawa Men*, 10–13.
5 Several historians have noted the tendency of the Mounted Police to be severely critical of the fur traders' exploitation of the Inuit. Morrison, *Showing the Flag*, 142–61; and Diubaldo, *The Government of Canada and the Inuit*, 61–62.
6 The British-born scientists who remained in Canada included, among others, Patrick Baird, Graham Rowley, Tom Manning, and Trevor Lloyd. Diamond Jenness was New Zealand born, but received his postgraduate degrees at Oxford, England.
7 NAC, Parkin Papers, vol. 37, file "Arctic," Parkin to J. S. Willets, 24 June 1943.
8 Patrick Baird, "Pat Baird's Arctic Journal," *Northward Journal* 38 (1986): 8.
9 Terry Cook, *Records of the Northern Affairs Program*, General Inventory Series, Federal Archives Division, NAC (Ottawa 1982), 8–11.
10 Joanne Overvold, ed., *Our Metis Heritage: A Portrayal* (Yellowknife, NWT: Métis Association of the Northwest Territories 1976), 105. In his biography, Camsell did not acknowledge the Métis ancestry of his mother, yet his nephew claims that Sarah Foulds Camsell, wife of Julian Stewart Camsell, was a Métis. Her picture is included in this book, which traces the family ties of the Mackenzie Valley Métis.
11 R. Finnie, *Canada Moves North*, 69. Both Trevor Lloyd and J. Lewis Robinson have confirmed that Camsell was considered to have been out of touch with the social problems in the north during the 1940s.
12 "Roy A. Gibson Helped Develop Rich Mineral Wealth in Canada," *Ottawa Journal*, 12 September 1950.
13 Correspondence, J. Lewis Robinson to S. Grant, 10 November 1981; and M. J. Dunbar to S. Grant, 25 November 1981.
14 NAC, Department of Indian Affairs and Northern Development Records, RG 22, vol. 278, file 99-2-81, Gibson to Major McKeand, 25 June 1943; and NAC, Parkin Papers, vol. 31, file "Trevor Lloyd." Copy of letter from Tom Manning to Trevor Lloyd, 10 June 1943.
15 Correspondence, J. L. Robinson to S. Grant, 10 November 1981.
16 Correspondence, M. J. Dunbar to S. Grant, 25 November 1981.
17 Correspondence, J. L. Robinson to S. Grant, 10 November 1981. In his "Arctic Journal" Pat Baird refers to Major D. L. McKeand as the "fatuous Major."
18 NAC, Parkin Papers, vol. 31, file "T. Lloyd," Lloyd to Parkin, 9 May 1934.
19 Special Joint Committee of the Senate and the House of Commons, appointed to examine and consider the Indian Act, *Minutes of Proceedings and Evidence*, No. 7, 21 June 1946 (Ottawa 1947), 343.
20 NAC, RG 22, vol. 270, file 40-10-1 (pt. 1), "Political Development of the North-

west Territories and Yukon," Appendix to a Memorandum for the Minister of Resources and Development, 8 May 1950. See also F. B. Fingland, "Administration," 145.

21 Richard Stuart, "Impact of the Alaska Highway on Dawson City," paper prepared for the 40th Anniversary Alaska Highway Symposium, Fort St. John, British Columbia, 18 June 1982, 4.

22 This legal interpretation of powers and duties of the commissioner was put forth in a paper prepared for the Hon. Robert Winters, minister of resources and development, March 1950 (DIAND Records, RG 22, vol. 270, file 40-10-1 [pt. 1]).

23 Jenness, *Eskimo Administration II*, 49. See also R. Finnie, *Canada Moves North*, 69.

24 Morris Zaslow, "Prelude," 4. See also Jenness, *Eskimo Administration II*, 49–50.

25 Prince of Wales Northern Heritage Centre, Yellowknife, Northwest Territories Council Minutes (hereafter NWT minutes), vol. 9, 2 April 1940, 2202–3.

26 Ibid., vols. 7 and 8, for years through 1937 to 1939.

27 Canada, *Census of Canada—1941* (Ottawa 1946), 318–19.

28 Stuart, "Impact," 1–4.

29 Robert G. McCandless, *Yukon Wildlife: A Social History* (Edmonton: University of Alberta Press 1985), 32–42, 122–28.

30 M. J. and J. L. Robinson, "Exploration and Settlement of the Mackenzie District, N.W.T." *Canadian Geographical Journal* (June–July 1946), reprint, 16–17.

31 Overvold, *Our Métis Heritage*, 7, 41, 135.

32 J. Lewis Robinson, "Eskimo Population in the Canadian Eastern Arctic," *Canadian Geographical Journal* 29 (September 1944): 130–31 and 138–42.

33 Jenness, *Eskimo Administration II*, 59–64.

34 NAC, Parkin Papers, vol. 24, file "Manning," Tom Manning to Parkin, 10 June 1941. Manning claimed that "the missionaries are anxious to keep all white men out of the north and prevent its development," as it would hinder their crusade to convert the heathens. At the same time, the fur traders were reluctant to encourage development "because uneducated natives will accept lower prices for their fur than the whiteman." Also see F. H. Kitto, *The Northwest Territories* (Ottawa: King's Printer 1930), 15; and D. C. Scott, *The Administration of Indian Affairs in Canada* (Toronto: Canadian Institute of International Affairs 1931), 27, for other views on the future of the native peoples.

35 R. Finnie, *Canada Moves North*, 57.

36 Jenness, *Eskimo Administration II*, 45, 67. For a more recent analysis of the harmful effects, see Diubaldo, *The Government of Canada and the Inuit*, 85–93.

37 Interview with John Nerysoo at Tuktoyaktuk, 15 August 1981.

38 This opinion was expressed by two former Hudson's Bay Company factors, Sam Mackie, 16 August 1981, at Aklavik; and Alex Forman, 17 August 1981, at Inuvik.

39 NAC, Parkin Papers, vol. 24, file "Manning," copy of report from T. Manning to R. Gibson, 10 June 1941, 6.

40 Canada, *Report of the Department of Mines and Resources for the fiscal year ending March 31, 1940* (Ottawa: King's Printer 1940), see reports of the Bureau of Northwest Territories and Yukon Affairs, 60–75, and Indian Affairs Branch, 150ff. Also Keith J. Crowe, *A History of the Original Peoples of Northern Canada* (Montreal: McGill-Queens University Press 1974), 166–67; Andrew Moore, "Survey of Education in the Mackenzie District," *Canadian Journal of Economics and Political Science* 11 (February 1945): 70; Lloyd, "The Geography and Administration of

Northern Canada," appendix, "Yukon Territorial School Enrollments of Indians 1942–1943," and chapter 7: 24–25.

41 Diubaldo, *The Government of Canada and the Inuit*, 86.

42 Lloyd, "Geography and Administration," chapter 6: 2.

43 Jenness, *Eskimo Administration II*, 50.

44 NAC, Parkin Papers, vol. 24, file "Manning," A. Steinmann to Manning, 29 September 1943.

45 Diubaldo, *The Government of Canada and the Inuit*, 94–95.

46 G. J. Wherett, "Survey of Health Conditions and Medical and Hospital Services in the North West Territories," *Canadian Journal of Economic and Political Science* 11 (February 1945): 54–58.

47 Copland, *Livingstone of the Arctic*, 109–10, 124–25.

48 Diubaldo, *The Government of Canada and the Inuit*, 94–99. Also Jenness, *Eskimo Administration II*, 46, 50–54, 70–71; the *Annual Reports* of the Department of Mines and Resources from 1936 to 1940.

49 Canada, *Report of the Department of Mines and Resources for the fiscal year Ending March 31, 1940* (Ottawa: King's Printer 1940), 63.

50 Diubaldo, *The Government of Canada and the Inuit*, 72.

51 Copeland, *Livingstone*, 123–24, 168.

52 Diubaldo, *The Government of Canada and the Inuit*, 94–99.

53 Wherrett, "Survey of Health Conditions," 54–55.

54 Interview with Dr. J. Harry Ebbs, 31 October 1981. See also Helen Burgess, "Health by Remote Control," *Beaver* (Winter 1970): 50; and various reports in NAC, Department of National Health and Welfare Records, RG 29, vol. 181, file 300-2-1 (pt. 3).

55 NWT Council Minutes, vol. 9, February 1940, 2165–66.

56 Diubaldo, *The Government of Canada and the Inuit*, 70–73; and Crowe, *A History*, 173. For quote see Jenness, *Eskimo Administration II*, 53.

57 Jenness, *Eskimo Administration II*, 55.

58 Ibid., 54–55; and NAC, Parkin Papers, vol. 24, file "Manning," A. Steinmann to T. Manning, 29 September 1943.

59 Copeland, *Livingstone*, 124.

60 Lloyd, "Geography and Administration," chapter 5, "Native Peoples." Also *Annual Report of the Department of Mines and Resources for year ending March 31, 1940*.

61 O. S. Finnie, "Introduction" in A. E. Porsild, *Reindeer Grazing in North West Canada*, (Ottawa: King's Printer 1929).

62 As quoted in Crowe, *A History*, 168.

63 Diubaldo, *The Government of Canada and the Inuit*, 68–69.

64 Ibid., 112–14. Lloyd, "Geography and Administration," chapter 8:4.

65 Diubaldo, *The Government of Canada and the Inuit*, 73–75; also Lloyd, "Geography and Administration," chapter 8: 40.

66 Heather Robertson, *A Gentleman Adventurer: The Arctic Diaries of Richard Bonnycastle* (Toronto: Lester and Orpen Dennys 1984), 103–44.

67 Jenness, *Eskimo Administration II*, 51–53.

68 Crowe, *A History*, 173. Trevor Lloyd offers a variety of explanations for this apparent advancement of the Inuit elsewhere. Government sponsored education and intermarriage were advanced as general reasons in all three instances. It was also noted that there was no racial prejudice in Russia and that the United States government

had controlled the fur trade by arranging for the pelts to be sent to Seattle, thus preventing exploitation by the traders ("Geography and Administration," chapter 5, 65, 66, and 73).

69 NAC, Parkin Papers, vol. 24, file "Manning," Manning to Parkin, 10 June 1941.
70 R. Finnie, *Canada Moves North*, 85.
71 For the best account of the mining booms at Great Bear and Yellowknife, see Ray Price, *Yellowknife* (Toronto: Peter Martin Associates 1967), chapters 5–12.
72 Ibid., 117.
73 Kenneth Coates, *Canada's Colonies: A History of the Yukon and Northwest Territories* (Toronto: James Lorimer 1985), 103–4.
74 David Judd, "Seventy-five Years," 800. See also Fumoleau, *As Long as This Land Shall Last*, 20.
75 Information supplied by Dr. W. Scott, formerly of the Geological Survey.
76 Greenaway and Dunbar, "Aviation in the Arctic Islands," 79–83; and Dunbar and Greenaway, *Arctic Canada from the Air*, 403–5.
77 Morris Zaslow, *Reading the Rocks: The Story of the Geological Survey of Canada, 1842–1972* (Toronto: Macmillan 1975), 367–71.
78 Douglas, *The Creation of a National Air Force*, see chapter 1.
79 Jenness, *Eskimo Administration II*, 50.
80 R. A. Gibson to W. W. Cory, February 1936, as quoted in Jenness, *Eskimo Administration II*, 54.
81 NWT Council Minutes, vol. 9, 11 March 1940, p. 2175; and vol. 12, 24 February 1942, 2121–22.
82 Ibid., vol. 9, 2 April 1940, 2201.
83 Ibid., 9 January 1940, 2098–2100; and 2 April 1940, 2205.
84 Crowe, *A History of the Original Peoples*, 163.
85 Department of Mines and Resources, *Annual Report for year ending March 1939*, 8–9; and Jenness, *Eskimo Administration II*, 70.
86 C. C. Lingard, "Administration of the Canadian Northland," *Canadian Journal of Economics and Political Science* 12 (February 1946): 71.
87 Zaslow, "Prelude," 98–99.
88 Ibid., 97.
89 NWT Council Minutes, vol. 8 (1939), 1462–64, 1910–17.
90 Ibid., vol. 10, January 1941, 2449.
91 Zaslow, *Reading the Rocks*, 374.
92 James Eayrs, *In Defence of Canada: Appeasement and Rearmament* (Toronto: University of Toronto Press 1964), 218.
93 Robin Fisher, "T.D. Pattullo and the British Columbia to Alaska Highway," 12–22, and David Remley, "The Latent Fear: Canadian-American Relations and Early Proposals for a Highway to Alaska," both in *The Alaska Highway: Papers of the 40th Anniversary Symposium*, ed. Kenneth Coates (Vancouver: University of British Columbia Press 1985), 1–7.
94 Eayrs, *Appeasement and Rearmament*, 183–84.
95 Fisher, "T. D. Pattullo and the British Columbia to Alaska Highway," 20.
96 Ibid., 16.
97 NA, RG 59, PJBD series box 2, file "Alaska Highway." See the various and letters and maps sent to the American section of the Permanent Joint Board on Defence within weeks of this joint committee's creation.
98 C. P. Stacey, *The Military Problems of Canada* (Toronto: Ryerson Press 1940), 37.

99 Vilhjalmur Stefansson, "The American Far North," *Foreign Affairs* 17 (April 1939): 521.
100 William Franklin, "Alaska, Outpost of American Defense," *Foreign Affairs* 18 (October 1940): 249–50.

NOTES TO CHAPTER THREE

Epigraph: NAC, Escott Reid Papers, (hereafter Reid Papers) MG 27 III 65, vol. 9–10 (unsorted at time of research), memorandum, Reid to Loring Christie, 3 December 1938.

1 Hugh Keenleyside, "Canada's Department of External Affairs," *International Journal* 1 (July 1946): 205.
2 Owram, *The Government Generation*, 256–58.
3 Shelagh Grant, "Search for a Northern Policy, 1940–1950: Impact of the Canadian Institute of International Affairs," unpublished manuscript, 1981, copy in the CIIA National Library, Toronto, 23–24.
4 Granatstein, *The Ottawa Men*, 275.
5 Ibid., xii.
6 Owram, *The Government Generation*, 256, 260.
7 Arnold Heeney, *The Things That Are Caesar's: Memoirs of a Public Servant* (Toronto: University of Toronto Press 1972), 12. As noted by Pearson, an Oxford education tended to promote an English-Canadian nationalism (Granatstein, *Ottawa Men*, 79fn).
8 Heeney, *Things That Are Caesar's*, 5–14, 33.
9 Hugh L. Keenleyside, *Memoirs of Hugh L. Keenleyside, Volume 1, Hammer the Golden Day* (Toronto: McClelland and Stewart 1981), 499.
10 Keenleyside's failure to advance to more senior offices in the public service, as did his colleagues Norman Robertson and Lester Pearson, has given rise to diverse speculations. Granatstein claims he "blotted his copy-book in the prime minister's view by supporting the Japanese Canadians too enthusiastically." Gordon R. Robertson, who was assistant secretary of the Privy Council in 1949, suggests that the strong idealism of such civil servants as Keenleyside gave rise to some rigidity in their views and perhaps, at times, to "a tunnel vision." This created unease in the minds of senior politicians, who would give final approval to the top appointments (interview with Gordon R. Robertson, 10 September 1982; Granatstein, *The Ottawa Men*, 95; also Keenleyside, *Memoirs*, 1:98; and *Memoirs of Hugh L. Keenleyside, Volume 2: On the Bridge of Time* [Toronto: McClelland and Stewart, 1982], 20–21).
11 Holmes, *Shaping of Peace*, 1: 27.
12 T. B. Millar, "Commonwealth Institute of International Affairs," *International Journal* 33 (Winter 1977–78): 20–21, and 25.
13 John Holmes, *The Better Part of Valour: Essays on Canadian Diplomacy*, Carleton Library Series, no. 49 (Toronto: McClelland and Stewart 1970), 57.
14 NAC, Canadian Institute of International Affairs Papers, (hereafter CIIA papers), MG 28 I 250, vol. 7, file 1, "Report of the Nineteenth Annual Study Conference."
15 Holmes, *The Better Part of Valour*, 31.
16 Ibid., 30, 157.
17 Claus-M. Naske, "Building the Alaska Highway," *The Northern Engineer* 16:1 (Spring 1984): 29–30.
18 Christopher Thorne, *Allies of a Kind: The United States, Britain and the War against*

Japan, 1941–1945 (New York: Oxford University Press 1978), 96–98 and 212–14; Dean Acheson, *Present at the Creation: My Years in the State Department* (New York: W. W. Norton 1969), 29–33; Cordell Hull, *The Memoirs of Cordell Hull*, vol. 2 (London: Hodder and Stoughton 1948), 831–43.

19 University of Durham, England, Malcolm MacDonald papers (hereafter MacDonald Papers) 12/6/39–41. Report to the Dominions Office, Summer 1944.

20 Acheson, *Present at the Creation*, 11, 38.

21 Thorne, *Allies of a Kind*, 113–14.

22 Ibid., as quoted on 92. See also 117.

23 Ibid., 97.

24 As quoted in Robert Sherwood, *Roosevelt and Hopkins: An Intimate History*, rev. ed. (New York: Grosset and Dunlap 1950), 266.

25 As quoted in Thorne, *Allies of a Kind*, 98.

26 NA, State Department Records, RG 59 "Research and Analysis Reports," Intelligence Service for the British Empire Section, microfiche #738a, 128.

27 MacDonald papers, 12/2/9, 8 August 1941, and 12/2/1-5, April 1941. Memos to Dominions Office forwarded to Churchill.

28 Sir Alexander Cadogan, *The Diaries of Sir Alexander Cadogan*, ed. David Dilks (New York: G. P. Putnam), 63.

29 Reported in the *Toronto Daily Star*, 6 September 1924.

30 Heeney, *Things That Are Caesar's*, 91–92; J. L. Granatstein, *A Man of Influence: Norman A. Robertson and Canadian Statecraft, 1929–1968* (Ottawa: Deneau 1981), 111.

31 MacDonald Papers, transcripts of taped interviews by journalist Narain Singh in Kenya, 22 May 1969 (unassigned file), tape no. 11: 6 and tape no. 12: 1–4.

32 Library of Congress (hereafter LC), Cordell Hull Papers, Microfilm-reel no. 28, "Conversations with Canada," Hull and Loring Christie, 13 April 1940.

33 Eayrs, *Appeasement and Rearmament*, 188–202.

34 Ibid., 206.

35 Ibid., 205.

36 NAC, CIIA Papers, vol. 1, file "1939–1941," correspondence John Baldwin to Edgar Tarr, 4 July 1940.

37 Keenleyside, *Memoirs*, 2: 48–51.

38 C. P. Stacey, *Arms, Men, and Governments: The War Policies of Canada, 1939–1945* (Ottawa: Department of National Defence 1970), 337.

39 As quoted in R. D. Cuff and J. L. Granatstein, *Ties That Bind: Canadian American Relations in Wartime, from the Great War to the Cold War* (Toronto: Samuel Stevens Hakkert 1977), 99. Berle was also Chairman of the Foreign Policy Subcommittee of the Postwar Economic Committee.

40 Department of External Affairs (hereafter DEA), Historical Records Division, vol. 781, file 394, memo "An Outline Synopsis," 17 June 1940, as cited in J. L. Granatstein, *Canada's War: The Politics of the Mackenzie King Government 1939–1945* (Toronto: Oxford University Press 1975), 479.

41 Cuff and Granatstein, *Ties That Bind*, 98.

42 MacDonald Papers, 12/2/5, report to the Dominions Office, forwarded to Churchill, April 1941. Quote as cited in the report.

43 H. L. Keenleyside, "The Canada-United States Permanent Joint Board on Defence, 1940–1945," *International Journal* 16 (Winter 1960–61): 52–56.

44 Stanley Cohen, *The Forgotten War* (Missoula, MT: Pictorial Histories Publishing Company 1981), 10, 44–45.

45 F. H. Soward et al., *Canada in World Affairs: The Pre-War Years* (Toronto: Oxford University Press 1941), 4.

46 Franklin, "Alaska," 247–50.

47 Cohen, *The Forgotten War*, 3–4.

48 LC, Cordell Hull Papers, Reel #28, King in conversation with Hull, 17 April 1941.

49 M. V. Bezeau, "The Realities of Strategic Planning: The Decision to Build the Alaska Highway," in *The Alaska Highway*, ed. Coates, 26.

50 Naske, "Building the Alaska Highway," 30.

51 NA, RG 59, PJBD series, vol. 2, file "Alaska Highway," Hickerson to La Guardia, 21 July 1941, and meeting 11 August 1941.

52 V. Stefansson, "The American Far North," 511.

53 Stanley Cohen, *Trail of 42: A Pictorial History of the Alaska Highway* (Altona, Manitoba: Friesen Printers 1981), 2.

54 NA, RG 59, PJBD series, vol. 2, file "Goose Bay," secret memo from La Guardia to Col. Biggar, 16 June 1941; and NA, Charles Hubbard Papers, RG 401/17, vol, 5, file "Crystal Force Reports." In preparation for the proposed airfields, weather and radio communication bases were built in October 1941 at Frobisher, Chimo and Padloping, apparently under blanket authorization, but without specific approval or knowledge of the Cabinet War Committee. (See report, "Crystal Force Expedition," dated 11 November 1941.) All three sites were chosen as potential air bases by Elliott Roosevelt, the president's son.

55 Ibid., memo of conversation between Lewis Clark and O. M. Biggar, 11 August 1941; and memo from Bissell, General chiefs of staff to Hickerson, 11 August 1941; see also correspondence August-September 1941.

56 Trevor Lloyd, "Aviation in Arctic North America and Greenland," *Polar Record* 5 (November 1947): 165–68; C. C. Lingard and R. Trotter, *Canada in World Affairs 1941–1944* (Toronto: Oxford University Press 1950), 28–29. See also Stacey, *Canada and the Age of Conflict*, vol. 2 (Toronto: University of Toronto Press 1981), 308–9.

57 Adolf Berle, *Navigating the Rapids 1918–1971* (New York: Harcourt, Brace Jovanovich 1973), 356.

58 PRO, Cabinet Records (hereafter CAB), 122/624, JB #325, Serial 717, noted as approved 28 October 1941 by chiefs of staff, and by the War Cabinet, 8 December 1941.

59 NAC, King Papers, MG 26 J 4, vol. 350, file 3788, memo from Wrong to King, 21 October 1941.

60 Ibid., 24181–87.

61 Berle, *Navigating the Rapids*, 365–66.

62 Keenleyside, *Memoirs*, 2:91.

63 Stacey, *Age of Conflict*, 2: 315–16. See also Holmes, *Shaping of Peace*, 1: 166.

64 NAC, King Papers, MG 26 J 4, vol. 350, file 3788/C241773, quote from original signed document, "Done by Mackenzie + FDR at Hyde Park on a grand Sunday, April 20 1941."

65 MacDonald Papers, 14/4/4, memo to Lord Cranborne, 24 April 1941.

66 Lingard and Trotter, *Canada in World Affairs*, 10; Cuff and Granatstein, *Ties That Bind*, 102–3; and Holmes, *Shaping of Peace*, 166–67.

67 Canada, House of Commons, *Debates*, 22 February 1943, 610–11.

68 NA, International Conferences, Commissions, and Expositions Records, Wartime Commissions Series, RG 43, vol. 1, Carl Goldenburg to R. A. C. Henry, 21 June 1941. Henry was to be the chairman of the Canadian section, but he suffered a fatal

heart attack just prior to the first joint meeting. He was replaced by W. A. Mackintosh, already a member (see Keenleyside, *Memoirs*, 2:84).

69 R. Warren James, *Wartime Economic Cooperation: A Study in Relations between Canada and the United States* (Toronto: Ryerson 1949), 26–31; and Keenleyside, *Memoirs*, 2: 82–91.

70 NA, Wartime Commissions Series, RG 43, vol. 4. For example, see memoranda and "The Problem of Eliminating British Imperial Preferences with special reference to Canada" by E. Dana Durand, 14 January 1943.

71 Acheson, *Present at the Creation*, 27–35, 39–41, 64; Hull, *Memoirs*, 1: 830–43. Original American members included E. Dana Durand, of the Tariff Commission, W. Batt of the U.S. War Production Board, Harry D. White, chief negotiator for Treasury, and Will Clayton, who later became assistant under-secretary of state for economic affairs. According to Dean Acheson's biographer, "Clayton was convinced that war sprang from colonial-style imperialism and that open markets and multilateral trade were panaceas for war" (David McLellan, *Dean Acheson: The State Department Years* [New York: Dodd, Mead & Company 1976], 71).

72 Keenleyside, *Memoirs*, 2: 90–91. Keenleyside places most of the blame for the Canadian committee's lacklustre performance on W. A. Mackintosh, who, he claimed, "didn't really believe in the task he had inherited," 85.

73 NA, RG 43, vol. 4, "J. Rettie File," draft of "Long-run Economic Collaboration between Canada and the United States," 2 September 1941, Kindleberg to Alex Skelton. Numerous other studies are scattered throughout the files, particularly in vol. 7, file "406." Of special note is a 105-page study titled "Canadian–United States Relations" (tentative draft) prepared by the Joint Economic Committee. The concluding paragraphs admit it is too early to make any concrete recommendations.

74 As cited in Cuff and Granatstein, *Ties That Bind*, 103.

75 Most of these articles were found in the news clipping files located in the CIIA National Library. The dates and origins in some cases were obscure. Those cited are identified at least by month and year. "Discounts Arctic Air Attack," *Vancouver Province*, 24 January 1941; "Arctic Attack Bases Urged," ibid., 1 March 1941; "Arctic Anxiety: Axis Unlikely to Get Bases Bishop Fleming Declares," ibid., April 1941.

76 *Montreal Gazette*, 15 November 1941. There is no author's name attached to this article, but the information supplied on the map and in the text would indicate the source might be related to the United States Army or Navy. The phraseology is similar to that used by Stefansson, who was then attached to the War Department as Arctic Adviser.

77 NAC, Reid papers, vols. 9–10, "Interview with Don Page, 21 July 1944."

NOTES TO CHAPTER FOUR

Epigraph: Vincent Massey, *What Is Past Is Prologue* (Toronto: Macmillan 1963), 371.

1 Holmes, *Shaping of Peace*, 1: 164.

2 As cited in Granatstein, *A Man of Influence*, 118.

3 NAC, Reid Papers, vols. 9–10, "The United States and Canada: Dominance, Cooperation and Absorption," 12 January 1942.

4 DEA, Historical Records Division, file 3265-A-40C, Wrong to Lester Pearson, 3 February 1942, as cited in J. L. Granatstein, *Canada's War: The Politics of the Mackenzie King Government, 1939–57* (Toronto: Oxford University Press 1975), 196.

5 NAC, King Papers, MG 26 J 4, vol. 350, file 3788, memo from Wrong to King, 7 April 1942.
6 *DCER* 9/957 F. H. La Guardia to Col. O. M. Biggar, 2 January 1942. La Guardia claimed the request had been made by the president and required an immediate reply. The request was forwarded to the prime minister, with reasons for refusal (*DCER* 9/959, Biggar to Mackenzie King, 13 January 1942).
7 NAC, Reid Papers, vols. 9–10, "The United States and Canada: Dominance, Cooperation and Absorption," 12 January 1942.
8 Holmes, *Shaping of Peace*, 1: 23.
9 Earl Parker Hanson, "Fighting at 50 below Zero," *This Week*, 7 December 1941.
10 NAC, Parkin Papers, vol. 37, file "Arctic," Finnie to W. S. Rogers, 26 December 1941. See also NWT Council Minutes, vol. 12 (1942), 2718, 2740.
11 As reported in the *Winnipeg Free Press*, 4 December 1940.
12 V. Stefansson, "Routes to Alaska," *Foreign Affairs* (July 1941): 868. While Stefansson preferred "Route D," the United States military chose to follow the path of the proposed Northwest Staging Route from Edmonton to Fairbanks via Whitehorse. Note that none of the routes Stefansson proposed bypassed Dawson, the capital of the Yukon.
13 Cohen, *The Forgotten War*, 92. See also David Breen, "Wartime Oils Limited: Canada's First Public Petroleum Corporation and Canadian Petroleum Policy, 1939–45," paper presented at the annual meeting of the Canadian Historical Association, June 1983, 3–6. Breen also points out that once the Americans entered the war, they initiated measures aimed at conserving the United States crude upon which the Canadian west coast depended.
14 NAC, Parkin Papers, MG 30 D 77, vol. 39, "Clipping file." Notes on discussion with V. Stefansson, 28 February 1943. Stefansson claimed that opposition to development of Mackenzie River oil came from Standard Oil of California, which had interests in Venezuela.
15 V. Stefansson, *The Arctic in Fact and Fable*, Headline Series, no. 51 (New York: Foreign Policy Association 1945), 88.
16 An excellent detailed account is found in Bezeau, "The Realities of Strategic Planning," 25–35. The details correlate with the memos and correspondence of the American files of the Permanent Joint Board on Defense (NA, RG 59, PJBD series, vol. 2, "Alaska Highway"). For commercial aviation interests, see correspondence related to dispute over use of the staging route by the newly formed Trans-Canada Airlines and American commercial airlines in NA, RG 59/811.79642, nos. 280–94, particularly A. A. Berle to J. P. Moffat, 25 June 1942.
17 Bezeau, "The Realities of Strategic Planning," 29–31. Also see *DCER*, 9/979, memo of conversations by J. P. Moffat with N. A. Robertson and J. D. Hickerson, 13 February 1942.
18 *DCER*, 9/980, report of meeting of various government officials and Canadian members of the PJBD, 17 February 1942.
19 *DCER*, 9/982, Keenleyside to Robertson, 3 March 1942.
20 From notes in King's diary, 21 March 1942, as cited in Granatstein, *Canada's War*, 321–22.
21 NAC, Reid Papers, vols. 9–10, "Oral Interview with Don Page, 21 July 1944," 21.
22 NAC, RG 2/18, vol. 43, file D-19-2, Cabinet War Committee Document no. 101, 2 March 1942. Also related report and memos of the Permanent Joint Board on Defence.
23 Cohen, *Trail of 42*, 11–18. The estimated cost in 1942 is stated in Keenleyside's report to Robertson, 3 March 1942, *DCER*, 9/982.

24 Naske, "Building the Alaska Highway," 33–34.
25 The full details of the requests, concerns, debates and final agreements are documented in the memos, correspondence, and extracts from CWC minutes and the Journal of Discussions and Decisions of the PJBD, published in *DCER*, 9/1019-32, covering the period from 24 March 1942 to 13 January 1943.
26 Ibid., nos. 9/1033-34.
27 Ibid., 9/1035, Excerpts from the Journal of Discussion and Decisions, 25 February 1943.
28 NA, RG 59, PJBD series, vol. 10, file "Correspondence January–March 1943," Clark to Hickerson, 3 February 1943 and Hickerson to Maj. Gen. Guy Henry, 8 February 1943.
29 YTA, YRG 1, vol. 61, as examples, see files 35355-6, 35365, 35386, 35401-5.
30 Ibid., file 35386, LeCapelain to Gibson, 6 March 1943.
31 NWT Council Minutes, vol. 12, 3863–66, report on Camsell's tour. For MacDonald's observations, see trip diary in the MacDonald papers or Malcolm MacDonald, *Down North* (Toronto: Oxford University Press 1943), 83–84.
32 Dwight Oland, "The Army Medical Department and the Construction of the Alaska Highway," in *The Alaska Highway*, ed. Coates, 65–73.
33 Ibid., 66–67. Also for more detailed account of impact on native health and social life, see Kenneth Coates, "The Alaska Highway and the Indians of the Southern Yukon, 1942–50: A Study of Native Adaptation to Northern Development," in ibid., 151–68.
34 YTA, YRG 1, vol. 61, file 35386, Jeckell to Gibson, 5 March 1943, proposed study dated 12 April 1943.
35 Ibid., various correspondence, see Gibson to Jeckell, 5 January 1944 and 18 July 1944; petition (n.d.); Jeckell to Gibson, 24 March 1944, 29 June 1944, 24–25 October 1944.
36 Oland, "The Army Medical Department," 66, 71.
37 *DCER*, 9/992-998, various teletypes passing between the prime minister as secretary of state and the legation in Washington, 26 March to 10 July 1944.
38 Special precautions were taken with the agreement to allow improvements to the Northwest Staging Route. Americans could pay for accommodation for their own men and aerodromes for their planes, but construction on the runways themselves would be financed by the Canadian government (*DCER* 9/1023, "Extract from Cabinet War Committee Minutes," 22 April 1942).
39 Ibid., 9/988-91, with special reference to "Extracts from Minutes of Cabinet War Committee," 11 and 26 March 1943.
40 Ibid., 9/1239-50, various memoranda and correspondence between External Affairs, the prime minister, and legal advisers. Note 9/1241, Attorney General R. L. Maitland to Ian Mackenzie, minister of pensions and national health, 20 January 1942.
41 Green, *The Boundary Hunters*, 142, 178
42 Cohen, *The Forgotten War*, 66. For more complete details on the Canol Project, see Shelagh Grant, "Canol: A Ghost from the Past," *Alternatives* 9:2 (Spring–Summer 1981): 22–28; and Richard Diubaldo, "The Canol Project in Canadian-American Relations," *Historical Papers*—1977 (Ottawa: Canadian Historical Association 1978): 179–96.
43 NWT Council Minutes, vol. 12, Special Report by Charles Camsell, May 1942, 2788–90. Meeting with Hudson's Bay Company officials took place 4 March 1942 before final approval by the Canadian government.
44 MacDonald, *Down North*, 177.

45 *DCER*, 9/999-1007, includes Camsell's report to Robertson, 15 June 1943. Also very complete details of all aspects of the project are found in NAC, Special Commissioner Records, RG 36/7, vol. 4, files 22–23. Of particular note, see the special report by the Wartime Information Board on Canol, 8–9 and appendix 37–72. Reference to the meeting 16 May 1942 is found in the "War Cabinet" file, the "Summary of the War Committee Decisions." Other references in Canada, House of Commons, *Debates*, 15 May 1942, 2696, and NWT Council Minutes, vol. 12, 2 June 1942, 2822.

46 NWT Council Minutes, vol. 12, "Canol Reports" dates 25 August 1942, and 8 December 1942.

47 Ibid., meeting of 28 August 1942. Camsell reported on his northern trip commencing 5 August 1942. Keenleyside was absent from this meeting and would not likely have received a copy of the minutes for several weeks. The Cabinet War Committee was not advised until October of the unauthorized airfields along the Mackenzie River as noted in the August minutes.

48 NAC, Special Commissioner's Records, RG 36/7, vol. 4, file "Summary of War Cabinet Decisions," entry 7 October 1942.

49 DEA, Historical Records Division, file 4349-40C, Keenleyside to Robertson, 6 October 1942, as quoted in Diubaldo, "The Canol Project in Canadian-American Relations," 181.

50 NAC, Reid Papers, vols. 9–10, "Oral History Interview with Don Page, 21 July 1977," 20.

51 Richard Finnie, "The Origins of Canol's Mackenzie Air Fields," *Arctic* 33 (June 1980): 274–77.

52 *DCER*, 9/952, Keenleyside to Robertson, 14 April 1942. Keenleyside also cites an incident where a U.S. Army officer phoned the general manager of the CNR to ask for sixty Canadian engineers to help locate and construct a railway from Prince George to Fairbanks before the idea had even been suggested to the PJBD.

53 The misunderstanding related to "blanket authorization" was apparently widespread, with the Senior U.S. Army member of the PJBD inquiring of American Secretary John Hickerson if he would clarify the terms of the agreements. Hickerson replied that the United States did not "have blanket authority for construction of all war projects in Canada" and that "special permission of the Canadian government must be obtained for the construction of any proposed airfields" (*NA*, RG 59, PJBD series, vol. 10, Hickerson to Maj. Gen. Guy Henry, 3 March 1943).

54 *DCER*, 9/1008, Moffatt to Robertson, 27 November 1942. Also NAC, Special Commissioner's Records, RG 36/7, vol. 4, file "Summary of War Cabinet Decisions" under Appendix K—Canol, see letter from Lewis Clark to the secretary of state, 28 December 1942.

55 *DCER*, 9/1009, Cottrelle to Keenleyside, 7 December 1942.

56 NAC, Trevor Lloyd Papers, MG 30 B 97 (hereafter Lloyd Papers), vol. 1, file 9, Stefansson to Lloyd, 13 March 1943.

57 James Eayrs, *In Defence of Canada: Peacemaking and Deterrence*, vol. 3 (Toronto: University of Toronto Press 1977), 349.

58 NWT Council Minutes, vol. 12, Meeting 12 April 1942. The problems of finding construction workers and technicians had already been discussed in relation to the Northeast Staging Route.

59 Ibid., vol. 13, letter, 14 January 1943, A. F. Totzke to Gibson, 3026.

60 Ibid., 3023; and vol. 12, 20 August 1942, 2895.

61 Ibid., vol. 12, McKeand to Gibson, 20 August 1942, 2895.

62 Ibid., 2932–33.
63 Ibid., 4 September 1941; 2584; 2 June 1942, 2833ff., and 3 September 1942, Eastern Arctic Patrol Report, 2933.
64 Ibid., memorandum, 18 December 1942, 2884–88; the official report from telephone message, 3 September 1942, 29332–33; and his verbal report delivered at council meeting, December 1942, 2915–23.
65 Ibid., report of 18 December 1942, 2884–85.
66 Ibid., vol. 13, January 1943, 3019; and 4 April 1943, 3072.
67 Ibid., vol. 12, 2801–2. See also 2825.
68 Ibid., 2846. As an example, Dr. Pett of the Department of Pensions and Health was asked to conduct a study on nutrition in the Arctic after reports that similar studies were being conducted by the doctors of the Hospital for Sick Children for the Hudson's Bay Company. See also vol. 13, 26 January 1943, 2946; and 22 June 1943, 3095–97.
69 Ibid., vols. 12 and 13, 2943, 3057, and 3065.
70 Ibid., vol. 12, report, 18 December 1942, 2887–88.
71 Ibid., 2920.
72 Ibid., vol. 13, 3134–37.
73 Ibid., vol. 12, 28 August 1942, 2864, 18 December 1942, 2921, and vol. 13, 26 January 1943, 2943–49.
74 NA, RG 43, Wartime Commissions Series, vol. 5, file "James E. Rettie," report to Federal Reserve System by Wendell Thorne, 4 June 1943; file 405, press release, 25 January 1943.
75 DCER, 9/1184 Mackintosh to Heeney, 17 December 1942.
76 NA, RG 43, Wartime Commissions Series, vol. 5, file "James Rettie-1," confidential study on "Trans-Canada–Alaska Railway," 8 October 1941; and "Notes on Conversations with Canadian Officials," 12–17 October 1941.
77 Ibid., vol. 5, file 405. This clipping file included the two pages of The Sunday Oregonian containing the article by Mel Arnold.
78 Ibid., file "B. Kizer," includes a lengthy outline titled "Suggested Draft for Mr. Kizer's IPR Presentation." Details of Kizer's presentation are found in correspondence from Kizer to Alvin Hansen, chairman of the American section of the Joint Economic Committees, 22 December 1941. Maps and negatives are in a separate file.
79 Maps used in the presentation are also published in Benjamin Kizer, The US-Canadian Northwest: A Demonstration Area for International Post War Planning and Development (Princeton, NJ: Princeton University Press 1942). This expanded terms of reference is also stated by Charles Camsell, co-director of the North Pacific Planning Project (NWT Council Minutes, April 1943, 3064).
80 Benjamin Kizer, "The North Pacific International Planning Project," American Council Paper no. 2, for the Eighth Conference of the Institute of Pacific Relations, Mont Tremblant, Quebec, December 1942. See also "Preliminary Outline of the North Pacific Planning Project." Copy on file in NAC, Special Commissioners Records, RG 36/7, vol. 47, file "North Pacific Planning Project."
81 DCER, 9/1183, Mackintosh to Heeney, 17 December 1942. The message was forwarded immediately (NAC, King Papers, MG 26 J 4, vol. 350, file 3788, Heeney to King, 12 December 1942).
82 J. W. Pickersgill, The Mackenzie King Record, vol. 1 (Toronto: University of Toronto Press 1960), 436.

83 *DCER*, 9/1184-85, extracts from minutes of Cabinet War Committee, 23 and 30 December 1942.

84 *DCER*, 9/1186, Mackintosh to Hansen, 4 January 1943; NA, RG 43, Wartime Commissions Series "James Rettie" file, Hansen to Rettie, Rettie to Hansen, 8–12 January 1943.

85 Ibid., 9/1187, extracts from the minutes of the Cabinet War Committee, 13 January 1943.

86 NAC, RG 36/7, vol. 47, file NPPP, "Preliminary Outline of the North Pacific Planning Project."

87 Ibid., "North Pacific Planning Project: Report of Progress, May 1943."

88 *Vancouver Daily Province*, 25 and 26 January 1943, and the *Edmonton Journal*, 25 and 26 January 1943.

89 *New York Times*, 25 and 26 January 1943.

90 *Financial Post*, 17 April 1943.

91 *Vancouver Sun*, 3 April 1943.

92 NA, Wartime Commissions Series, RG 43, vol. 5, file "B. Kizer," Mackintosh to Col. R. F. Bessey, 26 January 1943.

93 Kizer, *The US–Canadian Northwest*, 28–38.

94 NAC, Parkin Papers, vol. 37, file "Arctic," list of quotes relating to the Arctic sent to Parkin by J. S. Willets, 5 November 1943. Quote attributed to Isaiah Bowman by annotations.

95 John Hughes, "The Great Northwest," *Far Eastern Survey* (8 February 1942): 28. When asked about the "John Hughes" article, Keenleyside appeared quite at a loss, admitting he had completely forgotten that he had written it. He did recall being enthusiastic about the project, with an admitted personal bias because of his British Columbia background (interview, 10 June 1980).

96 Keenleyside, *Memoirs*, 2: 91–92.

97 NWT Council Minutes, vol. 13, 3108; see also correspondence, Wilgress to Keenleyside, 4 May 1943, and Keenleyside to Wilgress, 3 March 1943.

98 Interview with Trevor Lloyd, 2 November 1980.

99 Correspondence Maxwell J. Dunbar to S. Grant, 25 November 1981.

100 Interview with Mrs. Louise Parkin, Raleigh Parkin's widow, September 1981.

101 NAC, Parkin papers, vol. 32, file "Montreal Dinner Correspondence," paper entitled "The Institute of Current World Affairs."

102 Ibid., vol. 2, file "General Correspondence," under "Notes to Wife"; and vol. 37, file "Arctic," Parkin to W. S. Rogers, 15 April 1941.

103 Ibid., vol. 41, file "CIIA," Parkin to R. Trotter, 14 January 1943; vol. 39, file "North Atlantic Studies," in addition to vol. 32, file "Montreal Dinner Correspondence."

104 NWT Council Minutes, vol. 11, meeting 22 April 1941, 2519–20.

105 NAC, Parkin Papers. See the numerous correspondence files: for example, Parkin to Brooke Claxton and Keenleyside regarding Tom Manning; vol. 21, file "Claxton," and vol. 24, file "Manning."

106 Ibid., vol. 37, file "Arctic," notes on interview with Trevor Lloyd, 15 November 1942.

107 Interview with Lloyd, 15 November 1980; and correspondence, Lloyd to author, 14 July 1982.

108 NAC, Parkin Papers, vols. 20–26, 31–33, 37–39. See correspondence files, "ICWA," "AINA," "Arctic," "CIIA," and "Arctic Study" files.

109 Ibid., vol. 37, file "Arctic," Parkin to Kizer, 17 March 1942.
110 CIIA National Library, Minutes of the Canadian Institute of International Affairs, special minutes of the 3rd meeting of the National Research Committee, 18 March 1943 (volume 6, 1943–44).
111 NAC, Parkin Papers, vol. 41, file "Arctic Study," Parkin to R. Adamson, 27 July 1943.
112 Ibid., vol. 31, "Trevor Lloyd," Lloyd to D. Maclennan, 16 October 1943.
113 Douglas, *The Creation of a National Air Force*, 2: 419–20. The entire Aleutian campaign is described in Cohen, *The Forgotten War*.
114 Douglas, *The Creation of a National Air Force*, 2: 415–20, and Cohen, *The Forgotten War*.
115 Massey, *What Is Past*, 371.
116 *DCER*, 9/1034, extract from minutes of the Cabinet War Committee, 24 February 1943.
117 Berle, *Navigating the Rapids*, 427.
118 R. G. Riddell to Professor George Brown, 20 February 1943, as quoted in Granatstein, *A Man of Influence*, 120.
119 NAC, King Papers, MG 26 J 4, vol. 350, file 3788, "Certain Developments in Canada–United States Relations," Pearson to Leighton McCarthy, 18 March 1943.

NOTES TO CHAPTER FIVE

Epigraph: NAC, King Papers, MG 26 J 4, vol. 309, file 3282, "Notes on Developments in North-Western Canada," 6 April 1943.

1 PRO, Foreign Office Records, (hereafter FO) FO 954/48, 100660, MacDonald to Attlee, 7 April 1943.
2 Margaret Gowing, "Britain, America and the Bomb," in *Retreat from Power*, ed. David Dilks, vol. 2 (London: Macmillan 1979), 50–56.
3 James Eayrs, *Peacemaking and Deterrence*, 258–59.
4 Quote cited in ibid., 259.
5 Complete narratives of the events are found in Eayrs, *Peacemaking and Deterrence*, 258–61; and Margaret Gowing, *Britain and Atomic Energy, 1939–1945* (London: Macmillan 1964), 179–83. For further details, refer to correspondence, telegrams, and minutes of meetings in PRO, Records of the Atomic Energy Authority (hereafter AB), AB 1/80 and 81, as well as AB 1/128, 271, 357, and 416. Mackenzie King mentions the issue of secrecy in his diary, referring only to a "mineral" needed for the manufacture of explosives and saying that it was agreed that no one else in government be told (Pickersgill, *Mackenzie King Record*, 1: 412–14). MacDonald suggested in August that Ilsley and Ralston might be brought into the picture, but there is no subsequent note that this occurred (PRO, AB1/80, MacDonald to Dominions Office, 4 August 1942).
6 *DCER* 9/411. As stated in letter from Gilbert Labine, president of Eldorado, to C. D. Howe, 28 May 1943.
7 PRO, AB 1/80/1624, 1697, 1698. Copies of telegrams between MacDonald and the Dominions Office, 15 July to 4 August 1942. Also Eayrs, *Peacemaking and Deterrence*, 259–61.
8 David Breen, "Anglo-American Rivalry," *Canadian Historical Review* 62 (September 1981): 287–98; also Breen "Wartime Oils," 7.

9 NWT Council Minutes, vol. 9, 1 June 1940, 2303; and vol. 12, 28 August 1942, 2865.
10 MacDonald Papers, 14/9; cited by MacDonald in correspondence, 12.
11 Ibid., 79/5, "Diary of Travels in the Canadian Far North," 7.
12 NAC, King Papers, MG 26 J 4, vol. 305, file 3146, C211424. "Remarks by Prime Minister," 27 March 1946. See also Heeney, *Things That Are Caesar's*, 91–92.
13 MacDonald Papers, 79/5, "Diary of Travels."
14 PRO, War Cabinet Records, (hereafter CAB), CAB 66, W.P. (42) 465, 13 October 1942, "Report on a Visit to North-West Canada and Alaska," by the United Kingdom high commissioner with memorandum by Clement Attlee, copy #9 in MacDonald Papers, 12/14/66–67.
15 All references of MacDonald's tour are found in "Report on a Visit to North-West Canada and Alaska."
16 MacDonald Papers, 79/5, "Diary of Travels," 68.
17 Gowing, *Britain and Atomic Energy*, 131.
18 PRO, AB 1, file 416, Ackers to Howe, 4 December 1942. Ackers claimed to have received his information from MacDonald.
19 Gowing, *Britain and Atomic Energy*, 155–57, "The Conant Memorandum," 13 January 1943.
20 PRO, AB 1/357, as related in Akers to Perrin, 21 December 1942.
21 Gowing, *Britain and Atomic Energy*, 149–52, 156–59.
22 PRO, AB 1/128, Report on status up to end January 1943. The most important files were still closed in summer of 1987 (e. g. CAB 98/47-51 on "Br-US planning—Tubes Alloy," as well as DO 127/43, MacDonald correspondence to Dominions Office, and DO 127/975 [6], "Tubes Alloy—Uranium supply"). There is enough material in peripheral files AB1/137, AB1/80, AB1/81, AB1/128, AB1/357; and the Premier 3 files, 366/11 and 12, and 83 (6) to piece the story together. These records all fit with the accounts by Gowing, *Britain and Atomic Energy*, 157–62; Kimball, *Churchill and Roosevelt*, vol. 2, *The Complete Correspondence*, (Princeton, NJ: Princeton University Press 1984), 214; *Foreign Relations of the United States* (hereafter *FRUS*), *Washington Conference, 1943*, 630–53; Sherwood, *Roosevelt and Hopkins*, 703; and Eayrs, *Peacemaking and Deterrence*, 258–66.
23 Kimball, *Roosevelt and Churchill*, 2: 155–56.
24 Thorne, *Allies of a Kind*, 213–14.
25 Gowing, *Britain and Atomic Energy*, 147–64.
26 MacDonald Papers, 14/1, MacDonald to Claxton, 9 March 1943.
27 Ibid., 12/5, 20–27, memorandum, 23 February 1943.
28 Eayrs, *Peacemaking and Deterrence*, 259, 262–75. See also NAC, Privy Council Records, RG 2/18, vol. 50, file W-46-A (pt. 2). Memos and correspondence indicate that by April 1944 the Cabinet War Committee were cognizant at least of the general purpose of the research. Heeney was aware by August 1943.
29 PRO, AB 1/81. Evaluation of the positions of Howe and Mackenzie are outlined in letter from Ackers to Perrin, 23 July 1943. Also in Eayrs, *Peacemaking and Deterrence*, 269.
30 MacDonald Papers, 14/8/29. MacDonald to Viscount Halifax, 26 February 1943. MacDonald's sister recalls that her brother was still recovering from a hernia operation but insisted he must take another trip north in spite of the doctor's disapproval.
31 Ibid., 14/8/29, MacDonald to Viscount Halifax at the British embassy in Washington, 26 February 1943.

32 Ibid., 12/5, MacDonald to Eden, addressed to the British embassy in Washington, 13 March 1943.

33 MacDonald, *Down North*, 254–56.

34 MacDonald Papers, 79/5, "Diary of Travels." Reference to the second trip in the diary is limited to brief notes of arrival and departure. More details are described in letter to Attlee which indicate that it was perhaps Costley-White who did the notetaking for the second trip (PRO, FO 954/48, 100660, MacDonald to Attlee, 7 April 1943).

35 W. L. M. King, diary, 29 March 1943 as cited by C. Nordman, "The Army of Occupation," in *The Alaska Highway*, ed. Coates, 87.

36 *DCER*, 9/1251, Robertson to the prime minister, 30 March 1943.

37 NAC, Minutes of the Cabinet War Committee, RG 2/7, vol. 12, 31 March 1943.

38 PRO, FO 954, 48/100600/527–749. Memo attached to the report indicated it had been read by Churchill, Eden, and the air ministry among others, 26–30 May 1943.

39 Ibid., 528–29, MacDonald to Attlee, 7 April 1943.

40 Eayrs, *Peacemaking and Deterrence*, 262.

41 NAC, King Papers, MG 26 J 4 vol. 309, file 3282, Norman Robertson to King, 8 April 1943. Memo is annotated "Withheld by PM," but there is no indication for how long or from whom.

42 Ibid., "Note on Developments in North-Western Canada," 6–7.

43 NAC, Privy Council Records, RG 2/18, vol. 50, file W-34-1-5, "WIB Survey No. 7: Study of Public Attitudes re: Canadian Nationhood," 27 March 1943.

44 DEA, Historical Records Division, file 52-B(s), Hugh Keenleyside, "U.S. Activities in Northwestern Canada," 9 April 1943.

45 Ibid., memo by John Baldwin, "Situation in Canadian Northwest," 12 April 1943.

46 Ibid., file 52-B(s), Robert Beattie, "Memorandum on Trip to Northwest," 12 April 1943.

47 Ibid., Keenleyside's reply is written at the end of Beattie's report; the note to Norman Robertson is dated 15 April 1943.

48 NAC, King Papers, MG 26 J 4, vol. 309, file 3282, Heeney to King, 13 April 1943, and 20 April 1943. Also *DCER*, 9/1255–8.

49 *DCER*, 9/1258, extracts from Minutes of Cabinet War Committee, 16 April 1943.

50 *DCER*, 9/1037-39, memo from External Affairs, 5 April 1943; and excerpts from CWC minutes, 7 and 28 April 1943.

51 NAC, Cabinet War Committee minutes, RG 2/7, vol. 12, 3 March 1943. See also various correspondence in Privy Council Records, RG 2/18, vol. 21, file A-15-4 (1942–1943), Reid to Norman Robertson, 19 March 1943; memos 30 March 1943 and 7 April 1943; in addition to telegram from Wershof to Keenleyside, 20 April 1943.

52 NAC, RG 2/18, vol. 21, file A-15-4 (1942–1943), Maj.-Gen. Guy Henry to J. E. Hickerson 10 February 1943; and Heeney to Keenleyside, 26 February 1943. See also King Papers, vol. 350, file 3788, Robertson to King, 14 February 1943; Keenleyside to Clark, 22 June 1943; and Cabinet War Committee minutes, RG 2/7, vol. 12, 18 February 1943; and 24 February 1943; 3, 11 and 25 March 1943; 2, 18 and 23 June 1943.

53 *DCER* 9/975, Robertson to King, 27 May 1943.

54 *DCER* 9, documents 988-91 cover the issue of post war use of the Alaska Highway, documents 1039-47, the clarification of control of the airfields.

55 *DCER*, 9/410-11 Howe to Labine, 26 May 1943, and Labine to Howe, 28 May 1943; also Eayrs, *Peacemaking and Deterrence*, 263–65.

56 Pickersgill, *Mackenzie King Record*, 1: 503.

57 *FRUS: Washington and Quebec Conferences, 1943*, 630–753; and Kimball, *Churchill and Roosevelt*, 2: 214.

58 MacDonald papers, 12/6, MacDonald to Attlee, 6 August 1943; and Gowing, *Britain and Atomic Energy*, 197–99.

59 *DCER*, 9/415-16, Churchill to King, 11 and 19 August 1943; *FRUS: Washington and Quebec Conferences 1943*, 1117–19; and PRO, Dominions Office Records (hereafter DO), DO 127/61/100379, copy of draft articles of the Quebec Agreement signed 19 August 1943. Howe was reported to have claimed that the committee meetings were "so secret that I have never been able to attend a formal meeting." Eayrs, *Peacemaking and Deterrence*, 266.

60 Ibid., 266–79; see also Holmes, *Shaping of Peace*, 1: 198–202; Robert Bothwell, "Radium and Uranium: Evolution of a Company and a Policy" *Canadian Historical Review* 64 (June 1983): 143–45; PRO, DO 127/61/100879, draft copy of "Declaration of Trust," signed 13 June 1944.

61 As examples, see Stacey, *Age of Conflict* 2: 362; Donald Creighton, *The Forked Road* (Toronto: McClelland and Stewart 1976), 74; and Granatstein, *Canada's War*, 322.

62 *DCER* 9/1261, King to Foster, 20 May 1943.

63 Heeney's memoirs make little reference to any interest in the north despite his Privy Council files of accumulated data. The reason for this omission was clarified somewhat by C. P. Stacey's review of his book. Stacey claims that Heeney meant to revise the whole work after further research ("It is sad that the account of the war years in this book is so thin and inadequate. Obviously Heeney was writing from memory, his memories were growing dim, and he never had a chance to check his draft against those invaluable minutes [CWC]," review of *The Things That Are Caesar's*, *Canadian Historical Review* 55 [March 1974]: 92–94).

64 NAC, Special Commissioner's Records, RG 36/7, vol. 47, file "NPPP," personal memo, Heeney to Foster, 2 August 1943.

65 Ibid., "Memorandum for Brigadier Foster on Research Re: Resources of Northwest Canada."

66 Ibid., vol. 4, "Cabinet War Committee Incoming Mail," copies of correspondence, 10 July 1943.

67 NAC, RG 2/18, vol. 50, file D-19-D-R. See Heeney correspondence files in RG 2/18, vols. 20 and 22; and the many correspondence files in the Special Commissioner's Record files, RG 36/7.

68 *DCER* 9/1263, Keenleyside to Clark, 4 June 1943.

69 NA, RG 59, PJBD Series, vol. 10, April–June Correspondence, 1943, memo, dated Ottawa, 27 May 1943.

70 NAC, Records of the Special Commissioner, RG 36/7, vol. 4, "First Report of the Special Commissioner."

71 NAC, Privy Council Records, RG 2/18, vol. 50, file D-19-D-5-R, "Recommendations from Special Commissioner's Office," 1 March 1945.

72 NAC, Records of the Special Commissioner, RG 36/7, vol. 4, "Second Report of the Special Commissioner," recommendation no. 15, 28 July 1943. See also vol. 1, "Fire Hazards," report by Dr. Urquhart, 23 July 1943 from observations of W. J. Taylor and others.

73 Ibid., vol. 4, "Fifth Report of the Special Commissioner," recommendation no. 19. See also Department of Mines and Resources *Annual Report 1946*, 80, 93.

74 Heeney, *Things That Are Caesar's*, 72.

75 Keenleyside, *Memoirs*, 2:160. The connection is of greater significance in light of the fact that in later years, Foster was Keenleyside's predecessor, once removed, as chairman of the British Columbia Power Commission.

76 NAC, King Papers, MG 26 J 4, vol. 350, file 3788, "Speech at the Canadian Club," by Maj. Gen. W. W. Foster, Ottawa, 18 January 1945 with "Introduction" by Keenleyside.

77 Ibid., vol. 309, file 3282, Keenleyside to Robertson, 24 May 1943.

78 George Drew, "Where We Fit in the Global Air Map," *Financial Post*, 3 April 1943.

79 "Will Develop Area on Alcan Highway," *Montreal Gazette*, 15 April 1943.

80 Granatstein, *Canada's War*, 322.

81 NAC, RG 36/7, vol. 13, file 2-4, D. Dunton to Norman Robertson, 29 May 1943.

82 NAC, RG 2/18, vol. 50, file W-34-1-5, "WIB Survey No. 13," 2.

83 NAC, RG 36/7, vol. 13, file 2-4, D. Dunton to N. A. Robertson, 29 May 1943. See also Lloyd Papers, vol. 37, file 798. The lengthy report on the development of the Russian Arctic was also found in the King Papers, MG 26 J4, vol. 233, file 2274.

84 NAC, Wartime Information Board Records, RG 36/31, vol. 6, file 2-1-3, "Origins."

85 Interview with T. Lloyd, 2 November 1980.

86 NAC, Lloyd Papers, vol. 9, file 223, memo from Lloyd to Grierson, 4 June 1943, and memo titled "Information Centre on Northern Canada."

87 NAC, RG 2/18, vol. 21, file A-25-2. Memo signed by T. Lloyd, 8 June 1943.

88 Ibid., Brooke Claxton to Heeney, 18 June 1942. See also Parkin Papers, vol. 31, file "Trevor Lloyd," Lloyd to Parkin 10 June 1943, and Hanna to Lloyd, 12 June 1943.

89 NAC, Parkin papers, vol. 31, file "T. Lloyd." The remark was made by Tom Manning, who was on a special assignment with the Northwest Territories and Yukon Branch of Mines and Resources (Lloyd to Parkin with enclosure of Manning correspondence, 5 August 1943).

90 NAC, Lloyd Papers, vol. 9, file 223, J. D. Ketchum to Lloyd, 24 June 1943.

91 "Roaring Days in Edmonton," from article reported by the *Winnipeg Free Press*, in the *Edmonton Bulletin*, 23 June 1943.

92 "Alaska Highway, Opening up the Canadian North-West," *The Times*, 5 July 1943.

93 *Maclean's*, 1 July 1943. See articles by Trevor Lloyd, Grant Dexter, and Leslie Roberts.

94 MacDonald, *Down North*, 177, 233, 240.

95 Ibid., viii.

96 MacDonald papers, vol. 14, file 14, 8 January 1943, 23–27.

97 NAC, RG 36/7, vol. 13, file 2-4, External Affairs teletype, Washington embassy, 21 June 1943; also Dunton to Foster, 24 September 1943. Other articles also appeared, such as one on 19 June 1943 in the *New York Times* under the headline "U.S. Army Tapping Canada's Oil."

98 NAC, RG 2/18, vol. 50, file W-34-2-5, WIB Survey No. 14, 3 July 1943.

99 Ibid., vol. 21, file A-25-3, Keenleyside to F. Doyle, acting secretary for the Northwest Territories Council, 19 July 1943. See also the NWT Minutes, 23 June 1943, 3112–13.

100 NAC, DIAND Records, RG 22, vol. 278, file 99-2-81, Gibson to McKeand, 25 June 1943; Gibson to Camsell, 28 June 1943.

101 NAC, Parkin Papers, vol. 31, file "Lloyd," Lloyd to Parkin, 5 August 1943, with enclosures from Manning correspondence.

102 NAC, RG 36/7, vol. 7, "Second Report of the Special Commissioner," 638; and

Eayrs, *Peacemaking and Deterrence*, 349.

103 NAC, RG 2/18, vol. 43, file D-19-2, Keenleyside to Mackenzie King, 29 July 1943.

104 *DCER* 9/1064, Robertson to Lewis Clark, 7 September 1943, regarding ownership of property by the U.S. government; and document no. 1069, Heeney to W. C. Clarke, 24 November 1943, regarding "Reimbursement to the United States for Defence Construction in Canada."

105 "Editorial," *Maclean's*, 15 November 1943.

106 NAC, RG 36/7, vol. 47, file "NPPP," copies of "Outline of the North Pacific Planning Project" and the "Preliminary Report."

107 YTA, YRG 1, vol. 61, file 3540, Jeckell to Gibson, 2 August 1943.

108 NAC, RG 2/18, vol. 21, file A-25-3 (pt. 1), Escott Reid to Norman Robertson, 30 July 1943.

109 Ibid., Reid to Heeney, 24 February 1944: see also "The Company of the North," 7 February 1944.

110 Richard Diubaldo, "Canada Reasserts Herself," 8. Diubaldo cites DEA 463-B-40, Foster to Heeney, 30 August 1943.

111 NAC, RG 36/7, vol. 4, file "War Cabinet," memo from Heeney to Cabinet, 6 October 1943.

112 Ibid., vol. 13, file 2-4, copy of letter, Foster to Heeney, 8 October 1943.

113 *DCER* 9/1072 and 9/1073. Department of Finance memorandum, 1 December 1943 and 9/1075, Keenleyside to Robertson, 11 December 1943. See also "Roosevelt Maps Aviation Policy," *Journal of Commerce*, 2 October 1943.

114 As quoted in Diubaldo, "The Canol Project," 183.

NOTES TO CHAPTER SIX

Epigraph: NAC, Parkin Papers, vol. 41, file "CIIA," Parkin to Adamson, 24 July 1944.

1 Correspondence, Trevor Lloyd to S. Grant, 14 July 1982.

2 NAC, RG 36/7, vol. 4, file "War Cabinet—incoming mail," Heeney to Foster, 1 July 1943.

3 *DCER* 9/1015, minutes of meeting in preparation for discussions with U.S. officials, 30 November 1943; 91016, memo, Hanna to Keenleyside, 1 December 1943.

4 NAC, RG 2/18, vol. 70, file D-17-2, "Minutes of Meeting to Discuss the Canol Development," 2 December 1943.

5 NAC, RG 2/7, vol. 12, 3 December 1943.

6 NAC, King Papers, MG 26 J 4, vol. 350, file 3788, Keenleyside to Robertson, 11 December 1943.

7 United States, Senate, *Additional Report of the Special Committee Investigating the National Defense Program: The Canol Project* (Washington: Government Printing Office 1944), 7.

8 Pickersgill, *Mackenzie King Record*, 1: 644.

9 Massey, *What Is Past*, 396.

10 NAC, RG 2/18, vol. 70, file D-17-2 (1944), King to Atherton, 25 February 1944.

11 Pickersgill, *Mackenzie King Record*, 1: 645.

12 NAC, King Papers, MG 26 J 4, vol. 309, file 3282, "Exchange of Notes," and related memos, C21378-87.

13 Ibid., vol. 350, file 3788. File includes correspondence, lists of estimated costs, minutes of meetings, and copies of "Exchange of Notes," 27 June 1944 and 31 March 1946. Lists of airfields and weather stations constructed by or on behalf of the

United States are found in two memos, "United States Defence Projects and Installations in Canada," 12 January 1944, and 6 May 1943 (NAC, RG 36/7, vol. 14, file 28-6).

14 Diubaldo, "Canada Reasserts," 20–24.

15 Diubaldo, "The Alaska Highway in Canadian-United States Relations," in *The Alaska Highway,* ed. Coates, 112–13.

16 Diubaldo, "Canada Reasserts," 14.

17 Holmes, *Shaping of Peace,* 1: 62.

18 For example, see NAC, Reid Papers, vols. 9–10, "Some Problems in Relations between Canada and the United States," 16 April 1943.

19 *DCER* 9/642. In a letter to Vincent Massey as Canadian high commissioner to Britain, Hume Wrong enclosed two studies on aviation issues in the far north, 4 October 1943.

20 NA, Wartime Commissions Series, RG 43, vol. 7, file 406, "United States–Canadian–Airway Cooperation," 15 June 1943, secret document prepared by the Research and Analysis Division of the Economic Bureau, 8.

21 "Roosevelt Maps Aviation Policy," *Journal of Commerce* (New York), 2 October 1943.

22 MacDonald papers, 14/4, MacDonald to Lord Cranborne, 29 August 1944.

23 Ibid., "Origins and Development of the Northeast Staging Route."

24 Kimball, *Churchill and Roosevelt,* 2: 226.

25 NAC, RG 2/18, vol. 21, file A-15-1-6, "Outline for the Montreal Conversations," 3 May 1944.

26 NAC, Reid Papers, "The United States and the Peacemaking," 16 June 1944.

27 Holmes, *Shaping of Peace,* 1: 64–71.

28 NAC, Parkin Papers, vol. 37, file "AINA—General Correspondence 1936–1967." In particular, see copies of letters to J. Willets, 24 June 1943 and to W. S. Rogers, 2 July 1943, in which Parkin notes the various people he had contacted.

29 Ibid., Parkin to Willets, 24 June 1943.

30 Ibid., vol. 37, "AINA." Quotes and reference to his letter to MacDonald appear in Parkin's letter to Lloyd, 10 July 1943.

31 Raleigh Parkin, "The Origin of the Institute," *Arctic* 20 (March 1966): 13–15. In an interview, J. Lewis Robinson talked of an invitation he had received in the spring of 1944 to attend an informal discussion in an Ottawa hotel room. Among those present were Claxton, Heeney, and Keenleyside. The topic of conversation was the future of the Canadian north.

32 Parkin, "Origin," 9.

33 NAC, Arctic Institute of North America Records (hereafter AINA Records) MG 28 I79, vol. 1, file "Organization," informal notes on "Meeting 31 March 1944."

34 Ibid. See also Parkin, "Origin," 13–14.

35 Parkin, "Origin," 11. See also NAC, Lloyd Papers, vol. 37, file 782, "The Arctic Institute of North America as a Regional Research Institute," draft of speech given by Lloyd at the University of Saskatchewan, 1 May 1969.

36 NAC, AINA Records, vol. 1, file "Organization," minutes of meeting, 31 March 1944.

37 NAC, Lloyd Papers, vol. 17, file 381-88, "Draft of GRP Article." See also Parkin, "Origin," 11.

38 Grant, "Search for a Northern Policy, 1940–1950," Appendix 1: H.

39 Parkin, "Origin," 13–16.

40 Interview with Hugh Keenleyside, 29 May 1980.

41 NAC, Parkin Papers, vol. 2, file "Organizations," notes to wife, January 1971.
42 Ibid., vol. 37, file "AINA," Parkin to Rogers, April 1944.
43 Ibid., copy of a letter from Anne Bezanson of the Rockefeller Foundation to Dr. R. H. Coats of the Canadian Social Science and Research Council was forwarded to Parkin by a third party "for your interest," dated 20 July 1943.
44 Harold A. Innis, "Arctic Survey—Foreword," *Canadian Journal of Economic and Political Science* 11 (Winter 1944–45): 48.
45 NAC, Parkin Papers, vol. 37, file "Arctic," memo from J. Lewis Robinson, 20 March 1944.
46 Ibid., copy of letter from D. Jenness to H. A. Innis, 21 March 1944.
47 Innis, "Foreword," 48.
48 G. J. Wherrett, "Survey of Health Conditions," 59.
49 Andrew Moore, "Survey of Education in the Mackenzie District," 61–82.
50 NWT Council Minutes, 2 November 1944, 3170–72.
51 Compare the 1944 and 1946 *Annual Reports for the Department of Mines and Resources* (Ottawa: King's Printer 1945–47), 62–63 and 78 respectively.
52 C. C. Lingard, "Administration of the Canadian Northland," 45–72.
53 NAC, Parkin Papers, see, for example, vol. 21, file "Claxton," Parkin to Claxton, 26 March 1943; and vol. 31, file "Lloyd," Lloyd to Parkin, 26 October 1943. See also DIAND Records, RG 22, vol. 278, file 99-1-81, Keenleyside to Norman Robertson, 23 March 1944.
54 NAC, Parkin Papers, vol. 31, file "Lloyd," Lloyd to D. Maclennan, 17 August 1943. Gibson's quote cited by Lloyd. See also Gibson to Lloyd, 14 April 1944.
55 Correspondence, Lloyd to S. Grant, 11 January 1981.
56 Correspondence, J. Lewis Robinson to S. Grant, 10 November 1981.
57 NAC, Parkin Papers, vol. 41, file "CIIA," "Report on Progress of Research," June 1944.
58 Ibid., vol. 41, Parkin to R. T. Adamson, 24 July 1944.
59 Lloyd, "The Geography and Administration of Northern Canada," chapter 8: 19–22.
60 NAC, Parkin Papers, vol. 41, file "CIIA Study," Parkin to Adamson, 25 July 1944, 3.
61 Ibid., vol. 31, file "Lloyd," Lloyd to Parkin, 9 May 1943. This view was confirmed by Lewis Robinson, who was employed by the bureau from 1943 to 1945. With exceptions, Robinson claimed the Department of Mines and Resources was inundated with older civil servants who were more or less putting in time until their retirement (interview, 11 November 1982).
62 Ibid., vol. 41, file "CIIA Study." The knowledge he acquired when posted to Greenland is noted in letter from Lloyd to Lingard, 14 November 1945, Those people who received portions of the manuscripts in various stages of completion were referred to in a number of letters. For example, see Heeney to Parkin, 3 May 1946; and in vol. 23, file "Lloyd," Lloyd to Lingard, 27 December 1946, and 10 February 1947.
63 Lloyd, "Geography and Administration," chapter 1: 34.
64 Ibid., chapter 5: 26–27.
65 Ibid., chapter 12: 1–24.
66 NAC, Parkin Papers, vol. 41, file "CIIA Study," Lloyd to Parkin, 11 January 1946.
67 S. Grant, "Search for a Northern Policy," 72–79, 101–15, and appendix 12.
68 NA, Wartime Commissions, RG 43, vol. 1, file 400, "Minutes of the November 5–6, 1943, meetings of the Joint Economic Committees" and copy of progress re-

port, October 1943. Detailed back-up report for the water resources report is found in vol. 6, file "Water Resources." Other specific reports are found scattered throughout vols. 5 and 7.

69 Ibid., vol. 7, file 406, "United States–Canadian Postwar Civil Aviation Relationships in the North Pacific," February 1944.

70 Ibid., vol. 4, file "J. Rettie," Camsell to Rettie, 16 May 1944.

71 NAC, RG 36/7, vol. 14, file 22-3, "Press release" on expanded field studies for development of the northwest, issued 21 June 1944 by the Department of Mines and Resources.

72 Trevor Lloyd, "Mainstreet of the Air," *Maclean's*, 1 July 1943.

73 Charles Camsell, "The New North," *Canadian Geographical Journal* 33 (December 1946): 277. Also published in *The Beaver* (June 1944): 7.

74 Lewis Robinson stated that Camsell had a speech writer in the department who also wrote articles and some reports.

75 Lt. Col. Charles J. Hubbard, "The Arctic Isn't So Tough," *Saturday Evening Post*, 16 October 1944.

76 The Finnie films are available from the Prince of Wales Northern Heritage Centre at Yellowknife; Lorne Greene's "Look to the North" is still available from the National Film Board.

77 NAC, RG 2/18, vol. 50, file W-34-2-5, radio press releases. The policy to promote Canadian participation was approved by the Cabinet War Committee in an attempt to offset any adverse publicity arising from the Truman Commission (*DCER* 9/1068, excerpts from the minutes of the Cabinet War Committee, 17 November 1943).

78 L. B. Pearson, "Canada Looks 'Down North,'" *Foreign Affairs* 24 (Winter 1945–46): 638–47.

79 NAC, RG 36/7, vol. 5, file "11th Report," 30 April 1944.

80 NAC, RG 2/18, vol. 21, file A-25-3 (pt. 1), memo from Keenleyside, 23 December 1943.

81 Ibid., W. E. D. Halliday to Heeney, 10 March 1944.

82 NAC, RG 36/7, vol. 4, file "War Cabinet Recommendations," Foster to Camsell, 27 April 1944.

83 NAC, RG 2/18, vol. 21, file A-25-3 (pt. 1), Camsell to Heeney, 5 May 1944; Heeney to Camsell, 20 May 1944; and Keenleyside to Heeney, 18 May 1944.

84 Ibid., Keenleyside to Heeney, 24 May 1944.

85 NAC, RG 36/7, vol. 4, file "War Cabinet Recommendations (outside)," Heeney to Foster, 26 May 1944; Foster to Heeney, 23 May 1944.

86 NAC, RG 2/18, vol. 21, file A-25-3, see correspondence from November 1944 through to February 1945. See also file A-35-3 (pt. 1), C. J. Powers to Heeney, 16 May 1944; and file A-25-1 (pt. 1), Halliday to Heeney, 10 March 1944.

87 NAC, RG 22, vol. 270, file 40-10-1 (pt. 1), personal memorandum from Keenleyside to Gibson, 7 July 1944.

88 NAC, RG 36/7, vol. 15, file 28-12, minutes of meeting of a Special Committee of the Joint Defence Construction Projects, 12 September 1944.

89 Ibid., Jeckell to Gibson, 17 October 1944; and W/C Stewart to Foster, 16 December 1944.

90 Ibid., Camsell to P. A. Cumyn, 19 September 1944; Foster to Heeney, 24 October 1944; Jeckell to Gibson, 17 October 1944; and minutes of meeting, 15 November 1944.

91 NAC, RG 2/18, vol. 50, file D-19-D-5-R, Foster to Heeney, 31 July 1944.

92 Ibid., vol. 22, file A-25-3 (pt. 2), Foster to Heeney, 26 August 1944; and Foster to

Heeney, 12 December 1944.

93 "Ottawa Officialdom Again," *Alaska Highway News*, 13 July 1944: residents protested against lack of health care and the absence of settlement planning. See also NAC, Special Commissioner's Records, RG 36/7, vol. 6, "25th Report," 641.

94 NAC, RG 2/18, vol. 22, file A-25-39 (pt. 2), memo from Keenleyside to the Northwest Territories Council, 19 January 1944, and Keenleyside to Heeney, 19 January 1944.

95 NWT Council Minutes, vol. 13, 25 April 1944, 3185. In the minutes of subsequent meetings there were no reports of any external studies being conducted other than the Arctic Survey by the Canadian Social Science and Research Council.

96 NAC, King Papers, MG 26 J 4, vol. 350, file 3788, Heeney to King, 7 April 1945.

97 NAC, RG 36/7, vol. 6, file "22nd Report," 224.

98 NAC, RG 2/18, vol. 72, file D-19-D-5-1, Gibson to the secretary of the chiefs of staff, 1945. See also RG 36/7, vol. 7, file "32nd Report," 638.

99 Keenleyside, *Memoirs*, 2: 217–19.

100 Ibid., 219–20.

101 Holmes, *Shaping of Peace*, 1: 72.

NOTES TO CHAPTER SEVEN

Epigraph: Trevor Lloyd, *Frontier of Destiny, 1*.

1 Holmes, *The Better Part of Valour*, 35.

2 F. H. Soward, *Canada in World Affairs, 1944–1946*, 50.

3 John Holmes, *Life with Uncle: The Canadian-American Relationship* (Toronto: University of Toronto Press 1981), 18.

4 Igor Gouzenko defected 5 September 1945. King diary entry, 11 September 1945, as cited in Eayrs, *Peacemaking and Deterence*, 320.

5 Holmes, *Shaping of Peace*, 1:197, citing C. A. Ritchie, 8 September 1945, "Control of the Atomic Bomb by the United Nations Organization.

6 Ibid., 288; New York speech reported in *Globe and Mail*, 8 February 1946.

7 NA, RG 59, PJBD series, vol. 10, file "Correspondence 1946," report published by AC/S Intelligence "Problems of Canadian–United States Cooperation in the Arctic," 29 October 1946, 10.

8 Holmes, *Shaping of Peace*, 1: 172. This sensitivity to "potential derogation to Canadian sovereignty" is also noted by R. Sutherland, "The Strategic Significance of the Canadian Arctic," in *The Arctic Frontier*, ed. MacDonald, 261; and David Judd, "Canada's Northern Policy: Retrospect and Prospect," *Polar Record* 14 (May 1969): 595.

9 Holmes, *The Better Part of Valour*, 13.

10 Holmes, *Shaping of Peace*, 1: 188.

11 MacDonald Papers, 12/6, report to Dominions Office, February 1944, 6–9.

12 PRO, CAB 120/843, file 100819, MacDonald to Viscount Addison, secretary of state for dominion affairs, 1 October 1945.

13 Trevor Lloyd, "Canada's Strategic North," *International Journal* 2 (Spring 1947): 149.

14 NAC, RG 2/18, vol. 50, file W-34-2-5, Wartime Information Board Survey, 4 December 1943.

15 NAC, Brooke Claxton Papers, MG 32-B-5, (hereafter Claxton Papers) vol. 224, "Memoir Notes." See also vol. 174, "Research on Health and Welfare," and vol.

164, "Research on Family Allowances." Most memos and reports were dated 1944. According to Arnold Heeney, King relied heavily on Claxton for the creation of his new welfare state (*Things That Are Caesar's*, 82). Born and raised in Montreal, Claxton was a veteran of World War I and a graduate of McGill Law School. A close friend of both Arnold Heeney and Raleigh Parkin, he actively participated in the Montreal Branch of the Canadian Institute of International Affairs, the "Montreal Group," and the Canadian League. He was also a close associate of many members of the League of Social Reconstruction and a strong advocate of constitutional reform. Claxton was first elected to Parliament in 1940 and within a year was appointed parliamentary secretary to Mackenzie King.

16 Robert Bothwell and William Kilbourn, *C.D. Howe: A Biography* (Toronto: McClelland and Stewart, 1979), 199–200.
17 NAC, Parkin Papers, vol. 24, file "Manning," Parkin to Manning, 15 May 1941.
18 Heeney, *Things That Are Caesar's*, 32.
19 "Revision Is Urged for Indian Affairs," *Montreal Gazette*, 10 September 1944.
20 Copeland, *Livingstone*, 168.
21 NAC, King Papers, MG 26 J 4, vol. 281, file 2927, "Memorial on Indian Affairs." Also see p. C192262ff, memo from Pickersgill to King (n.d.).
22 NAC, Claxton Papers, vol. 184, "Speeches," delivered 29 October 1945.
23 Special Joint Committee to Investigate the Indian Act, 1946, *Minutes*, 76.
24 Ibid., 281–82 and 291.
25 YTA, YRG 1, Series 2, vol. 44, file 35563. See correspondence and directives, 1945. Although the programme was established in May 1945, the new regulations under the Department of Health and Welfare did not change this policy. Also see PWNHC, Northwest Territories Council minutes, vol. 14, 12 March 1946, 3264.
26 H. L. Keenleyside, "Recent Development in the Canadian Northwest," *Canadian Geographical Journal* 36 (October 1949): 175.
27 NWT Council Minutes, vol. 14, March 1946, 3266, correspondence Gibson to Dr. Brock Chisholm.
28 NAC, RG 2/18, vol. 22, file A-25-3 (pt. 2), "Memorandum on Air Ports," 15 June 1945.
29 Special Joint Committee to Investigate the Indian Act, 1946, *Minutes*, 275.
30 NAC, RG 22, vol. 125, file 99-2-1-122, speech delivered at Winnipeg, 23 April 1946.
31 Department of Mines and Resources, *Annual Report*(s) for years ending March 1945, 1946, and 1947.
32 NAC, RG 22, vol. 125, file 99-2-1-122, speech delivered by the Hon. J. A. Glen at Winnipeg, 23 April 1946.
33 Charles Camsell (dir.), *Canada's New North-West: Report of the North Pacific Planning Project* (Ottawa: King's Printer 1947), 7.
34 Ibid., 6.
35 Ibid., 17.
36 Charles Camsell, *Son of the North* (Toronto: Ryerson Press 1954).
37 Copy of letter from the Labour Progressive party of Yellowknife to the prime minister, 17 October 1945, is located in the Northwest Territories Council minutes (vol. 14, 3246–47).
38 NAC, RG 2/18, vol. 57, file A-25-3 (pt. 1), Camsell to Mackenzie King, 5 January 1946.
39 Ibid., and also vol. 46, file D-17, Camsell to Heeney, 5 August 1945.

40 Ibid., "Memo to Cabinet," 1 March 1946.

41 Ibid., W. E. D. Halliday to Heeney, 6 March 1946; and L. H. Phinney to Heeney, 6 March 1946.

42 Ibid., "the Administration of the Northwest Territories," signed Meredith Glassco, Privy Council Office, 11 April 1946.

43 Ibid., memo from Heeney, 23 March 1946.

44 M. Dunbar, "Science in the North," radio broadcast, 9 June 1946.

45 J. Lewis Robinson, "Land Use Possibilities in the Mackenzie District, N.W.T.," *Canadian Geographical Journal* 31 (July 1945): 37.

46 NAC, RG 22, vol. 125, file 99-2-1-122, Wilson to Camsell, 9 May 1944.

47 Ibid., Gibson to Camsell, 17 May 1944.

48 Eayrs, *Peacemaking and Deterrence*, 320–22.

49 Colonel J. H. Jenkins as cited in Eayrs, *Peacemaking and Deterrence*, 322.

50 Ibid., 331.

51 NA, RG 59, file 842.20 Defense 5.445, Clayton to Atherton, 4 May 1945. See also McLellan, *Dean Acheson: The State Department Years*, 71. According to the author, Clayton was one of the more avid free traders who were known for their "good old American, 'get Britain' mentality."

52 NA, RG 59, file 842.20 Defense 5-934, memorandum of conversations, including quotation of Howe's verbal agreement, sent by Atherton to Clayton, 9 May 1945.

53 Holmes, *Shaping of Peace*, 176, 180.

54 R. D. Cuff and J. L. Granatstein, *American Dollars: Canadian Prosperity* (Toronto: Samuel Stevens 1978), 25–26.

55 PRO, FO 127/61/100379, S. Holmes of the Foreign Office to Makins, U.K. ambassador to Washington, 30 November 1945. There is full documentation in the file of all meetings, the various drafts, the printed final report of proceedings and correspondence related to both the "Declaration" and the memorandum. The role played by MacDonald as liaison between the Canadians and British is described in a letter from a member of the U.K. embassy in Washington, Cockram to Sedgwick of the Dominions Office, 20 November 1945. Description of the meetings which involved drafting the memorandum to the Combined Policy Committee were attached to correspondence from Makin to Rickett, 17 and 19 November 1945.

56 PRO, CAB 120/843/100879, MacDonald to Viscount Addison, 1 October 1945, including attached "note" of conversations.

57 Ibid., "Imperial Co-operation in Defence," document C.O.S (45) 625 (O), 4.

58 *DCER* 12/750, "Minutes of a meeting on Commonwealth Defence," 7 June 1946.

59 NA, State Department Records, RG 59, vol. 842.20 Defense/10-2645, J. Graham Parsons to Colonel Francis Graling, military attaché at the American embassy in Ottawa, 30 October, 1945.

60 Ibid., 842.20 Defense/11-345, Graling to Parsons, 3 November 1945.

61 PRO, CAB 120/843/100879, MacDonald to secretary of state for the dominions, 2 October 1945.

62 Heeney, *Things That Are Caesar's*, 117.

63 Holmes, *Shaping of Peace*, 1: 208–9.

64 S. W. Dzuiban, *Military Relations between the United States and Canada, 1939–1945*, United States Department of the Army, Office of Military History Series (Washington: United States Government Publications 1960), 34.

65 John Swettenham, *McNaughton, Volume III, 1945–1946* (Toronto: Ryerson Press, 1960), 34. Although his biographer gives McNaughton the credit for resistance to American pressure, A/M Leckie claimed that McNaughton when temporarily a

pointed minister of national defence had recommended that Canadian troops acquire American equipment at a cost of $700 million and become "virtually units of the U.S. contingent" in the second stage of the war. It was only on the vehement opposition of Leckie and Ilsley that the motion was defeated by the Cabinet War Committee (PRO, CAB 120/843/100879, MacDonald to Viscount Addison, Dominions Office, 1 October 1945). Presumably, McNaughton's later position was at the direction of the Defence Committee.

66 A. M. Schlesinger, Jr., *A Thousand Days: John F. Kennedy in the White House* (Boston: Houghton Mifflin 1965), 165; also see NA, RG 59, 842.20 Defense/6-2745. See correspondence and attached memos by Maj. Gen. Guy Henry, 8 June 1945, which suggests the advantage of "Canada being incorporated into the military family of American nations."

67 Kendrick Lee, "Arctic Defenses," *Editorial Research Reports*, Washington, vol. 2, no. 5 (1946): 503. Also see NAC, RG 2/18, vol. 22, file A-25-3, memos from Heeney to Crerar and McNaughton, 19 January 1945.

68 Lee, "Arctic Defenses," 513.

69 Trevor Lloyd maintains this code word applied only to the weather station plans, but author's discussion 19 June 1982 with Dr. S. Harris, historian for the Department of National Defence, and Dr. John Greenwood, historian for the United States Army Corps of Engineers, seemed to confirm that the code name applied to the army's "extended plans" for the weather stations that involved aerial photography. In the view of these historians, "Arctops" was short for "Arctic Topography."

70 NA, Charles Hubbard Papers, RG 410/17, vol. 5, files 1 through 11; NAC, RG 2/18, vol. 74, file D-19-2, Maj. Gen. Henry to the Permanent Joint Board on Defence, 9 September 1946.

71 Ibid., Cabinet Document no. 125, "Post War Defence Collaboration with the United States," 13 December 1945.

72 Ibid., memo from Heeney to Norman Robertson, 1 February 1946.

73 Ibid., "List of Recent United States and Permanent Joint Board on Defence Proposals for Joint Defence Projects and Cooperation Measures," 30 June 1946.

74 *DCER* 12/909, memo from R. Macdonnell to Legal Division, 6 May 1946.

75 As cited in J. W. Pickersgill and D. F. Foster, *The Mackenzie King Record,* vol. 3 (Toronto: University of Toronto Press 1970), 219.

76 NAC, RG 2/18, vol. 56, file A-15-2, Colin Gibson to Mackenzie King, 7 May 1946.

77 NA, RG 59, PJBD series, vol. 2, files "Postwar Defense," "Military Cooperation Committee," and "Basic Security Plan." There is no indication whether the confidential Canadian documents came from the MCC or were submitted by Canadians, with or without consent.

78 *DCER* 12/956, "Appreciation" and "Basic Security Plan" from meetings 20–23 May 1946.

79 Eayrs, *Peacemaking and Deterrence*, 329.

80 NA, RG 59, PJBD series, vol. 10, file "Correspondence—1946," AC/S intelligence report, "Problems of Canadian-United States Cooperation in the Arctic," 29 October 1946, 8–10.

81 "Canada Another Belgium in U.S. Air Bases Proposal," *Financial Post*, 29 June 1946. See NAC, Privy Council Records, RG 2/18, vol. 46, file A-25-1, Barclay to Heeney, 29 June 1946; and *DCER* 12/924, Norman Robertson memo, 28 June 1946.

82 NAC, RG 2/18, vol. 74, file D-19-2, memo from secretary of the Privy Council Office, G. W. T. Gill to Heeney, 4 June 1946. Gill suggests refusal to consider plan until next year would relieve growing pressure of United States demands.

83 *DCER* 12/925, "USAAF Weather Stations in Eastern Canada," 3 August 1946; 12/926, confidential memo from Macdonnell to Heeney, 31 August 1946; 12/927, E. W. T. Gill to Cabinet Defence Committee, 9 September 1946.

84 Ibid., 12/968, chiefs of staff to Cabinet Defence Committee, 9 September 1946. For full correspondence between Henry and the American secretary of the PJBD, see NA, State Department Records, RG 59, PJBD series, vol. 2, file "Fort Churchill—1," correspondence, 22 August—November 1946.

85 *DCER* 12/914, memorandum by Wrong to Cabinet Defence Committee, 30 May 1946.

86 Ibid., 12/913, memorandum from Department of National Defence to Cabinet Defence Committee, "Sovereignty in the Canadian Arctic in Relation to Joint Defence Undertakings" (n.d., circa May 1946).

87 NAC, King Papers, MG 26 J 4, vol. 309, file 2274, Robertson to Camsell, 1 April 1946.

88 *DCER* 12/916, Pearson to Wrong, 5 June 1946.

89 NA, RG 59, series PJBD, vol. 10, file "Correspondence—1946," Top secret memo, "United States–Canadian Relations," signed by Maj. Gen. Guy V. Henry, U.S. Army, 28 August 1946. See also related correspondence.

90 Ibid., vol. 2, file "Basic Papers," memoranda, Dean Acheson to President Truman, 1 and 26 October 1946, and attached "Oral message."

91 *DCER* 12/975, Wrong to King, with attached memo, 26 October 1946.

92 NAC, RG 2/18, vol. 74, file D-19-2 contains copy of the "Oral Message," handed to King on 28 October 1946; for the off-the-record comment, see PRO, CAB 122/629, memo by Group Captain Braithwaite, "United States Air Bases in Canada," 1 November 1946. Included were details of the conversation between Truman and King as related to him by St. Laurent.

93 PRO, CAB 122/629, report of conversation between Bevin and St. Laurent, 12 November 1946.

94 *DCER* 12/757, King to Attlee regarding changes in proposed white paper, 3 October 1946; 12/764, telegram, Attlee to King, 9 November 1946; documents 750-70 reflect the annoyance of the prime minister and members of External Affairs over the assumption that Canada would be willing to participate in a new "imperial defence scheme."

95 PRO, CAB 122/624/100867, copy of report by Clutterbuck (British high commissioner) to Dominions Office, 15 November 1946.

96 Ibid., CAB 120/629, telegram from Bevin to Attlee and Attlee to Bevin, 9 and 11 November 1946, respectively.

97 Ibid., telegram from Attlee to Bevin in New York, 12 November 1946. Attlee claimed that the proposed air bases would provide little protection to the Dominion, but only serve to force Canada and hence Britain "to follow the United States lead in any further crisis with the Soviet Union."

98 Ibid., telegram, Bevin to Attlee, 13 November 1946, in which the foreign secretary describes the conversation with St. Laurent.

99 *DCER*, 12/983, memo from Norman Robertson to Mackenzie King, 12 November 1945.

100 *DCER*, 12/984, minutes of Cabinet Defence Committee meeting, 13 November 1946.

101 *DCER* 12/989, Cabinet Conclusions, 15 November 1946. See also report by A/VM Curtis to State Department's Graham Parsons, NA, RG 59, PJBD series, vol. 2, file "Basic Papers," memorandum of conversation, 21 November 1946.

102 NA, RG 59, PJBD series, vol. 2, file, "Joint Defense Discussions," 21 November 1946, 3.

103 Ibid., 2

104 J. T. Jockel, "The Canada-United States Military Cooperation Committee and Continental Air Defence, 1946," *Canadian Historical Review*, 64 (September, 1983): 365–68. Jockel also sees a disparity, similar to that of the PJBD, in the reporting structure of the MCC, with the Canadian secretary reporting directly to Heeney, secretary to the Cabinet, 369.

105 NA, RG 59, PJBD series, vol. 2. The PJBD files of the State Department contain frequent correspondence between Atherton and the American secretary, indicating that the United States ambassador was fully apprised of the strategy in attempts to influence Ottawa in favour of continental defence, as well as details of the proposed plan. See various memos of conversation and correspondence in the "Basic Papers" files and others. Atherton was directly involved in various attempts to promote continentalism, both military and economic. Although his continentalist sympathies were also helpful in facilitating more friendly Canadian-American relations, in some quarters he was perceived as a threat to Canadian hopes for independence (Holmes, *Shaping of Peace*, 2: 90, 95.

106 NA, RG 59, PJBD series, vol. 2, file "Basic Papers," two memos from Maj. Gen. Guy Henry to Maj. Gen. Lauris Norstad, both dated 25 November 1946.

107 Ibid., "Joint Defense Discussions," 21 November 1946, 3.

108 Ibid., top secret memo by Maj. Gen. Guy Henry, 28 August 1946. Henry recognized the drastic changes involved in moving from a loosely aligned commonwealth military commitment to an integrated involvement in North American defence. In his report on "United States–Canadian Relations," he outlined the concerns and probable resistance, and added six recommendations on the appropriate themes to emphasize when talking with "important Canadian officials." Included was the directive to state "that the United States wishes in every way to respect Canadian sovereignty."

109 Ibid., "Memorandum of Conversation" between Curtis and Parsons, 21 November 1946.

110 Ibid., "Joint Defense Discussions," 21 November 1946.

111 Ibid., see memo of conversation, 21 November 1946; minutes of meetings, 21 November and 16–17 December 1946; also "Working Papers for use in Discussion with the United States,," n.d.

112 Ibid., memorandum of Canadian–United States Defense Conversations, 16–17 December 1946.

113 NAC, RG 2/18, vol. 74, file D-19-2, telegram from Magann to Menzies, Washington, 17 October 1947, "Directive concerning publicity relating to joint Canadian–United States defence plans and operations in the Far North."

114 Ibid., vol. 46, file A-25, F. T. Davies, "The Sector Principle in Polar Claims," 11 February 1947.

115 NA, RG 59, PJBD series, vol. 10, file "Correspondence 1946," intelligence report of the Army Air Force headquarters, 29 October 1946, 9–10.

116 NAC, RG 2/18, vol. 57, file A-25-5, "Summary of U.S. Military Activities in Canada," 28 January 1948.

117 NA, RG 59, PJBD series, vol. 6, file, "Press Clippings," *New York Tribune*, 6 March 1947, annotated notes by Graham Parsons, American secretary of the PJBD.

118 Jockel, "Continental Air Defence," 372–74.

119 Canada, House of Commons, *Debates*, 12 February 1947, 343–48.

120 PRO, CAB 122/624/100867, telegrams from Foreign Office to Lord Inverchapel, 20 February and 7 March 1947, respectively.
121 James Reston, *New York Times*, 13 February 1947, 17.
122 Canada, House of Commons *Debates*, 1947, vol. 1, 12 February 1947, 347–48.
123 Ibid., vol. 4, 4–5 June 1947, 3796–3858.

NOTES TO CHAPTER EIGHT

Epigraph: H. L. Keenleyside, "Recent Developments in the Canadian North," speech delivered at McMaster University, 14 May 1949, 2.

1 Interview with Hugh Keenleyside, 29 May 1980. In his autobiography, he notes his own request to Jack Pickersgill that he would *"really"* like the post, but he also quotes a letter from Lester Pearson that stated "the Prime Minister is so anxious you take this responsibility on" (*Memoirs*, 2: 280–81). In a later interview, 29 February 1988, Keenleyside admitted to knowledge of Pearson's and Heeney's strategy of "civilianizing" various military activities, that he understood the reasoning and supported them fully.
2 Canada, House of Commons, *Debates*, 1946, 6 June 1946, 2264–66.
3 Ibid., 1947, 13 February 1947, 372.
4 Ibid. The issue was brought forward on 21 February 1947; discussed further on 16 March; 25 and 30 April; on the 1, 6, 7, and 12 of May; and 26 June 1947, 3393–4685.
5 Ibid., 15 July 1947, 5657ff.
6 NAC, RG 2/18, vol. 57, file A-25-3 (pt. 1), Heeney to Pearson, 15 February 1947; Heeney to St. Laurent, 18 February 1947.
7 NAC, RG 22, vol. 270, file 40-10-1 (pt. 2), Heeney to Glen, 21 February 1947. See also NWT Council Minutes, vol. 15, 16 April 1947, 3326.
8 NWT Council Minutes, vol. 14, 15 April 1947, 3326ff. One notable exception to the "serious" discussion was the protest by new military members on council over the restrictive liquor regulations affecting the legions in the Northwest Territories.
9 Department of Mines and Resources, *Annual Report* ending March 1947, 76, and ending March 1948, 162.
10 Interview with H. Keenleyside, 29 May 1980.
11 Keenleyside, *Memoirs*, 2: 270.
12 Keenleyside, McMaster speech, 6. The last sentence did not appear in the nearly identical article, "Recent Developments in the Canadian North," *Canadian Geographical Journal* 39 (October 1949): 156–76.
13 NAC, RG 22, vol. 270, file 40-10-1 (pt. 1). As an example, see correspondence of Dr. Harvey to Keenleyside, 5 October 1947.
14 NAC, RG 2/18, vol. 70, file D-17, Keenleyside to Glen, 29 September 1947; Keenleyside to Heeney, 6 October 1947; and Keenleyside to King, 29 September 1947.
15 Department of Mines and Resources, *Annual Report* ending March 1948, 7, 150.
16 Ibid., 162. Also NWT Council Minutes, vol. 17, 9 December 1948, 3605.
17 Ibid., vol. 15, 22 October 1947, 3404.
18 NAC, RG 22, vol. 270, file 40–10-1 (pt. 1), "Political Democracy in the Northwest Territories," 16 March 1950. This report was produced with the assistance of the department's legal adviser.
19 NAC, RG 2/18, vol. 57, file A-25-3 (pt. 1), Cabinet document no. 475, 17 June 1947.

20 YTA, YRG I, Series I, "Council History." Details of this period are sketchy owing to loss of documents in the transfer of the capital from Dawson to Whitehorse. See also Series 2, Votes and Proceedings, vol. 43 and 44, session 50, 22 October 1949, 2.

21 Ibid., 2d session, 5–22 October 1949, 2.

22 Ray Price, *Yellowknife* (Toronto: Peter Martin Associates 1967), 204–29.

23 Ibid., 208.

24 NWT Council Minutes, vol. 15. 8 October 1947, 3340ff.

25 Ibid.

26 NAC, RG 22, vol. 270, file 40-10-1 (pt. 1), Keenleyside to McMeekan, 8 December 1948.

27 Ibid., vol. 275, file 85-4-1, "Estimates of the Northwest Territories and Yukon Budget 1949–1950," including accumulative costs since 1946.

28 Ibid., vol. 270, file 40-10-1 (pt. 1), "Political Democracy," 2 and 4.

29 *Montreal Gazette*, 30 November 1944.

30 NWT Council Minutes, vol. 18, 3 November 1949, 3715; and vol. 19, 1950, copy of letter from Keenleyside to Dr. O. L. Stanton, 14 April 1950, 3791. Further correspondence is found in the NAC, Northern Affairs Records, RG 85, vol. 730, file 18-1; and RG 22, vol. 270, file 40-10-1 (pt. 1). Racial segregation was not limited to Yellowknife. Norman Wells, a totally white community, provided hospital services for the white residents of Fort Norman and Fort Franklin. Natives from this area were sent to Fort Simpson (see report on health service, Northwest Territories Council Minutes, session 190, April 1949). Perhaps it was only a coincidence, but the request from Norman Wells to set up a Local Administrative District was not granted.

31 NWT Council Minutes, vol. 18, 3 November 1949, 3713. Report by the committee set up to investigate the financial relationship of Yellowknife to the territorial government. The committee was composed of representatives from the Bank of Canada, Mines and Resources, and the Northwest Territories Council. See also NAC, RG 22, vol. 270, file 40-10-1 (pt. 1), "Political Democracy," 11.

32 Ibid., vol. 153, file 5-0-1-35 (pt. 5), press release no. 3196, 20 December 1949.

33 Ibid., vol. 270, file 40-10-1 (pt. 1), "Political Democracy," 11–12.

34 Keenleyside, McMaster speech, 7.

35 "A Bouquet for Keenleyside," *News of the North*, Yellowknife, 6 October 1950.

36 Interview with Keenleyside, 29 May 1980.

37 NWT Council Minutes, vol. 14. special session, 3338; 1 June 1947, 3353; and 18 June 1947, 3352; Also NAC, RG 22, vol. 153, file 5-0-1-35 (pt. 5).

38 NWT Council Minutes, vol. 16, closed session, 17 November 1947, 3408–9.

39 NAC, RG 22, vol. 153, file 5-0-1-35 (pt. 6), "Personnel Required for Northern Schools," April 1949.

40 Keenleyside, McMaster speech, 8.

41 NAC, RG 22, vol. 165, file 5-2-1-2- (pt. 1), report dated 9 December 1948, 26.

42 NWT Council Minutes, vol. 17, special session, 4 June 1948, 3545.

43 Department of Resources and Development, *Annual Report ending March 1950*, 80.

44 Ibid., 80–81, and *Annual Report* for year ending March 1951, 88.

45 Department of Resources and Development, *Annual Report* for the year ending March 1950, 80.

46 YTA, YRG 1, Series 1, "Council History."

47 NAC, Northern Affairs Records, RG 85, vol. 159, file 510-1-1 (pt. 1), Fraser Commission Report, July 1952.

48 NAC, Geographical Branch Records, RG 92, vol. 15, file 506-1-1 (pt. 2), report to

the Geographical Bureau by B. J. MacLeod, 15 (n.d., circa 1950).

49　NAC, RG 22, vol. 165, file 5-2-1-2 (pt. 1), "Recent Developments in Northern Canada," 9 December 1948.

50　YTA, Government Administration Series, vol. 1, file 1–37, *Annual Reports* for 1949–1950 and 1951–1952.

51　Lloyd, "Geography and Administration," chapter 5, "Native Peoples," 1, 30.

52　Department of Mines and Resources, *Annual Report* for years 1946 through 1949. In particular, see *Annual Report* 1948, pp. 152–53, and *Annual Report* 1949, 138–39.

53　Department of Resources and Development, *Annual Report* ending March 1950, 11.

54　Department of Mines and Resources, *Annual Report* for year ending 1944, 8. Total expenditure by the northern administration on the Yukon and Northwest Territories was $261,800.

55　NWT Council Minutes, vol. 17, May 1948; and vol. 19, 22 December 1949, 3750.

56　NAC, RG 22, vol. 153, file 5-0-1-35 (pt. 4), press release, 26 October 1948.

57　NWT Council Minutes, vol. 17, session 190, 21 April 1949.

58　NAC, RG 22, vol. 153, file 5-0-1-35 (pt. 4), press release, 26 October 1948.

59　*Arctic Circular* 3, no. 2 (February 1950): 17.

60　NAC, RG 22, vol. 165, file 5-2-1-2 (pt. 1), "Recent Developments in Northern Canada," 32.

61　NWT Council Minutes, vol. 17, session 187, report for fall of 1848; and *Arctic Circular* 1 (February 1948).

62　NWT Council Minutes, vol. 18, 22 September 1949; and vol. 19, 7 December 1949, 3742.

63　NAC, RG 22, vol. 153, file 5-0-1-35 (pt. 5), press release, "Northwest Game Ordinance."

64　*Arctic Circular* 2 (October 1949): 76–88.

65　NWT Council Minutes, vol. 17, 15 April 1948, 3510–11.

66　Ibid., 28 March 1948, 3487; and 15 April 1948, 3519.

67　NAC, RG 85, vol. 298, file 1009-2[2-A]. Memo to R. Gibson "Northern Tour of the Arctic Research Committee of the Defence Research Board," February 1950, 8–9.

68　Ibid., file 1009–2[2]. Minutes of meeting of Arctic Research Advisory Committee, 6 June 1950.

69　NAC, RG 22, vol. 153, file 5-0-1-35 (pt. 5), press release no. 3084, 19 March 1949.

70　Ibid., vol. 47, file 5-0-1-17, report by Colin Gibson, n.d.

71　Ibid., vol. 275, file 85-4-1, Cabinet directive, 7 May 1948.

72　NWT Council Minutes, vol. 17, 22 June 1948.

73　For example, see NAC, RG 22, vols. 147 and 153.

74　NWT Council Minutes, vol. 17, 21 October 1948; and vol. 18, May 1949.

75　Peter Larkin, "Science and the North: An Essay on Aspiration," in *Northern Transitions*, ed. R. Keith and J. B. Wright, vol. 2 (Ottawa: Canadian Arctic Resources Committee, 1978), 119; and P. Baird and J. L. Robinson, "Research in the Canadian Eastern Arctic," *Canadian Geographical Journal* 35 (March 1945): 45ff.

76　Keenleyside, "Recent Developments," 161.

77　NAC, RG 2/18, vol. 70, file D-17-3, Keenleyside to Heeney, 27 April 1947; Heeney to E. W. T. Gill, 6 May 1947; and J. Rutherford to secretary of the chiefs of staff, 10 May 1947.

78　NAC, RG 92, vol. 1, file 1–2, "Establishment."

79　NAC, RG 22, vol. 147, file 5-0-1-17, Keenleyside to A. Day, secretary of the Royal Commission on National Development in the Arts, Letters, and Sciences, 16 June 1949.

80 Ibid., vol. 153, file 5-0-1-35, press release no. 1981.
81 NWT Council Minutes, vol. 18, 1 December 1949.
82 *Arctic Circular* 1 (February 1948): 5.
83 Ibid., 9.
84 Department of Resources and Development, *Annual Report* for year ending March 1950, 12.

NOTES TO CHAPTER NINE

Epigraph: Hugh L. Keenleyside, "Recent Developments in the Canadian North," McMaster speech, 1.

1 MacDonald, *Down North*, ix.
2 Joseph Jockel, "The United States and Canadian Efforts at Continental Air Defense, 1947–1957" (Ph.D. diss. John Hopkins University 1978), 46.
3 NAC, RG 2/18, vol. 57, file A-25-5, "Summary of United States Military Activities in Canada," January 1948.
4 NA, RG 59, PJBD series, vol. 2, file "Basic Papers," memorandum of meetings, 16–17 December 1946. In the United States version of the notes for the December 1946 meetings, Heeney claimed that it was Cabinet who "was anxious to have as much civilian 'cover' for defense projects as possible."
5 Eayrs, *Peacemaking and Deterrence*, 92.
6 R. D. Cuff and J. L. Granatstein, *American Dollars and Canadian Prosperity*, 7–78, 84–102. Also see Holmes, *Shaping of Peace*, 1: 181; and Bothwell and Kilbourn, *C.D. Howe*, 249–50.
7 NA, RG 59, PJBD series, vol. 7, file "U.S. Weather Stations," Henry to Graham Parsons, 14 February 1947; also Macdonnell to Henry, 6 May 1947; Henry to Macdonnell, 19 May 1947; and NAC, RG 2/18, vol. 57, file A-25-5, report by A. R. Kilgour to Heeney, 1 December 1947.
8 NAC, RG 2/18, vol. 57, file A-25-5, reports submitted by Captain W. W. Bean, secretary to the chiefs of staff committee, 13 November 1947; 25 January and 28 April 1948; and report by A. R. Kilgour, 1 December 1947.
9 Ibid., "Summary of United States Military Activities in Canada," 28 April 1948, 2.
10 Ibid., Bean to Heeney, 13 November 1947.
11 Ibid.: and NA, RG 59, PJBD series, vol. 11, "Correspondence, July–December 1948," report dated 30 June 1948.
12 PRO, CAB 122/624, file 100867, report of Royal Air Force forwarded to Cabinet, 15 August 1947. Also NAC, RG 2/18, vol. 57, file A-25-5, report by A. R. Kilgour to Privy Council, 1 December 1947.
13 NAC, RG 85, vol. 298, file 1009-2(2-A), J. G. Wright to Roy Gibson, 17 March 1950. Gerald Waring, "White Elephant in the Arctic," *Montreal Standard*, 24 June 1950.
14 David Judd, "Canada's Northern Policy," *The Polar Record* 14 (May 1969): 595; J. Tuzo Wilson, "Exercise Musk-Ox," *The Polar Record* 5 (December 1947): 14–25; Swettenham, *McNaughton*, 3:183; and H. W. Hewetson, "Arctic Survey V," *Canadian Journal of Economic and Political Science* 11 (1945): 465.
15 NAC, RG 2/18, vol. 57, file A-25-5, reports by secretary of the chiefs of staff committee to Heeney, 28 January 1948 and 23 April 1948.
16 NA, RG 59, PJBD series, vol. 2, file "Fort Churchill," DMO & P memo, 19 May 1947. Expansion fell short of plan, reaching accommodation for only 1,299 single

men and 201 in married quarters (report to American secretary of the PJBD, 16 February 1952).

17 NAC, RG 2/18, vol. 57, file A-25-5, reports of 1 December 1947 and 28 January 1948.

18 NA, RG 59, PJBD series, vol. 2, file "Fort Churchill," PJBD memo, 2 September 1947.

19 Ibid., Gen. Henry to director, Research and Development Division of War Department General Staff (WDGS) 3 February 1947.

20 Ibid., War Department General Staff to Graham Parsons, American secretary of the PJBD, 23 January 1947.

21 Ibid. In addition to correspondence, see booklet, "Fort Churchill Experimental Centre," produced by the U.S. Directorate of Weapons and Development, 1951. First official report of rocket launchings were by the Canadian Army in 1954. A permanent launching range was built in 1956 and turned over to the United States Army in 1959. In 1966, the facilities were transferred to the National Research Council of Canada. *Handbook for Range Users, no. 95, Churchill Research Range* (Ottawa: National Research Council 1967), 1-2-1.

22 Eayrs, *Peacemaking and Deterrence*, 68–72.

23 Ibid., 54–56.

24 D. J. Goodspeed, *A History of the Defence Research Board of Canada* (Ottawa: Queen's Printer 1958), 14, 29, 63–65.

25 Ibid., 177–84; and NAC, RG 85, vol. 298, file 1009-2[2] "Summary of Activities of the Arctic Research Advisory Committee," 1949.

26 NAC, RG 85, vol. 298, file 1009 (pt. 1), "Report of the Arctic Research Advisory Committee," December 1948.

27 Ibid., file 1009 (pt. 2A), "Constitution," Arctic Research Advisory Committee, December 1950; and "Activities in the Canadian North During 1950–1951," report by the Arctic Research Advisory Committee.

28 Swettenham, *McNaughton*, 3: 185.

29 Eayrs, *Peacemaking and Deterrence*, 112.

30 Ibid., 113–14.

31 Ibid., 108.

32 Swettenham, *McNaughton*, 3: 184.

33 NAC, Lloyd Papers, vol. 18, file 381–98, "Report on the Arctic Institute of North America Research Committee, 1949–1950."

34 NAC, RG 2/18, vol. 74, file D-19-2, teletype from the Canadian ambassador to the secretary of state for external affairs, 17 October 1947, "draft of Directive concerning publicity relating to Joint Canadian–United States defence plans and operations in the Far North."

35 Ibid., vol. 70, file D-17-3; for example, see J. A. Rutherford to Gill, 10 May 1947. The Joint Intelligence Committee was a sub-committee of the Chiefs of Staff Committee.

36 Ibid., Heeney to Gill, 6 May 1947.

37 Ibid., F. W. T. Lucas to Heeney, 8 July 1947.

38 NAC, RG 92, vol. 1, file 1-1, Halliday to Matheson, 19 April 1948.

39 Ibid., file 1-1, "Strategic Intelligence Study of Canada," tentative layout, 8 April 1946. Also see NAC, Lloyd Papers, vol. 34, file 780, correspondence and reports.

40 NAC, RG 92, vol. 13, file 400, Lloyd to Keenleyside, 12 May 1948, and other related correspondence; and vol. 4, file 5-25, Lloyd to Keenleyside, 1 May 1948.

41 NWT Council Minutes, vol. 15, September 1947, 3394.

42 NAC, RG 22, vol. 370, file 40–10-1 (pt. 1), "Draft," November 1947.
43 NAC, RG 2/18, vol. 57, file A-25-5, 8 November 1947; and correspondence Keenleyside to Heeney.
44 Ibid., Rowley to Heeney, 15 November 1947; and Bean to Heeney, 13 November 1947.
45 Ibid., correspondence from Heeney to heads to various departments, November and December 1947.
46 Ibid., Heeney to Keenleyside, 21 November and 12 December 1947. Keenleyside's contribution was certainly major, as is evidenced in such phrases as "our views" and "many of the changes you propose" appearing in Heeney's personal letters to the deputy minister.
47 Ibid., draft of "Northern Canada Development and Policy," 21 November 1947.
48 Ibid., Cabinet Document no. 588, 16 January 1948, "Northern Development Policy."
49 NAC, RG 85, vol. 300, file 1009-3-1, "Minutes of the Advisory Committee on Northern Development." Note that Solandt and McNaughton were not present at the first two meetings.
50 Ibid., meeting 2 February 1948, 1.
51 No copy of Lloyd's original paper could be found despite numerous memo references and correspondence referring to attached copies. Criticisms and comments are from notations in the minutes and related correspondence. A copy of the Privy Council report is found in NAC, RG 2/18, vol. 57, file A-25-5, "Northern and Arctic Projects," 28 January 1947.
52 NAC, RG 85, vol. 300, file 1009-3-1, minutes of the Advisory Committee on Northern Development, 23 April 1948.
53 NAC, RG 2/18, vol. 57, file A-15-5, memo to the ACND, 23 April 1948.
54 Ibid., memo to Heeney, 13 November 1947.
55 NAC, RG 85, vol. 300, file 1009-3-1, minutes of the second meeting, 1 June 1948; also memo from chiefs of staff to Keenleyside, 13 August 1948.
56 Ibid., minutes of meeting, 23 November 1948. Although file by that name is listed in the NAC finding aid, it is nowhere to be found in the volume indicated.
57 NAC, RG 2/18, vol. 74, file D-19-2, "U.S. Service and Service Employed Personnel in Canada" (as of 30 April 1948), from Chiefs of Staff Committee to Heeney, copy to Pearson. See also NAC, RG 59, PJBD series, vol. 11, file "Correspondence July–December 1948," simple sheet without identification of origin, "Military Personnel," 30 June 1948. Totals are curiously similar, but numbers do not in any way relate to break down by location. One explanation may be in the possible movement of personnel, but both listings are incomplete.
58 NAC, RG 22, vol. 278, file 99-2-81, Keenleyside to Lloyd, 28 June 1948.
59 Minutes of the research committee of the Canadian Institute of International Affairs, vol. 8, letter from Lloyd, 28 May 1948, 947–48. Lloyd had completed his manuscript prior to accepting the position with the Geographical Bureau, but he advised the research committee against its publication. "Among other things" he claimed, "the change in the Administration of the North has been so radical that by the time the book appeared it would give a false impression of conditions." Raleigh Parkin also believed that the study had achieved "its original purpose" because of the "considerable influence" it had had on the developments which came about "under Keenleyside's inspiration" (NAC, Parkin Papers, vol. 23, file "Lloyd," Parkin to Lloyd, 6 November 1951).

60 NAC, RG 2/18, vol. 57, file A-25-5-T, planning documents June-August 1948.

61 Ibid., file A-25-5, Heeney to Chipman regarding agenda of the third meeting of the ACND, 9 November 1948.

62 Ibid.

63 NA, RG 59, PJBD Series, vol. 7, file "SANACC, 1947–1948," correspondence and signed copy of the 34th recommendation.

64 Ibid., vol. 2, file "Defence Research Board," report by O'Donnell, 17 August 1948; also vol. 7, files "SANAAC" and "Release of Information to Canada," various correspondence from June 1947 to 16 May 1949.

65 Ibid., vol. 11, file "July–December 1948," correspondence, memo for Forrestal, "United States–Canada Defense Plans and Operations," 13 August 1948.

66 NAC, RG 2/18, vol. 57, file A-25-5-T, report 10 August 1948.

67 Ibid., file A-25-5, "Aide Memoire to General A. G. L. McNaughton," 2 June 1948; and RG 85, vol. 300, file 1009-3-1, Minutes of Meeting 28 December 1948, report of the Sub-Committee on Transportation.

68 NAC, RG 2/18, vol. 57, file A-25-5-B, memo from C. C. Eberts to Heeney, 19 November 1948.

69 NAC, RG 85, vol. 300, file 1009-3-1, minutes of the third meeting of the ACND, 22 November 1948.

70 Ibid., minutes of the fourth meeting of the ACND, 9 March 1949.

71 NAC, RG 85, vol. 302, file 1009-4 (pt. 1), "Security Recommendations for the Canadian Arctic Regions," Privy Council Office, 29 June 1949.

72 NWT Council Minutes, vol. 18, May 1948, 3555.

73 Eayrs, *Peacemaking and Deterrence,* 358–59 and 123; also Jockel, "The United States and Canadian Efforts," 115–29.

74 *Arctic Circular,* 1 (January 1948): 2; 1 (May 1948): 45; (January 1950): 11–12; and 2 (September 1949): 66. For information on the Loran stations, see NAC, RG 85, vol. 298, file 1009-2[2-A] "Northern Tour of the Arctic Research Advisory Committee."

75 Jens Brøsted and Mads Faegeteborg, "Civil Aspect of Military Installations in Greenland," *Information North* (Winter 1986): 15.

76 NAC, RG 22, vol. 153, file 5-0-1-35 (pt. 7), press release 3199, 25 January 1950.

77 J. Pickersgill, *My Years with Louis St. Laurent* (Toronto: University of Toronto Press 1975), 104.

78 NAC, RG 22, vol. 270, file 40-10-1 (pt. 1); see correspondence February–March 1950.

79 Ibid., as stated in letter from Keenleyside to Herbert, February 1950.

80 Ibid., "Political Democracy in the Northwest Territories," confidential report by Keenleyside to Robert Winters, 18 March 1950, 8–13; also see NAC, RG 85, vol. 298, file 1009-2[2], "Activities in the Canadian North during 1949," December 1949.

81 NAC, RG 22, vol. 270, file 40-10-1 (pt. 1), C. W. Jackson to Robert Winters, 8 May 1950.

82 Ibid., Gibson to Keenleyside, 18 August 1950.

83 Ibid., original memo was sent by Robert Winters to Acting Deputy Minister C. W. Jackson, 1 August 1950.

84 Ibid., Gibson to Robert Winters, 25 September 1950.

85 Keenleyside, *Memoirs,* 2: 354–59. '

86 NAC, RG 22, vol. 270, file 40-10-1 (pt. 1), Winters to Keenleyside, 13 Sept. 1950.

87 Keenleyside, *Memoirs,* 2: 357–58.

88 Ibid., 1:462.

89 NAC, RG 22, vol. 148, file 5-0-1-17 (pt. 5), "Speeches," speech delivered by Keenleyside at the University of British Columbia, 1 April 1948.

90 NWT Council Minutes, vol. 20, 10 November 1950. It was also noted that Winters brought with him his jurisdiction over Central Mortgage and Housing from his previous post as minister of reconstruction and supply. It also followed him to Public Works in 1953.

91 NAC, RG 22, vol. 148, file 5-0-1-17 (pt. 3), biographical sketch of Gen. Hugh A. Young.

92 Department of Resources and Development, *Annual Report* for year ending March 1951.

93 Canada. House of Commons, *Debates,* 1951, 2 April 1951, 1538–42.

94 Richard Laing et al., "The Political Development of the Northwest Territories," in *Northern Transitions,* vol. 2, eds. R. Keith and Janet Wright (Ottawa: Canadian Arctic Resources Committee 1978), 316. Winters's definition of a "more democratic form of government" held until 1959, at which time all natives of the Northwest Territories were granted the territorial franchise.

95 NAC, RG 22, vol. 270, file 40-10-1(1), M. A. Hardie to Gen. H. A. Young, 28 November 1951.

96 Ibid., "Matters to be submitted to the Council of the Northwest Territories at its December 1951 Session."

97 See Minutes of the Northwest Territories after November 1950.

NOTES TO CHAPTER 10

Epigraph: Lester B. Pearson, *Mike: The Memoirs of the Rt. Honourable Lester B. Pearson,* Volume II, 1948–57 (Toronto: University of Toronto Press 1973), 24.

1 John Holmes made only passing reference to "giving civilian cover to Arctic developments" to avoid "provoking further tension with the Russians" and "frightening Canadians" (*Shaping of Peace*), 2:86. Similarly, James Eayrs only touches on the subject when he suggested that Heeney and Pearson were casting about for "protective colouration" to account for the use of Goose Bay and Churchill as American offensive bases (*Peacemaking and Deterrence,* 354–55).

2 Holmes, *Better Part of Valour,* viii.

3 Ibid., 49.

4 Carl Berger, *The Sense of Power* (Toronto: University of Toronto Press 1970), 120–31; see also Robert D. Page, "The Canadian Response to the "Imperial' Idea during the Boer War Years," in *Canadian History since Confederation: Essays and Interpretations,* 2d ed., eds. B. W. Hodgins and R. D. J. Page (Georgetown, Ontario: Irwin-Dorsey 1979), 331. Page questions the importance of anti-American sentiment in the late 19th-century imperial movement in Canada. If viewed not as anti-American, but as fear of American dominance, then comparison of this period to the 1940s would have more direct relevance.

5 Pearson, "Canada Looks 'Down North,'" 638.

6 Camsell, "Opening the Northwest," 277.

7 M. MacDonald, *Down North,* 264.

8 Keenleyside, McMaster speech, 8–9.

9 *Journal of Commerce,* 9 March 1944.

10 *DCER,* 12/908-9. Macdonnell to Hopkins, 6 May 1946; Hopkins to Macdonnell, 8 May 1946.
11 NAC, RG 85, vol. 65, file 164-1 (pt. 3), "Estimate Report on Population Increase," (White pop. only).

	Yukon	Mackenzie District
1941	3,414	2,113
1949	7,148	5,041

Expenditures on northern administration of the Yukon and NWT rose from $384,346 in 1940 to $4,671,479 in year ending 30 March 1950. This compared to a revenue increase from $250,920 to $781,330 over the same period. See *Annual Reports* of the Department of Mines and Resources, 1940, and Department of Resources and Development, 1950.
12 NA, RG 59, PJBD series, vol. 5, file "Military Cooperation Committee," extracts from PJBD Journal, April 1953 and 22 July 153.
13 Ibid., memo from U.S. Air Force to the MCC, 29 March 1954.
14 Canada, House of Commons, *Debates,* 1953, 1: 698.
15 Canada, House of Commons, *Debates,* 1950, second session, 6 September 1950, 324.
16 An oldtimer in Fort Smith used this phrase when he referred to the more prosperous section of town where the "government people" lived. "Welfare Row," as he termed it, meant that the residents were living off the welfare of the government (interview, Henry Geisbrecht, August 1981).
17 As quoted in Annette Fox Baker and Alfred O. Hero, Jr., "Canada and the United States: Their Binding Frontier," in Annette Fox Baker et al., *Canada and the United States: Transnational and Transgovernmental Relations* (New York: Columbia University Press 1976), 402.

Selected Bibliography

PRIMARY SOURCES

Manuscript Sources

Canadian Institute of International Affairs Library—Toronto
    Minutes, Volumes 3–6
    Clipping files
    Records

Department of External Affairs—Canada
    Historical Records Division

Library of Congress—Washington
    Cordell Hull Papers

National Archives of Canada
(1)   *Federal Archives Division*
    Department of External Affairs Records, RG 25
    Department of Indian Affairs and Northern Development Records, RG 22
    Department of Mines and Resources Records, RG 21
    Department of National Health and Welfare Records, RG 29
    Geographical Branch Records, RG 92
    Indian Affairs Branch Records, RG 10
    Northern Affairs Program Records, RG 85
    Privy Council Office Records, RG 2/18
    Cabinet War Committee Records, RG 2/7
    Special Commissioner of Defence Projects in Northwest Canada Records, RG 36/7
    Wartime Information Board Records, RG 36/31

(2)   *Manuscript Division*
    Arctic Institute of North America Papers, MG 28 I 77
    Canadian Institute of International Affairs Papers, MG 28 I 250
    Brooke Claxton Papers, MG 32 B 5

Arnold Heeney Papers, MG 30 E 144
W. L. M. King Papers, MG 26 J 4
Trevor Lloyd Papers, MG 30 B 97
Raleigh Parkin Papers, MG 30 D 77
Escott Reid Papers, MG 27 III 65

(3)   *National Photography Collection*

National Archives—Washington DC
International Conferences, Commissions and Expositions Records, RG 43
State Department Records, RG 59
William S. Carlson Papers, RG 401/100
Charles Hubbard Papers, RG 401/17

Prince of Wales Northern Heritage Centre, Archives Division—Yellowknife
Northwest Territories Council Minutes, Volume 8–20
Records
Richard Finnie Photograph Collection

Public Record Office—London
British Atomic Energy Authority Records, AB series
Cabinet Records, CAB series
Dominions Office Records, DO series
Foreign Office Records, FO series
Records of the Prime Minister's Office, PREM 3 and 4

Royal Commonwealth Society Library, London
Malcolm MacDonald Papers—(now transferred to University of Durham, England)

Trent University Archives
Northwest Service Command, United States Army Air Force Records
(microfilm)

Yukon Territorial Archives, Whitehorse
Central Registry Files, YRG 1
    Records
    Votes and Proceedings
Yukon Government Administration Records

Interviews and Correspondence

Alexander Brady
Maxwell J. Dunbar
René Fumoleau, OMI
John Holmes

Sheila (MacDonald) Lougheed
Louise Parkin
Escott Reid
Margaret Gowing

Hugh Keenleyside   J. Lewis Robinson
Trevor Lloyd   Graham Rowley
and various long-time residents of the Yukon and Northwest Territories

SECONDARY SOURCES

Unpublished Theses, Papers, and Speeches

Breen, David. "Wartime Oils Limited: Canada's First Public Petroleum Corporation and
    Canadian Petroleum Policy 1939–1945." Paper presented to the Annual Meeting of
    the Canadian Historical Association, Vancouver, June 1983
Canada. "Foundation of Canada's Sovereignty over the Arctic Region." A study
    prepared by the Research Branch of the Library of Parliament, May 1969
Diubaldo, Richard. "Canada Reasserts Herself in the North." Paper presented at the
    Alaska Highway Symposium. Fort St. John, B.C., June 1982
Dunbar, Maxwell. "Science in the Canadian North." Radio broadcast, CBC, Saturday, 9
    June 1946
Grant, Shelagh D. "Search for a Northern Policy, 1940–1950: Impact of the Canadian
    Institute of International Affairs." Unpublished paper, copy in CIIA library, 25 Febru-
    ary 1981
Jockel, Joseph T. "The United States and Canadian Efforts at Continental Defence,
    1947–1957." Ph.D. diss., Johns Hopkins University, 1978
Keenleyside, Hugh. "Recent Developments in the Canadian North." Speech delivered at
    McMaster University, 14 May 1949
Kizer, Benjamin. "The North Pacific International Planning Project." American Council
    Paper No. 2, for the Eighth Conference of the Institute of Pacific Relations, Mont
    Tremblant, Quebec, December 1942
Lloyd, Trevor. "The Geography and Administration of Northern Canada." Unpublished
    manuscript for the Canadian Institute of International Affairs, 1947
Morrison, William R. "Showing the Flag: The Mounted Police and Canadian Sovereignty
    in the Western Arctic 1903–1924." Paper presented at the Canadian Historical Asso-
    ciation Annual Meeting, Vancouver, June 1983
Stuart, Richard. "Impact of the Alaska Highway on Dawson City." Paper presented at
    the Alaska Highway Symposium, Fort St. John, B.C., June 1982

Published Government Documents and Reports

Canada. *Census of Canada, 1931*, Vol. 2. Ottawa: King's Printer 1935
————. *Census of Canada, 1941*, Vols. 1 and 3. Ottawa: King's Printer 1946
————. Department of External Affairs. *Documents on Canadian External Relations*,
    Vols. 9 and 12. Ottawa: King's Printer 1977–80
————. Department of the Interior. *Estimates,* and *Annual Reports.* For years 1922
    through 1929
————. Department of Mines and Resources, *Annual Report.* For years 1938 through
    1949. Ottawa: King's Printer

————. *An Outline of the Canadian Eastern Arctic*. Ottawa 1944

————. *The Northwest Territories: Administration, Resources and Development*. Ottawa 1943

————. Department of Mines and Technical Surveys, Geographical Branch. *An Introduction to the Geography of the Canadian Arctic*. Canadian Geography, Information Series no. 2 Ottawa 1951

————. Department of Resources and Development. *Annual Report*. For years 1950 through 1953. Ottawa: King's Printer

————. House of Commons. *Debates*. Ottawa 1930, 1946–53

————. North Pacific Planning Project, Charles Camsell, dir. *Canada's New Northwest*. Ottawa: King's Printer 1947

————. Royal North West Mounted Police. *Report of the Commissioner*. Ottawa 1918

————. Special Joint Committee of the Senate and the House of Commons appointed to Investigate the Indian Act. *Minutes of Proceedings and Evidence 1946*. Ottawa: King's Printer 1947

United States. Department of State. *Foreign Relations of the United States*. For years 1940–50. Washington, DC: United States Government Printing Office 1969–79

————. *Public Papers of the Presidents of the United States: Harry S. Truman, 1947*. Washington, DC: United States Government Printing Office. 1963

————, Senate. *Hearings before a Special Committee Investigating the National Defense Program*. United States Senate, Seventy-eighth Congress, first session, September 11–December 2, 1943. Washington, DC: United States Government Printing Office 1944

Published Reports of Private Institutions

Canadian Institute of International Affairs. *Annual Reports* for years 1938 through to 1951. Toronto

Institute of Pacific Relations. *War and Peace in the Pacific: A Preliminary Report of the Eighth Conference of the Institute of Pacific Relations*. Mont Tremblant, Quebec, December 1942. Published at Washington, DC 1943

Morton, W. L. *Building Post War Canada: Report of a Conference of the Western Branches of the Canadian Institute of International Affairs*. Toronto: Canadian Institute of International Affairs 1943

————. *Prepare for Peace: A Report of the Institute's Eleventh Annual Study Conference on Canada and the Commonwealth in the World*. Toronto: Canadian Institute of International Affairs 1944

Articles and Periodicals

Adams, John Q. "Settlements of the Northeastern Canadian Arctic." *Geographical Review* 31 (1941): 112–23

Arctic Circular. Vols. 1 through 4 (1948–1951)

Baird, P. "Pat Baird's Arctic Journal, 1936–1938." *Northward Journal* 38 (Fall 1986):

5–19; and 39 (Winter 1986): 5–24

Baird, P., and J. L. Robinson. "A Brief History of Exploration and Research in the Canadian Eastern Arctic." *Canadian Geographical Journal* 30 (March 1945): 135–43

Barry, P. S. "The Prolific Pipeline: Getting Canol Underway." *Dalhousie Review* 56 (1976): 255–61

Berger, Carl. "The True North Strong and Free." In *Nationalism in Canada,* ed. Peter Russell. Toronto: McGraw-Hill 1966

Blanchet, Guy. "The Canol Project." *Canadian Surveyor* 8 (November 1944): 2–7.

Bothwell, Robert. "Radium and Uranium: Evolution of a Company and a Policy." *Canadian Historical Review* 64 (June 1983): 142

Breen, D. H. "Anglo-American Rivalry and the Evolution of Canadian Petroleum Policy to 1930." *Canadian Historical Review* 62 (1981): 283–303

Bucksar, R. G. "The Alaska Highway: Background to Decision." *Arctic* 21 (1968): 215–22

Burgess, Helen. "Health by Remote Control." *The Beaver* (Winter 1970): 50–55

Camsell, Charles. "The New North." *Canadian Geographical Journal* 33 (1946): 265–77

———. "Opening the North West." *The Beaver* (June 1944): 4–9

Cohen, Maxwell. "The Arctic and the National Interest." *International Journal* 26 (1970–71): 52–63

Collins, Henry, and W. E. Taylor, Jr. "Diamond Jenness." *Arctic* 23 (June 1970): 71–81

Dawson, C. A. "Arctic Survey VI: The New North West." *Canadian Journal of Economics and Political Science* 11 (1945): 578–96

Diubaldo, Richard. "The Absurd Little Mouse: When Eskimos Became Indians." *Journal of Canadian Studies* 16 (Summer 1981): 34–41

———. "The Canol Project in Canadian-American Relations." *Historical Papers 1977.* Ottawa: Canadian Historical Association 1978, 179–96

Dunbar, Maxwell. "Common Cause in the North." *International Journal* 1 (October 1946): 358–64

———. "Greenland During and Since the Second World War." *International Journal* 5 (Spring 1950): 121–40

Ebbs, J. Harry. "Historic Airplane Trip to the Western Arctic." *Moccasin Telegraph* (Winter 1970): 62–64

Ebbutt, Frank. "The Gravel River Indians." *Canadian Geographic Journal* 2 (April 1931): 311–22

Finnie, O. S. "Canada's Land of the Midnight Sun." *Natural History* 28 (1928): 353–66

Finnie, Richard J. "The Epic of Canol." *Canadian Geographical Journal* 34 (1947): 136–39

———. "Joseph Elzéar Bernier." *Arctic* 39 (September 1986): 278

———. "The Origin of Canol's Mackenzie Air Fields." *Arctic* 33 (June 1980): 273–79

Franklin, William. "Alaska, Outpost of American Defence." *Foreign Affairs* 21 (October 1940): 245–50

Grant, Shelagh. "Canol: A Ghost from the Past." *Alternatives* 9 (1981): 21–31

———. "Escott Meredith Reid: The Makings of a Radical Diplomat." *Queen's*

Quarterly 91 (Autumn 1984): 594

Gowing, Margaret. "Britain, America and the Bomb." In David Dilks, ed., *Retreat from Power,* Volume 2. London: Macmillan, 1981.

Green, L. C. "Canada and Arctic Sovereignty." *Canadian Bar Review* 48 (December 1970): 740–75

Heeney, A. D. P. "Cabinet Government in Canada." *Canadian Journal of Economics and Political Science* 12 (August 1946): 296–314

Hewetson, H. W. "Arctic Survey V: Transportation in the Canadian North." *Canadian Journal of Economics and Political Science* 9 (1945): 450–89

———. "The Future of Canada's North Country." *Public Affairs* (Winter 1945)

Hodgins, B. W., and Shelagh D. Grant. "The Canadian North: Trends in Canadian Historiography." *Acadiensis* 26 (Autumn, 1986): 173–88

Hopkins, Oliver B. "The Canol Project: Canada Provides Oil for the Allies." *Canadian Geographical Journal* 27 (November 1943): 138–49

Hubbard, C. J. "The Arctic Isn't So Tough." *Saturday Evening Post,* 26 June 1944, 19–20 and 61

Hughes, John (alias for Hugh Keenleyside). "The Great Northwest." *Far Eastern Survey,* 8 February 1943, 28–29

Inglis, Alex. "The Institute and the Department." *International Journal* 33 (Winter 1977–1978): 88–101

Jockel, J. T. "The Canada–United States Military Cooperation Committee and Continental Air Defence, 1946." *Canadian Historical Review* 64 (September 1983): 352

Johns, Robert E. "A History of St. Peter's Mission and of Education in Hay River. N.W.T. Prior to 1950." *Musk-Ox* 13 (1973): 22–33

Jones, Kenneth. "How Canada Almost Claimed Wrangel Island." *Canadian Geographic* 102 (August–September 1982): 56–63

Judd, David. "Canada's Northern Policy: Retrospect and Prospect." *Polar Record* 14 (1969): 593–602

———. "Seventy-five Years of Resource Administration in Northern Canada." *Polar Record* 14 (1969): 791–805

Kazurak, Peter. "American Foreign Policy Officials and Canada, 1929–1941." *International Journal* 32 (Summer 1977): 546

Keenleyside, Hugh L. "Canada's Department of External Affairs." *International Journal* 1 (July 1946): 189–214

———. "The Canada–United States Joint Board on Defence, 1940–1945." *International Journal* 16 (Winter 1960–1961): 50–75

———. "Critical Mineral Shortages." *International Journal* 4 (1949): 327–41

———. "The International Significance of Canadian Resources." *International Journal* 5 (Spring 1950): 109–20

———. "Recent Developments in the Canadian North." *Canadian Geographical Journal* 39 (1949): 157–76

Koenig, L. S., and K. R. Greenaway, Moira Dunbar, G. Hattersley-Smith. "Arctic Ice Islands." *Arctic* 5 (1952): 67–103

Lee, Kendrick. "Arctic Defenses." *Editorial Research Reports* (1946): 503–18

Lingard, C. C. "Arctic Survey VII: Administration of the Canadian Northland." *Cana-*

dian *Journal of Economics and Political Science* 12 (1946): 45–73

Lloyd, Trevor. "Activity in Northwest Canada." *Journal of Geography* 42 (May 1943): 161–74

———. "Aviation in Arctic North America and Greenland." *Polar Record* 5 (1947): 163–71

———. "Barges." *The Beaver* (June 1943): 21–23

———. "Canada: Mainstreet of the Air." *Maclean's*, 1 July 1943, 1–4

———. "Canada's Strategic North." *International Journal* 2 (1946–1947): 144–63

———. "The Mackenzie Waterway: A Northern Supply Route." *Geographical Review* 33 (1943): 415–74

———. "New Perspective on the North." *Foreign Affairs* 42 (January 1964): 293–308

———. "Oil in the Mackenzie Valley." *Geographical Review* 34 (1944): 273–307

Lower, A. R. M. "Canada and the New Non-British World." *International Journal* 3 (1948): 208–21.

———. "Canada and the New World Order." *Canadian Forum* 19 (January 1938): 204

———. "Canada—Next Belgium?" *Maclean's*, 15 December 1947, 51–53

———. "Canada, and the Second Great War and the Future." *International Journal* 2 (1946): 97–111

MacLulich, T. D. "Reading the Land: The Wilderness Tradition in Canadian Letters." *Journal of Canadian Studies* 20 (Summer 1985): 29–44

Madill, R. Glenn. "The Search for the North Magnetic Pole." *Arctic* 1 (Spring 1948), reprint for the Dominion Observatory, Ottawa

Marriott, R. S. "Canada's Eastern Arctic Patrol." *Canadian Geographical Journal* 20 (March 1940): 156–61

McKeand, D. L. "The Annual Eastern Arctic Patrol." *Canadian Geographical Journal* 17 (July 1938): 37–38

Miller, T. B. "Commonwealth Institutes of International Affairs." *International Journal* 33 (Winter 1977–1978): 5–27

Moore, Andrew. "Arctic Survey II: Survey of Education in the Mackenzie District." *Canadian Journal of Economics and Political Science* 11 (1945): 61–82

Morton, W. L. "Canadian-American Partnership in the Pacific Northwest." *Far Eastern Survey*, 26 January 1944.

———. "The 'North' in Canadian Historiography." *Transactions of the Royal Society*, series 4, 8 (1970): 31–40

Naske, Claus-M. "Building the Alaska Highway: The Political Background." *Northern Engineer* 16 (Spring 1984): 25–35

Neary, Peter F. "Newfoundland and the Anglo-American Leased Bases Agreement of 21 March 1941." *Canadian Historical Review* 67 (December 1986): 491

Neuberger, R. L. "Great Canol Fiasco." *American Mercury* 66 (April 1948): 415–21

Oswalt, Wendell H., and James W. Vanstone. "The Future of the Caribou Eskimo." *Anthropologica II* 2 (1960): 1–23

Page, Don, and D. Munton. "Canadian Images of the Cold War 1946–1947." *International Journal* 32 (Summer 1977): 577

Page, R. J. D. "Norman Wells: The Past and Future Boom." *Journal of Canadian Studies* 16 (Summer 1981): 16–33

Parkin, Raleigh. "The Origin of the Institute." *Arctic* 19 (March 1966): 5–18

Pearson, L. B. "Canada Looks 'Down North.'" *Foreign Affairs* 24 (1945–46): 638–45.

Pierce, S. D., and A. F. W. Plumptre. "Canada's Relations with Wartime Agencies in Washington." *Canadian Journal of Economics and Political Science* 11 (1945): 402–19

Pratt, Wallace E. "Oilfields in the Arctic." *Harper's Magazine,* January 1944, 107–11

Reed, John. "Yesterday and Today." *Arctic* 19 (1966): 19–33

Robinson, J. Lewis. "Agriculture and Forests and Yukon Territory." *Canadian Geographical Journal* 31 (August 1945): 30–47

———. "A Brief History of Exploration and Research in the Canadian Eastern Arctic." (With P. D. Baird.) *Canadian Geographical Journal* 30 (March 1945): 136–57

———. "Canada's Western Arctic." *Canadian Geographical Journal* 37 (December 1948): 242–60

———. "Conquest of the Northwest Passage by the RCMP Schooner *St. Roch.*" *Canadian Geographical Journal* 30 (February 1945): 52–73

———. "Eskimo Population in the Canadian Eastern Arctic." *Canadian Geographical Journal* 29 (September 1944): 128–42

———. "Exploration and Settlement of Mackenzie District, NWT." (With M. J. Robinson.) *Canadian Geographical Journal* 32 (June 1946): 246–55, and part 2, 33 (July 1946): 43–49

———. "Fur Production in the Northwest Territories." (With M. J. Robinson.) *Canadian Geographical Journal* 37 (January 1946): 34–48

———. "Land Use Possibilities in Mackenzie District, N.W.T." *Canadian Geographical Journal* 31 (July 1945): 30–47

———. "Mineral Resources and Mining Activity in the Canadian Eastern Arctic." *Canadian Geographical Journal* 29 (August 1944): 55–75

———. "Resources of the Arctic." *The Beaver* (December 1949): 48–51

———. "RMS *Nascopie:* Veteran of the Seas." *Canadian Geographical Journal* 35 (October 1947): 196–97

———. "Water Transportation in the Canadian Northwest." *Canadian Geographical Journal* 31 (November 1945): 236–56

———. "Weather and Climate of the Northwest Territories." *Canadian Geographical Journal* 32 (March 1946): 124–39

Rowley, G. W. "Settlement and Transportation in the Canadian North." *Arctic* 7 (1954): 336–42

Soward, F. H. "Inside a Canadian Triangle: The University, the CIIA and the Department of External Affairs." *International Journal* 33 (Winter 1977–78): 66–81

Stefansson, Vilhjalmur. "The American Far North." *Foreign Affairs* 17 (1939): 508–21

———. "Routes to Alaska." *Foreign Affairs* 19 (1941): 861–69

Taylor, Griffith. "Parallels in Soviet and Canadian Settlement." *International Journal* 1 (1946): 144–58

Trotter, R. G. "Canada as a Colonial Power." *International Journal* 1 (1946): 215–17

Vipond, Mary. "The Nationalist Network." *Canadian Review of Studies in Nationalism* 7 (1980): 32–52

Webster, C. J. "The Growth of the Soviet Arctic and Sub-Arctic." *Arctic* 4 (1951): 27–45

Wherrett, G. J. "Arctic Survey I: Survey of Health Conditions and Medical and Hospital Services in the North West Territories." *Canadian Journal of Economics and Political Science* 11 (1945): 49–60

Wilson, J. Tuzo. "Exercise Musk-Ox, 1946." *Polar Record* 5 (1947): 14–25

Zaslow, Morris. "A Prelude to Self-Government: The Northwest Territories, 1905–1939." In *The Canadian Northwest and its Potentialities*. Edited by Frank Underhill. Toronto: University of Toronto Press 1959

General Works

Acheson, Dean. *Present at the Creation: My Years in the State Department*. New York: W. W. Norton 1969

Baker, Annette Fox, et al. *Canada and the United States: Translational and Transgovernmental Relations*. New York: Columbia University Press 1976

Barry, P. S. *The Canol Project: An Adventure of the U.S. War Department in Canada's Northwest*. Edmonton: Private Printing 1985

Berger, Carl. *The Sense of Power*. Toronto: University of Toronto Press 1970

Berle, Adolf A. *Navigating the Rapids, 1918–1971*. New York: Harcourt, Brace Jovanovich, 1973

Bernier, J. E. *Cruise of the "Arctic" 1908–9*. Ottawa: Department of Marine and Fisheries 1910.

———. *Master Mariner and Arctic Explorer*. Ottawa: *Le Droit* 1939

Bethune, W. C. *Canada's Eastern Arctic*. Ottawa: Department of the Interior 1934

Bothwell, Robert. *Eldorado: Canada's National Uranium Company*. Toronto: University of Toronto Press 1984

———, and William Kilbourn. *C. D. Howe: A Biography*. Toronto: McClelland and Stewart 1979

Burwash, L. T. *Canada's Western Arctic*. Ottawa: Department of the Interior 1931

Cadogan, Sir Alexander. *The Diaries of Sir Alexander Cadogan*. Edited by David Dilks. New York: G. P. Putman 1972

Campbell, Colin. *Canadian Political Facts, 1945–1976*. Toronto: Methuen 1977

Camsell, Charles. *Son of the North*. Toronto: Ryerson Press 1954

Coates, Kenneth. *Canada's Colonies: A History of the Yukon and Northwest Territories*. Toronto: Lorimer 1985

———, ed. *The Alaska Highway: Papers of the 40th Anniversary Symposium*. Vancouver: University of British Columbia Press 1985

Cohen, Stan. *The Forgotten War*. Missoula: Pictorial Histories Publishing Company 1981

———. *The Trail of '42: A Pictorial History of the Alaska Highway*. Altona: Friesen Printers 1981

Compton, A. H. *The Atomic Quest*. London: Oxford University Press 1956

Conn, Stetson, Rose C. Engelman, and Byron Fairchild. *United States Army in World War II: The Western Hemisphere, Guarding the United States and Its Outposts*. Washington, DC: Department of the Army 1964

Copeland, Dudley. *Livingstone of the Arctic*. Lancaster, Ont.: Canadian Century Publishers 1978

Creighton, Donald. *The Forked Road: Canada 1939–1957*. Toronto: McClelland and Stewart 1976

Crowe, Keith. *A History of the Original Peoples of Northern Canada*. Montreal: McGill-Queen's University Press 1974

Cruikshank, Julie. *Their Own Yukon*. Whitehorse: Yukon Press 1975

Cuff, R. D., and J. L. Granatstein. *American Dollars and Canadian Prosperity*. Toronto: Samuel Stevens Hakkert 1978

———. *Ties That Bind: Canadian-American Relations in Wartime, from the Great War to the Cold War*. Toronto: Samuel Stevens Hakkert 1977

Dawson, C. A., ed., *The New Northwest*. Toronto: University of Toronto Press 1947

Diubaldo, Richard. *The Government of Canada and the Inuit, 1900–1967*. Ottawa: Indian Affairs and Northern Development 1985

———. *Stefansson and the Canadian Arctic*. Montreal: Queen's-McGill University Press 1979

———, and S. J. Scheinberg. *A Study of Canadian–American Defence Policy, 1945–1975: Northern Issues and Strategic Resources*. Extra-mural paper no. 6. Ottawa: Department of National Defence 1978

Dorion-Robitaille, Y. *Captain J. E. Bernier's Contribution to Canadian in the Arctic*. Ottawa: Indian and Northern Affairs 1978

Dosman, E. J., ed. *The Arctic in Question*. Toronto: Oxford University Press 1976

Douglas, W. A. B. *The Creation of a National Air Force: The Official History of the RCAF*. Vol. 2. Toronto: University of Toronto Press 1986

Driscoll, Joseph. *War Discovers Alaska*. New York 1943

Dunbar, Moira, and Keith Greenaway. *Arctic Canada from the Air*. Ottawa: Defence Research Board 1956

Dzuiban, S. W. *Military Relations between the United States and Canada 1939–1945*. Washington, DC: United States Department of the Army, Office of Military History Series, U.S. Government Publications 1959

Eayrs, James. *In Defence of Canada: Appeasement and Rearmament*. Vol. 2. Toronto: University of Toronto Press 1965

———. *In Defence of Canada: Peacemaking and Deterrence*. Vol. 3. Toronto: University of Toronto Press 1972 (1977 edition)

Edelstein, Julius. *Alaska Comes of Age*. New York 1943

Finnie, Richard. *Canada Moves North*. Toronto: Macmillan 1947

———. *Canol*. San Francisco: Taylor and Taylor 1945

Foulkes, Charles. *Canadian Defence Policy in a Nuclear Age*. Toronto: Canadian Institute of International Affairs, Behind the Headlines Series 1961

Fumoleau, René. *As Long as This Land Shall Last*. Toronto: McClelland and Stewart 1973

Glazebrook, G. P. de T., ed. *A History of Canadian External Relations*. Vol. 2. Toronto: McClelland and Stewart, Carleton Series 1965

Godsell, Philip. *Romance of the Alaska Highway*. Toronto: Ryerson 1944

Goodspeed, D. J. *A History of the Defence Research Board of Canada*. Ottawa: Queen's
Printer 1958
Gowing, Margaret. *Britain and Atomic Energy, 1939–1945*. London: Macmillan 1964
————. *Independence and Deterrence: Britain and Atomic Energy, 1945–1952*. London: Macmillan 1974
Granatstein, J. L. *Canada's War: The Politics of the Mackenzie King Government
1939–1945*. Toronto: Oxford University Press 1975
————. *A Man of Influence: Norman A. Robertson and Canadian Statecraft 1929–1968*.
Ottawa: Deneau Publishers 1981
————. *The Ottawa Men: The Civil Service Mandarins, 1935–1957*. Toronto: Oxford
University Press 1982
Green, Lewis. *The Boundary Hunters*. Vancouver: University of British Columbia Press
1982
Griffin, Harold. *Alaska and the Canadian Northwest: Our New Frontier*. New York:
W. W. Norton 1944
Griffiths, Franklyn, ed. *Politics of the Northwest Passage*. Montreal: McGill-Queen's
University Press 1987
Haliburton, R. G. *The Men of the North and Their Place in History*. Montreal 1869
Hall, D. J. *Clifford Sifton, Volume 2, A Lonely Eminence, 1901–1929*. Vancouver: University of British Columbia Press 1985
Hamelin, Louis-Édmond. *Canadian Nordicity: It's Your North, Too*. Montreal: Harvest
House 1978
Harrison, W. E. C. *Canada in World Affairs 1949–1950*. Toronto: Oxford University
Press, 1957.
Heeney, Arnold. *The Things That Are Caesar's: Memoirs of a Public Servant*. Toronto:
University of Toronto Press 1972
Hewlit, R. G., and O. E. Anderson. *The New World 1939–1946 : Volume 1 of A History
of the U.S.A.E.C.* Philadelphia: Pennsylvania University State Press 1962
Holmes, John. *The Better Part of Valour: Essays on Canadian Diplomacy*. Toronto:
McClelland and Stewart, Carleton Library Series 1970
————. *Life with Uncle: The Canadian-American Relationship*. Toronto: University of
Toronto Press 1981
————. *The Shaping of Peace: Canada and the Search for World Order, 1943–1957*.
Volume 1. Toronto: University of Toronto Press 1979
————. ————, Volume 2. Toronto: University of Toronto Press 1982
Honderich, John. *Arctic Imperative: Is Canada Losing the North?* Toronto: University of
Toronto Press 1987
Horn, Michiel. *The League for Social Reconstruction*. Toronto: University of Toronto
Press 1979
Hull, Cordell. *The Memoirs of Cordell Hull*. Vols. 1 and 2. London: Hodder and
Stoughton 1948
Hunt, Barbara, ed. *Rebels, Rascals and Royalty: The Colourful North of LACO Hunt*.
Yellowknife: Outcrop 1983
Hunt, W. R. *Stef: A Biography of Vilhjalmur Stefansson, Canadian Arctic Explorer*.
Vancouver: University of British Columbia Press 1986

James, R. Warren. *Wartime Economic Co-operation: A Study of Relations between Canada and the United States*. Toronto: Ryerson 1949

Jenness, Diamond. *Eskimo Administration II: Canada*. Montreal: Arctic Institute of North America, Technical Paper no. 14, 1964

Keenleyside, Hugh L. *Canada and the United States*. New York: Alfred A. Knopf 1929

——. *Hammer the Golden Day: Memoirs of Hugh L. Keenleyside. Volume 1*. Toronto: McClelland and Stewart 1981

——. *On the Bridge of Time: Memoirs of Hugh L. Keenleyside. Volume II*. Toronto: McClelland and Stewart 1982

——, ed. *The Growth of Canadian Policies in External Affairs*. London: Cambridge University Press 1960

Keith, Robert, and Janet B. Wright. *Northern Transitions*. Vol. 2. Ottawa: Canadian Arctic Resources Committee 1978

Kimball, Warren F., ed. *Churchill and Roosevelt: The Complete Correspondence. Volume II, Alliance Forged, November 1942–February 1944*. Princeton: Princeton University Press 1984

——. *Churchill and Roosevelt: The Complete Correspondence. Volume III. Alliance Declining, February 1944–April 1945*. Princeton: Princeton University Press 1984.

Kitto, F. H. *The Northwest Territories*. Ottawa: King's Printer 1930

Kizer, Benjamin H. *The U.S.–Canadian Northwest: A Demonstration Area for International Post War Planning and Development*. Princeton: American Council of the Institute of Pacific Relations, Princeton University Press 1943

Lingard, C. C. *Territorial Government in Canada*. Toronto: University of Toronto Press 1946.

——, and R. G. Trotter. *Canada in World Affairs, September 1941 to May 1944*. Toronto: Oxford University Press 1950

Lloyd, Trevor. *Canada's Last Frontier*. Toronto: Canadian Institute of International Affairs, Behind the Headline Series 1943

——. *Frontier of Destiny: The Canadian Arctic*. Toronto: Canadian Institute of International Affairs, Behind the Headlines Series 1946

——. *The New North*. Ottawa: Wartime Information Board, Canadian Affairs Series 1944

McCandless, Robert G. *Yukon Wildlife: A Social History*. Edmonton: University of Alberta Press 1985

McClellan, Catherine. *My Old People Say: An Ethnological Survey of the Southern Yukon Territory*. Ottawa: National Museum of Man 1975

MacDonald, Malcolm. *Down North*. Toronto: Oxford University Press 1943

MacDonald, R. St. J., ed. *The Arctic Frontier*. Toronto: University of Toronto Press 1966

McLellan, David. *Dean Acheson: The State Department Years*. New York: Dodd Mead 1976

Marwick, Arthur. *War and Social Change in the Twentieth Century: A Comparative Study of Britain, France, Germany, Russia and the United States*. London: Macmillan 1974.

Massey, Vincent. *What's Past Is Prologue*. Toronto: Macmillan 1963

Millard, P. E. *Southern Baffin Island*. Ottawa 1930

Morissonneau, Christian. *La Terre promise: Le Mythe du nord québécois*. Montreal:

Cahiers du Québec, Hurtubise 1978

Morris, Alexander. *The Hudson's Bay and Pacific Territories*. Montreal, 1859.

———. *Nova Britannia*. Montreal, 1858

Morrison, David R. *The Politics of the Yukon Territory, 1898–1909*. Toronto: University of Toronto Press 1968

Morrison, W. R. *Showing the Flag: The Mounted Police and Canadian Sovereignty in the North, 1894–1925*. Vancouver: University of British Columbia Press 1985

Nash, Roderick. *Wilderness and the American Mind*. 3d ed. New Haven: Yale University Press 1982

National Museum of Man. *The Athapaskans*. Toronto: Southam-Murray 1974

Overvold, Joanne, ed. *A Portrayal of Our Metis Heritage*. Yellowknife: Mackenzie District Metis Association 1976

Owram, Doug. *The Government Generation: Canadian Intellectuals and the State, 1900–1945*. Toronto: University of Toronto Press 1986

———. *Promise of Eden: The Canadian Expansionist Movement and the Idea of the West, 1856–1900*. Toronto: University of Toronto Press 1980

Page, Robert. *Northern Development: The Canadian Dilemma*. Toronto: McClelland and Stewart 1986

Pearson, Lester B. *Mike: The Memoirs of the Right Honourable Lester B. Pearson. Volume II, 1948–1957*. Toronto: University of Toronto Press 1973

Pemberton, J. S. B. *Ogdensburg, Hyde Park and After*. Toronto: Canadian Institute of International Affairs 1941

Phillips, R. A. J. *Canada's North*. Toronto: Macmillan 1967

Pickersgill, J. W. *The Mackenzie King Record, Volume I. 1939–1944*. Toronto: University of Toronto Press, 1960

———. *My Years with Louis St. Laurent: A Political Memoir*. Toronto: University of Toronto Press 1975.

———, and D. F. Foster. *The Mackenzie King Record*. Vols. 2, 3, and 4. Toronto: University of Toronto Press 1970

Porsild, A. E. *Reindeer Grazing in Northwest Canada*. Ottawa: Department of the Interior, King's Printer 1929

Price, Ray. *Yellowknife*. Toronto: Peter Martin Associates 1967

Rea, Kenneth J. *The Political Economy of the Canadian North*. Toronto: University of Toronto Press 1968

———. *The Political Economy of Northern Development*. Ottawa: Science Council of Canada, Background Study no. 36 1976

Reid, Escott. *Time of Fear and Hope*. Toronto: McClelland and Stewart 1977

Robertson, Heather, ed. *A Gentleman Adventurer: The Arctic Diaries of R. H. G. Bonnycastle*. Toronto: Lester and Orpen Dennys 1984

Schlesinger, A. M. J. *A Thousand Days: John F. Kennedy in the White House*. Boston: Houghton Mifflin 1965

Scott, Duncan Campbell. *The Administration of Indian Affairs in Canada*. Toronto: Canadian Institute of International Affairs 1931

Sherwood, Robert. *Roosevelt and Hopkins: An Intimate History*. Rev. ed. New York: Grosset and Dunlap 1950

Index

Index